Russian Political Philosophy

Edinburgh Studies in Comparative Political Theory & Intellectual History
Series Editor: Vasileios Syros

Edinburgh Studies in Comparative Political Theory & Intellectual History welcomes scholars interested in the comparative study of intellectual history/political ideas in diverse cultural contexts and periods of human history and Comparative Political Theory (CPT).

The series addresses the core concerns of CPT by placing texts from various political, cultural and geographical contexts in conversation. It calls for substantial reflection on the methodological principles of comparative intellectual history in order to rethink of some of the conceptual categories and tools used in the comparative exploration of political ideas. The series seeks original, high-quality monographs and edited volumes that challenge and expand the canon of readings used in teaching intellectual history and CPT in Western universities. It will showcase innovative and interdisciplinary work focusing on the comparative examination of sources, political ideas and concepts from diverse traditions.

Available Titles:
Simon Kennedy, *Reforming the Law of Nature: The Secularisation of Political Thought, 1532–1689*
Lee Ward, *Recovering Classical Liberal Political Economy: Natural Rights and the Harmony of Interests*
Evert van der Zweerde, *Russian Political Philosophy: Anarchy, Authority, Autocracy*

Forthcoming:
Leandro Losada, *Machiavelli in Argentina and Hispanic America, 1880–1940: Liberal and Anti-Liberal Political Thought in Comparative Perspective*
Filippo Marsili and Eugenio Menegon, *Translation as Practice: Intercultural Encounters between Europe and China and the Creation of Global Modernities*

Russian Political Philosophy

Anarchy, Authority, Autocracy

EVERT VAN DER ZWEERDE

EDINBURGH
University Press

Edinburgh University Press is one of the leading university presses in the UK. We publish academic books and journals in our selected subject areas across the humanities and social sciences, combining cutting-edge scholarship with high editorial and production values to produce academic works of lasting importance. For more information visit our website: edinburghuniversitypress.com

Edinburgh University Press Ltd
The Tun – Holyrood Road
12(2f) Jackson's Entry
Edinburgh EH8 8PJ

First published in hardback by Edinburgh University Press 2022

Typeset in 11/13 Adobe Sabon by
IDSUK (DataConnection) Ltd, and
printed and bound by CPI Group (UK) Ltd
Croydon, CR0 4YY

A CIP record for this book is available from the British Library

ISBN 9781474460378 (hardback)
ISBN 9781474460385 (paperback)
ISBN 9781474460392 (webready PDF)
ISBN 9781474460408 (epub)

Contents

Introduction   vii
Acknowledgements   xv
Glossary of Russian Concepts   xvi
Timeline   xx

1. The Origins of Political Philosophy in Russia   1

2. First Debates in Russian Political Philosophy –
   'What Is to be Done?'   18

3. Socialism and Marxism in Russia: The Peasant Commune
   is Dead – Long Live the Peasant Commune!   37

4. Christian Political Philosophy in a Modernising
   World – Preparing for God's Kingdom   55

5. Russian Liberalism Revisited – Between a Rock and
   a Hard Place   75

6. The Long Russian Revolution – Signposts for a
   Roller Coaster   92

7. Soviet Marxism–Leninism and Political Philosophy –
   Never Mind the Gaps!   109

8. Christian Political Philosophy in Exile – Between
   Sobornost' and Theocracy   129

9. Counter-Soviet Political Philosophy in Emigration –
Beyond the Pale   147

10. Late Soviet and Early Post-Soviet Political
Philosophy – Licking the Wounds   165

11. Political Philosophy for a New Russia –
New Wine in Old Bottles?   185

Conclusion – Mediation Beyond Duality and Immediacy   202

Afterword   211
Bibliography   212
Index   245

Introduction

I beg you in advance, please don't think that all the charlatans of
the world are living in your country. They are everywhere! Forget,
generally, about Russia's exclusivity.

Aleksandr M. Piatigorskii, *Chto takoe politicheskaia filosofiia:
razmyshleniia i soobrazheniia* (Piatigorskii 2007: 38)

The topic of this book is political philosophy in Russia. The fact
that, to date, there is no monograph on this topic, is suggestive,
not of the absence of the phenomenon it seeks to address, but of
its intrinsic sensitivity. Whenever philosophy becomes political, it
is looked upon with suspicion by the authorities in place. Although
Russia is not unique on this point, it certainly is extreme. For long
periods of time, philosophy generally has been either forbidden or
subordinated by the incumbent regime (tsarist or Soviet), while
political philosophy as a separate academic discipline is almost
non-existent. This implies that one has to look for political philosophy in unexpected places. Sources include diaries, letters and
prison writings; authors include activists, novelists and a nun. At
the same time, it means that one needs a flexible understanding of
political philosophy.

Many of the authors discussed in this book use concepts that
may appeal to some while others abhor them. This applies both
to the political–theological language of Orthodox-Christian thinkers and to the political-philosophical categories used by socialists
and revolutionaries. The key categories of modern political theory,
from sovereignty to bright communist future, are 'secularised'
political–theological concepts (Schmitt). However, 'secular' is itself

a religious category that makes full sense only within the Latin–Christian tradition, and, second, political theology is already an attempt to articulate the political dimension of human existence. If, therefore, Christian thinkers detect, at some point, the Antichrist, while Marxists point to a class enemy, they are employing different, yet functionally equivalent concepts. In both cases, they identify the opponent as an enemy that has to be defeated or even destroyed, rather than as an adversary who can be convinced in a debate.

In order to present and analyse so widely diverse currents, authors and texts within a single framework, without burdening the book with elaborate arguments of my own, I apply a simplified, yet specific, conception of political philosophy. The basic, axiomatic premiss of this conception is that reality, at least as far as humans are concerned, is populated by an indeterminate number of finite beings, each with their limited physical, mental and symbolic powers and capacities. Between these beings there is, always and everywhere, the possibility of both conflict and concord. Where conflict prevails, alternatives are always available, and where consensus seems achieved, contestation always remains a possibility. Also, while agreement requires at least two persons, one suffices for polemics. In principle, this political dimension, as a potentiality, is present in anything human, from economic relations via art works and potable water to religiously obligated garments.

This ubiquitous and permanent possibility of conflict and concord I label 'the political' (following Mouffe, but adding concord). Given this first definition, I define politics as 'dealing with the political'. Politics comes in a large variety of forms, ranging from denial, via suppression and canalisation, to mobilisation and unchaining. In any concrete situation, politics stabilises into some form of political order or overall political form of society, which I call, using classical terminology, *politeia*. This *politeia* is of an objective and seemingly unassailable nature, but it is inevitably political and, therefore, contestable and vulnerable. One of its possible fortifications is a state-supported religion or ideology. The result is a given political system, surrounded by other entities that act as its constitutive others (Mouffe). Externally, it is surrounded by any number of similar entities with which it can stand in a number of different relations (enmity or friendship, war or trade, and so on), but which in any case act as its constitutive outside others that, among other things, shape its identity as being alike or different. Internally, it is surrounded by any number of explicitly or implicitly oppositional forces and positions, from critical voices to terrorist organisations.

While the system is the constitutive inside other of these forces and positions, they are, in their turn, its determined negations [*bestimmte Negationen*]. Similarly, factions within a political party, for example, are each other's inside constitutive other.

In this whole constellation, I distinguish, very traditionally, three dimensions. The first is theory, which can be religious, theological, philosophical or scientific, and that reflects upon, but also seeks to influence the existing socio-political situation broadly understood, and yields the concepts in which the humans that populate that situation understand themselves and articulate their differences. The second is praxis, understood as action, including protest and speech, but also any number of more or less stable repertoires and practices. Agents of such praxis are both a regime or government and indigenous or foreign oppositional groups and individuals. The third, often underrated, dimension is *poièsis*, understood as the making and maintaining of institutions, from laws and tax systems to political parties and concentration camps. This whole political constellation of more or less stable theoretical, practical and poiètical elements forms an internally harmonious or antagonistic and externally open or closed whole. It exists over time and thus obtains a life and logic of its own, with a 'political memory' that contains crucial events in the past, perceived dangers and opportunities, theoretical, practical and poiètical elements – from key concepts to perceived pitfalls – and a number of political and intellectual traditions. Since this constellation is itself political, it is intrinsically vulnerable, which explains the demand for ideological fortification and for clear markers of certainty (Lefort).

Simultaneously, if such a constellation has a long history of statehood and a self-referring intellectual tradition, it becomes recognisable and typical. This applies to those entities that we habitually call countries, represented by colourful patches on a political world map. In any such country, questions of power, authority, obedience and protest, and of the legitimacy or illegitimacy of each of these, arise and are resolved in one way or the other. Since humans also have the capacity to think independently and hence critically, political philosophy is likely to emerge in any society and to develop gradually from more rudimentary and implicit to more complex and explicit forms. Human thought, by default, transcends its own immediate situation in the direction of more general conceptualisations, even if universality remains an unreachable goal.

To the extent to which all forms of human society share a number of 'political issues', different traditions of political philosophy share a common ground and can engage in communication as a matter of principle, even if in practice it may be hard, for people from different backgrounds, to understand one another. In practice, this functions as the *tertium comparationis* in any endeavour in the field of comparative political philosophy. The central question then becomes: how do philosophers, from different traditions, relate to and deal with the basic issues that are part of their political reality? At this point, I use a triple concept of political philosophy. The first, most traditional, meaning is that of a branch of philosophy that has existing political reality as its object of conceptual analysis and normative judgement. The second meaning relates to the ontological question of why and how, if politics is the totality of ways of dealing with the political, our reality is political in the first place. The third and final meaning relates to the articulation, or concealment, of the fact that philosophy itself is inevitably political, too. This triple understanding is helpful in assessing political philosophy in Russia, or anywhere else for that matter. The aim of this book is to facilitate, on this conceptual basis, communication between Western and Russian political philosophy, building a bridge from one to the other.

This bridge consists of eleven arches: eleven chapters that are both chronological and topical. The underlying assumption is that this is the best way to build up gradually the elements that have shaped political philosophy in Russia and to highlight the features that determine it to this very day. The first two chapters sketch, first, a long pre-history that introduces a number of theoretical, practical and poiètical elements that are still recognisably there: an indigenous republican tradition, Byzantine and Tatar legacy, traditional forms of religious protest and opposition, and the impact of the West European Enlightenment. Second, an overview of the short eighteenth century focuses on the emergence of recurrent questions and debates, such as the traditionally opposed Westernising and Slavophile motifs, and on the genesis of radical political movements.

The following three chapters discuss, synchronically, several strands of political thinking: agrarian, Marxist, *narodist* and anarchist socialism; Christian political philosophy with a focus on four towering figures; and liberalism in its growth and maturation. Separate chapters on anarchism and *narodnichestvo* (often mistranslated as 'populism') were a possibility. I have, however, integrated a discussion of these trends in the second and third chapters, linked to the radicalisation of political philosophy in the nineteenth century and to the struggle over socialism in which Marxism was engaged.

The sixth chapter is the pivot of the book. It focuses on what was both a period of unprecedented cultural and philosophical bloom (the Silver Age), a politically explosive period with two revolutions and a Bolshevik takeover, and a period in which new *vekhi* (landmarks or signposts, comparable to Lefortian markers of certainty) were sought and finally set by a new, Soviet regime.

The next three chapters branch out synchronically, discussing, first of all, the gradual transformation, in the USSR, of a heavily politicised but lively Marxist philosophy into an official and orthodox Marxism–Leninism as an integral part of the Soviet system, both during the Stalin period and during the revitalisation of philosophy after World War II. Next, the eighth chapter addresses the still influential Russian religious philosophy that took shape outside the USSR, in exile, with positions that can be roughly identified as right, left and centre. The ninth chapter, finally, highlights a number of thinkers who left the USSR and became influential in Western academia, but whose Russian backgrounds are often overlooked, also because, contrary to the Russian religious philosophers, they did not emphasise it.

The two concluding chapters discuss, first, the later Soviet and early post-Soviet period, from the moment, around 1968, when the system started losing its credibility, via the period of *perestroika*, to the El'tsin years when Russian philosophers were seeking to deal with the Soviet past, but also with the uncertainties that came with neoliberal shock therapy. The eleventh chapter, finally, highlights a number of elements and motifs in the field of political philosophy that took shape during the first two decades of the twenty-first century, as part of a new, more self-confident Russia.

As a whole, these eleven chapters serve, for Western readers, as a bridge to largely unfamiliar territory. But why is Russian political philosophy so little known? With a number of noticeable exceptions, such as the notion of *sobornost'* or the dual concept of truth as *pravda* versus *istina*, Russian political-philosophical terminology has the same roots as other Indo-European languages. For Europeans, moreover, Russian is not a particularly difficult language to learn. Finally, many texts by Russian philosophers exist in translations into major West European languages, and the scholarly journal *Russian Studies in Philosophy* has existed since 1961. Russian philosophy is, in fact, widely read, but more by scholars in linguistics, Russian studies, literary studies and theology than by professional philosophers.

Part of the aim of this book, then, is to lower the threshold, but part of it is also to understand why that threshold is high in the first place. The shortest answer is Russia's otherness: while this otherness is attractive for cultural historians or literature specialists, for philosophers it seems to be a barrier. Russian philosophy is, simultaneously, too different and not different enough: too different to be accessible without background knowledge, but not different enough for the attraction of the exotic. Students of comparative political philosophy are therefore likely to focus on African or Chinese, rather than on Russian philosophy. Political philosophers, moreover, tend to concentrate on authors that are important within their own tradition: Bakunin and Kropotkin are classics in the anarchist tradition, and Lenin and Bogdanov are standard reading among Marxists, while religious philosophers and theologians have found their way to Bulgakov and Frank. Kojève and Rand are widely read, but often with complete neglect of their Russian roots. Il'in and Dugin have been claimed by the European extreme right for their own purposes, while Horujy and Bibikhin are in the process of being discovered.

With this book, I try to bring together in a comprehensible narrative a considerable number of authors and currents, in an attempt both to situate them in their shared background and to do justice to their originality and differences, while at the same time highlighting patterns and red threads. This has yielded a study that may serve at least three audiences: non-Russian political philosophers who want to gain relatively easy access to a largely unknown field; scholars in Russian and Soviet studies who want to add a political-philosophical perspective to their competence; and students in a broad range of disciplines who want to read about unknown thinkers and sometimes familiar, sometimes disturbing ideas such as the physical resurrection of all of humankind.

Given this broad approach, the book inevitably is selective. Not only have many authors been left out – this applies, for example, to Belinskii and Gradovskii – but all of them are discussed on a few pages while, in most cases, library shelves are filled with monographs and edited volumes. In making defensible selections and choices, I have tried to strike a balance between paying attention to the 'usual suspects' like Herzen or Solov'ëv, and highlighting less well-known figures, including a relatively large number of female thinkers such as Kollontai, Skobtsova and Dunayevskaya. Likewise, the bibliography is also highly selective: it is limited to those texts that I actually refer to, in the hopeful expectation that readers will find their own way if they want to learn more. In order to increase accessibility, I refer to translations, mostly into English, of the discussed texts, or to both original and translation (separated with a slash in the references). Unless indicated otherwise, translations are mine. I also refer to a number of my earlier publications, but have avoided repetition and overlap.

Where appropriate, I have tacitly adapted spelling and transliteration, especially in quotations. Transliteration is a complex issue in its own right. Throughout, I have used the simplified version of the Library of Congress system, without diacritical signs, thus writing Solov'ëv, Chernyshevskii and Kistiakovskii. Exceptions are made for widespread popular renderings – Tolstoy, Dostoevsky – and for authors who have mostly not written in Russian: Dunayevskaya and Groys rather than Dunaevskaia or Grois. Where confusion is possible, I have added between square brackets the spelling of names as they appear on book covers: Losev [Lossev], Chubais [Tschubais]. Key Russian concepts, often hard to translate unambiguously, have been included in a Glossary at the beginning of the book, while a Timeline should provide a general frame of reference.

What I have largely tried to refrain from is evaluation. Not only am I not inclined to pass judgement on the arguments of my Russian colleagues, but also I do not judge their conclusions, leaving both to them. I present arguments and conclusions as they present themselves to us in the texts at hand, bringing out contrasts and parallels. Nor is the point of this book to pass judgement on Russia. When it comes to Russian politics throughout the centuries, it is easy to point to a number of black, or at least dark grey, pages. However, this has little to do with a comparative evaluation, as if criticising Russia or the USSR implies a justification of situations elsewhere. If this book takes a side, it is with political philosophy, understood as unassisted critical thought, not with this or that political system or ideology.

To end on a personal note, this book is nourished by a life-long fascination with the USSR and Russia. Like Boris Kagarlitskii, I was born in 1958, and I can repeat his words to the effect that the Prague Spring of 1968 'was my first political experience' (Kagarlitsky 1989: 349). However, I experienced it from the other side of the Iron Curtain, shocked by the television footage that I was looking at from a safe spot, not as a witness to the discussions of the same events among Moscow dissidents. This was the starting point of an interest in international politics and, increasingly, the Europe on the other side of the Curtain. Also, the enigmatic combination of the familiar and the exotic of the letters CCCP on the suits of athletes from the USSR started a fascination with the Russian language. Prolonged stays in the USSR and Russia led to the clichéd 'love–hate relationship' with Russia that, surprisingly, many Russians share. Becoming familiar with the philosophical culture of this huge country and engaging in friendly dialogue with Russian colleagues who proved always ready to engage in discussion, implied a permanent search for points of comparison. This has been a most enriching experience in political philosophy, with one leg firmly rooted in the Western tradition and with the other foot testing the waters of that other European tradition. The aim of this book is, not least of all, to communicate that experience.

Acknowledgements

My gratitude is due, first of all, to series editor Vasileios Syros, who suggested writing this book in the first place, and to the very helpful staff at Edinburgh University Press.

Then there are the many people who, one way or another, assisted in the preparation of this work: students who participated in seminars that I taught, PhD students working on neighbouring topics, several student assistants, and many colleagues in the Netherlands, in Russia, and elsewhere. I am very grateful to all of them!

I want to thank in particular Janneke Toonders and Pam Tönissen for their critical, reliable and untiring assistance during the production process, and the staff at the Netherlands Institute in St Petersburg for their hospitality and help.

Most of all, I owe a big thank you to my wife, Godelief de Jong, for putting up with a husband who was periodically absent and frequently cranky during the writing of this book – unfortunately for her, the two did not always coincide. Whatever value this book may have, there is a great woman behind it.

Finally, I dedicate this book to two life-long friends, Jeroen Jongmans and Rinus van de Warreburg, who had no idea that their 1982 birthday present, a now worn and torn copy of Isaiah Berlin's *Russian Thinkers*, would have such long-term effects.

Glossary of Russian Concepts

aktsiia	акция	political action (small-scale and short-term)
artel'	артель	artisan cooperative
bogochelovechestvo	богочеловечество	Godmanhood, Divine Humanity, Theanthropy
bogochelovek	богочеловек	God-man [Jesus Christ]
bogoiskatel'stvo; bogoiskatel'	богоискательство; богоискатель	God-seeking; God-seeker
bogostroitel'stvo; bogostroitel'	богостроительство; богостроитель	God-building; God-builder
chelovekobozhestvo	человекобожество	deified humanity
glasnost'	гласность	openness, publicness [one of Gorbachëv's reform aims]
intelligentsia; intelligent(y)	интеллигенция; интеллигент(ы)	highly educated, often radical, layer of society; its member(s)
istina	истина	truth / verity
iurodivyi; iurodstvo	юродивый; юродство	'Fool in Christ', 'holy foolishness'
kukhnia	кухня	kitchen, symbol of private discussions that were impossible in public
kul'turologiia	культурология	cultural studies
lichnost'	личность	person(ality), personhood
mir	мир	political form of the peasant commune [*obshchina*]
narod	народ	people / nation, ordinary people / folk

narodnichestvo; narodnik(i)	народничество; народник	*narodism*, 'populism', betting on the *narod*; representative of this trend
narodnost'	народность	'people-ness'
neopochvennichestvo	неопочвенничество	revival of *pochvennichestvo*
oberprokuror	оберпрокурор	highest official in the Russian Orthodox Church during the synodal period (without patriarch)
obozhestvlenie	обожествление	deification, making/becoming divine; θεωσις
obshchestvennost'	общественность	sociality, societality [S. Frank]
obshchina	община	peasant community
pomestyi sobor	поместный собор	national (church) council
pochvennichestvo; pochvennik(i)	почвенничество; почвенник(и)	'return to native soil [*pochva*]' movement; adherent to this trend
perestroika	перестройка	reconstruction (one of Gorbachëv's reform aims)
pravda	правда	truth / justice
pravo	право	right [*droit, Recht*]
pravoslavie	православие	Orthodox Christianity
prosveshchenie	просвещение	education, (the) enlightenment
publitsistika	публицистика	opinion journalism, essays on current affairs
raskol; raskol'nik(i)	раскол; раскольник(и)	schism of the Russian Orthodox Church; schismatics
raznochinets, raznochintsy	разночинец, -цы	person of mixed social rank
rossiiskii	российский	Russian [statehood]
russkii	русский	Russian [ethnicity / language]
samizdat	самиздат	clandestine publication [self + publish]
samobytnyi; samobytnost'	самобытный; самобытность	specific, original; specificity
samoderzhavie	самодержавие	autocracy
sbornost'	сборность	collectivity
shestidesiatnik(i)	шестидесятник(и)	'people of the sixties': influential post-Stalin generation of philosophers
simfoniia	симфония	harmonious division of tasks between worldly and ecclesiastical authorities

slavianofil'stvo; slavianofil	славянофильство; славянофил	Slavophilism, 'love of things Slavic'; adherent to this trend: Slavophile
smutnoe vremia, vremia smuta	смутное время, время смута	time of troubles
sobor	собор	council [church], cathedral
sobornost'	соборность	depending on context: catholicity, conciliarity [eccl.]; communality, community spirit [societal]
sovet	совет	council, soviet
spetskhran	спецхран	*spetsial'noe khranenie*, closed department of a library
spravedlivost'	справедливость	justice
starets, startsy [pl.]	старец, старцы	religious elder, spiritual leader (often in a monastery)
starovertsy, staroobriadtsy	староверцы, старообрядцы	Old-Believers, Old-Ritualists: Orthodox Christians who rejected the reforms
svoboda	свобода	freedom, liberty
tamizdat	тамиздат	publication abroad [yonder + publish]
veche	вече	traditional popular assembly at town level
vekha, vekhi [pl.]	веха, вехи	signpost, landmark, buoy
volia	Воля	freedom, licence
zakon	Закон	(positive) law [*loi, Gesetz*]
zapadnichestvo; zapadnik	западничество; западник	Westernising trend; adherent to this trend: Westerniser
zemstvo	земство	local representative government

Abbreviations

KD	*Konstitutsionnye Demokraty; 'Kadety'*	Constitutional Democrats
KPRF	*Kommunisticheskaia Partiia Rossiiskoi Federatsii*	Communist Party of the Russian Federation
KPSS / CPSU	*Kommunisticheskaia Partiia Sovetskogo Soiuza*	Communist Party of the Soviet Union
NÈP	*Novaia Èkonomicheskaia Politika*	New Economic Policy

PSR	*Partiia Sotsial-Revoliutsionerov; 'Èsèry'*	Social-Revolutionary Party
ROC	*Russkaia Pravoslavnaia Tserkov'*	Russian Orthodox Church
RSDRP	*Rossiiskaia Sotsial-Demokraticheskaia Rabochaia Partiia*	Russian Social-Democratic Labour Party
RSFSR	*Rossiiskaia Sovietskaia Federativnaia Sotsialisticheskaia Respublika*	Russian Soviet Federative Socialist Republic
USSR	*Soiuz Sotsialisticheskikh Sovetskikh Respublik*	Union of Socialist Soviet Republics
VKP(b)	*Vserossiiskaia Kommunisticheskaia Partiia (bolshevikov)*	All-Russian Communist Party (Bolshevik)

Timeline

This timeline is largely 'conventional' and contested on several points; here, it merely serves orientation.

482:	founding of Kiev [according to legend]
859:	first mention of Novgorod
862:	founding of Kiev as capital of Rus'
903:	first mention of Pskov
988:	adoption of Orthodox Christianity in Kiev
1237–1481:	Mongol–Tatar 'yoke'
1453:	conquest of Constantinople by Mehmet II
1533–84:	*Tsar'* Ivan IV Groznyi ['the Terrible']
1552:	conquest of Kazan'
1598–1613:	*smutnoe vremia*
1613:	establishment of autocracy; start of Romanov dynasty
1613–45:	*Tsar'* Mikhail
1649:	introduction of serfdom
1652–66:	reforms of the Russian Orthodox Church
1670–1:	Razin uprising
1682–1725:	*Tsar'* Pëtr I Velikii ['the Great']
1700–1917:	synodal period ROC [no patriarch]
1724:	founding of Academy of Sciences
1755:	founding of Moscow (State) University
1762–96:	*Tsarina* Ekaterina II Velikaia ['the Great']
1771:	plague riot [*chumnoi bunt*]
1773–4:	Pugachëv uprising
1789:	French Revolution
1790:	exile of Radishchev

1801–25:	*Tsar'* Aleksandr I
1814–15:	Congress of Vienna
1825–55:	*Tsar'* Nikolai I
1825:	Decembrist uprising
1833:	'Orthodoxy, Autocracy, Nationality' official slogan
1833–63:	effective ban on philosophy
1836:	publication of Chaadaev's first 'philosophical letter' – author declared insane
1843–51:	lecture series by Granovskii
1844–5:	*zapadnichestvo – slavianofil'stvo* controversy
1848:	liberal revolution in many European countries
1849:	near-execution of Dostoevsky
1853–6:	Crimean War
1855–81:	*Tsar'* Aleksandr II
1857–67:	Herzen's *Kolokol* appearing in London
1861–4:	Great Reforms
1863:	*Chto delat'* (Chernyshevskii)
1869:	*Katekhizis revoliutsionera* (Nechaev, Bakunin [?])
1874:	*khozdenie v narod*
1878:	Trepov affair (Zasulich)
1880–1905:	Pobedonostsev *oberprokuror* of the ROC
1881:	assassination of Tsar Aleksandr II
1881–94:	*Tsar'* Aleksandr III
1881:	letter exchange Zasulich–Marx
1894–1917:	*Tsar'* Nikolai II
1898:	founding of RSDRP
1900:	founding of PSR
1901:	excommunication by the ROC of Tolstoy
1902:	edited volume *Problemy idealizma*
1904–5:	Russo-Japanese War
1905:	January Revolution
1905:	founding of KD
1905:	October Manifesto
1906–12:	Elections 1st–4th Duma [March]
1909:	edited volume *Vekhi*
1910:	edited volume *Intelligentsia v Rossii*
1914–18:	World War I
1917:	February (8 March) and October (7 November) Revolutions
1917:	Provisional Government and Petrograd Sovet
1917–24:	Vladimir I. Lenin [Ul'ianov] first Soviet leader
1917:	Elections Constituent Assembly [November]

1917–18:	National Council of the ROC, election patriarch Tikhon
1918:	Constituent Assembly disbanded [January]
1918:	killing of Tsar Nikolai II and his family in Ekaterinburg
1918:	edited volume *Iz glubiny*
1918:	assaults on Lenin and on Moisei Uritskii (Cheka leader) [August]
1918:	Red Terror [August–October]
1918–21:	Military Communism and Civil War
1921:	Kronshtadt uprising
1921–8:	NĖP
1921:	edited volume *Smena vekh*
1922:	'Philosophy Steamer'
1924–53:	Iosif V. Stalin [Dzhugashvili]
1929:	Lev Trotsky exiled
1929–31:	Grand Turning Point [*velikii perelom*], leading to official Marxism–Leninism
1929:	first five-year plan
1930–60:	GULag
1936–8:	Great Purge [*Bol'shaia chistka*] / Great Terror / show trials
1939–45:	World War II
1941–5:	Great Patriotic War
1942:	rehabilitation of the ROC, patriarchate re-established
1947:	'philosophical discussion', founding of *Voprosy filosofii*
1953–64:	Nikita S. Khrushchёv general secretary [*gensek*], period of 'thaw [*ottepel'*]'
1956:	20th CPSU Congress; 'destalinisation'
1958:	founding of *Filosofskie nauki*
1962:	Novocherkassk Massacre
1964–82:	Leonid I. Brezhnev *gensek*
1965:	process against Daniel' and Siniavskii
1965–85:	period of 'stagnation [*zastoi*]'
1968:	suppression of Prague Spring
1974:	edited volume *Iz-pod glyb*
1985–91:	Mikhail S. Gorbachёv *gensek*, period of 'reconstruction and transparency [*perestroika i glasnost'*]'
1991:	founding of *Logos*
1991–9:	Boris N. El'tsin president
1996:	contest for a new 'Russian idea'
2000:	publication of the ROC's *Osnovy sotsial'noi doktriny*
2000–8:	Vladimir V. Putin president

2008–12:   Dmitri A. Medvedev president
2012:   Pussy Riot's 'blasphemous' performance
2012–:   Vladimir V. Putin president
2013:   founding of *Stasis*
2014:   President Putin handing out copies of Solov'ëv, Berdiaev and Il'in

Chapter 1

The Origins of Political Philosophy in Russia

[P]easants, Cossacks, and schismatics, yearning for their old way of life, had long hoped that a good tsar would someday appear and by the stroke of his pen grant them freedom, happiness, and prosperity.

Paul Avrich, *Russian Rebels* (Avrich 1972: 185)

In *Rossiia i Evropa* (1869), the pan-Slavist thinker Nikolai Iakovlevich Danilevskii (1822–85) defined Europe as 'a Western peninsula of Asia, initially distinguishing itself from it less than the other Asiatic peninsulas, but gradually, towards its extremity, more and more splitting up and partitioning itself' (Danilevskii 1995: 47 / 2013: 47). The absence of any clear border explains why Europe and Asia define themselves in relation to each other (van der Zweerde 2007: 53f). From the European perspective, Russia has always been a partly frightening, partly fascinating, European Big Other. Often perceived as backward or barbarian, Russia has always impressed through its sheer size, natural richness (from furs to carbohydrates) and military force, moving deep into the heart of Europe at the end of two great wars (1815 and 1945). The opposition of a 'barbarian' Russia and a 'perverted' Europe is a simplification (Scheidegger 1993), but the two have frequently been each other's constitutive (outside) other. The construction of a barbarian Eastern Europe has been instrumental in the self-instalment of an Enlightened and liberal West (Wolff 1994; De Custine 1975 [1839]), while the construction of a perverted West has been equally instrumental in the Orthodox East's self-identification (Demacopoulos and Papanikolaou 2013).

One major factor in Russia's political history is indeed geography. The largely flat Russian lands are easily swept by cold winds from the North and by scorching heat and drought from the South. This makes agriculture vulnerable in spite of the fertile soil and explains the repeated famines. Russia's limited access to open sea accounts for its traditional fear of encirclement. Flatness, openness and a sparse population make it vulnerable to invasion from the Eastern steppes and, from the West, by Sweden, Poland, France and Germany, some of which have managed to reach Moscow (Polish forces in the sixteenth century, Napoleon Bonaparte in 1812), while others (the *Wehrmacht* in World War II) just failed. This explains the desire to break through encirclement and establish extensive buffer zones, including the Western buffer zone, aptly called 'bloodlands' by Timothy Snyder (Snyder 2011). The expansion that followed the defeat of the Tatar Golden Horde turned Russia into the largest country on Earth by far, covering eleven time zones and thirty latitudes.

In order to understand political philosophy as it developed in Russia, we need to know where it came from. What has shaped its points of departure and reference? What accounts for its specifics? Even if major sources are the same in Western Europe and the other, Russian, Europe – namely, Ancient Greek philosophy and Christianity – different conditions and circumstances have facilitated other developments and trajectories, which then obtained lives of their own. This chapter traces the origins of political-philosophical thought in Russia from its inception until well into the nineteenth century, and in three big steps: the period until the start of the Romanov dynasty, the period of modernisation that ended with Peter the Great [Pëtr I] and the period of Russian Enlightenment [*Prosveshchenie*].

Three Defining Elements: *Veche, Simfoniia, Khanate*

Russian political history is mostly shaped by three major factors: the 'republican' *veche* and *zemstvo* tradition, the Byzantine heritage and the Tatar legacy of a centralised state. Concerning the first factor, early Russian political history is often linked to the foundational narrative of the Slavonic tribes asking the Vikings to rule over Kiev because they themselves were incapable of doing so. This no doubt partly mythical story depicts Russians as somewhat anarchic people, averse to government and regarding political power as never their own. The political life of the Slavonic and Finno-Ugric tribes that populated the area was probably organised, like that of their Germanic neighbours, around an assembly of warriors and household leaders: the *veche*.[1] This assembly contains democratic, or republican, elements that have remained part of Russia's political tradition. In Medieval Russia, the *veche* was the primary form of political organisation, and it coexisted in Russian cities with the rotational system of princes from the Rurikid dynasty – allegedly of Viking origin – the oldest member of which would be Prince [*gosudar'*] (or, rarely, Princess [*gosudarynia*]) of Kiev. Both institutions ended with the Tatar invasions and the sacking of Kiev (1240), but the *veche* continued to exist in the areas outside Tatar rule. Novgorod [Newtown], which ruled over the entire Northern part of Russia, and in its smaller Western neighbour, the Republic of Pskov, developed into prosperous aristocratic republics.

The *veche* in Novgorod and Pskov degenerated into an oligarchy even before the two cities were incorporated in Muscovy. However, the free peasantry of Northern Russia [*pomor'e*], liberated from Novgorod and not colonised by Moscow, retained a political system of local self-government. It ranged from the local *mir* (the political form of the *obshchina* [commune] (Beecher 2013: 383)), via the larger *zemstvo*, to the national *zemskii sobor* [land assembly], which functioned well into the seventeenth century until it was abolished by Pëtr I (Solzhenitsyn 1995: 6–10; Platonov 1985).

The *veche* is easily idealised because of its stark contrast with the just as easily demonised 'Mongol-Tatar Yoke' [*tatarskoe igo*] (1237–1481), as well as with later absolutism and autocracy. Certainly, the Russian *veche* was a far cry from an all-inclusive democratic republic, but the existence of a tradition of shared political rule by a city's military and economic elites (a continuation of the warriors and heads of households from tribal times), and the existence of local self-rule in the North, undermine the suggestion that Russians are naturally predisposed both to accept and to exercise authoritarian rule. The *veche* has always been invoked, down to the present day, in the argument for democracy or, more accurately, republicanism. A line thus runs from the *veche*, and the guilds in Novgorod and Pskov, via the emerging *zemstvo* liberalism of professionals in the late nineteenth century, to today's liberals within the political elite.

A second major factor in the shaping of Russia's political reality is Orthodox Christianity. Kievan Rus' was top-down baptised in 988 by Vladimir the Great (*Povest'* 1997: 86f; Dennes 1987: 31). For a long time, Christianity remained an elite phenomenon that met with folk resistance, and it became a national religion only at the end of the Tatar period (Fedotov 1965–6: vol. I, 346; Trepanier 2010: 11). With the adoption of Christianity from Byzantium, Russia also imported the political theology of the Eastern Roman Empire that combined Christian and neo-Platonic elements. Recent scholarship has challenged the view that Neoplatonism did not contain a political philosophy. It could draw, for example, on the contrast between Plato's 'first best' *Politeia* and his 'second-best' *Nomoi* (O'Meara 2003: 85). Also questioned is the received view that the Byzantine tradition was purely neo-Platonic and ignored Aristotle: 'a number of Byzantine intellectuals, including emperors and other figures of political experience and importance, had studied the *Politics* carefully, and did make use of its concepts, arguments and images in formulating their own ideas about politics', often as a way of expressing 'dissident opinion' (Kaldellis 2011: 123, 137). Contrary to one-size-fits-all Platonic idealism, the Aristotelian paradigm implies that different countries can have different constitutions, and highlights the man-made nature of the earthly city, which subverts the ideologeme of a divine sanction of worldly authority. Clearly, the Platonic model better fits a monotheistic political theology, and the Byzantine state, as Christian continuation of the Roman Empire, 'had an extraordinarily stable, resilient, and so long-lasting political system' (ibid.: 123); its 'theocratic constitution' remained 'essentially unchanged' during eleven centuries (Runciman 2003: 164).

The official Russian Orthodox political theology that took shape continued the Byzantine tradition of dual rule by an emperor and a patriarch. Even if, in caesaropapist practice, the emperor was the actual ruler and patriarchs were elected by his intercession, the principle was that of *simfoniia* between the two. Consequently, the patriarch never became a worldly ruler. The concept of 'two swords' in one pair of hands is a specifically Latin Christian idea, which could never have possibly entered the mind of a Byzantine patriarch or emperor. In the Eastern Christian world, the 'Constantinian' idea of an empire which was itself Christian, with a Christian *caesar / basileus*, went along with the concept of a harmonious, symphonic division of labour between the heads of state and church, respectively, and thus, ideally, a separation of powers civil and ecclesiastical (Demacopoulos and Papanikolaou 2017). Even if the reality did not match the ideal, this division of labour excluded the legitimate power of any third body or function.

The third major factor is the occupation of the Russian lands by the Tatars, invading on horseback from the endless steppes. Christian Europeans have ascribed successful Tatar domination to fast horses and ruthless cruelty alone, overlooking their military organisation, sophisticated long-distance mail system, effective unitary tribute system prefiguring tax collection, census [*perepis'*] of the population and religious toleration (Halperin 1985: 24). Russian discussions of the 'Tatar Yoke' often exaggerate its oppressive nature and understate the extent to which Russia has adopted elements of the Tatar–Mongol political system which introduced several assets of the modern centralised state (Zamaleev 1987: 170; Halperin 1985: 89, 93). Muscovy benefitted from Tatar–Mongol domination because it removed two major obstacles, the *veche* and the independent nobility (boyars). When Tatar domination was ended in 1480 by Ivan III (the Great) of Moscow, Muscovy had become the main principality, thanks to close cooperation with the Tatar Golden Horde. It reunited the Russian lands, conquered the North West that had not been under Tatar domination (Novgorod and Pskov), and rapidly expanded in Eastern and Southern directions, incorporating the territory of the Golden Horde and its predominantly Muslim population. When the Golden Horde's capital, Kazan', was conquered by the troops of Ivan IV ('The Terrible' [Groznyi] (b. 1530, r. 1533–84)) in 1552, it was a thriving commercial, cultural and administrative centre. It is more than likely that Muscovy adopted much of the Tatar system of rule, including its vertical organisation with a 'sovereign' *Khan* who ruled through a system of vassals (Thompson 1987: 100; Halperin 1985: 87–9).

Against the background of these three factors, Moscow became the centre of a new Russia that inherited from the Second Rome the Byzantine model of, ideally, a symphonic relationship between state and church, emperor and patriarch. When, in 1453, Constantinople was conquered, Sultan Mehmet (Muḥammad) II (1432–81), named al-Fātiḥ – literally, 'the opener' (for Islam), called himself *kayser-i-Rum*, thus adopting the title of Roman Caesar. At that time, Muscovy already was the major power, both ecclesiastical and civil, over the Russian lands (Fedotov 1965–6: I, 346). It became a *mitropoliia* [part of a patriarchate] in 1448, declared itself autocephalous in 1461 and was recognised as patriarchate in 1589. Ivan IV officially adopted the name of *tsar'*, also derived from *caesar*, in 1547. From Ivan IV onwards, and reinforced with Pëtr I, who adopted the title of *imperator*, the Russian tsar started to resemble the Sultan and the Tatar *khan* as a single authority above the law. In practice, the relation of *simfoniia* tended towards caesaropapism, as it had in Constantinople.

Political antagonism was expressed in political–theological terms. An important early instance of this is the controversy that arose in the late fifteenth century between the followers of Iosif Volokolamskii (1439/40–1515) and those of Nil Sorskii [Maikov] (1433–1508). The first group, called 'possessors', endorsed monastic property and actively supported tsarist rule, which implied military and economic functions of monasteries as well as the persecution of heretics. This group, which advocated a political theology that presented the state church of Muscovy as the Kingdom of God on Earth, came out victorious. The result was a hegemonic 'theocratic absolutism' (Zamaleev 1987: 169), a variant of representative political theology in which the tsar, God's vicar on Earth, has divinely sanctioned authority. This 'political–theological rationalism' supported the tsar's authority as well as the close bond between state and church (Zamaleev 1987: 173, 180), and matched the ideologeme of Moscow as the 'Third Rome' after Rome and Constantinople, and hence the legitimate heir of both – all three being built on seven hills added to the symbolism.

The second group advocated retreat from this world, separation of state and church and renunciation of monastic property: hence their name of 'non-possessors'. Sorskii is a key figure in the development of hesychasm [from Greek ἡσυχία – being silent], a long-standing and often oppositional tradition in Orthodoxy associated with Gregory of Palamas (c. 1296–1357/9) (Payne 2011: 81–107). These non-possessors stood for monastic contemplation, opposed serfdom, opted for voluntary conversion of heretics, perceived the church as a temporary and worldly institution, and emphasised the inner relation between human being and God (van den Bercken 2018: 387). They retreated into the province as hermits and *startsy*, and continued the hesychast traditions and the teaching of Sophia, both of which emerged later to play a role in political philosophy (Stahl 2019: 128). This second position, which turns away from worldly affairs and politics, has acted as an undercurrent in Russian Orthodoxy ever since, making it the more political of the two: the refusal to identify positively with the existing order opens the possibility of negatively rejecting it (Jubara 2000: 81–2). Hegemonic political theology thus was challenged by an anti-political mysticism and irrationalism which was inevitably political itself. Increasingly, it was accompanied by anti-clerical, heretical and sectarian sentiments and positions, due to the state's tightening control over church and religion, which contrasted sharply with the regime of relative religious toleration that the Tatars had practised (Halperin 1985: 24; Zamaleev 1987: 181).

Furthermore, hesychasm often went along with the phenomenon of *iurodstvo*, a recurrent phenomenon since the Kievan period. It is particularly in the fourteenth to seventeenth centuries that the *iurodivyi* – 'God's fool' or 'fool for Christ'[2] – is an important figure with political significance. Contrary to the embedded court jester or the scheduled ritual of carnival, the holy fool articulates radical rejection of this wicked world. Radical as they may be, holy fools are not crazy or mentally ill: denouncing poverty and injustice makes their activity political, particularly when other ways of articulating the political dimension of society are lacking. There is a significant difference between a court jester and a 'fool for Christ'. The jester is typically part of the court entourage as the voice of unorthodox, unruly, impolite and incorrect opinions that never must, but always can, inspire those in power. The jester is the outside of the box that the rulers cannot think beyond, at least not publicly, and as such is an integral part of the political order. The 'fool in Christ', by contrast, is not part of the court or of any institution – not even, as a rule, of the church. Not limited or inhibited by social convention or religious ritual, the divine fool can do and say anything he or she likes, confronting the authorities not only with unpleasant truths, but also with the very contingency of socio-political order. The jester, like a stand-up comedian, is the constitutive other inside the existing order, a parasite fed by its host, assisting the powers-that-be in affirming their realism and reasonability. The 'fool in Christ', by contrast, is the constitutive outside other, living at the margin of society and politics, eating the crumbs from the table (Novakshonoff 2017: 6). While the jester can be allowed, or even invited, to speak, but also be summoned to shut up, thus falling under a regime of toleration and control, the divine fool speaks with or without permission, subject to no rule at all except that of his own mind and conscience, a free manifestation of the absolute. The role of the jester is political in an 'embedded' sense, turning protest into laughter, while the holy fool represents the ineradicability of the political. The most famous *iurodivyi* was Vasilios Blazhennyi [The Blessed] (1459[?]–1557[?]), who openly criticised Ivan IV. The Cathedral on Red Square, just outside the Kremlin, built on Ivan IV's orders to commemorate his conquest of Kazan', was named St Basil's Cathedral after him, and Pussy

Riot's performance in front of it in 2012 explicitly referred to the *iurodstvo* tradition.

Iurodstvo is a legitimate form of religious piety in the Orthodox tradition, but in order for the person to be canonised, the church must determine whether a *iurodivyi* is genuine or fake. This becomes difficult when the *iurodivyi* is a possible, perhaps the only possible, oppositional role in society, since canonical status effectively means political immunity. Until Pëtr I, the ROC wielded autonomous authority, canonising a few dozen *iurodivye* and recognising in them possible weapons in the ongoing power struggle with the tsars. When Pëtr I replaced the Patriarch by a Holy Synod, the ROC stopped recognising and canonising *iurodivye* and started to suppress the phenomenon generally, albeit only with partial success (Likhachëv and Panchenko 1991: 127, 170; Ivanov 2005: 317–30). Moderniser Pëtr I, in line with imported West European absolutism, thus effectively reduced the political arena – Terrible as Ivan IV may have been, Pëtr I is the first absolute monarch in Russian history, completing a period of political modernisation.

Autocratic Modernisation

The *smutnoe vremia* [Time of Troubles], a period of political crisis from 1598 to 1613 with competing pretenders to the throne, ended with the enthronement of Mikhail Romanov in 1613. He was elected by an ad hoc national assembly [*zemskii sobor*], followed by the establishment, in 1649, of serfdom as the socio-economic basis of society, and of service gentry (against the boyars) as the political basis. In 1613, absolute monarchy was formally ratified, and if the corresponding charter is not an eighteenth-century fabrication, it can be considered an early Russian constitution (Riasanovsky 1993: 171; von Rimscha 1983: 230; Pipes 1966: 61, and Karamzin in Pipes 1966: 213–14). This 'marked nothing less than the great divide between medieval Muscovy and modern Russia', replacing a patrimonial regime by a modern state (John T. Alexander in Platonov 1985: x). Russian autocracy combined absolute monarchy with the modern concept of the centralised state. Reformist tsars like Pëtr I, Catherine the Great [Ekaterina II] and Aleksandr II used the powerful state to reform society from above, while reactionary tsars like Nikolai I, Aleksandr III and Nikolai II retained the first, but rejected the second. Ever since, reformism and conservatism have been competing forces within the government, precisely because the government was largely the only dynamic force, claiming the role of enlightened reformer against church, gentry and, often, peasantry; only intellectuals and later *intelligenty* were its natural, but often more radical, partners.

The church reform by Patriarch Nikon (1652–66) in the mid-seventeenth century led to a major schism [*raskol*] among Russian Orthodox Christians. The so-called Old-Believers [*starovertsy*] or Old-Ritualists [*staroobriadtsy*], pejoratively called schismatics [*raskol'niki*], opposed not only the turn to the Byzantine rite of the official church, but also the Latinising influences from the West (Eastern Ukraine, which had been under Polish rule, became part of Muscovy in 1654), which brought along humanism, scholasticism and the study of 'philosophy' (notably Aristotle). Too easily denounced as peasant obscurantism, the schismatics' resistance was rather 'an intellectual rejection of a bifurcation of cultures [popular and elite, EvdZ], unthinkable in their scheme of one Redeemer, one true Faith, one Salvation, and one holy God-ordained Tsar' (Okenfuss 1995: 45). Heavily persecuted, the *raskol'niki* fled from urban centres and split into a large number of groups which recognised neither each other nor the official church, and have continued to live in secluded communities, partly returning to economic and cultural prominence in the late nineteenth and early twentieth centuries: their illegality was lifted only in 1905, while the ROC dropped its anathema against the *raskol'niki* as late as 1971.[3]

The model of two tokens of power, sword and staff, in the hands of a single sovereign, as symbolised in the well-known cover of Thomas Hobbes's *Leviathan*, became a Russian reality in 1700, when Pëtr I decapitated the ROC by not allowing the election of a successor to Patriarch Adrian, and replacing the Patriarch by a Holy Synod based on the Swedish model. Absolute monarchy included subordination of the church under the state and centralisation of the state's structures. An absolutist regime founds itself on the exclusive authority of, in this case, the tsar, legitimised by a monotheistic political theology, but the political dimension of such a construction has to be systemically denied as it disturbs the normative order. Ever since, both the ROC and the Orthodox community in a broader sense have been struggling to define their religious identity and their position vis-à-vis the authorities in a long series of switches.

In both East and West, the possible tension between worldly and ecclesiastical powers was resolved by a form of monarchy. In the West, the solution was absolutism, which allowed for a single sovereign power (first royal absolutism, as theorised by Thomas Hobbes and others, then later democratic absolutism, elaborated philosophically in Jean-Jacques Rousseau's *Du contrat social*). In the East, the solution was autocracy [*samoderzhavie*], with the crucial difference that, while in the West the sovereign monarch or an assembly was expected, 'ideal-theoretically', to rule according to natural law and to be enlightened by Reason or steered by a *volonté générale*, the sovereign *tsar'* in the East was expected, again 'ideal-theoretically', to rule by divine sanction and to be enlightened by Revelation rather than Reason. From this angle, 'European' rulers like Pëtr I and Ekaterina II, both 'Great', are exceptions rather than the rule.

Smutnoe vremia is not only a negative notion: 'There were moments not only of uncertainty but also of opportunity and hope for positive change, promising better times' (Obolonsky 2019: 124f). Later, *smutnye vremena* like the 'long revolution' (1905–22) and the late 1980s to early 1990s are similarly two-sided. After such crises, retrospectively labelled 'time of troubles' by the victors and 'time of glory' by the defeated, the new reality may be similar to the old one in some respects (order, domination, hierarchy), while different in others (legal, centralised, autocratic). Russia's seventeenth century was such a period. At this time, in line with developments elsewhere in Europe, a shift took place from the idea of a Christian monarch accountable to the religious authorities to that of an absolute monarch accountable only to God. With Pëtr I, this shift towards a West European model of absolute monarchy was completed, and *samoderzhavie* became the trademark of the Russian Empire.

Under Pëtr I, Russia also emerged 'as a major philosophical and scientific, as well as naval and military, power in the Baltic', and the newly founded St Petersburg Russian Imperial Academy of Sciences (1724, still existing) 'became the scene of some of the continent's most acrimonious philosophical strife' (Israel 2001: 561). In the eighteenth century, Russia was perhaps backward socio-economically and politically, but not philosophically or scientifically. Innovations, however, remained superficial, as most academics were foreigners and instruction was mostly in foreign languages (Tschiżewskij 1974: 188). They did not, moreover, extend into the field of politics, but served the 'enlightening' of a 'despotic' regime. At the same time, these academic battles were deeply political as part of Peter's struggle against the independent power of the ROC.

Still, absolutist modernisation met with fierce resistance. One of the many misconceptions about Russia is the alleged political apathy of its population. In fact, Russia has an impressive record of popular uprisings, starting with the violent resistance by 'heathen masses instigated by the *volkhvi* [shamans]' against the imposition of Christianity in 988 (Fedotov 1965–6: vol. I, 344). In the seventeenth century, the persecution of religious sects, especially that of the *staroobriadtsy*, who did not accept the church reforms of 1666 [*sic!*], turned them into pockets of resistance (Tschiževskij 1974: 196) and yielded a leader, Priest Avvakum Petrov (1620–82), whose militancy puts him at the level of Puritans and Presbyterians in Western Europe. The introduction of serfdom in 1649, adopted from the West and abolished in 1861, meant that more than half of the peasant population had no political rights at all; it met with resistance as it 'deepened the enslavement of the peasantry' (Solzhenitsyn 1995: 8f; Wirtschaftler 2008: 93). In the seventeenth and eighteenth centuries, rural Russia was the scene of large-scale rebellions, of which those led by Stenka Razin in 1670–1 and Emel'ian Pugachëv in 1773–4 are the most widely known (Avrich 1972).

These uprisings all originated in the Southern borderlands of the Russian Empire, were led by charismatic Don Cossacks and were not oriented against the tsar or central government, but against local nobility and bureaucrats. Religious and social myth played an important role:

> The lower classes were hungry for a messiah, and the ground swell of popular support that arose around the rebel leaders owed much to the belief that the promised saviour had arrived to punish the wicked and purge the land of sin and suffering. (Avrich 1972: 1)

The followers of Pugachëv expected a good tsar to take the place of the wicked incumbent (Solzhenitsyn 1995: 25). The perception of political power as 'either an evil means for good ends, or [. . .] a source of sin' combined with the wishful expectation of a just [*pravednyi*] or 'White Tsar [*Belyi tsar*']' has become a recurrent motif in Russian political thought (Dobrokhotov 2001: 519, 526–7). The persecuted *staroobriadtsy* played an important role in these uprisings, and Avvakum became a hero of many critical currents and authors, while his auto-hagiography, entitled *Zhitie*, could not appear in Russia until 1861 (Avvakum 2001: 16; Ronin 2001: 164). To the great rebellions, many smaller revolts can be added. They include the religiously flavoured popular uprising in 1654, against both state and church authorities (Alexander 2003: 18f), and especially the 1771 Plague Riot [*chumnoi bunt*]: when the bubonic plague had killed some

50,000 Muscovites, a large crowd gathered in central Moscow, collecting money for a silver covering for an icon they believed to possess miraculous healing powers.

Between Enlightenment and Despotism

Russia's autocratic appearance concealed remarkable diversity: visitors in the eighteenth century noted 'an absolute monarchy that appeared to function as a federal empire' with a variety of local political regimes, including 'the military democracy of the Kozaks' (Whatmore 2013: 309). While Medieval Rus' had been a relatively homogeneous polity, this changed rapidly when Muscovy became the motor of rapid expansion, leading to the inclusion of numerous ethnic and religious minorities. Although Russia has generally identified itself as an Orthodox Christian nation, it houses a remarkable religious and ethnic diversity due to the inclusion of – in historical order – Muslim, shamanistic, Buddhist and Jewish populations as a result of Russia's expansion, and the invitation of West Europeans (Germans, Dutch) and East Asians (Koreans in particular) to assist in the modernisation of commerce and agriculture. Russia became, among other things, a colonial empire, with the predictable effect that its unity had to be ideologically underpinned with a civilisational narrative. A clear example is Ekaterina II, who 'gave liberties to non-Orthodox Christians in her search for migrants to colonise the East'; at the same time, she was cautious, being of German descent herself, not to hurt her subjects' feelings and thus had to appear as Orthodox as possible (Goldie and Wokler 2016: 107; Tschiževskij 1974: 193). The Russian Empire displayed the paradox of the colonised coloniser, employing often more advanced populations for its own expansion. This situation lasted until the end of the empire, when, for example, the Grand Duchy of Finland had a constitution and a parliament that mainland Russia was lacking.

Two key motifs in the philosophy of politics and law in Russia from the eighteenth century onwards can be connected to the names of Aleksandr Nikolaevich Radishchev (1749–1802) and Mikhail Vasil'evich Lomonosov (1711–65) (Osipov 2014: 3). Although Lomonosov and Radishchev did not elaborate political philosophies in the full sense of the term, they took clearly diverging political stances vis-à-vis existing political reality. Lomonosov, from the perspective of the ideology of enlightened despotism [*prosveshchënnoe samoderzhavie*], advocated the realisation, top-down by the state, of necessary socio-economic and cultural reforms, starting a line of thinking all the way down to Gorbachëv. Radishchev, by contrast, from a natural rights perspective, advocated a democratic rule-of-law state without feudal law and despotism, thus pointing in the direction of a bottom-up political self-organisation of the people; yet he did not give priority to private life, as mainstream Western liberalism would do, but rather insisted, as a republican, on the unity of private and public life, thus starting another line of development that would form the backbone of Russian liberalism.

Still in the eighteenth century, Russia became a self-evident and self-conscious part of Europe, and several of the French *philosophes* set part of their hopes on the Russian court, rightly so when it came to supporting and stimulating the sciences, or to introducing military and mining techniques, but wrongly when it came to political reform. Enlightenment thinkers like Voltaire and Diderot had, in fact, every reason to bet on enlightened monarchs rather than on democratic government, let alone clergy or gentry, and Russia, with its tradition of top-down modernisation, was a case where it made sense to try to convince an autocratic ruler who could invoke the authority of reason while overruling that of tradition or religion, suppressing anarchy and uprising where necessary. This tells us something about Russia, but also about the flawed assumptions of despotic Enlightenment. A hopeful Diderot proposed, in his *Mémoires pour Cathérine II* (1773), intermediate institutions but, after she rebuffed him, humbly suggested, in *Observations sur le Nakaz* (1774; published only in 1920), 'a representative body, to meet every five years so as to judge whether the sovereign had observed the laws' (Beales 2016: 519; Fetscher 2016: 581). Politically, Ekaterina II was sympathetic to the ideas of the Enlightenment thinkers, but she was not immune to the logic of centralised power: if reform is not top-down, it undermines the top by default. She herself composed a Regulation [*Nakaz*] based on Montesquieu, Beccaria and others, which she allowed to be widely discussed (Beales 2016: 508), and she offered Diderot the possibility of publishing the remaining volumes of the *Encyclopédie* in Russia if French censorship were to block it (Fetscher 2016: 580), an offer which Diderot declined, despite his sympathies for the tsarina.

The Russian tsars continuously oscillated between, on the one hand, acquiescence to the traditional faith of the *narod* [people, folk] and the vested interests of the nobility, and, on the other, a perceived need for top-down reform and modernisation. Empress

Ekaterina II received her enlightenment not only from *philosophes* like Voltaire, with whom she exchanged 185 letters between 1763 and 1778 (Stroev 2006), or Diderot, with whom she met on an almost daily basis in 1773–4 (Zaretsky 2019), but also, and increasingly, from Russian intellectuals who had been sent abroad to study. They introduced thinking on matters political by what Leo Strauss has famously called 'the unassisted human mind' – unassisted by any other authority than that of the author's own reason (Strauss 1988: 13). Apart from the German (Leibniz, Wolff) and French Enlightenment, Russia also experienced, through academics like Semën Efimovich Desnitskii (1760–98), a pupil of Adam Smith, the impact of the Scottish Enlightenment, which, broadly speaking, mitigated German metaphysics and French rationalism with British common sense. Finally, as the eighteenth turned to the nineteenth century, Russian as a an academic and literary language took shape (Koyré 1976: 35, 44, n. 59, and 113–14, n. 4, 15).

One major representative of the Russian Enlightenment was Ekaterina II's friend, Princess Ekaterina Romanovna Vorontsova-Dashkova (1743–70), who was sent to Paris and Edinburgh to meet Voltaire and Diderot, Smith and Ferguson, and many others. Upon her return, she was appointed head of the Academy of Sciences. The historical puzzle is how it was possible that a strong, autocratic empress like Ekaterina, who was at the forefront of the European Enlightenment, was not able to implement all the reforms that Russia needed, both in her own eyes and in those of her critical compatriots. One answer could be that she was afraid to lose her own position in the process, another that she simply did not have the leverage to do so. In fact, these answers do not exclude each other, and the important lesson to be drawn from their combination is that there is no such thing as an absolute monarch, an all-powerful dictator or, indeed, an enlightened despot, that avatar of the Philosopher–King (Beales 2016: 507). The absoluteness of absolute monarchy resides not in omnipotence, but in a monopoly on the legitimacy of power.

Enlightenment ideas spread in Russia as they did elsewhere, and 'hints of revolutionary sentiment appear[ed] in Russia as early as 1790', with the appearance of Radishchev's badly written and pedantic book *Puteshestvie iz Peterburga v Moskvu* [Journey from St Petersburg to Moscow] (Claeys and Lattek 2013: 229). Radishchev, who had published and distributed the book himself, was sentenced to death, a punishment that Ekaterina II transformed into Siberian exile, making Radishchev an early example of the Russian traditions of *samizdat* and exile (Radishchev 2018: 8, 13). The regime's reaction initiated a tradition of radically critical thinking, and Radishchev later became one of the heroes of the Soviet narrative relating to 'revolutionary democrats'. A second, softened edition of the book could only appear in English, published in 1868 by Herzen (ibid.: 7). Radishchev had been sent abroad for five years to study law in Leipzig because good lawyers were needed, but he absorbed the literary and philosophical works of the time. In fact, Radishchev did not even advocate regime change or revolution, but merely called attention to a number of social evils that he observed during his trip between the two big cities: corruption, uprisings, diseases and the dire living conditions of the peasantry (ibid.: 8). This occasioned Berdiaev to locate the birth of the Russian *intelligentsia* in Radishchev's famous words that 'I looked around me and my soul was lacerated by the sufferings of mankind' and to qualify him as 'the first parent of the radical revolutionary tendencies of the Russian intelligentsia' (Berdiaev 1992: 45–6 / Berdiaev 2004a: 36–7; Radishchev 2018: 11 / Radishchev 1994: 11).

Gradually, the idea of regime change took shape. Earlier forms of protest and rebellion, such as *iurodstvo*, *staroobriadstvo* and peasant uprisings, had tended to field a 'true' Christian tsar (or priest) against a 'false' or corrupted one, without questioning the political regime as such. However, the idea of revolution, inspired by the American and French Revolutions of 1776 and 1789, aimed at radical reform, if not outright replacement of the autocratic regime, in the name of reason and / or popular sovereignty. Conspiratorial political organisations came into being, turning Russia into a hotbed of oppositional political theories and practices that inspired people far beyond its borders. In the early nineteenth century, private Masonic and literary circles were founded, some of them with political agendas, all of them hidden from the public eye (Karenovics 2015: 121–4).

The first serious illegal political organisation was that of the Decembrists, led by Pavel Ivanovich Pestel' (1793–1826) (Breckner 1996): they plotted the assassination of the tsar and his family, and the 'Jacobin' Pestel'

> wedded ideas of representative government based on universal suffrage to a proto- or quasi-totalitarian state which was to rely on a powerful clergy and secret police [. . .] Serfdom was to be abolished, half the land nationalised, public morals regulated and private associations, as well as drinking and card-playing, banned. (Claeys and Lattek 2013: 230; Ulam 1998: 35)

With this, further recurrent elements enter the stage of political philosophy in Russia: a vision of the good society in radical opposition to the existing one and a readiness to reach for illegal, clandestine and, if need be, violent means to reach political goals. Lacking possibilities for political opposition, the relation between state and a substantial part of society was one of enmity. Military officers like Pestel' and the Society of United Slavs organised a military uprising in 1822, a precursor of the Decembrist coup of 1825. Both failed and most participants were exiled to Siberia, but the impression on the minds of many Russians was decisive, and 'from this point onwards, [. . .] radicalism and socialism were virtually inseparable in Russia' (Claeys and Lattek 2013: 230). Still, the Decembrist uprising of 1825 bore a republican, not a liberal, character (Kharkhordin 2018: 2). It was much more a revolution of republican aristocrats than of liberal bourgeois, who started to play a prominent political role in Russia only towards the end of the nineteenth century, taking central stage in the 1905 Revolution that, according to Martin Malia, was a liberal one (Malia 2006: 266).

Conclusion

This chapter has been dedicated to the pre-history of what really begins in the next chapter. Up until the emergence of political philosophy as a recognisable field of intellectual activity, we have seen several forms of disruption and subversion of the normative political order: theological debates which bring in religious motives against worldly power and opportunistic politics, the recurrent phenomenon of *iurodstvo*, repeated attempts at political reform and popular uprisings. Also, we have traced the genesis of a defining triangle in Russian society in the nineteenth century: that of the autocratic regime, including its ranks of civil servants; the service nobility, including an increasingly enlightened intelligentsia; and the mass of the *narod* or ordinary people.

The predominant political system in Russia is a merger of the Byzantine and the Tatar models, infused with the West European Enlightenment, along with two undercurrents: one a 'republican' undercurrent that, with varying strength, articulated itself, the other a long tradition of popular uprisings, especially by the peasantry, and of 'anarchy'. This political reality was framed, at the symbolic level, by a predominantly representative political theology. Both the permanence and the vulnerability of centralised power in Russia have become constant elements in later political philosophy. At the same time, the legacy of both *veche* and *mir* has been claimed by republicans and liberals on the one hand, and *narodniki*, anarchists and socialists on the other.

Notes

1. The *veche* is comparable to the *ting* or *ding* in Germanic languages (*Folketing* in contemporary Danish, *þing* for parliament in Icelandic).
2. The term μωροι δια Χριστον / *mōroi diá Christòn* was coined by the Apostle Paul in application to himself (1 Cor. 4: 10; 1 Cor. 1: 18ff; 2 Cor. 11: 30), and, arguably, Jesus of Nazareth himself was a first 'fool for Christ' (Mark 3: 21, 5: 40, 27: 39). Similar figures can be found in other traditions (Saward 1980: 1).
3. Today, the Old-Believers constitute 0.2 per cent of the population of the Russian Federation, with small communities existing in other countries, including the USA and Canada.

Chapter 2

First Debates in Russian Political Philosophy – 'What Is to be Done?'

> Yes, those were precious tears: with some of them I believed in Russia, with others in Revolution.
>
> Aleksandr Herzen, *My Past and Thoughts*
> (Herzen, *PSS*: IX, 127)

> The Russian thinkers of the nineteenth century, pondering over the destiny of Russia and its vocation, [. . .] believed that the Russian people will, in the long run, say its word to the world and reveal itself.
>
> Nikolai Berdiaev, *The Russian Idea* (Berdiaev 1992: 22)

Anyone interested in Russia will come across two 'eternal' questions: 'Kto vinovat [*Who's to Blame*]?' and 'Chto delat'?' [*What Is to be Done?*]'. The questions are the titles of an 1846 novel by Aleksandr Ivanovich Herzen (1812–70) and an 1863 novel by Nikolai Gavrilovich Chernyshevskii (1828–89). The second title was repeated for programmatic texts by Vladimir Il'ich Lenin in *Chto delat'?* (1902) and, with a variation, Lev Tolstoy: *Tak chto zhe nam delat'?* [So what should we do?] (1886). Such questions, expressing a sense of moral protest and practical urgency, dominated the scene in the nineteenth century. Also, given the lack of opportunities to participate in political affairs, the question of alternatives arises: one alternative is to make one's ideas public, which implies struggle with the censorship or *tamizdat* [publishing abroad]; another is to go underground and establish conspiratorial revolutionary organisations.

Overall, nineteenth-century Russian intellectuals were obsessed by the question of political agency: in a situation of official autocracy, suppression of the political, exclusion of the opposition and absence of political participation, there is only one political authority and only one legitimate agent: the tsar. Consequently, the question as to whether a given tsar is a reformer or a reactionary, a liberal or a conservative, becomes crucial, and direct appeal to the tsar becomes an obvious political act. Mikhail Aleksandrovich Bakunin (1814–76) addressed the tsar (Nikolai I) in writing with his 1851 *Confession* [*Ispoved'*] (Bakunin 1977). Herzen could count the tsar (Aleksandr II) among the readers of his underground journal *Kolokol* [The Bell]. The Decembrists and the members of *Narodnaia Volia* [People's Will] frequently plotted to kill the tsar, finally succeeding in 1881 (Aleksandr II). In reaction, Solov'ëv called upon the murdered Tsar's son (Aleksandr III) to spare the lives of his father's assassins. All of these actions, and many more, reflect the concentration of political authority in a single person.

Connected to this was the question of 'what Russia should do' in order to play its role in history. Two possible answers – namely, 'follow the West' and 'stick to our roots' – lie at the basis of the split into '*Zapadniki* [Westernisers]' and '*Slavianofily* [Slavophiles]'. Rather than looking at *zapadnichestvo* and *slavianofil'stvo* as currents or schools of thought, we should view them as tendencies or orientations that organised Russia's political-philosophical debates and reflections. The advocates of the two positions shared the idea of Russia as a potential historical factor, but were aware of their own utter impotence as political agents. The 'Slavophiles' added to this the idea of Russia's unique, Orthodox-Christian national character; the Westernisers added a positive appreciation of the attempts at modernisation by some of Russia's rulers. All of this took place against a background of widespread reception of West European thought, especially of German philosophy (Fichte, Schelling, Hegel, Feuerbach, Büchner) and of French socialism (Saint-Simon, Blanc, Charles Fourier, Proudhon), and later also positivism (Auguste Comte) and British authors like J. S. Mill, Charles Darwin and Herbert Spencer.

While the following three chapters address three major currents that arose in the period after 1881, this one focuses on the dramatic middle part of the nineteenth century, which starts after the failed Decembrist uprising of 1825; with 3,000 participating officers, this had demonstrated both the possibility of revolution and the violently repressive nature of the regime. The uprising was organised in protest against the contested accession of Tsar Nikolai I as successor to the relatively liberal Aleksandr I, who had abolished serfdom in the Baltic provinces and had asked for the drawing up of a constitution. The Decembrists had favoured Konstantin, *de facto* viceroy of Congress Poland, which, at least on paper, was a constitutional monarchy. However, Konstantin had already secretly resigned in 1823. The crackdown on the Decembrists started a period of oppression and conservative reaction which lasted until the Great Reforms, begun in 1861 by Tsar Aleksandr II. The European Revolution of 1848 not only remained without effect in Russia, but it increased repression and led to Russian interference in neighbouring Central Europe. The period discussed in this chapter includes the dramatically unsuccessful Going to the People [*khozhdenie v narod*] (1874) by *intelligenty* and students. It ends with a wave of terrorist attacks (1878–81) (Claeys and Lattek 2013: 240). In 1881, at the seventh [*sic!*] attempt on his life (Fediashin 2012: 108), Nikolai's son, reformer-Tsar Aleksandr II, was killed on the very day that he had signed a decree introducing constitutional reforms; they were instantly turned back. At the same time, the earlier Great Reforms – abolition of serfdom (1861), university liberalisation (1863), judiciary reform (1864), introduction of limited local self-government [*zemstvo*] (1864) – facilitated societal and economic dynamics that, in the long run, might point to political participation. Therefore, 1881 can be seen as a turning-point.

As a whole, this chapter makes clear what happens when political awareness increases among a well-informed population, while the political system does not offer opportunities for canalisation of the political, thus reducing the alternatives to suppression by the state and its apparatuses on the one hand, and unchaining the political in the form of uprising and political murder on the other. Apart from the question of agency, the systematic political-philosophical issues that dominate political philosophy in Russia in the nineteenth century are the question of universalism (including internationalism) versus singularism (including nationalism), with particularism as an intermediate position, and the question of revolution versus reform.

'Slavophiles' versus 'Westernisers'

We can date the beginning of political philosophy in Russia to around 1825–30. Since the 1810s, the Russian government had increasingly excluded philosophy from gymnasium and university curricula. After the formulation of the official state ideology of 'Orthodoxy, Autocracy, Nationhood' in 1833, a mandatory course for all institutions of higher education was introduced, which allegedly was 'freed from the absurdities [*neleposti*] of the latest philosophers' (Pustarnakov 2003: 99–116; Karenovics 2015: 64–77). The teaching of philosophy was largely banned from Russian universities, to be permitted again only in 1863, and state control over intellectual activity was tightened. The coincidence of the beginning of political philosophy in Russia with the banning of philosophy in general suggests not only that free thought was considered a threat to the existing tsarist order, but also that philosophy does not have to be 'political philosophy' in order to be political: it is the conjuncture and the regime, not the participants, that decide whether or not ideas are dangerous.

Until late in the nineteenth century, political philosophy was extra-governmental and extra-academic: it took place in the circles of the educated nobility and, later, in clandestine networks. Private literary salons, intellectual circles [*kruzhki*], which could meet up to three times a week (Krasikov 2011: 72), and the so-called 'thick journals [*tolstye zhurnaly*]' made up the space of public debate in most of nineteenth-century Russia. Censorship was severe and political participation excluded, but the financially independent nobility had the possibility to travel and to import literature from abroad. Most of the protagonists of this chapter come from that layer of society. Many of them were exiled during parts of their career; such exile, though uncomfortable, as a rule did not keep them from working. For well-off persons, it most of all meant being geographically distant from the centres of power, and performing government tasks in faraway towns and provinces [*gubernii*], where they formed small, local networks. At the same time, there was – as there is today – considerable continuity and osmosis between oppositional intellectual circles and reformists of various orientations within the state apparatuses. Interestingly, the tsarist regime itself often leaned towards constitutional reform as part of the ongoing modernisation of the state, but it also relied on the support of the land- and serf-owning nobility [*dvorianstvo*] 'to staff the government and command the armed forces' (Compton 2016: 9), and it feared that the mass of the population was not ready for anything but a quasi-divine Father Tsar.

Around 1815, Russia, having defeated Napoleon at the Battle of Borodino in 1812 and having led the coalition that took Paris in 1814, rose to prominence as a major European power. Its political backwardness as an absolutist autocracy turned into an advantage when Russia initiated the conservative Holy Alliance with Prussia and Austria and became the anti-revolutionary *gendarme d'Europe*, up to the point of interfering with revolutionary movements in neighbouring countries in 1848. Russia clearly was a force to be reckoned with; it was less clear which direction this giant would or should take. This is mirrored by the heated debates in Russia between so-called *zapadniki* and *slavianofily*. The two labels were each other's constitutive other in 'the great ice drifting [*ledokhod*] of Russian thought' that was the shock effect of a single event: the publication in 1836 of Chaadaev's *Philosophical Letters* (Krasikov 2011: 73), in which he lamented that Russia had yet failed to contribute to humanity's development and was, in socio-political terms, a *tabula rasa* (Chaadaev 1991: I, 96, 330). Few thinkers can, in fact, be qualified as 'pure' *zapadniki* or *slavianofily*, and this first major figure, Pëtr Iakovlevich Chaadaev (1794–1865), already defies the very opposition, since the motivation for his outcry is a passionate patriotism: he wants Russia to have its own identity and to play a specific role (Shchukin 2001: 58; Mrówczyński-Van Allen et al. 2018). Upon publication of the first letter, he was officially declared insane and placed under house arrest, with a life-long ban on publishing.

Also, the contrast between a Westernising and a Slavophile trend resulted not simply from the reception of German idealism on a *tabula rasa*. It was also rooted in the tradition of 'Eastern Orthodox religious thinking about the nature of human community', which departed from a '*theocentric*' instead of an '*anthropocentric* personological paradigm' (Horujy 2010: 28–9). In fact, *slavianofil'stvo* emerged as a reaction to the *zapadnichestvo* of those who, following Chaadaev's outcry, looked to West European philosophy, particularly that of Schelling and Hegel, for food to put on this empty plate and for cutlery to tackle it with. Westernisers and Slavophiles had much in common, and they were fighting in a single arena. Working from a common conceptual apparatus largely derived from German idealism, they shared a concern about Russia's present and future, and put the emphasis on the collective, rather than the individual subject of political consciousness and action: the Russian nation, divided into state apparatus, serf-owning gentry, critical intelligentsia and ordinary people [*narod*].

In literary salons and intellectual circles of the 1830s, there was heated discussion within what Herzen labelled 'the educated minority [*obrazovannoe men'shinstvo*]' (Levandovskii 2010: 55). In 1844–5, this educated minority split over several questions: whether or not Western Europe showed Russia its future; whether or not Christianity generally, and Orthodoxy in particular, was a hindrance or a help in Russia's historical development; whether the modernisation initiated by Pëtr I was a positive or negative example; and, last but not least, whether revolution was an inevitable means for political change. Russia's Orthodox-Christian identity played an important role in these debates. Westernisers deplored the absence, in Russian history, of an independent church with its canonical law and society-oriented religious orders, and of Reformation and revolution. Slavophiles, by contrast, loathed the corrupting political role of the Vatican, the Inquisition, the destruction of Constantinople by the Crusaders, and the rise of *Spießbürgertum* [fuddy-duddy bourgeoisie] (ibid.: 63). In *O starom i novom* [About the Old and the New] (1838–9), self-made philosopher and lay theologian Aleksei Stepanovich Khomiakov (1804–60) pointed to Russia's past and to those traditions, including the *veche*, that had been cut off by imposed modernisation and centralisation, Pëtr I being identified as the main culprit (Khomiakov 1994: I, 461–9). Khomiakov's much-debated notion of *sobornost'* [conciliarity, communality], which brings together religious communion and traditional rural life, has become an important point of reference down to the present day (Mrówczyński-Van Allen et al. 2019). Their opposition to bureaucracy and unitary statehood explains Berdiaev's qualification of the Slavophiles generally as 'peculiar [*svoeobraznye*] anarchists' (Berdiaev 1996: 118). In the 1830s, an explicitly Christian political philosophy thus came into being, largely outside the ROC and under the impact of Schelling.

The emergence of a Christian political philosophy was a political reaction to the realisation that Christianity no longer self-evidently 'defined' Russia. In 1833, Sergei Semënovich Uvarov (1786–1855) launched the triad 'Orthodoxy, Autocracy, Nationality [*Pravoslavie, Samoderzhavie, Narodnost'*]' as the ideological basis of the expanding Russian Empire. Both *zapadniki* and *slavianofily* had this official ideology as their constitutive other: the first by opposing the first two elements, and the second by endorsing all three, but denying the incumbent regime's pretention to their materialisation. In more general terms, the opposition is between, not two, but three positions: first, a rationalistic universalism, in a tradition stretching from Plato to Lenin, which holds that there exists one best model for all societies, even if different societies may be at different stages of historical development towards this model or follow different trajectories; second, a naturalistic particularism, reaching from Aristotle to Montesquieu, which holds that, although political systems can be compared and ranked on a single set of parameters, different circumstances, such as climate, size, being land-locked or having sea access, and so on, account for a plurality of different systems, suitable to specific situations; and third, an essentialist singularism, found among Romantics and all the way down to present-day Heideggerians like Dugin, which holds that each culture or civilisation is unique and must stick to its own unique and distinctive [*samobytnyi*] socio-political model. Slavophile thinkers differed fundamentally from their Westernising colleagues on one major point: they tended towards singularism, believing in the 'innate specificity (not to say intrinsic supremacy) of Russia' due to its adherence to true, Orthodox Christianity (Shanin 2018: 8). Later thinkers like Chernyshevskii or Pëtr Lavrovich Lavrov (1823–1900) would, in a particularist vein, also emphasise Russia's specificity, but within the context of global development, denying any innate superiority, yet at the same time also avoiding the idea of an intrinsic superiority of Europe or the West.

The impact of Hegel is crucial here. The fact that Russia had, according to him, hardly played a substantial role in history (Hegel 1971: XII, 422) could appear to be an explanation for its lagging behind, but could also be an omen of its future significance. Hegel's dialectical method thus offered both inspiration and self-explanation to the radical and 'maximalist' Russian critics of the existing order. At the same time, however, Hegel's emphasis on the state as the unifying moral whole that would limit the fragmenting character of bourgeois society [*bürgerliche Gesellschaft*], keep a nation together and give it purpose, suited conservative and statist positions, including those that advocated a gradual transition towards constitutional monarchy. Bearing in mind that the Russian word for state, *gosudarstvo*, is derived from *gosudar'* [ruler, prince, sovereign] and, contrary to its Western European counterparts [*Staat, état, estado*], does not refer to a stable situation or to institutions, but 'to the person of the ruler' (Antonov 2019: 39), we can understand the predominance of a 'decisionist dimension' in Russian understandings of state and law. The actual state of affairs is attributable to the good or bad decisions of the good or evil persons holding power, not to a neutral warrant of rights and liberties, and not to political institutions.

One of the most original early Russian political philosophers is Herzen, whose thought 'eludes all attempts at categorisation' (Kelly 1999: 17), and who 'stands apart as the most versatile, flexible, passionately persuasive and ironically disconcerting figure in that strange galaxy of original intellectuals thrown up by nineteenth-century Russia' (Hare 1951: 212). Herzen has been qualified as 'the true founder of Populism' (Venturi 2001: 1; Baluev 1995: 25), as one of Russia's 'utopian socialists' (Volodin and Shakhmatov 1985) and as the founder of agrarian socialism (Kudiukin 2013: 192–3). Soviet-era encyclopaedias qualified Herzen as a 'revolutionary democrat' (Konstantinov et al. 1960–70: I, 358; Alekseev 1995: 133), others classify him as a liberal (Kara-Murza 2018: I, 269–78), while still others call him 'partly liberal, partly radical' (Fischer 1969: 17). Like many great thinkers, Herzen was a displaced person in various ways, but he is also proof of the fact that habitual categories in Western academia do not easily apply to Russian thinkers. For this, there are three reasons. First, for long stretches of time, philosophy was academically marginal and not divided into sub-disciplines. Second, the vast majority of Russian thinkers were not employed by academic institutions, but were either economically independent or part of conspiratorial circles. Finally, many of the relevant figures were simultaneously politically engaged and active in literature and philosophy.

Herzen also defies the *slavianofily* versus *zapadniki* opposition, describing himself as occupying, in his own words:

> a sort of involuntary *juste milieu* on the Slavic question: the Slavophiles see me as a man of the West; to their opponents I am a man of the East. It follows from this that these one-sided definitions have no place in our time. (Kelly 2016: 228)

However, the important question is not whether a particular thinker can be called, without reservation, a Westerniser or a Slavophile. After all, most thinkers of the period whose relevance has survived show elements of both positions, so that the real issue here is the predominance of the 'Slavic question' that Herzen mentions. Herzen's own main contribution to political philosophy is his rejection of historical determinism: Aileen Kelly credited him with the 'discovery of chance' (Kelly 2016), and Isaiah Berlin did not tire of underlining the consequences of his claim that history not only does not have a libretto, but also would be utterly meaningless and boring if it did (Berlin 1978: 92). In Herzen's own words in *S togo berega* [From the Other Shore] (1847–51):

> If mankind went straight to any particular goal, that would be not history but logic [. . .]. The animal organism develops its instinct little by little. In man his development goes further – it attains

reason, though slowly and with difficulty. Reason does not exist either in nature or outside of it; it has to be attained, to be somehow adjusted, for there exists no ready libretto to follow. And if it did, history would become dull, unnecessary, and ridiculous. (Herzen 2003: 364)

Herzen and his contemporary and friend Bakunin both exemplify the profound influence of Hegel, whose work they knew well (Planty-Bonjour 1974: 41; Volodin 1973; Kelly 2016: 149, 189, 213–14). Both fell victim to the tsarist regime and spent much of their life in exile or prison; both became prominent figures in revolutionary movements in Europe, Bakunin entering into competition with Karl Marx over leadership of the International, Herzen engaging with liberals and moderate socialists in Italy, France and Great Britain – his rightly famous *Byloe i dumy* [My Past and Thoughts] opens a fascinating window on both Russian and European political history. Contrary to Bakunin, Herzen never became an important political activist (von Beyme 2001: 103–12), but his journal *Kolokol* [The Bell], published in London from 1857 until 1867, was the first fully independent Russian journal, illegally but widely circulated and well respected in Russia.

If Herzen famously labelled Hegelian dialectics 'the algebra of the revolution' (Herzen, *PSS*: IX, 23), it was Bakunin who turned Hegel's retrospective justification of violence as the birthplace of a new order, freer than the previous one, into a prospective legitimisation of the violent destruction of existing institutions like state and church, thus performing a switch from theory, as a call for understanding, to praxis as a call for change, under simultaneous neglect of *poièsis*. It is abundantly clear that Bakunin is not advocating destruction for the sake of destruction, but as a condition for the realisation of freedom and a future 'collective anarchist' society, which, after a successful revolution that would remove hindrances like state, church and private property, would enjoy an 'undisturbed development of society that one could not imagine at the time' (Lausberg 2017: 28).

Although destruction of the old order may be a necessary condition for the creation of a free and just society, it certainly is not a sufficient one: the 'real passion for destruction' that inspires a popular uprising is, as Bakunin famously put it, 'a creative passion, too', but it is 'far from sufficient for achieving the ultimate aims of the revolutionary cause' (Bakunin 1990: 28; 1973: 58). Bakunin's emphasis on revolutionary violence easily overshadows his idealistic programme.

The label of 'nihilists' for the radical revolutionaries in Russia is misleading, as if they did not have any positive plans or beliefs:

> Deriving as it does from Latin *nihil*, the name Nihilist seems to imply a belief in nothing at all or in destruction for its own sake. In fact [. . .], Nihilists [. . .] mostly believed passionately in something, if only in a hotch-potch involving revolution, the Russian peasant, Chernyshevskii, some kind of socialism, the idea of progress, science, materialism, and so on. They preached destruction often enough, but chiefly as a means to an end, the necessary prelude to some dimly conceived, but fervently desired new order. (Hingley 1967: 57)

Therefore, 'annihilists' would be a better label, as they were convinced that a just society presupposed the eradication of the old order, in terms of both domination and hegemony.

The reproach that radical political philosophy does not have a clear plan for a future society misses an important point: a free, self-determining society cannot, by definition, be planned, but must be left to those who freely determine it. In Bakunin's words: 'The future social organisation must be built from below upwards, by the free association or federation of workers, first in associations, then in communes, then in regions, in nations, and, finally, in a great international and universal federation' (Bakunin in Edie et al. 1976: I, 412). This excludes any blueprint. In line with this, Bakunin also believed that the Reformation had destroyed all authority, other, that is, than that of reason or experience. In 'What is Authority?' (1871), he claimed to 'bow before authority' only if his own reason told him so: for example, when an engineer is an expert in constructing canals or railways, rejecting any idea of a 'fixed, constant and universal authority' (such as a tsar or a church). He rejected any authority that comes with power, especially that of state or church, but also 'the *government of science*' when science exceeds its limits, since the task of science is to point out 'the *general causes of individual suffering*' and 'the *general conditions necessary to the real emancipation of the individuals living in society*', not to tell human society what to do: 'It is time to have done with all popes and priests; we want them no longer, even if they call themselves Social Democrats' (Bakunin 1973: 162, 165, italics in the original).

In sum, it would be a serious mistake to equate *zapadnichestvo* with revolution and socialism or *slavianofil'stvo* with conservatism and nationalism. Rather, *slavianofil'stvo* is the other largely progressive and oppositional trend next to *zapadnichestvo*. The difference between the two is not situated on a simplified left–right spectrum, but in different appreciations of aspects of modernisation, such as the development of a modern bureaucratic state, which took off in Russia in the late eighteenth and especially the early nineteenth centuries and reached its completion a century later (Wirtschaftler 2008: 203; Raeff 1966: 107; Philippot 1991: 13). Nor were the Slavophiles necessarily anti-Western. As Berdiaev, quoting Herzen from *Byloe i dumy*, eloquently put it:

> Speaking of the Westernisers and Slavophiles of those times Herzen said: 'We had one love [*odna liubov'*], but it was not the same love [*odinakovaia liubov'*].' He called them a two-faced Janus, and both sides loved freedom, and both sides loved Russia. The Slavophiles loved her as a mother, the Westernisers as a child (Berdiaev 1992: 56 / Berdiaev 2004b: 47; also Walicki 1989b: 394).

From University to Village and Back

While the early nineteenth-century thinkers mostly belonged to the economically self-sustaining nobility, the most characteristic social group in Russia in the nineteenth century is undoubtedly the *intelligentsia*, one of those Russian words that have made it into many languages. Hard to pin down sociologically, by 1860 this layer of society measured some 20,000 out of a population of 60 million (Chernyshevskii 1989: 2). The shortest description of them goes as follows: of mixed background (born from parents of different rank, so-called *raznochintsy*), highly educated, often impecunious, and with few opportunities other than service to an oppressive state that left little space for public debate, let alone political participation or action. In a sense, autocratic regime and critical intelligentsia were each other's constitutive other. They mirrored each other, in their inflexibility and in their similar top-down attitude towards a joint excluded third: the distant, illiterate and 'backward' *narod*, meaning both the people or nation at large and the ordinary people or 'folk'.

As already mentioned above, Chernyshevskii is the ideal-typical *intelligent*. A *raznochinets*, he was the son of a well-educated priest in Saratov but did not become a member of the clergy himself, knew ancient and modern languages at the age of fourteen, went to study history and languages in St Petersburg, and absorbed the works of Schelling, Hegel, Feuerbach, J. S. Mill, Smith, Ricardo and Malthus (Edie et al. 1976: II, 11–12). One of Russia's strongest intellectuals, he was among the many who gave up on reform and believed that only a revolution could 'overcome Russia's social and economic problems' (Chernyshevskii 1989: 21). His affinity with British utilitarianism – he introduced J. S. Mill to a Russian audience with an annotated translation of Mill's *Principles of Political Economy* (Edie et al. 1976: II, 13) – led him to develop a conception of art and literature as a means of educating and uplifting the people, a 'manual of life for man' that serves its purpose by 'explaining it [reality] for his [man's] benefit', very much in line with developments elsewhere in Europe.

Thinkers like Chernyshevskii were ahead of society's actual development; they were leaders without a constituency, revolutionaries without a mass. Could the *intelligentsia* connect with the *narod*, educate it, transform it into a revolutionary force? When, in the 1870s (1874 in particular), large numbers of students decided 'to go towards the people [*khozdenie v narod*]' to educate them and to mobilise them in an anti-tsarist spirit, they met with resistance and rejection (Kołakowski 2005: 612). If the people are not easily mobilised, the idea of a vanguard intellectual elite becomes plausible, especially in light of the perceived urgency of socio-political change. Of course, this is a general idea of the Enlightenment – the difference between Russia and the rest of Europe is not the existence of political movements led by small conspiratorial groups, but the fact that such groups became ideologically hegemonic and, in one case, politically successful. In this nexus, theory played a key role.

The nineteenth century is, among other things, a century of grand historical and evolutionary narratives (of the kind Herzen and Bakunin were critical of), many of which claimed to replace 'philosophy' as 'love of wisdom' or 'quest for truth' by 'scientific philosophy' (Hegel), 'science' (Comte, Marx, Spencer) or 'integral knowledge' (Solov'ëv). Hegel's philosophy of history was highly influential in Russia in the first half of the century, but in the second half, the 'intellectual arch-model' was 'evolutionism'. Later nineteenth-century Russian intellectuals generally shared this scientific evolutionism, which included an evolutionary conception of science itself, thought to play a crucial role in this evolution. Karl Marx, Auguste Comte and Herbert Spencer, among many others, suited this role (Gordin 2016). Towards the end of the century, however, domestic authors like Solov'ëv, Danilevskii and Konstantin Nikolaevich Leont'ev (1831–91) could be added to the list. Exceptions to this quest for a 'general science of society'

(Vucinich 1976) include Herzen, rightly highlighted by Berlin as a rare opponent to any 'great despotic vision' (Berlin 1978: 86), and Bakunin. Evolutionism was, however, central to the outlook of Chernyshevskii, Lavrov, Mikhailovskii, Solov'ëv, Fëdorov and the Russian Marxists.

A significant part of political philosophy in Russia was articulated outside Russia, in emigration and exile. The first wave of emigration consisted mostly of economically independent members of the nobility without clear political agendas (Herzen and his friend, Nikolai Platonovich Ogarëv (1813–77), are the exception rather than the rule). The second wave, which started in the 1860s after 'the student disorders (1861), the activities of the first *Zemlia i Volia* [Land and Freedom] group (1861–62), and the Kazan' Conspiracy (1863)', consisted mostly of *raznochintsy* who had fewer resources to fall back on and had already engaged in oppositional political activity, which they continued abroad (Miller 1986: 111). A recent estimate arrives at a number of 200–225 active Russian revolutionaries in Europe (mostly in Geneva, Paris and London) in the 1880s (ibid.: 207–8). If we add to this the long list of people imprisoned in Russia or exiled to Siberia, it comes as no surprise that emigration and/or exile was a reality for the vast majority of thinkers discussed in this book.

Fatal Turning Point

Chernyshevskii wrote *What Is to Be Done?* in prison in 1862–3, and the novel appeared in 1863 in the 'thick journal' *Sovremennik* [The Contemporary], of which he himself was editor. A cult hero in his day, he was sentenced to fourteen years of hard labour, later reduced to seven, and permanent exile, lifted only in 1889, shortly before his death (Chernyshevskii 1989: 22–3, 14–15). The author became a martyr and the book an inspiration for an entire generation. The tsarist regime showed its violently oppressive face in the 1860s, with the crackdown on student protests in the early 1860s, the crushing of the January Uprising in Poland in 1863–4, and the completion in 1864 of the conquest of the Caucasus with the genocidal Circassian massacre that killed or expelled 90 per cent of the population. After the 1866 assault on his life by Karakazov (Ulam 1998: 1–9), Aleksandr II switched to a more conservative and repressive course. While reform of the criminal law system continued, the many crimes that were considered 'politically motivated' met with harsh persecution, and after 1867, 'Russia reverted, all but in name, to the custodial model of "Police State"' (Nethercott 2007: 23). At the same time, academic education continued to develop in a country that needed state officials and experts.

The predictable result was a radicalisation of the *intelligentsia* and the student protest movement, well-known leaders of which included Pëtr Nikitich Tkachëv (1844–86) and Sergei Gennadievich Nechaev (1847–82). In 1873, Bakunin asked in *Gosudarstvennost' i anarkhiia* [*Statism and Anarchy*]: 'In such a situation, what can our intellectual proletariat do, our honest, sincere, utterly dedicated social-revolutionary Russian youth?' (Bakunin 2014: 662 / Bakunin 1990: 212). An early answer could be found in the *Katekhizis revoliutsionera* [Catechesis of a Revolutionary] (1869), which advocated a life completely dedicated to the sacred cause of revolution, and is one of the most notorious texts in the history of political thought. It is usually ascribed to Nechaev, who has since figured as the prototypical dedicated terrorist and consistent 'nihilist': 'We have an entirely negative plan, which no one can modify: utter destruction' (Hingley 1967: 57; Venturi 2001: 373).

This text is not to be confused with Bakunin's much more balanced and realistic *Catéchisme révolutionnaire* [Revolutionary Catechesis] of 1865 (Bakounine 2009). In Switzerland, in the late 1860s, Nechaev and Bakunin briefly formed another conspiratorial organisation, of which they were the only two members. It is a moot point whether Bakunin, who later explicitly distanced himself from Nechaev, actually assisted in writing the *Katekhizis* (Avrich 1988: 40; Masaryk 1992: II, 109), but it is clear that Nechaev was inspired by Bakunin as well as by Tkachëv (Marks 2003: 12). After arrest and exile in 1873, Tkachëv left Russia for Geneva, where he published the journal *Nabat*, the 'organ of the radically extremist wing within *narodnichestvo*', and founded a conspiratorial 'Society for the Liberation of the People [*Obshchestvo narodnogo osvobozhdeniia*]' (Alekseev 1995: 593). Nechaev also was the architect of the murder in 1869 of a student who had questioned his credentials – inspiring Dostoevsky to write his anti-revolutionary novel *Besy* [Demons] (Steiner 1996: 114).

The *Katekhizis* strikes with the total dedication, self-sacrifice and political self-instrumentalisation that it demands from a revolutionary, but also with an extreme ascetic subjectivism. Its twenty-six numbered paragraphs are divided into four chapters, entitled 'The relation of the revolutionary to him/herself', 'The relation of the revolutionary to the revolutionary comrades [*k tovarishcham po revoliutsii*]', 'The relation of the revolutionary to society' and

'The relationship of the revolutionary fellowship [*tovarishchestvo*] to the people' (Nechaev 1871). Nechaev qualifies the revolutionary as 'doomed [*obrechënnyi*]', as having only a single goal and passion – namely, the revolution [art. 1], as knowing only 'the science of destruction' [art. 3], and as being free of 'any romanticism, any sentimentality, enthusiasm [*vostorzhennost'*], and passion [*uvlechenie*]' [art. 7]. Three things are most striking: first, the explicit and radical instrumentalisation of human beings, whom the text divides into categories depending on how they should be used [art. 6]. Second, the radical subjectivism is striking: being a revolutionary starts from a relationship to oneself [*k samomu sebe*] and is a matter of will, discipline and self-determination. Nechaev articulates an absolutely subjective political voluntarism that is simultaneously a self-subjection to an absolutely objective goal, paired with a radical utilitarianism [art. 11]. Third, the world-view of these early terrorists displays more than a whiff of Gnosticism: they, the elect, know for certain where the world should be going, even if the rest of the world has no idea. They are therefore entitled to take the lead in humankind's road towards salvation.

Terrorism came to the fore as a possible alternative to the apparently impossible revolution (Murray-Miller 2020: 187–213), and although 'Russian terrorism was intimately interwoven with anarchist doctrine, this does not as such explain its character' (Claeys and Lattek 2013: 239). Certainly, political violence is as old as politics itself; systematic violence in order to intimidate a population, suppress revolt or reprimand a segment of society is a feature of all times, too, and the excessively oppressive character of the tsarist regime explains violent reaction. However, terror, understood as a repertoire of organised and planned violence aimed at overthrowing a regime or at firmly establishing a new order, is a distinctive feature of modernity: it is a Jacobin invention turned into a principle of revolutionary organisation by Russians like Bakunin and Nechaev, later adopted by the Bolshevik faction of the Social Democrats. The Red Terror deployed by the Bolshevik regime after 1918 was not only quantitatively unprecedented, but also qualitatively different, in its sheer instrumentality and deliberate planning, from the Jacobin Terror, but no different at all in its underlying conviction that truth legitimises all means.

As Marks rightly suggests, *Narodnaia Volia*, which split off from *Zemlia i Volia* in the late 1870s, was the prototype of later terrorist movements such as the German *Rote Armee Fraktion* (Marks 2003: 16) – or *al-Qā'idah*, for that matter. However, as *Narodnaia Volia* gained momentum, more 'moderate' voices started to dominate. For example, Vera Nikolaevna Figner (1852–1942), a prominent member, condemned the assassination of US President James Garfield in 1881, indicating Russia's exceptional situation:

> In a land where personal freedom gives an opportunity for an honest conflict of ideas, where the free will of the people determines not only the law but also the personality of the ruler, in such a land political murder as a means of struggle presents a manifestation of that despotic spirit which we aim to destroy in Russia. Personal despotism is as condemnable as group despotism, and violence may be justified only when it is directed against violence. (Figner 1991: 7)

Fifteen years after its invention by Alfred Nobel, the explosive potential of dynamite was used by Russian revolutionaries to kill Tsar Aleksandr II with cleverly designed bombs (Venturi 2001: 711); the landmark Saviour on the Blood church in St Petersburg was built to commemorate the event, and in Soviet times the streets around this location were named after the terrorists. The effect was not the disappearance of the widely hated tsarist regime, but a conservative twist of the government and the start of a period of heavy repression of any kind of political opposition. One of the striking characteristics of authoritarian regimes is that if they are organised around a single person, this person becomes the key target of attempts to change the regime. Russian autocracy did not consist, of course, of only the tsar, but was composed of a large, hierarchically organised state apparatus. However, its declared autocratic nature made the tsar the obvious addressee not only of pleas and letters, but also of revolutionary action. Aleksandr Dmitrievich Mikhailov (1855–84), a prominent member of both *Zemlia i Volia* and *Narodnaia Volia*, wrote about revolutionary change: 'There is only one way to do this: fire at the centre' (quoted from Venturi 2001: 708; cf. Figner 1991: 6).

After the assassination of Aleksandr II, *Narodnaia Volia* published a letter in which the new Tsar was confronted with the choice between either continued violence and revolution or a 'voluntary transference of supreme power to the people' (Venturi 2001: 717; text in Figner 1991: 307–12). Ironically, on the morning of his assassination, the Tsar had signed a decree in which, on the basis of ideas from his reformist minister of the interior, Mikhail Loris-Melikov (1824–88), cautious steps were taken in a more liberal, democratic and constitutional direction. It was rejected (and Loris-Melikov dismissed) by Aleksandr III, who, persuaded by his tutor, the arch-conservative jurist and later *oberprokuror* of the ROC Konstantin Petrovich Pobedonostsev (1827–1907), 'chose absolute power and embarked on the policy of reaction which character-ised his entire reign' and that of his successor Nikolai II (whose tutor was the same Pobedonostsev) until 1905 (Venturi 2001: 719; Pipes 2005: 140–1). His father's assassins were sentenced to death despite the pleas made to the new Tsar by prominent intellectuals like Tolstoy and Solov'ëv to show himself a truly Christian mon-arch and not reply with an eye for an eye. The executive commit-tee of *Narodnaia Volia* was effectively executed and a period of increased repression inaugurated. As Figner puts it: 'The Executive Committee perished to the last person, the party was smashed, but its significance in the history of the revolutionary movement was extraordinary' (Figner 1991: 6). Figner herself, who had tried to hold *Narodnaia Volia* together, was arrested in 1883 as the last of the Executive Committee and sentenced to life imprisonment; she was released in 1904, surviving as a Soviet citizen until her death (Figner 1991: xvi; Hartnett 2014).[1]

Terrorism in Russia came in two waves. The second wave preceded the 1917 Revolution, while the first, performed by *Narodnaia Volia* 1878–81, 'included the shooting of the gover-nor-general of St Petersburg [. . .] by Zasulich, the killing of the head of the tsarist secret police, General Mezentsev [. . .] and the assassination of Tsar Alexander II himself on 1 March 1881' (Claeys and Lattek 2013: 240). Vera Ivanovna Zasulich (1849–1919), who inspired Oscar Wilde to write his first play, *Vera; or, The Nihilists* (1880), became famous because of the Trepov affair. In 1878, she shot Dmitrii F. Trepov (1855–1906), gover-nor-general of St Petersburg and known for his cruelty, wound-ing but not killing him. Her trial, presided over by the liberal Judge Aleksandr Koni, started with the prosecutor demanding capital punishment, but ended with her being found not guilty by a sympathising jury; thousands celebrated her acquittal on the streets of St Petersburg (Ely 2010: 186). This was, in fact, a rare demonstration of independence of the judiciary and an effect of the legal reforms in Russia. Zasulich fled to Switzerland, where she turned to Marxism, co-founded the *Osvobozhdenie Truda* [Liberation of Labour] movement, one of the forerunners of the RSDRP [Russian Social-Democratic Labour Party], and started the revolutionary Marxist newspaper *Iskra* [The Spark].

Renouncing terrorism, she later also opposed the October Revolution, like most Mensheviks, and died at the margins of political events (Bergman 1983; Koni 2015).

Conclusion

Many of the themes that had started to dominate the political-philosophical agenda were there to stay: reform versus revolution, universalism versus particularism, Westernising versus Slavophile orientation, the triangle of *tsar'* – *intelligentsia* – *narod*, the relationships between state and church and between politics and religion. In this sense, there is a strong continuity that stretches all the way into the twenty-first century – and this also gives the authors discussed in this chapter their present-day relevance. At the same time, political philosophy in Russia after 1881 begins to feel more serious, both philosophically and politically, also due to fundamental societal changes: 'Until the 1890s in Russia almost nobody wanted a bourgeoisie' (Monas 1991: 28), but in the latter part of the nineteenth century, this bourgeoisie nonetheless slowly became a reality for political philosophers, as it did elsewhere. What comes to the fore most clearly is the contrast between realistic and open-minded positions, of which Herzen, 'the first really effective champion of a free public opinion in Russia' (ibid.: 29), is an early example, and more 'Gnostic' and close-minded stances. This takes us back to the discussions of Hegel and the left-Hegelians that thinkers like Herzen, Bakunin and Chernyshevskii started with: does history evolve according to a libretto? If so, who or what wrote this libretto, who is entitled to read and interpret it, and, last but not least, who is elected to turn the libretto into action?

In the following three chapters, three currents are addressed that provided elaborate answers to the burning question 'What Is to Be Done?' The first, Russian Marxism, was marked by a contrast between historical determinism and the desire for revolutionary change. The second was a Christian social and political philosophy that oscillated between social protest and an irenic denial of the political. The third, Russian liberalism, vainly tried to reconcile reform and stability. Compared to the radicalism highlighted in this chapter, all three appear as moderate. Still, to the extent to which Russia's political history is characterised by lengthy periods of suppression, not only of oppositional groups, but also of the political as such, the position of radical rejection of the existing order continues to serve as an important chapter in humankind's handbook of political philosophy.

Note

1. As late as 1968, Margarita Figner, Vera Figner's niece, expressed her hopeful wish that one little alley would be named after her aunt. In 1987, in another part of St Petersburg, a small street was indeed named after Figner.

Chapter 3

Socialism and Marxism in Russia: The Peasant Commune is Dead – Long Live the Peasant Commune!

> The analysis in *Capital* therefore provides no reasons either for or against the vitality of the Russian commune.
>
> Karl Marx, Letter to Vera Zasulich, 1881
> (Shanin 2018: 124; *MEW*: XIX, 243)

It is impossible to discuss political philosophy in Russia without discussing Marxism, just as it is impossible to discuss Marxism without paying attention to Russia. It is not least in (connection to) Russia that Marxism took shape in the first place: 'It was in Russia that Marxism had its greatest impact and produced some of the most well-known Marxist theoreticians: men like Plekhanov, Lenin, Bukharin and Trotsky' (White 2019a: vi). Also, Russia urged Marx to specify his theory on significant points. In Russia, finally, socialism was never exclusively, or even predominantly, Marxist (until claimed as such by official Soviet Marxism–Leninism); nor was the impact of Marxism limited to revolutionary movements. Marxist political economy made its way into the university, and Russia was the place where Marxism was transformed into a dogmatic system of dialectical and historical materialism, combined with innovative theories of party and revolution.

In the second half of the nineteenth century, Russia was quickly modernising, urbanising and industrialising, but the country remained predominantly agricultural (Hussain and Tribe 1983: 156). The abolition of serfdom in 1861 had liberated the peasants, but the uneven distribution of the land between peasants and land-owning gentry forced the former to work for the latter or seek work in mines and factories (Wirtschaftler 2008: 211). The results were striking: heavy and light industry increased annually by between 5 and 10 per cent, and the state-owned railway network grew from 917 km in 1855 to 50,881 km in 1905. Yet, at the same time, the Russian population remained largely rural and overall very poor. In all of this, the role of the state was very strong, warranting a qualification as 'capitalism from above' – which places this development in the tradition of top-down modernisation. State investment in heavy industry and infrastructure for economic and military purposes, the harsh repression of political opposition after the assassination of Tsar Aleksandr II in 1881, and an active policy of russification started by Aleksandr III mark this period. The ethnic–national twist given to the principles that Uvarov had formulated in 1833 – *Pravoslavie, Samoderzhavie, Narodnost'* – accompanies the transition of Russia from a 'federal empire' into a large nation-state (Whatmore 2013: 309).

Spontaneously, readers may frame the emancipation of the serfs within broader progressive movements, such as the abolition of slavery (which, in the Russian Empire, was realised in 1723), the stepwise extension of the franchise or the introduction of equal civil rights, all as a result of bottom-up pressure, growing public consensus and top-down reforms to match new realities. But this is not the whole story. Like the abolition of slavery in the USA (1863) or the Netherlands (1863, effectively 1873), the emancipation of the serfs often meant deterioration of, rather than improvement in, their economic situation – widespread peasant protest against the Emancipation Act was not a sign of conservatism or backwardness, but of legitimate protest against a poisoned gift (Hussain and Tribe 1983: 161).

Three factors need to be taken into account if we want to understand the reception and 'fate' of Marxism in Russia: first, the strong home-grown tradition of agrarian socialism with its emphasis on the village community [*obshchina*], its political organisation [*mir*] and, more broadly, the (ordinary) people [*narod*]; second, the fertile academic ground that welcomed the Marxian framework as an innovative theory in the field of political economy, rather than as a practically oriented revolutionary theory; and third, the tradition of political organisation and 'nihilist' terrorist action, best viewed as bottom-up Jacobinism, which Russian Marxism inherited from Nechaev, Bakunin and Tkachëv (Kołakowski 2005: 616–17). Accordingly, this chapter is divided into three sections: the first section focuses on agrarian socialism in Russia as the soil – partly fertile, partly resistant – on to which Marxism fell; the second section addresses the competition between theories of socialism; and the third section addresses the struggle over Marxist 'orthodoxy' within the Russian Social-Democratic movement.

Socialism: Agrarian or Proletarian?

Socialism in the nineteenth century was an umbrella notion for a wide range of currents. Jonathan Beecher has distinguished four types of socialism: 'democratic state socialism' (Louis Blanc, Ferdinand Lassalle), 'anarchist socialism' (Pierre-Joseph Proudhon, Mikhail Bakunin), 'Russian agrarian socialism' (Aleksandr Herzen, Nikolai Chernyshevskii, Pëtr Lavrov, Nikolai Mikhailovskii) and 'Marxism' (Beecher 2013: 376–89). Of these four, one was exclusively Russian, one has Bakunin and Kropotkin as international leaders, and one, Marxism, became more prominent in Russia than anywhere else. This shows, first, the close connection between different European political milieus of which Russia was a self-evident part; second, the importance of socialism as an intellectual and political current in Russia; and third, that socialism was not brought to Russia by Marxism: it fell on already tilled soil, where it was one among several options.

Herzen was the pioneer of agrarian socialism: 'Herzen held that the indigenous peasant commune, with its traditions of self-government and communal land ownership, could provide the foundation for the building of a utopian society free of injustice, exploitation, class conflict, and nationalistic strife' (Wirtschaftler 2008: 234). Agrarian socialism developed in several directions, connected to different conceptions of this *obshchina*. First, it moved in a Slavophile and potentially nationalistic direction, which perceived it as a specifically Russian type of community, based on unique economic principles and the Orthodox notion of *sobornost'* and compatible with a 'White Tsar'. Second, it followed the conception of sociologists and economists like Maksim Maksimovich Kovalevskii (1851–1916), who 'showed that the *obshchina* was not a unique Russian community but a typical community for a particular phase of universal social development' (Vucinich 1976: 175–6). This conception, which presupposes global progressive development, albeit with local variations, comes closest to the Marxist conception and Marx indeed strongly appreciated Kovalevskii's work. Third, it embraced the conception of the *obshchina*, as the Russian variant of a communal form of society that was possible anywhere and at any time: already present in Bakunin, this conception was elaborated most of all by Kropotkin.

Russian agrarian socialism was strong, and Marx (more than Engels) was sensitive to the argument on the part of Russian socialists that socialism might be founded on a village commune that had never known private ownership of the means of production, thus bypassing the vale of tears of capitalist industrialisation. In 1875, Engels, invoking empirical economic data, refuted Tkachëv's claim that, although there indeed was no proletariat in Russia, there also was no bourgeoisie, so that the peasant workers needed only to overthrow a state that 'has no roots in the economic life of the people' (*MEW*: XVIII, 557). First of all, Engels argued, a socialist revolution presupposed both a proletariat and a bourgeoisie, so that a revolution in Russia would not yield socialism. Second, there was a ruling class, the nobility, which owned the better half of the farmland and had every reason to support the tsar. Thirdly, a merchant and entrepreneurial bourgeoisie was in the making (ibid.: 559). Over the course of the nineteenth century, Russia rapidly became an industrial country, which placed Russian socialists in a serious dilemma: wait for an industrial proletariat to develop, or forge a subject of revolution on the basis of workers, peasants and soldiers?

Russian agrarian socialism is habitually linked to *narodnichestvo*, often misleadingly translated as 'populism'. Like *zapadnichestvo*, it connotes a 'turning to' or 'betting on' the *narod*. Rendering it with '*narodism*' is more accurate, or, to avoid the suggestion of a full-blown ideology, one can stick to *narodnichestvo* and *narodnik*. Indeed, we should emphasise 'the amorphous nature of "*narodism*"', and the fact that it 'was more a state of mind than a finished doctrine' (White 1996: xi; White 2019a: 72–4). Andrzej Walicki, partly following Richard Pipes, has made a useful distinction between two meanings of *narodnichestvo* (Walicki 1989a: 2–5; Pipes 1964). In a narrow sense, it points to the 'movement to the people [*khozhdenie v narod*]' of the mid-1970s, organised by the Chaikovtsy Circle – named after one of its leaders, the 'grandfather of the Russian Revolution' Nikolai Vasil'evich Chaikovskii (1850–1926) – of which Kropotkin was a member; by *Zemlia i Volia* [Land and Freedom], which included Lavrov, editor of the illegal *narodnik* journal *Vperëd* [Forward], Zasulich and Georgii Valentinovich Plekhanov (1856–1918); and by many Bakuninists. After the failure of the *khozhdenie v narod*, and the 1878 shooting of Governor Trepov by Zasulich, *Zemlia i Volia* was subject to increased persecution. Zasulich had earlier served a jail sentence because of her association with Nechaev, but considered 'terrorism [. . .] justifiable only as a gesture of moral conscience' (that is, not as a general form of political action) and later renounced political violence altogether (Bergman 1983: 61–2; White 2019a: 65). In 1879, the *Narodnaia Volia* [People's Will] group, which advocated political violence, including assassination and terror, split off, and the remaining organisation called itself *Chërnyi Peredel* [Black Repartition], after an agreement that neither group would use the name *Zemlia i Volia* (Bergman 1983: 68). *Chërnyi Peredel*, 'representing the non-political *narodnik* orthodoxy' that Plekhanov and Zasulich (returning from exile in 1879) stood for (White 2019a: 65), adopted a policy of propaganda and agitation instead of political activism.

In a broader sense, *narodnichestvo* points to 'a certain body of ideas, certain attitudes towards capitalism' and a tendency to point to Russia's unique opportunity to 'by-pass capitalism' in order to reach socialism (Walicki 1989a: 5). In this sense, *narodnichestvo* became part of the outlook of the social-revolutionaries, organised in the *Partiia Sotsialistov-Revoliutsionerov* [Party of Socialist Revolutionaries, PSR, f. 1900], which continued to advocate agrarian socialism. They split over October 1917, into a left wing, led by Mariia Aleksandrovna Spiridonova (1884–1941 [executed]), which supported a second revolution, and a right wing, led by Viktor Mikhailovich Chernov (1873–1952 [in exile]), which opposed it. The latter came out victorious in the only fully free elections in Russia in the early twentieth century: those for the Constituent Assembly, held shortly after the Bolshevik takeover (Immonen 2015: 236–50). Chernov continued to refer to the Russian tradition of agrarian socialism, particularly to Herzen, Mikhailovskii and Lavrov, criticising their individualistic inclinations but approving of their understanding of socialism, and insisting that the concept of *narod* 'means the totality of the labouring classes' (Chernov 1997: 206, 572; Mendel 1961: 7).

The key to understanding the impact of Marxist thought in Russia is its claim to transform socialism from utopian (philosophical, speculative, moralising) into scientific (demonstrable, objective, sober). On the one hand, his scientific outlook forced Marx to take Russian realities seriously. On the other hand, one of Marx's rhetorical tricks – namely, to disqualify other forms of socialism as utopian – found application in Russia, too. Indeed, Russia's indigenous agrarian socialism was a serious competitor: until the arrival of Marxist theory, which placed full emphasis on an industrial proletariat as the main driver towards a socialist revolution, socialism in Russia was largely associated with the peasant village community [*obshchina*]. This was an ambiguous phenomenon: on the one hand, common ownership of the arable land was a prefiguration of socialist ideals. Yet, on the other hand, it continued to tie the majority of emancipated serfs to the land, thus assisting the regime in preventing the development of a proletariat that could overturn the existing order, as it threatened to do in Western Europe (1848, 1871).

Both Marxists and Russian socialists were in exile during most of their career:

> Many of the foremost Russian socialists – Herzen and Bakunin, Lavrov, Kropotkin and Tkachëv, the Marxists from Plekhanov to Trotsky – actually were émigrés most of their adult life, thus adding the expatriate's physical displacement to the political vacuum created by autocracy. (Fischer 1969: 88)

They also knew each other: Marx was personally acquainted with Herzen, Bakunin and Lavrov. Also, many Russian socialists were of noble descent and, like Marx and Engels, were neither workers nor peasants, but *intelligenty* (Carpi 2015: 104). They shared an intense hatred of bourgeois society and a resistance against the '*oburzhuazivanie* [becoming-bourgeois]' of society that was typical of the entire nineteenth-century *intelligentsia* (Arndt 2012: 84–5; Baluev 1995: 81). The bourgeois revolutions of 1848 had not brought socialism, but they did yield liberal and democratic reforms and constitutions in Western Europe that offered space for political organisation and participation. Not so, however, in Eastern Europe. Contrary to Marx and Engels, who enjoyed some freedom of movement, organisation and publication, the Russian socialists had no alternative than to organise themselves abroad or underground, and had limited access to their potential constituency of peasants and workers. This is one reason why the dynamics of the socialist movement in Western Europe, which resulted from the interaction between workers, who articulated short-term demands (from higher wages to the abolition of child labour), and intellectuals, who urged organised labour to look beyond short-term objectives at the long-term aim of socialism, were largely absent in Russia, where 'socialism [. . .] lacked not only an internal but also an external check on the intellectual' (Fischer 1969: 87).

Marx, for his part, took an active interest not only in the Russian reception of his work, but also in Russia's socio-economic reality and revolutionary potential. His interest in Russia was motivated by the challenge it presented to his theory: it seemed to defy his idea that expanding capitalism necessarily absorbed all earlier types of social and economic formations. The Russian case forced Marx to abandon the idea of a universal sequence of modes of production, and to adopt instead a more flexible model that allowed for local variations. In fact, Marx came close to recognising the possibility of agrarian socialism: that is, a transition from a feudal to a socialist society that would bypass capitalism. For Marx, in principle, both a developed capitalist economy and an agrarian communal economy could be the basis of a transition to socialism, but only if the second had not yet been invaded by the first – a process that he suspected was taking place in Russia.

'Narodism', Anarchism and Marxism in Competition

Since the reforms of the 1860s, Russian intellectuals across a wide political and professional spectrum had become concerned with economic questions (Vucinich 1976: 175). Generally, Marx's works were received in Russia as a major enterprise in the field of political economy, especially in the theory of capitalism, much more than as revolutionary or political writings. Nikolai Ivanovich Ziber (1844–88), the first Russian Marxist, was an academic economist. The first volume had been translated by anarchist Bakunin and *narodnik* revolutionary German Aleksandrovich Lopatin (1845–1918). Nikolai Frantsevich Daniel'son (1844–1918), who translated and published, very shortly after their appearance in German, the second (1885 German, 1886 Russian) and third (1894, 1896) volumes of *Das Kapital*, belonged to the so-called liberal *narodniki* (Baluev 1995: 21, 173–5). This gave Marxist theory the status of a legitimate academic affair.

Given a situation in which serious opposition was excluded but academic freedom increasing, a split occurred between these 'legal' theoreticians and their 'non-legal' colleagues. The period after 1881 generally saw the appearance of 'legal' manifestations, as opposed to illegal or underground ones, of currents like *narodism*, Marxism and liberalism. Although the state suppressed political opposition, the space for alternative ideas widened: 'legal' *narodniki* and 'legal' Marxists stayed within the boundaries set by law. They taught at universities, expressed their ideas in publications appearing in Russia and advocated reform instead of revolution, even if a socio-economic revolution was still their aim (Baluev 1995: 171). The 'non-legal' theorists were active in private circles, underground organisations and the émigré community, even if, on a personal level, many participated in both legal and non-legal activities, making 'the greatest possible use of legally printed books' in order to 'spread Socialist ideas', while at the same time also 'having their illegal printing presses' (Venturi 2001: 470). The very label of 'legal Marxism' was introduced, in a pejorative sense, by Lenin and others who lived an 'illegal life' of underground publications, imprisonment, exile and false names (Kołakowski 2005: 647; Carpi 2015: 102f).

While, in the academic domain, Marxism became a respectable theory, in the political field it was contested. It had its main competitors in the *narodniki* and the anarchists. One of the prominent *narodniki* who engaged in a debate with Marxism was Nikolai Konstantinovich Mikhailovskii (1842–1904), whose position connects two points: an emphasis on the desirability of socialism on moral grounds and a rejection of historical determinism. On the first point, his insistence on the 'inseparable connection [. . .] between justice [*spravedlivost'*] and truth [*pravda*]' has obtained classic status (Edie et al. 1976: II, 171). *Pravda* is one of the two Russian words for 'truth', the other being *istina*, and both are notorious 'untranslatables'. While *istina* [verity] has the connotation of objectivity, value-freedom and 'how things really are', *pravda* has the normative connotation of justice [*spravedlivost'*] and 'how things ought to be' (Cassin 2004: 980–7 / 2014: 813–19). Mikhailovskii criticised attempts to split *pravda* into objective, value-free *pravda-istina* and subjective, normative *pravda-spravedlivost'*, which would separate the realm of scientific investigation in terms of necessity from the realm of normative choice in terms of possibility. He insisted on the impossibility of such a split: truth meant the combination of both verity and justice, scientific knowledge and moral law (Utechin 1963: 133; Kistiakovskii 2003: 339–40). For Mikhailovskii, the category of (historical) possibility was crucially important for arguing that Russia had a real choice between a European, capitalist–industrial road to socialism and a Russian, agrarian-communal one. If, however, there is no historical determinism that necessitates the sequence feudalism – capitalism – socialism, there also is no historical necessity for socialism: it becomes a matter of free moral and political choice. The difference is between reading Marx as claiming that capitalism is itself historically inevitable (as a stage that precedes socialism), or as merely elaborating the inevitable logic of capitalism (leading to socialism) if and where it has emerged.

The second point brings Mikhailovskii's position close to Herzen's rejection of a historical libretto (Berlin 1978: 224). Marx's analysis of capitalism entailed an early warning for Russia, a 'how-not-to manual' (Masaryk 1992: II, 152; Fediashin 2012: 134). If capitalism is not historically inevitable, the question is whether Russia should follow 'the dolorous path of proletarianisation and the class struggle' of Western Europe (Kołakowski 2005: 613). Mikhailovskii was accused of 'subjectivism' and of a 'Romantic' critique of capitalism by Marxists (ibid.: 615), and there is a misleading parallel between his emphasis on moral preferences and the 'voluntarism' of the Bolsheviks. While, for the latter, the subjective factor was about seizing the right moment within an inevitable historical process, for the 'liberal *narodniki*' it was about free choice. 'Romantic' socialists like Mikhailovskii were attacked by both legal Marxists like Struve and 'orthodox' Marxists like Plekhanov: by the latter because of his naïve reformism, by both because of his resistance against capitalism. Not only did they regard capitalism as an historical fact in the making, but also they were convinced of the political potential of an industrial proletariat as compared to a peasant mass. By contrast, Mikhailovskii, and later Chernov, continued to defend the peasantry as a political agent, and to consider the possibility of a non-capitalist development in Russia (Baluev 1995: 171–2; Masaryk 1992: II, 170, n. 3). The 'legal *narodnik*' Daniel'son likewise advocated the peasant *artel'* [artisan cooperative] based on communal ownership as a continuation of the *obshchina*, in opposition to Marxists like Struve who, in order to accelerate the development of capitalism, applauded the free sale of land because it would drive poor peasants to the cities, where they could become a social-democratic constituency. Scholars such as Ziber and Struve are quoted as saying that the sooner 'the Russian peasant would be boiled in the factory cauldron [*vyvaritsia v fabrichnom kotle*]', the better it would be (White 2019a: 59; Baluev 1995: 172).

The key difference between *narodnichestvo* and Marxism is what initially led Marx and Engels to claim that Russia was not the place where a socialist revolution could take place. It was not a developed capitalist country with 'bourgeois' political institutions like France, Great Britain or even Germany, but a largely agricultural feudal society without an industrial proletariat. While the *narodniki* perceived this as an opening, the legal Marxists picked up this idea to use Marxist theory for the advocacy of a capitalist and bourgeois development, and they generally supported the state-capitalist industrialisation programme of politicians like

Count Sergei Witte. On this point, Marxists and the state stood side by side (Walicki 2010: 308). With the undeniable progress of capitalism in Russia, agrarian socialism gradually became a conservative and, ultimately, reactionary position (Baluev 1995: 80; Masaryk 1992: II, 169–70, n. 3, 195).

The *narodniki* knew about Marx's later nuanced views regarding the possibility of agrarian socialism. Marx and Engels consistently defended the position that developments in Russia and in Western Europe were interdependent and that a revolution in the West opened up the possibility of socialism in Russia on the basis of the *obshchina* (*MEW*: IV, 576). They had also become convinced that Russia was a crucial factor, either by politically repressing the revolution or by potentially accelerating it. The puzzle is not so much what exactly Marx and Engels were saying or writing about Russia, but why they enjoyed such tremendous authority among Russian socialists. The answer to this question is twofold. First, Russian socialists knew that Marx had started to include Russia in his empirical studies, learning Russian in order to read scholars like Chernyshevskii. Second, the Marxian claim to turn socialism from utopian into scientific offered Russian readers what they needed: a general science of society that pointed the way to socialism. Testimony to this mutual interest are Marx's prolonged discussions, in 1870–1, with Elizaveta Lukunichna Kusheleva-Tomanovskaia [ps. Élizabeth Dmitrieff] (1850[?]–1918[?]), later one of the IWA's envoys to the 1871 Paris Commune, of which she became a key protagonist (Braibant 1993: 90–102; Ross 2016: 23–7).

Next to *narodnik* and Marxist socialism, a third major strand of thought in nineteenth-century political philosophy is anarchist communism. The biologist Nikolai Dmitrievich Nozhin (1841–66) had insisted that 'cooperation, rather than struggle or competition, typically prevails among members of the same biological species', providing a Darwinist argument against the egoistic individualism of the social-Darwinists (Edie et al. 1976: II, 172; Masaryk 1992: II, 153). Following Nozhin, Pëtr Alekseevich Kropotkin (1842–1921) projected key ideas of evolution theory such as natural selection, struggle for life and survival of the fittest on to human society but, instead of struggle and competition, emphasised cooperation between members of the same species, in other words: *Mutual Aid* (1914). Contrary to the Marxists, who located the political in class struggle (a factor ultimately alien to human nature and to be overcome through a dialectical process of de-alienation), and also to the *narodniki*, who tended towards a moral rejection of egoism, socio-biological realists like Kropotkin situated the possibility of both conflict and concord inside human society, arguing that concord (cooperation, assistance, division of tasks, solidarity) generally prevails.

The latter quarter of the nineteenth century, a period of severe political repression, saw little anarchist activity, but Kropotkin was working hard as a scholar and activist, first in Russia, and then abroad between his escape from prison in 1876 and his return in 1917. A much more systematic thinker and writer than Bakunin, his works remain classics of anarchist theory. Echoing metaphors of revolutions as 'birthpangs' of history and of revolutionary organisations as 'midwifes', Kropotkin held that 'we may either advance or hold back' the inevitable development of history in the direction of complete liberty (Kropotkin 2002: 114). Not offering a blueprint, he focuses on the working principles of historical development; like Bakunin and unlike most Marxists, he sees the state (and the church), not as epiphenomena of an exploitative capitalist mode of production, but rather as minority positions that hinder the natural and rational organisation of society. An anarchist society is one in which, in Kropotkin's words,

> harmony would [. . .] result from an ever-changing adjustment and readjustment of equilibrium between the multitudes of forces and influences, and this adjustment would be the easier to obtain as none of the forces would enjoy a special protection from the state. (ibid.: 284)

Communism, as the organisation of society and economy on principles of cooperation and mutual aid, and anarchism, as the active abolition of the state, 'are therefore two terms of evolution which complete each other' (ibid.: 298).

Kropotkin 'made no concessions with Marxism', considering it 'a classic ideology of "state socialism"'– an ideology of mass economy inimical to the autonomy of local economic associations and favouring a centralised state apparatus (Vucinich 1976: 91–2). He rejected its dialectical method 'not only as a method of scientific inquiry but also as an explanation of social revolution' (ibid.: 298). The goal of social – more specifically, anarchist – revolution, for Kropotkin, was not, as for many Marxists, 'to install a new type of social relations' in a New Society populated by New (Wo)men, but to remove barriers, 'to eradicate the unnatural institutional arrangements working against the full realisation of the social potential of human nature' (ibid.: 92). From this perspective, there is no discussion about whether or not capitalism is a necessary stage that humankind has to go through in order to come out free and prosperous at the other end: capitalism simply stimulates the wrong potential within the human species.

To solve the debate between agrarian socialists and Marxists, Kropotkin proposed the same model of small, self-governing units for both agriculture and industry. In Kropotkin's view, local self-organisation becomes identical to 'revolution' and, in the long run, will replace vertical state-power by a federation of peasant communes and *artel*'s, and, at a higher aggregation level, organisations like the Hanseatic League (Kropotkin 1906: 20, 32). For Kropotkin, as for liberals and republicans, the model of the late Medieval city-state in Italy (Florence, Lucca and so on) or Russia (Pskov and Novgorod) continued to be a guiding light.

Kropotkin's anarchist communism differs from the Marxists' 'instrumentalist' understanding of the state, and also from liberalism: from Russian liberalism with its emphasis on a strong reformist state, from Western liberalism with its idea of a preferably small but still crucially important state, and from neoliberalism, which requires a strong state to warrant free market competition. It comes closer to the libertarianism of Robert Nozick or Ayn Rand, with its concept of maximum liberty with minimal state interference, but differs from it on one central point. While recognising a human instinct of self-preservation which can lead to an individual struggle for domination, Kropotkin forefronts a second instinct, that of sociability and mutual aid (Kropotkin 2002: 288). Kropotkin's opposition to the individualist competition of the social Darwinists – Thomas Huxley in particular – can be extended to the hyper-individualist liberalism of Rand.

The Rise of Orthodox Marxism

Zasulich and Plekhanov were key figures in the genesis of a Marx-inspired Social-Democratic movement in Russia. Plekhanov left Russia in 1880, Zasulich following suit, and in Switzerland they continued their activity together with Pavel Aksel'rod and others. During this period, Plekhanov started to study Marx's works seriously and he and Zasulich produced a new Russian translation of the *Communist Manifesto* (1882). In 1881, Zasulich wrote her famous letter to Marx, in which she asked him whether 'the rural commune [. . .] is capable of developing in a socialist direction' or, by contrast, 'the commune is an archaic form condemned to perish by history, scientific socialism and, in short, everything above debate' (Shanin 2018: 98–9). She presented this as 'a life-and-death question above all for our socialist party' and suggested that 'even the personal fate of our revolutionary socialists depends upon your answer', for two reasons: first, because 'the revolutionary socialist must devote all his strength to the liberation and development of the commune', and second, while:

> all that remains for the socialist, as such, is more or less ill-founded calculations as to [. . .] how many centuries it will take for capitalism in Russia to reach something like the level of development already attained in Western Europe. (quoted in Shanin 2018: 98–9)

Zasulich's letter shows Marx's authority, her assumption of an immediate connection between theory and praxis, the question of political strategy, and the question of political *poièsis*. What to create: a journal, a rural education network, an underground terrorist organisation, or a political party after the West European model? In 1880, Marx had expressed his sympathy for *Narodnaia Volia* over Zasulich's and Plekhanov's *Chërnyi Peredel* (White 2019a: 66), but this time, in 1881, he was hesitant: he felt that he needed to give a scientific answer, for which research was needed. In the letter he sent to Zasulich (after four draft versions; Shanin 2018: 99–123; *MEW*: XIX, 384–406) within a month of receipt of her letter (16 February and 8 March 1881, respectively), he gave the famous answer that the inevitability of the development sketched in *Das Kapital* was limited to Western Europe. Furthermore, he stated that 'the analysis in *Capital* therefore provides no reasons either for or against the vitality of the Russian commune' and that it was 'the fulcrum for social regeneration in Russia' – but also that, in order for it to fulfil this function, 'the harmful influences assailing it from all sides must first be eliminated' (Shanin 2018: 124; *MEW*: XIX, 242–3; Arndt 2012: 101). The exchange between Zasulich and Marx over the viability of the *obshchina* is more than a bump in the development of Marxist theory. It connects, first, to the contrast between a mono-linear historical trajectory, standardised in Soviet times as the 'five-stage sequence [*piatichlenka*]', and the possibility of a plurality of trajectories, as sketched by the *narodniki*; there was also a vision of small-scale cooperatives as a permanent possibility – a line of thought adopted by anarchists like Kropotkin. In retrospect, the nineteenth-century obsession with a 'libretto of history' not only overshadows many political-philosophical questions, but also shows the weakness of Marxism as a political philosophy.

Explicitly Marxist circles aside, Marxism became less prominent in the 1890s in academia, where it was regarded as one economic theory among many. As an ideology, however, it gained prominence among the *intelligentsia*. Plekhanov, the 'father of Russian Marxism', started as a *narodnik* and moved to a Menshevik position after adopting Marxism as his theoretical framework (Walicki 2010: 306; White 2019a: 63–9). He 'almost single-handedly introduced Marxism into Russia as a serious alternative to the populist ideology' (Billington 1970: 459). In texts in which he not only distanced himself from terrorism, but also articulated the switch from the wishful socialism of the *narodniki* to the idea of a socialism that would be based on economic science and realised by a workers' party, Plekhanov 'embodied orthodoxy itself'. Later Russian Marxists would criticise his views, but not dispute his model of a single, theoretically true and practically effective, world-view [*mirovozzrenie*] (Steila 1991: 62).

Plekhanov, in *Development of a Monistic View of History* [*K razvitiiu monisticheskogo vzgliada na istoriiu*] (1894), came close to a young-Hegelian teleology in which the historical process is the realisation of reason. According to him, 'once people knew the laws by which history operated they would be able to use them to transform history from an unconscious process to a conscious one' (White 2019a: 77), opening up 'for the first time in history the road to the kingdom of freedom' (Plekhanov 2004: I, 422–3). He was the initiator of the system of dialectical and historical materialism, in that order, implying that the second is an application to history of the universal laws of development articulated by the former. Plekhanov's 'reason' is not Hegel's impersonal Reason of History, but the collective reason of humankind, finally rationally mastering its own fate (Walicki 2010 : 307–8). This is why 'the Bolshevik Revolution was in his eyes a violation of the laws of history, caused by an irresponsible relapse into the populist dream of "by-passing capitalism"', which had been Plekhanov's own dream prior to turning from a *narodnik* into a Marxist (ibid.: 308).

Liubov' Isaakovna Aksel'rod-Ortodoks (1868–1946; b. Ėster Aksel'rod, Ortodoks being her pen-name) was Plekhanov's pupil and close friend. Until the late 1920s, she was second only to Plekhanov as an authority in matters of Marxist theory. Plekhanov's second-best pupil, Vladimir Il'ich Ul'ianov [Lenin] (1870–1924), like Aksel'rod-Ortodoks considered himself an 'orthodox' Marxist; the label Marxism–Leninism was invented in the late 1920s to indicate precisely that Leninism was the only true continuation of Marxism. Lenin did study Marx and Engels (as well as Hegel and Feuerbach) in the original: for example, in 1895 he wrote an extensive summary of the 1845 *Die heilige Familie: Kritik der kritischen Kritik* (Lenin, *PSS*: XXIX, 3–40). Though not the most important Marxist theoretician, Lenin certainly is a towering figure when it comes to Marxist political philosophy: it is difficult to think of any other thinker who made philosophy more directly political. With his explicit political philosophy, he filled in one of the major gaps in Marxist theory. Lenin's major contribution to Marxist theory was to develop a largely illegal and underground party led by 'hard-core professionals' like himself, appealing to workers while taking along the peasants. On its own, he claimed in *What Is To Be Done?* [*Chto delat'?*, a repetition of the title of Chernyshevskii's book], the proletariat would never move beyond trade unionism and thus would remain enslaved to the bourgeoisie. This made the role of intellectuals, again like himself, 'not simply auxiliary or catalytic, but [. . .] fundamental and indispensable' (Anderson 1967: 300; Sabine 1963: 809–12). Moreover, Lenin's model of the revolutionary party combined Marxist theory with the conspiratorial tradition of Nechaev and *Narodnaia Volia* (Sabine 1963: 812).

Towards the turn of the century, Marxism lost its academic status and became closely linked to the RSDRP (f. 1898). As a result, theoretical disputes became more closely entwined with party politics and the power struggle within it. The rivalry between Lenin and Bogdanov is the clearest case in point. Aleksandr Aleksandrovich Malinovskii [Bogdanov] (1873–1928) aimed to turn Marxist theory into a general social science. The well-known programmatic statement about basis, superstructure and corresponding societal forms of consciousness in the Preface to Marx's *Zur Kritik der politischen Ökonomie* (1859, Russian translations 1896 and 1907) contained, for Bogdanov, 'the essence of scientific sociology'. Four decades later, however, new scientific developments were urging Marxists to develop a new theory in place of a paradigm that 'continued to imitate the natural sciences' (Vucinich 1976: 208–9). For Bogdanov, this implied a distance from philosophy and a replacement of dialectics as a 'sort of universal method' by the notion of a 'dynamic equilibrium of changes [*podvizhnoe ravnovesie izmenenii*]' that underlies any state of apparent stability or 'conservation [*sokhranenie*]' (Bogdanov 1989: I, 197; White 2019b: 20–2). Dialectics proper he situated in the field of human interaction: for example, in the 'forming of a new, political or idea-oriented [*ideinaia*] social group' which, as an organisational process, can evolve both 'spontaneously or according to a plan [*stikhiino ili planomerno*]'

(Bogdanov 1989: II, 258; Jensen 1978: 90–4). In major works like *Ėmpiriomonizm* [Empiriomonism] (1904–6; Bogdanov 2003) and *Tektologiia: vseobshchaia organizatsionnaia nauka* [Tectology: A Universal Organisational Science] (1922; Bogdanov 1989), Bogdanov moved away from the orthodoxy of Plekhanov to become one of the founding fathers of systems theory.

Bogdanov was an important philosopher in his own right, but he was also Lenin's main competitor (Jensen 1978; Sochor 1988; Soboleva 2007; Plaggenborg and Soboleva 2008; Oittinen 2009; White 2019b). Lenin's heavily polemical and largely unfair *Materializm i ėmpiriokrititsizm* (1909) was meant to silence Bogdanov, who was at that point the more prominent Bolshevik (Sochor 1988: 6–7). Defeated politically, Bogdanov (a Bolshevik since 1903) did not want to have anything to do with the Bolshevik faction and left the RSDRP in 1911. In 1917 he gained new prominence as founder of the *Proletkul't* movement, which aimed at a complete break with bourgeois culture and science. Bogdanov played a pivotal role in the takeover of the scientific institutions in Soviet Russia as director of the Socialist Academy for Social Sciences, founded in 1918 and renamed the Communist Academy in 1924; it was set up 'as a "proletarian" antidote to the bourgeois-controlled Academy of Sciences', with which it was merged in 1936 (Jensen 1978: 6).

From a political-philosophical perspective, Bogdanov is interesting for two reasons. The first is his rejection of the idea of a system of dialectical and historical materialism, as elaborated by Plekhanov. Given the latter's status as the founding father of Russian Marxism, this led to a disqualification of Bogdanov as 'unorthodox' and a 'heretic' by both Lenin and Nikolai Ivanovich Bukharin (1888–1938), and made his theory anathema in the USSR (Bukharin, 'Funeral speech' (1828), in Bogdanov 1989: II, 345; Takhtadzhian, 'Slovo a tektologii', in ibid.: II, 348; Sochor 1988: 9–10). As late as 1989, a Soviet edition of *Tektologiia* contained the hint that 'republication of this book is aimed at the well-prepared reader who is familiar with Lenin's evaluation' (Bogdanov 1989: I, 4). In fact, Bogdanov was truer to the spirit of Marx, by criticising, supplementing and developing his theory, than Plekhanov, Lenin and other 'orthodox' Marxists. He obviously held Marx in high esteem and saw his own theory as a development of, among other things, historical materialism. But instead of identifying as a Marxist, he 'conceived of himself as a thinker independent of all trends in past thought' and aimed at a universal, synthetic theory of organisation (Jensen 1978: 18; Vucinich 1976: 210, 215–17). The second reason for Bogdanov's relevance is his alternative conception of the construction of socialism: namely, through education, enlightenment [*prosveshchenie*] and cultural revolution. As one of the architects and organisers of *Proletkul't* in the 1917–21 period, he opposed the Leninist idea of a succession of stages through which an all-powerful communist party would lead an ignorant proletariat (Sochor 1988: 40; Fitzpatrick 2002: 89–109; Jensen 1978: 9). In this sense, Bogdanov falls squarely within the category of idealists who believed that socialism and communism were not a matter of administration, let alone enforced collectivisation, but of facilitating the positive capacities and values set free by the breakdown of bourgeois capitalism. At the same time, Bogdanov's positivism tends to move Marxism away from political philosophy towards a social-scientific theory of politics.

Conclusion

There is no chapter in the history of Russian political philosophy that has been more strongly damaged by the Soviet reduction to a coming-to-be of Marxism–Leninism and a rewriting of the past from that perspective. This history is thus still in the process of being 'unrewritten'. For example, while the works of Plekhanov and Lenin fill bookshelves *ad nauseam* all over the world, Bogdanov is still being translated and studied. The yield of Russian Marxism is therefore mixed: the systematisation by Plekhanov and Aksel'rod-Ortodoks, the concept of the vanguard party consisting of professional revolutionaries, and the idea of the state as a mere instrument in the hands of the ruling class developed by Lenin are important, if contestable, components. Most importantly, the very idea of an 'orthodox' theory as itself an instrument in the class struggle has become a determining factor.

Marxist philosophy of politics is based on the essentially economic notion of class struggle, implying that an end to class struggle may, in the long run, make politics as we know it obsolete. Marxism thus belongs to the large family of political philosophies that ultimately aim to eradicate the political and, consequently, politics. Linking the political to class antagonism, Marxist theory is well suited to analysing political conflict in terms of material interests, but ill equipped for dealing with the political itself and utterly helpless when it comes to politics in a classless society. Marxism tends to start, not from the possibility of conflict and concord, but from the reality of class struggle as the root of all conflict, from the desirability of concord of the proletariat in the form of solidarity and determination, and from the possibility of a classless society from which conflict has disappeared. How political power is to be conquered, how the proletariat, once victorious, will be organised, or which institutions will govern a society in transition is of secondary importance and largely left open (Arndt 2012: 108; *MEW*: IV, 481).

Chapter 4

Christian Political Philosophy in a Modernising World – Preparing for God's Kingdom

> To become a real Russian, to become completely Russian, perhaps, means just (in the final analysis – bear that in mind) to become a brother to all people, a *panhuman*, if you like.
>
> Fyodor Dostoevsky, *A Writer's Diary*
> (Dostoevsky 1994: 1294 / 2017: 732)

The very fact that subsequent regimes in Russia have deemed it necessary to control church life strongly suggests the presence of critical potential. Readers may think, at this point, that 'Christian political philosophy' is a double oxymoron. Did not modern political philosophy come into being only when the Christian theological framework was left behind by thinkers like Machiavelli? Does philosophy not become theology as soon as it becomes Christian? Is Christianity not quintessentially a denial of the political? Paradoxically, however, it is the very attempt to move beyond politics and to deny the political that makes Christian thought, theological or philosophical, political.

From a traditional Christian point of view, history has, strictly speaking, secondary relevance: the historical time that humans live in is the period between the Fall and the End of Times. The modern discovery of historical progress, even if it develops dialectically, breaks with this tradition. A traditional position turns conservative when it finds itself in a historically developing, modernising world, and it becomes paradoxical when an established church finds itself subordinated to a regime that is a major agent of modernisation, secularisation and industrialisation. To an extent, this tension can be softened by emphasising the 'symphonic' division of labour between a church that is oriented on eternity, salvation and morality, and a state that has a monopoly over worldly politics. However, this extent ends where religious principles are felt to be applicable to society more generally and this particularly concerns the numerous burning issues indicated by the word *vopros*, which means both question and problem: the issues of national self-determination, for example, of the Polish people, of women's rights, of the position of Jews in the Russian Empire, of poverty and social inequality, and many more. As a result, the *pol'skii vopros*, *zhenskii vopros*, *evreiskii vopros*, *sotsial'nyi vopros* [Polish, Women's, Jewish, Social question] and others were high on the agenda of the thinkers discussed in this chapter.

In Russia, the combination of an autocratic regime and a 'disencephalised' church turned the latter into a conservative defender of the status quo, suppressing the critical socio-political philosophical potential of the Christian tradition. Meanwhile, the global phenomenon of modernisation and 'secularisation' (in the sense of a turn to society) in major religious traditions during the nineteenth century affected Muslims, Jews and (Orthodox) Christians in the Russian Empire, too. The Islamic reform movement of *jadidism*, derived from Arabic *jadīd* [جَدِيد], meaning 'present-day', took root in the predominantly Islamic regions, and pan-Turkism had one of its founders in Yusuf Akçura (1876–1935), a Russian Tatar born in Simbirsk [Ul'ianovsk], who also founded a Muslim Party in Russia in 1905. Also, several Jewish organisations flourished in the Russian Empire, including the well-known *Bund* that was among the founding members of the RSDRP. Given the direct subordination of the ROC to the tsarist regime, the modernisation movement took many forms: a revival of the traditionally oppositional ascetic and hesychast movement, society-oriented clergy and public debates outside the ROC (Valliere 2000). While each of those deserves study in its own right, this chapter focuses on representatives of the Orthodox-Christian tradition who attempted, outside the ROC, to accommodate modernity within a Christian framework.

If early Slavophile thinkers had largely accepted the Orthodox tradition as it existed, independently minded thinkers developed personal world-views which, though self-identifying as Christian, can be called 'orthodox' only at a stretch. This chapter focuses on four major thinkers who developed distinctly Christian political philosophies: Fëdor Mikhailovich Dostoevsky (1821–81), Lev Nikolaevich Tolstoy (1828–1910), Nikolai Fëdorovich Fëdorov (1829–1903) and Vladimir Sergeevich Solov'ëv (1853–1900). These four men opposed the conservatism of the Russian state–church tandem and, if anything, wanted to set free the moral and socio-political potential of Christianity as they perceived it, independently of the existing, Synodal Church. Because of this common denominator, this chapter, before discussing these thinkers individually, situates them in a broader context.

Reinventing Christianity in Order to Save the World

Unsurprisingly, all four thinkers ran into trouble with both worldly and ecclesiastical authorities, yet it should be emphasised, first of all, that they claimed to be more, not less, Christian than the official church. Second, the desire to stick to Christianity and avoid heresy was part of their intrinsic motivation and hence an inner barrier, not simply one imposed by a conservative church. Tolstoy was excommunicated in 1901 amidst turmoil and publicity; Fëdorov did not publish his writings, probably fearing excommunication;[1] Solov'ëv ran into several conflicts with the censorship of the Holy Synod (rather than that of the state) and had to publish several of his writings abroad; and Dostoevsky, after some initial conflict, came under the spell of the anti-Semitic, arch-conservative Pobedonostsev, who served as *oberprokuror* of the ROC for twenty-five years (1880–1905) (Stoyanov 2000).

Returning to what they saw as the core of the Christian teaching, these four merge, in different ways, the traditional Christian idea of a Second Coming like a flash of lightning (Matthew 24: 27), with the nineteenth-century idea of human progress. Each in their own way tried to steer clear of the blasphemous idea that God's Kingdom on Earth would be the effect of human activity, or that the Second Coming would inaugurate a new era in human history. Individual improvement and even perfection are possible by overcoming one's egoistic individualism and giving up one's individual life for the good of all. This will lead to a better world, from the small scale of a harmonious community to the large scale of a process of 'deification' of humanity in the direction of Godmanhood or Divine Humanity [*bogochelovechestvo*]. This, however, is preparation for, rather than realisation of, the Kingdom to come. The socialist idea of a 'New Man', populating a 'New Society', was, from these thinkers' point of view, the Promethean perversion of God's Kingdom on Earth. For this reason, they were critical not only of the state-bound church, but also of materialist and atheist socialism, as it denied a divine regulative order, put the creation of a just society in humankind's hands and, indeed, often invoked Prometheus, for which they could even quote both the young and the mature Marx (*MEW*: suppl. vol., pt 1, 263; *MEW*: XXIII, 675).

Christian political philosophy stands out with its reference to a situation of harmony: that is, absence of the political. For Christian political philosophers, the question is not whether this harmony is real, but if and how it relates to a world into which it is projected as an idea(l). If we assume that the ideal of 'true harmony' is itself a response to a reality of disharmony, we can read this as an ultimate denial of the political, but that begs the question of whether it is a denial of the political in this world or a rejection of this political world (Love 2018: 62–6). From an immanent perspective, these two options coincide, but from a transcendent one, they differ radically. The paradox of Christian political philosophy is that once it promotes freedom and participates in a pluralist market of positions, it jeopardises its own exclusive access to a truth that is its unique selling point. Both can fully thrive only in an environment in which their conception is shared by (nearly) all, and such a community of the truly faithful makes politics superfluous: ethics then takes priority over politics (Kaehne 2007: 114).

The protagonists of this chapter share this primacy of the ethical over the political. Solov'ëv's advocacy of free theocracy and Christian politics, Fëdorov's 'common cause', Tolstoy's pacifist socialism and Dostoevsky's universal compassionate love are elaborations of the Sixth Commandment, especially of the reformulation, in the New Testament, of the Decalogue as the Great Commandment: 'Thou shalt love the Lord thy God with all thy heart, and with all thy soul, and with all thy mind' and 'Thou shalt love thy neighbour as thyself' (Matthew 22: 35–40; Mark 12: 28–34; Luke 10: 27). Love, the central category in the political philosophy of these thinkers, is an anti-political principle in that it aims to overcome conflict generally. The question is not whether universal love would solve all conflicts between, and arguably within, all humans, or between humans and non-human animals and robots. Of course it would. As Carl Schmitt put it: 'In a good world among good people, only peace, security, and harmony prevail. Priests and theologians are here just as superfluous as politicians and statesmen' (Schmitt 2018: 196 / 2007: 65). Peace, love and understanding are always possible. Even if achieved, however, such love and peace would be continuous at best, not perpetual; general, not universal; ontic, not ontological – leaving open the possibility of renewed conflict.

All four thinkers rejected Marxist and materialist socialism, but adhered to an agenda of social justice – from a Marxist point of view, they could all be disqualified as Christian utopian socialists. They all rejected individualist liberalism, but adhered to a strong notion of individual and collective freedom, bordering on existentialism in Dostoevsky, on anarchism in Tolstoy, on technological self-enhancement in Fëdorov and on freely chosen integral life in Solov'ëv. They all related critically, yet appreciatively, to *slavianofil'stvo* and *narodnichestvo*, and they combined conservative and progressive elements, being both strikingly modern and strikingly traditional. All of this makes them hard to categorise, but if we follow Alexandre Christoyannopoulos, who called Tolstoy a Christian Anarcho-Pacifist Iconoclast (Christoyannopoulos 2020), we can label Dostoevsky a Christian Conservative-Socialist Prophet, Fëdorov a Religio-Technological Visionary, and Solov'ëv a Christian Synthetic Missionary.

What brings all four together is their rejection of individualism as it was gradually spreading in Russia as part of modernisation and 'bourgeoisification' – the matching ideology of which was liberalism. From this angle, the 'anti-political' call for brotherly love, asceticism and an exemplary life is also profoundly anti-bourgeois. In Dostoevsky, Tolstoy and Fëdorov, we witness a tortured, self-centred and escapist *imitatio Christi*. Solov'ëv offers a more moderate and synthetic version that accommodates the rights and liberties of the individual human being, if only because they are, as the indispensable basis of a free and open public sphere, the necessary condition for the appearance and activity of such potentially inspiring prophetic figures as they all four attempted to be. Explicitly anti-revolutionary even when demanding radical change, and generally monarchist, these Christian political philosophers called upon the authorities to stick to the Christian principles that they claimed to incorporate, and they called upon the tsar in particular to prove himself a truly Christian monarch. They advocated repentance, not punishment, and moral improvement, not retribution, tending to perceive the historical development of the world in general, and of the Russian Empire in particular, in terms of Christian eschatology.

Fëdor Dostoevsky – A Hedgehog Full of Foxes[2]

Michael Walzer has theorised humans as internally divided selves along three different parameters: their interests and roles, their identities, and their ideals, principles and values (Walzer 2012: 85–6). This dovetails with Chantal Mouffe's idea that antagonism is rooted not just in material interests or class relations, but also in the dynamics of the 'libidinal drives that he [Freud, EvdZ] calls Eros and Thanatos', which are sublated in collective identities (Mouffe 2013: 46–8). In Dostoevsky, even more radically, the reality of conflict and the possibility of concord (reconciliation) are mostly located, not in society or between humans, but inside each individual, as an inner struggle between opposing forces and contradictions. The potentially revolutionary reality, of which Dostoevsky was more than aware, becomes the domestic affair of a multitude of tormented souls, each the scene of a 'civil war'. His heroes typically engage in inner dialogue and the pronunciation of discourses that end up, not in communication, but in cacophony. Humans are, for Dostoevsky, fatally free in a proto-existentialist way, and universal brotherly love is a moral demand perceived from a position of utter loneliness. He lacks the confidence of later thinkers like Solov'ëv or Frank in an always-already existing fundamental connectedness between all humans.

Dostoevsky is famous for his 'polyphonic' capacity to give many different, often contradictory, voices a place, while he is also strikingly consistent in his own, broadly conservative, Slavophile and nationalist views. Although Dostoevsky was neither a professional philosopher, nor politically engaged (apart from his youthful affiliation with the *Petrashevtsy*[3]), his legacy is of considerable political-philosophical relevance and has been widely appreciated as such. Nobody has entered more profoundly into topics like political radicalism, revolutionary zeal, Christian reformism, nihilist rejection of the world or the perceived obligation to create the Kingdom of God on Earth. Dostoevsky addressed the flipsides of all those attitudes and projects, trying to come to grips with their underlying motivation. The ideas of inevitable progress, malleable society, absolute moral demand and ultimate self-sacrifice populate his literary masterpieces as much as do nihilism, murder, suicide, regicide and politicide. Novels like *Notes from the Underground* [*Zapiski iz podpol'ia*], *Demons* [*Besy*], *The Brothers Karamazov* [*Brat'ia Karamazovy*], *Crime and Punishment* [*Prestuplenie i nakazanie*] and *Notes from the House of the Dead* [*Zapiski iz mërtvogo doma*] have lasting global appeal because they address universal topics and dilemmas, while Dostoevsky's *Diary of a Writer* [*Dnevnik pisatelia*] expresses his often polemical political views on Russia, Christianity, socialism, progress and humankind.

All of this was exacerbated by his own experience as a 'target' of politics. In 1849 he was arrested and sentenced to death for reading aloud Vissarion Grigor'evich Belinskii (1811–48)'s famous letter to Gogol', which had been banned in Russia (Belinsky et al. 1976: 83–92). At the point of execution, Dostoevsky's sentence was changed to five years' hard labour [*katorga*] plus internal exile (Roosevelt 1986: 138). Dostoevsky spent a decade (1849–59) among convicts and ordinary people, with the Bible as his only reading material (Carter 2015: 59). He returned in 1859 to a Russia which, shifting (in 1855) from the oppressive regime of Nikolai I to the reformist era of Aleksandr II, had entered a period in which society's centrifugal forces were set free to interact and clash (Ruttenburg 2008: 97).

During his *katorga* years, Dostoevsky came to realise the gap between the *intelligentsia* to which he himself belonged and 'the people [*narod*]' that he had come to know and appreciate, and he discovered the importance of the religiosity of 'simple folk' (Carter 2015: 65–6; Walsh 2013: 10). He had also become convinced of the centrality of moral choice and individual freedom. However, this did not imply a turn from socialism to liberalism, but to a conservative notion of community close to the Slavophile idea of *sobornost'* (Carter 2015: 68–70). Dostoevsky has been described as a democrat (Ruttenburg 2008), but his democracy is more adequately understood as 'demophilia' – referring to 'the people' in the singular [*dèmos, narod*], not to 'people' [*liudi*] in the plural. Dostoevsky's democracy is Orthodox-Christian *dèmos*-rule, led by a virtuous Orthodox-Christian tsar. In such a case there is little left to rule: not only is rule [-cracy] absent, but a people [demo-] that is one (Dostoevsky 2017: 714) does not need politics, as the source of possible conflict has been deleted.

Since the Petrine reforms, the Russian population had been divided into, on the one hand, a state-employed society composed of fourteen ranks [*chiny*] and, on the other hand, a mass called 'the people [*narod*]' consisting first of serfs and, later, peasants and workers. Dostoevsky's political ideal repeats the Slavophile ideal of a *Belyi tsar'* combined with a pious *narod* as the basis of an Orthodox-Christian and predominantly ethnic Russian [*russkii*, not *rossiiskii*] community. At the same time, Dostoevsky's profound love of the Russian people has a universal messianic orientation:

I am simply saying that the Russian soul [*russkaia dusha*], the genius of the Russian people may have a greater capacity than other nations to embrace the idea of the universal fellowship of humans [*vsechelovecheskoe edinenie*], of brotherly love [. . .]. (Dostoevsky 1994: 1274 / 2017: 706; Berdiaev 1953: 25)

Russia thus owes to Dostoevsky the fateful idea of a 'Russian idea': the first explicit use of the phrase goes back to 1860, to a subscription announcement for the magazine *Vremia* [Time], published by his brother Mikhail. With unsurpassed paradox, Dostoevsky places the question in the mouth of an 'imaginary, disembodied, fantasised Frenchmen', whom he describes as hoping 'that in the future the Russian idea will become the synthesis of all those ideas which Europe has worked out so long and so persistently in its own separate nationalities' (Il'in 2004: 33–6). All the later motifs are there: Russia is expected to yield a Russian idea which is not yet there. This idea is not anti-European but, on the contrary, unites all earlier European ideas. The very idea of such a national idea is itself European. If Russia can come up with a unifying idea, it will reunite Europe – read: Christianity – but how such an idea should be articulated or where it should come from remains unclear. It is a promise, an idea *à venir*. Ever since, the idea of the 'Russian idea' has taken centre stage,

> [a] view of Russian culture as centred around some vision of final goals, whether religious or socialist [. . .]. Such an assertion is both an interpretation of Russian reality and the declaration of an ideal that should guide it. [. . .] Only a government and society based on such a deeper vision can be truly legitimate in the eyes of the Russian people. (McDaniel 1996: 33)

The Serial Hedgehog, Lev Tolstoy

What coexists schizophrenically in Dostoevsky, a broad-minded explorer of the human psyche and a narrow-minded nationalist, exists in temporal sequence in Tolstoy: first a great novel writer, then an insistent, self-righteous moralist. No less 'haunted by social and existential questions' and marked by a 'peculiar mix of inquisitiveness, perceptiveness, and sharp analysis with zealous conviction and stunning self-assurance', Tolstoy engaged with 'whatever he was suddenly throwing himself into with obsessive dedication' (Christoyannopoulos 2020: 12). Like Dostoevsky, Fëdorov and Solov'ëv, Tolstoy did *not* see himself as the founder of a new truth, but as a defender of the core of the old one. Already a world-famous author, he went through a serious existential crises in the late 1870s, which ended with his conversion to Christianity in 1879. Tolstoy overcame this crisis by stating, in his own manner, the core of Christianity in his deeply personal *My Confession* [*Ispoved'*] of 1879, through a critical *Investigation of Dogmatic Theology* [*Issledovanie dogmaticheskogo bogosloviia*] (1879–80) and with a unifying new translation of the Gospel. He turned the four canonical texts into a single one, stripping the Christian message of everything that he felt was not essential, such as the divinity of Jesus Christ and the dogmas of the Holy Trinity, the Immaculate Conception and the Resurrection: *Combination and Translation of the Four Gospels* [*Soedinenie i perevod chetyrëkh Evangelii*] (1880–1) (Lozowy in Tolstoï 2003: 9–11).

In distancing himself from all existing forms of organised Christianity, Tolstoy was the most radical among Christian political philosophers – up to the point where most Christians would deny him that title. For Tolstoy, 'the difference between Christian denominations was inessential if compared with their difference from true Christianity – all churched religion is a flagrant distortion of the initial teaching of Jesus Christ' (Evlampiev 2018: 92). Tolstoy, like Solov'ëv, Dostoevsky and Fëdorov, did not intend to develop a secret, Gnostic doctrine of the elect (Christoyannopoulos 2020: 188) but, on the contrary, to reach out to a global constituency in order to initiate a transformative movement. His reinvention of the Christian tradition, which went beyond denominations and sought common ground with non-Christian traditions (Islam and Hinduism, among others), led to his excommunication from the ROC (still in effect). It also turned him into one of the great thinkers, next to David Thoreau and Mahatma Gandhi, of pacifism, civil disobedience, non-violence, anarchist socialism and alter-globalism (Lozowy in Tolstoï 2003: 32; Christoyannopoulos 2020).

Among Tolstoy's heroes were the *dukhobory* [Spirit Wrestlers], a Christian sect in the Northern Caucusus who called themselves 'Christians of the Universal Brotherhood'. They were condemned by the ROC and persecuted by the tsarist government for their refusal of military service. Tolstoy, who admired their pacifism, vegetarianism and communitarian way of living, wrote in their defence and was instrumental in their emigration to Canada, where they still live (Tolstoy 1987: 232). Tolstoy highlighted the irresolvable conflict between 'governments who consider that Christianity is compatible with prisons, executions, and above all, with wars' and principled Christians such as the Dukhobors, who 'acknowledge as binding only the Christian law (which renounces the use of any force whatever, and condemns murder), and who therefore refuse to serve in the army' (ibid.: 225). Tolstoy's uncompromising rejection of violence and coercion equally defines his opposition to revolutionary socialism, which could only lead to 'more oppression and servitude, of an even more cruel kind', and his distance from anarchism, which, for a Russian in his day, was inseparable from terrorism (Lozowy in Tolstoï 2003: 19–21). The distancing was mutual: the anarchists admired 'his castigation of state discipline and institutionalised religion, his revulsion against patriotism and war, and his deep compassion for the "unspoiled" peasantry,' but it 'held no brief for Tolstoy's doctrine of non-resistance to evil' (Avrich 2005: 36; Lozowy in Tolstoï 2003: 20, n. 29).

Lastly, Tolstoy's struggle with the 'sexual question [*polevoi vopros*]' – the question of the relationship between the sexes – is well known. The core of this sexual question is the assumption (rejected by Tolstoy) that sexual attraction, desire and drive are natural and morally neutral. A sexual morality which turns around mutual consent and absence of harm was in the making in Russia around the turn of the century (Engelstein 1992; Matich 2005). Tolstoy was not the only thinker to struggle with the question what, from a Christian point of view, could be the possible justification (other than procreation) of love between the sexes, given the sinfulness of carnal love. Solov'ëv and Tolstoy broached this question from opposite perspectives, the first arguing, especially in *Smysl liubvi* [The Meaning of Love] (Solovyov 1985), that its justification was to be found in a path of transcendence from sexual, including carnal, love to the highest forms of spiritual love and mystical reunion, the second, on the contrary, arguing against any possible justification, with the implication of sexual abstinence. What unites them is the very idea that, without proper justification, sexual love is to be condemned (Tolstoy in Katz 2014: 298). In the view of both thinkers, everything stands in need of justification. Tolstoy's verdict is clear: 'And I maintain that it is bad. The conclusion that follows from this is that we should not do it' (ibid.: 298).

The Arch-Hedgehog: Nikolai Fëdorov

The 'uncanonised saint', Fëdorov (Lossky 1951: 75), a pious Christian and regular church-goer (Hagemeister 1989: 42), led an ascetic and humble life of abstinence from worldly and carnal pleasures, and of dedication to both his work as a librarian and his life-long project of '*obshchee delo* [common cause]'. He explicitly brought down to this world key elements of the Christian message as he understood it, in an attempt to repair 'the complete distortion of

Christianity, whose Covenant [*zavet*] involves precisely the uniting of the heavenly and the earthly, the divine and the human' (Fëdorov in Edie et al. 1976: III, 54 / Fëdorov 1982: 94). As Losskii phrased it: 'Fëdorov designates the resurrection planned by him as *immanent*; [. . .] The ideal he proposes is the realisation of God's Kingdom in this world' by means of 'the resurrection of man in a nontransfigured body' (Lossky 1951: 78–9). Fëdorov's major writing is the posthumously published and impossibly entitled *Vopros o bratstve, ili rodstve, o prichinakh nebratskogo, nerodstvennogo, t. e. nemirnogo, sostoianiia mira i o sredstvakh v vosstanovleniiu rodstva* [The Question of Brotherhood or Relatedness, and of the Reasons for the Unbrotherly, Dis-Related, that is Unpeaceful State of the World, and of the Means for the Restoration of Relatedness].

Fëdorov's *obshchee delo* project consisted of the spiritual and corporal resurrection [*voskreshenie*] of literally all humans who have ever lived. This implied, among other things, the creation of all-encompassing libraries and museums in order to preserve all past ideas and memories, and to use them as a material basis for resurrection (Hagemeister 1989: 39), and it also implied excavations that would collect the bodily remains of everybody who had ever existed (Lossky 1951: 76–80). Fëdorov's theory is not about zombies, but about immortality and universality. He stated emphatically:

> Life is (the) good [*dobro*]; death is evil. The giving back, by those who live, of life to all who have died in order to live forever is good without evil [*vozvrashchenie zhivushchimi zhizni vsem umershim dlia zhizni bessmertnoi est' dobro bez zla*]. The reconstruction from the earth of all the dead, their liberation from the power of the earth and the subordination of all earths and worlds to the resurrected generations – that is the highest task of humankind [. . .] and at the same time the supreme good [*vysshee blago*]. (Fëdorov 1982: 558, italics in the original)

Fëdorov's project also implies the radical denial of conflict. If death is the root of all evil, because fear of death leads to the drive towards self-preservation which proceeds at the expense of others, then the removal of death implies the eradication of the political. If humans rationally control nature and become immortal, they can take out the root cause of 'all vices, physical and moral, the vices of sexual love and of non-sexual hatred' (Fëdorov 1982: 557). If humankind is immortal, procreation becomes obsolete, and true brotherhood a possibility:

The mass of mankind will be transformed from a crowd, a jostling and struggling throng, into a harmonious power when the rural mass or common people [*narod*] become a union of sons for the resurrection of their fathers, when they become a relatedness, a psychocracy [*psikhokratiia*]. (Fëdorov in Edie et al. 1976: III, 26 / Fëdorov 1982: 65)

For this, however, they not only have to perfect themselves morally in a 'universal transformation involving a transformation of morality as well [*vsetselyi perevorot, sviazannyi i s nravstvennym perevorotom*]' (ibid.: 53 / 92), but also have to understand fully that overcoming death is the solution, because

> as soon as the earth is seen as a cemetery and nature as a death-healing force, just so soon will the political question be replaced by a question of physics; and in this context the physical will not be separated from the astronomical, that is, the earth will be recognised as a heavenly body and the stars will be recognised as other earths. (ibid.: 24 / 64)

Fëdorov was explicit about the this-worldliness of his project, criticising Christianity's otherworldliness and blaming it for not offering an alternative to socialism. Socialism, in Fëdorov's analysis of the early 1890s, 'is triumphing over the state, over religion, and over science', not because it is superior, but because Christianity is failing (ibid.: 52 / 91). Fëdorov echoed Dostoevsky and Solov'ëv when he wrote:

> [S]ocialism is a lie; it gives the name of relatedness, brotherhood, to the 'comradely' association of people [*tovarishchestvo liudei*] who are strangers to one another and are connected only by the external ties of utility, while real blood relatedness [*rodstvo deistvitel'noe, krovnoe*] connects people by an inner feeling. (ibid.: 52 / 91)

This takes us to the heart of the matter: brotherhood or – synonymous for Fëdorov – universal kinship or *rodstvo*, connoting *genus* [*rod*] and birth(-giving) [*rozhdenie, rody*]. Fëdorov's ideas took shape as early as 1851, in his early twenties (Hagemeister 1989: 25–7). His position strikes one as unpolished, but it is widespread among Russian thinkers of the period in question. *Égaliberté* [equaliberty], to use Étienne Balibar's term, which results from the subsequent 'bourgeois' revolutions (1789, 1848, 1905)

(Balibar 2012: 128 / 2014: 100), is an insufficient basis for social justice and moral improvement if true human brotherhood [*fraternité*] is lacking. Socialism offers the wrong version of such brotherhood – the actual development of socialism in its Soviet form arguably supporting this diagnosis. From this Christian perspective, solidarity and social justice depend on acknowledgement of the already existing brotherhood of all human beings as part of the same created humanity, not on division and class antagonism, or on the materialism and utilitarianism that socialists and communists emphasised.

In passing, Fëdorov also resolves the sexual question. As for the mature Tolstoy, erotic love does not have a place in his scheme of universal resurrection: an immortal humankind obviously does not need procreation and can hence do without 'divisive erotic love' (Love 2018: 97). We see here an affinity with the vision of Tolstoy (also in a persistent male chauvinism and misogyny: it is all about brothers, fathers and sons), who rejected Fëdorov's resurrection theory, but deeply admired his ascetic life, while Fëdorov loathed Tolstoy for not putting into practice the life of abstinence that he preached (Hagemeister 1989: 131–7). Fëdorov combines the Christian dogma of resurrection [ἀνάστασις] in both spirit and flesh with high expectations of scientific and technological progress, with a strict rationalism, and a deontological ethics that would make Kant shiver. His synthesis of practical and theoretical reason, called 'supermoralism' (Lossky 1951: 76; Fëdorov 1982: 473), implied a plan for the colonisation of the universe by the resurrected generations, thus ultimately humanising the whole of creation through science and technology.

Fëdorov, however, was not an admirer of modern, urban and industrial society. He opposed material progress and 'rapidity [*skorost'*]' in all forms, argued against the individuality, soullessness, artificiality and so on of modern life, which he, working and living in central Moscow, knew very well (Fëdorov in Edie et al. 1976: III, 44 / Fëdorov 1982: 84). He admired 'primitive mankind', which 'stubbornly spiritualised matter and materialised spirit', and was convinced that, in a similar vein, 'the new mankind [*novoe chelovechestvo*] will strive no less stubbornly toward the real control of blind force' (ibid.: 48 / 88). Instead of a 'back to nature' programme (which is, to an extent, what Tolstoy's vision is about), his is one of 'forward to brotherhood and immortality', with the help of asceticism and science.

A Foxy Hedgehog: Vladimir Sergeevich Solov'ëv[4]

Solov'ëv, a trained philosopher and, in fact, the first truly comprehensive philosopher in Russia (Obolevitch 2014: 109; Smart 2000: 258), is by far the most systematic and synthetic of these four Christian political-philosophical thinkers, much more so than the diagnostic Dostoevsky, the zealous Tolstoy and the self-educated Fëdorov. Solov'ëv wrote a considerable number of treatises in the fields of ethics, philosophy of law, philosophy of history and political philosophy, and in his *publitsistika* applied his philosophical and religious views to the issues of the day (De Courten 2004; Schrooyen 2006). Much of his work is available in translation (Solovyov 1990, 2001; Soloviev 2000, 2003, 2007). His genius expressed itself not only in his immense erudition and multilingualism, but also in his capacity to do at least some justice to almost any contemporary position, bringing together many strands of thought in a grand synthesis. This also includes his predecessors in the present chapter. With Dostoevsky he shared the idea of universal love and beauty, but without strife or strain; with Tolstoy he shared the universalist perspective, yet replacing pacifism by a moderate just war theory and accommodating traditional Christianity; and with Fëdorov he shared the idea of a reunified, Divine Humanity – not as a technological project in this world but as a spiritual transformation.

Deploying a strongly normative notion of 'normality', Solov'ëv took human beings, not as they are, but as they ought to be. 'Normal' for Solov'ëv is not what is common or habitual, but what corresponds to the highest achievable level of humanity: that is, Divine Humanity. Given the pivotal role of God-man Jesus Christ, a Christian anthropology must be a 'theanthropology'. This dimension is elaborated most clearly in his lecture series *Chteniia o bogochelovechestve* [Lectures on Godmanhood / Divine Humanity] (1878–81), which counted Dostoevsky and Tolstoy among its audience. God-man [*Bogochelovek*] is the traditional description of Christ's dual nature, and the idea of an *imitatio Christi* is also traditional. Indeed, Solov'ëv explicitly disclaimed originality, and experts assume that the notion of God-man [*Deus homo* / Богочеловек / *Θεανθρωπος*] that is central to his theory has its roots in Origen (Kojève 2018: 13, n. 6). This background explains the translation of *bogochelovechestvo* as Godmanhood, Theanthropy, Théandrie, Divine Humanity or Deohumanitas (Pribytkova 2011: 32; Smith 2011: 93; Kojève 2018: 52). The big step taken by Solov'ëv is the extension of the concept from the incarnated Jesus Christ on the one hand, and the spiritual *theōsis* of individual Christians on the other, to humanity as a single organism (Solovyov 2005: 351–403), one progressively becoming divine. Whether we should ascribe to Solov'ëv (or Dostoevsky) a literal interpretation of deification [ϑέωσις, *obozhestvlenie*] – that is, an 'immortalisation project' like Fëdorov's, as has been suggested – is debatable (Masing-Delic 1992: 105; Smith 2011: 4). What they do all agree about is that 'deification is the proper end of history – that history ends once human beings have become divine' (Love 2018: 71). From the Christian backbone of Solov'ëv's thought, this 'end of history' means the end of created time. It is the Kingdom of God which completely absorbs creation, and it is the reunification of created reality with its Creator.

The basis of Solov'ëv's world-view is provided by three personal, mystical encounters with the figure of Sophia, in which she revealed to him the secret of the world and of universal religion, the key notion being 'the one and all [ἕv και παv]' in which all coincides. In his unfinished and unpublished *La Sophia* (Soloviev 1978: 1–80), Solov'ëv elaborated these encounters with Sophia / Divine Wisdom / Eternal Feminity (van der Zweerde 2019a, 2020). It is the basis and inspiration of a 'life project' that can be labelled 'integral life [*tselnaia zhin'*]', consisting of three major parts: free theosophy, free theocracy and free theurgy. In more mundane terms, these are theory, praxis and *poièsis* (Kline 1974: 164).

Contrary to Plato and Hegel, who developed their wisdom as an unwritten doctrine and an all-encompassing system, respectively, Solov'ëv left us, untimely, with a very mixed legacy. It consists of, among other things, critical studies of Western philosophy, the *Lectures on Divine Humanity*, a broad range of poetic texts, polemical articles on a wide spectrum of publicly debated issues, theological and church-historical studies, close to 200 scholarly encyclopaedia articles, a Plato translation, a highly original treatise on *The Meaning of Love*, a fascinating set of dialogues, *Three Conversations*, that also contains *A Short Story of the Antichrist* (Solovyov 1990: 159–93) – part variant of, part reply to Dostoevskii's *Legend of the Grand Inquisitor* – and, last but not least, a philosophical system of which only the first part was finished: *Opravdanie dobra* [Justification of the Good] (1897), which contains his philosophical anthropology, ethics, social, legal and political philosophy (Solovyov 2005).

Solov'ëv was a synthetic thinker if ever there was one, and his thought is marked by nuance and moderation. His conception of positive law, for example, is moderate: Alexander Haardt locates him between Tolstoy, who rejected law in the name of Christian morality, and Chicherin, who denied that law had a moral meaning and insisted on its independent value (Haardt 2008: 171). For Solov'ëv, in contrast to both, positive law does have a moral meaning in that it orders society and minimises evil (crime), thus maximising space for a free affirmation of morality: 'The purpose of legal justice [*pravo*] is not to transform the world which lies in evil into the kingdom of God, but only to prevent it from changing *too soon* [*do vremeni*] into hell' (Solovyov 2005: 324 / Solov'ëv 1988: I, 454). A just society is also the place where preparation for the Kingdom of God can take place. From Kant's categorical imperative, which states that each person must always-also be treated as an end in itself and never-only as a means, Solov'ëv derives the unconditionality of individual rights, including freedom of religion, freedom of speech and property rights, while the rights of the community are conditioned by individual rights (Solovyov 2005: 229 / Solov'ëv 1988: I, 346). This implies protection of the individual person from the state, but it does not imply political rights of organisation or participation (Haardt 2008: 181). In this respect, Solov'ëv's political philosophy is not liberal, but remains 'aristocratic' – or, if one prefers, paternalistic.

Indeed, in a thinker like Solov'ëv one witnesses a split of conservative and progressive elements that is symptomatic of a situation with little to no place to transform political-philosophical ideas into practical proposals and programmes. On the one hand, in his utopian vision of a free theocracy, Solov'ëv adopted the Eusebian scheme of the 'three offices' of King, High Priest and Prophet, and defended tsarist monarchy, papal authority and the critical voice of the prophet, rather than that of the public at large (Solovyov 2005: 416 / Solov'ëv 1988: I, 542). On such points, his views strike one as conservative. On the other hand, Solov'ëv took a profound interest in the writings of 'utopian' socialists, and when he lived in London in 1975, he tried to get in touch with the *narodnik* socialist Lavrov, an acquaintance of Marx and editor of the revolutionary journal *Vperëd!* (Luk'ianov 1990: II [III], 123, 139; Nikol'skii 2000: 362, n. 4). Nor was this a childhood sin: as late as 1892, when the French journalist Jules Huret interviewed him, along with this same Lavrov [!], on the 'social question in Europe', Solov'ëv advocated state ownership of major industries, banks and infrastructure 'in order to ensure for everyone a *minimum* of material means, indispensable for the maintenance and development of their moral and intellectual capacities' (Huret 2007: 306–10 / Soloviev 1978: 302). On such points, Solov'ëv can be regarded as a forerunner, if not a representative, of Christian socialism. In the same context, he also expanded the Categorical Imperative to living beings, other than humans: 'he [the human being, EvdZ] has the duty to cultivate and perfect this nature for the good of the lower creatures themselves, who must consequently be considered not as a simple means, but also as an end', adding in a footnote that Kant had failed to recognise this (ibid. 312 / 303). Thus moving in the direction of deep ecology, Solov'ëv at the same time displays the very same patronising attitude with regard to non-human nature as he did with regard to humanity: it must not be left to develop freely, but led to perfection by those who know God's plan for His creation and can therefore know what is right and what is wrong.

The same logic applies to his views on violence and war. While Solov'ëv opposed violence, and certainly political violence, he did support a variant of just war theory and extended it to justifiable violence generally: for example, in penal justice. As long as there is evil, one is justified to fight it, even if that involves the use of violence. Also, peace is not good *per se*: 'War is not an unconditional evil, and [. . .] peace is not an unconditional good [. . .] it is possible to have a *good war*, it is possible to have a *bad peace*' (Solovyov 1990: 39). Violence should be countered with violence when inevitable, but with love when possible: hence his explicit, scandalous and ineffective public call upon Tsar Aleksandr III to forgive, as a truly Christian monarch, the terrorist members of *Narodnaia Volia* who had assassinated Aleksandr II (van der Zweerde 2020: 186–9). The assassins were murderers, yes, but a pious, forgiving tsar could understand the situation and repair the lost harmony of state and society, as well as the tensions and contradictions within the latter (Carrère d'Encausse 1988: 297). Solov'ëv generally rejected retributive violence and capital punishment. He replaced 'an eye for an eye, a death for a death' with a plea for a system of criminal justice that offered possibilities for repentance and re-education in one of his most 'liberal' writings, *Pravo i nravstvennost'* [Law and Morality] of 1897 (Soloviev 2000: 153–84; Marks 2003: 17). Recognising the presence of violence and evil in this world, and, by implication, the possible justification of violence as a necessary evil used by the state in domestic and international affairs, Solov'ëv was distant from any positive appreciation of violence as we find it in Bakunin or Il'in.

In Solov'ëv we find, in fact, all three meanings of political philosophy. First of all, in his later writings, we encounter an elaborate philosophy of politics, focusing on state, law and justice, though largely silent on political struggle and institutions. Second, his concept of *khristiianskaia politika* [Christian politics], which he elaborated most of all in his *publitsistika*, is an explicit attempt to make philosophy itself an effective political tool. Finally, he was well aware of the political dimension of his own activity. On all three points, Solov'ëv's political philosophy is ultimately anti-political: it considers politics as a necessary evil to repair a 'fallen' situation, of course presuming that that situation is rectifiable to begin with. However, in his practical philosophy, especially in *Law and Morality* [*Pravo i nravstvennost'*] and *Opravdanie dobra*, Solov'ëv moves beyond the sterile opposition of existing positive law and uncompromising morality, defining law as the balance of personal freedom and the common good, and prefiguring the notion of *sobornost'* that would become central to the thought of the Russian religious philosophers of the first half of the twentieth century.

Conclusion

If we bracket Christian metaphysics completely, the one outstanding message of the political philosophers discussed in this chapter is that the attempt to realise a perfect society inevitably leads to disaster. From this angle, they prophetically foresaw the outcome of the October 1917 Revolution and the victory of the architects of the human body and mind. Dostoevsky's *Legend of the Grand Inquisitor* and Solov'ëv's *Short Story of the Antichrist* are, from that angle, warnings against a (literally) anti-Christian scenario; their apocalyptic visions prefigure the Benefactor in Zamiatin's dystopian novel *My* (1921) and Big Brother in George Orwell's *1984* (1949). Fëdorov and Tolstoy come closer to the idea that Man can actually fulfil the Divine Plan in this world. Solov'ëv's normative conception of God-manhood arrives at the idea of maximum preparation for the Second Coming, as it were 'smoothening' the Apocalypse by creating an 'as-perfect-as-possible' state. If the end-state is the 'New Jerusalem' as

> not merely a particular political order that may itself yield to other political orders in an endless struggle from domination [. . .], but a political order that brings a close to all politics in a final apocalyptic transformation, in the establishment of a [. . .] final universal order, the heavenly city (Love 2018: 48–9),

then we are speaking of a politics that puts an end to everything political, a city that puts an end to all cities, one that is no longer political, hence no longer a city [*polis*]. The truth of the matter is that Christianity holds a tremendous potential for the conservative defence of the existing status quo, as well as for radical protest against injustice (Boer 2019). At the same time, this chapter has shown that releasing the critical potential of the Christian tradition remains impotent if it is not connected to some form of politics: that is, a way of dealing with the political.

Nineteenth-century Christian political philosophy in Russia developed against the backdrop of a rapidly changing society in which the old world of a traditional faith-based community was replaced by a new world of intellectual plurality and 'secular' urban culture. The legitimisation of the tsarist regime in premodern political–theological terms no longer sufficed; at the same time, it was increasingly unclear if or how this regime would be able to modernise itself. This explains a clear and apocalyptic urgency in the religious thinkers of the period: either the nostalgic urgency of preserving a past way of life or the activist urgency of offering a different direction from the one that society was taking. From the perspective of these thinkers, atheist socialism and individualist liberalism were, by and large, two sides of the same materialist and utilitarian coin. Contrary to liberalism, which rode the wave of society's transformation, the Christian political thinkers were trying to place markers of certainty, or *vekhi* [signposts / landmarks], that could point towards the direction that the Russian people should take. Their bad luck was that, while these *vekhi* did make a strong impression, at the same time they coexisted with many others, pointing in equally many different directions.

Notes

1. On the hypothesis that Fëdorov did not publish his writings fearing excommunication: https://www. e-flux. com/journal/88/176021/editorial-russian-cosmism/, p. 01/04 (last accessed 25 October 2020).

2. The famous distinction between goes back, via Isaiah Berlin, to the Greek poet Archilogus (Berlin 1978: 22). Foxes 'know many things' and hedgehogs 'know one big thing': the first are versatile and address many options, while the second work with one big idea that they apply everywhere.

3. *Petrashevtsy* was the name given to the members of a progressive discussion group in the 1840s in St Petersburg, organised by Mikhail Petrashevskii.
4. This section is relatively short because I have written at length about Solov'ëv elsewhere (see Bibliography), and also plan a book-length study of his political philosophy.

Chapter 5

Russian Liberalism Revisited – Between a Rock and a Hard Place

[L]iberalism in all its aspects developed in opposition to state power.
Michael Mandelbaum, The Ideas that Conquered the World
(Mandelbaum 2002: 74)

But regardless of the sphere in which we may move or the kind of law to which we may be subordinate, everywhere we are free beings, for liberty constitutes an inalienable characteristic of our spiritual nature.
Boris Chicherin, 'Property and State', in Liberty, Equality,
and the Market (Chicherin 1998b: 366)

Liberalism has been the most consistently oppositional political philosophy throughout Russian history. This probably also explains why it has received so much attention from Western scholars, often not without a whiff of wishfulness. The common denominator of nineteenth- and early twentieth-century liberalism in Russia is a negative one: rejection of arbitrary autocratic rule and struggle against the widespread 'legal nihilism' that includes the radicals and terrorists, the socialists and Marxists, and the Christian thinkers with the exception of Solov'ëv (Walicki 1992: 9–104). Russian political philosophers generally perceived the law as a mere instrument in the hands of state power, prioritised social justice and equality over individual civil and political rights, and rejected formal legality in the name of true, Christian morality. This contrasts with the undeniable progress of legal culture and penal law since the 1864 reforms, the development of the *zemstvo* practices of limited local self-government, reluctant moves towards popular representation and constitutionalism, and the increasing academic freedom that yielded 'legal *narodniki*', 'legal Marxists' and 'legal liberals' (Nethercott 2007; Medushevsky 2006).

There is no generally accepted definition of liberalism. Following Chantal Mouffe, I identify three key principles of the liberal tradition: individual liberty, human rights and rule of law [*Rechtsstaat, pravovoe gosudarstvo, gospodstvo zakona*] (Mouffe 2000: 2). The distinctive feature of liberalism is not simply the understanding, however crucial, of the human being as inherently free (Kara-Murza and Zhukova 2019: 13), but the idea that this inherent freedom should be the main organising principle of socio-economic and political order. If one links those two orders, the economic and the political, the result is the classical liberalism of John Locke and Isaiah Berlin. If it is posited as the only organising principle, implying full emphasis on negative liberty, the result is the libertarianism of Ayn Rand and Robert Nozick. If it is combined with the principle of a political community, implying not only civil rights but also civic duties, the outcome is the republican liberalism of Jean-Jacques Rousseau or Pëtr Struve. If it is combined with the principle of social justice, the result is the social liberalism of John Rawls or Pavel Novgorodtsev. If, finally, it is combined with the idea of an 'ethical' community in the Hegelian sense of *Sittlichkeit*, the outcome is the protective liberalism of Benjamin Constant and Boris Chicherin.

A good place to start is with Isaiah Berlin:

> I believe that it is human beings, their imagination, intellect and character, that form the world in which they live, not, of course, in isolation but in communities – that I would not deny – but that this is in a sense a free, unorganised development which cannot be causally predicted. It is not part of a deterministic structure, it does not march inexorably towards some single predestined goal, as Christians, Hegelians, Marxists and other determinists and teleologists have, in varied and often conflicting ways, believed and still believe to the present day. (Berlin 2013: 332–3)

Starting with Berlin's hero, Herzen, Russian liberals generally follow an anti-deterministic model of society as the unpredictable effect of the free action of a plurality of human beings. However, a rejection of determinism does not imply a rejection of teleology altogether. Under the impact of Hegel in particular, Russian liberals tended to believe in a vector of historical development pointing to a free and just society. Moreover, unlike Berlin and most Western liberals, their liberalism was less individualistic and less about negative liberty: they placed great value on positive liberty, including national self-determination. They also counted on the state and – paradoxically – even the autocratic tsar, to implement a modern legal system and to introduce political reforms, rule of law and constitutional monarchy. Positive appreciation of institutions generally, and of the state in particular, is what distinguishes the liberals from anarchists, who saw the state only as an instrument of oppression (Offord 1985: 75; Roosevelt 1986: xiii, 151–2, 161; Levandovskii 2010: 43), and from Christian political philosophers, who, like Solov'ëv, saw it as a necessary evil.

The search for a middle path between authority and anti-authority, autocracy and anarchy, is another distinct feature of Russian liberalism. Western liberalism aimed at a liberation of (civil/bourgeois) society from the state and a 'liberalisation' of the state itself (separation of powers, rule of law, representation). Its success turned liberalism into the centrepiece of the hegemonic ideological framework of Western polities. By contrast, Russian liberalism relied on the reforms undertaken by the autocratic government, or, alternatively, it had to opt for revolution. While it shifted depending on the actual conjuncture, the overall project was stable: a preference for reform over revolution, an emphasis on freedom of the press, public opinion and academia, a constitutional regime with rule of law instead of rule by decree, some form of representation and individual freedom. Private property rights were less prominent, though not absent from this agenda: liberalism may be the natural political philosophy of a rising bourgeoisie but Russian liberals rarely were 'bourgeois capitalists', and their constituency was mostly a combination of the growing class of 'professionals' employed at *zemstvo* level and that part of the nobility that went into business.

This chapter discusses, first, a formative stage of 'early' Russian liberalism, represented by Granovskii; second, a 'mature' stage represented by Chicherin, whose 'conservative liberalism' is best contrasted with the viewpoint of Solov'ëv; and third, a politically committed 'new liberalism' – a notion covering a broad spectrum of positions, including the 'rule-of-law socialism' of Kistiakovskii, the 'social liberalism' of Novgorodtsev and the liberal nationalism of Struve (Walicki 1992: 5–6, and *passim*). In terms of constituency, one can discern two major strands within Russian liberalism that continue into the twenty-first century. On the one hand, there is the more theoretical *intelligentsia* liberalism, consisting of liberal-minded groups working in 'free professions' (academics, lawyers, judges, physicians, engineers), generally lacking political experience, sceptical about the capability of the tsarist regime to reform itself and prone to engage in principled discussions over doctrine. On the other hand, there is the more 'hands-on' *zemstvo* liberalism, consisting of people who were active in local governance, had obtained political experience and continued to hope for renewal and expansion of the reforms of the 1860s (Karpovich 1997: 389–96).

Early Russian Liberalism

The appearance of liberalism in Russia is often connected with the name of Desnitskii, the first Russian university professor of law, the first professor to teach in Russian and 'one of the first representatives of moderate liberalism in Russia' (Antonov 2012: 55; Bowring 2013: 21). The key figure in early liberalism, however, is Timofei Nikolaevich Granovskii (1813–55). His career was made by three years as a student in Berlin, which turned him into a polyglot, a professional historian and a 'statist liberal' of the Hegelian kind (Levandovskii 2010: 16; Offord 1985: 46–9; Roosevelt 1986: 24–44). Like Herzen, Granovskii was deeply influenced by Hegel's philosophy of law, politics and history, but unlike the impatient and capricious Herzen, Granovskii was highly consistent in his constitutional liberalism. Like Hegel, who reportedly toasted the French Revolution every 14 July (Good 2006: 4), Granovskii remained true to the ideals of 1789, but expected their realisation from consistent reform in Russia in order to bring empirical reality closer to rational reality. As he said to Chicherin in 1844:

> Freedom, equality, brotherhood – it is not easy to achieve this. After a long struggle, the French finally obtained freedom; now they are struggling for equality, and when the two are consolidated, then brotherhood will appear. That is the highest ideal of humanity. (Roosevelt 1986: 133)

In these sentences, we see both Westernising universalism and an emphasis on human agency: the realisation of humanity's highest ideal is a matter of long-haul reform, not of swift revolution, and while history may not have a libretto, it does have a single plot. Russia, as a nation and as a state, was facing historical choices, but with, ultimately, a single possible outcome; hence, the choice was between facilitating or delaying a development that 'slowly, but truly has absorbed Russia' (Levandovskii 2010: 46).

In three immensely popular series of public lectures in 1843–4, 1845–6 and 1851, Granovskii used his authority as professor of modern history to provide progressive liberalism with a scientific basis. The first of these series was threatened with closure, which only added to its impact (Roosevelt 1986: 87, 90; Offord 1985: 53–4; Dmitriev 1987: 323–4). Granovskii rejected Belinskii's dictatorial 'Jacobinism', to which he opposed a 'Girondin' view on reform politics. This prefigured the position of a liberal *narodnik* like Mikhailovskii, including the anti-determinist emphasis on the crucial role of free and critically thinking individuals (Offord 1985: 66–71). Granovskii elaborated a broadly Hegelian view of history as a universal process of gradual improvement. Guided by the key ideas of freedom and unconditional human dignity executed by 'great people' like Charlemagne or Pëtr I, this process was always conditioned 'by the struggle of opposite forces' and hence manifested itself most of all in 'transitional periods [*perekhodnye periody*]' during which 'the Absolute operates, not only by way of creation, but also of destruction' (Levandovskii 2010: 26, 47).

Sharing Hegel's universalism but attentive to local specifics, Granovskii emphasised the importance of transitional periods, marked by revolutions and uprisings of the oppressed (Dmitriev 1987: 323). In the 1840s, transition was in the air, but it remained limited to liberal–bourgeois revolution in Western Europe and did not reach Eastern Europe. At this point, an 'orthodox' Hegelian position was a helpful source of hope. The *Weltgeist* has time on its side and has 'enough nations and individuals to spend' (Hegel, *Werke*: XX, 507), which, when applied to Russia, meant that, for a Westerniser like Granovskii: 'Russia's transformation in a Western spirit [. . .] was predetermined with complete inevitability – only the periods were not indicated' (Levandovskii 2010: 43). Shortly before Granovskii's death, the succession of Aleksandr II, when Nikolai I died, marked the beginning of such a transitional period in Russia.

The desire to be free does not necessarily make one a liberal. Liberals are those who desire not only freedom for themselves, but 'equal freedom for all' [*égaliberté*] (Balibar 2012), an expression in which the understanding of 'freedom' and the extension of 'all' can vary. The meaning of freedom can range from freedom of thought via property rights to freedom of political organisation. Moreover, the referents of 'all' can include all adult members of society, but can also be limited to male aristocrats: the distinctive feature of liberalism is that those falling under 'all' should equally enjoy the given catalogue of rights and liberties. Under Russia's absolutist autocracy, anybody claiming any kind of liberty, for anyone other than the monarch, was a liberal: even tsars like Aleksandr I or Aleksandr II could therefore be labelled liberals.

Many thinkers discussed in this book were 'liberal' in the sense of loving freedom but few explicitly endorsed a liberal political philosophy. If we start from a famous quip by Herzen – 'Despotism or socialism – there is no other choice' (Offord 1985: xi, quoting Herzen, *PSS*: IX, 151) – Russian liberals were those who, *pace* Herzen and against all odds, did try to find a middle way between the Scylla of tsarist autocracy and the Charybdis of revolutionary socialism. Even 'partly liberal, partly radical' Herzen himself was trying to find a way out of the 'haunting dilemma: in a backward society, can there ever be a third choice between cajoling concessions out of an autocratic state or forcing them through revolutions whose utility (for liberal goals) most nineteenth-century liberals came to doubt?' (Fischer 1969: 17, 41). While this still defines liberalism in broad, largely negative strokes, it does exclude, at one end, the absolutist model with its monarchic and Jacobin variants and, at the other, the idea of revolution. It also contrasts with, on the one hand, Christian and Slavophile visions of a tightly knit, religion-based community and, on the other, radical anarchist and communist visions of a fundamentally different society.

Mature Liberalism

Liberals in Russia became increasingly aware of their identity. Boris Nikolaevich Chicherin (1828–1904) was one of Granovskii's students, and an exceptional scholar who was 'the patriarch of Russian *gosudarstvennaia nauka* [state science, *Staatswissenschaft*]' (Osipov in Chicherin 1998a: 3), but also a loner, 'equally alien to all currents in Russian philosophical and political thought' (Walicki 21992: 106). Chicherin was professor of state law [*gosudarstvennoe pravo*] at Moscow university from 1861. He left his job in protest against violations of the university's autonomy in 1868, after which he established himself as an independent scholar (Osipov in Chicherin 1998a: 11). Actively participating as a junior member in the debates between 'Westernisers' and 'Slavophiles' of the 1840s, Chicherin emerged as an 'enlightened patriot' who wanted Russia to embark on the universal path towards a liberal and democratic rule-of-law state, but bearing in mind local specifics (ibid.: 6; Walicki 1992: 109–10). During an 1858 encounter in London, Chicherin tried to move the highly influential Herzen from a revolutionary socialist to a reformist liberal position. Herzen, as he wrote later, 'from the first words sensed [*pochuial*] that this was not an adversary, but an enemy', and their ensuing polemics planted the caricature of Chicherin as a right-Hegelian, 'for whom every existing polity was an object of veneration', while, in fact, it was Chicherin who was wary of Herzen's advocacy of socialism by whatever means (Chizhkov 2013: 98–9; Hamburg 1992: 195–8).

Chicherin distinguished three 'different types of liberalism'. The first, which he despised, is 'liberalism of the street', the position that 'does not want to know anything but its very own self-will [*sobstvennoe svoevoliia*]' and 'cannot stand authority' (Chicherin 1998a: 464f). The second type, and the main target of his polemics (Kelly 1998: 227), is 'oppositional liberalism', which limits itself one-sidedly to the negative dimension: 'To change, dissolve, to destroy – that is its whole system' (Chicherin 1998a: 467). While this liberalism can sometimes address injustices, it does not offer an alternative and is often simply parasitic: 'Many, many oppositional liberals are sitting on cushy jobs' (ibid.: 468). The third type, finally, is his own 'protective [or conservative – *okhranitel'nyi*] liberalism': a liberalism that preserves the existing order while aiming at gradual reform in the direction of a constitutional monarchy granting civil rights.

Chicherin's main contribution to political philosophy in Russia is a clear distinction between civil and political rights. The former, as in Hegel, are fundamental, sacred and, 'in our view, [. . .] essential for Russia's prosperity' (Chicherin 1998b: 134). In his programmatic *Sovremennye zadachi russkoi zhizni* [Contemporary Tasks of Russian Life] (1855), Chicherin lists seven civil rights: freedom of conscience,[1] emancipation from serfdom, freedom of speech, freedom of the press, academic freedom, publication of all governmental activities except inevitable *arcana imperii*, and public legal proceedings (ibid.: 134–9; Kokorev 2012: 250). These civil rights should have priority over political rights. In *O narodnom predstavitel'stve* [On Popular Representation] (1866), Chicherin asserted that 'political liberty is the culmination of individual liberty' (Chicherin 1998b: 159), yet he advocated slow implementation of such culmination in Russia since it presupposed, in his view, not only personal freedom and civil rights, but also competence (hence: literacy and education), an elevated level of morality and private property.

Chicherin thus makes political liberty, representative government and party pluralism dependent on the maturity of citizens (ibid.: 201). Relating representation to competence, Chicherin was as supportive of the *zemstvo* and the jury court system as he was opposed to a national assembly on the basis of universal suffrage, not as a matter of principle, but of realistic timing:

> In our time almost nobody will deny the enormous and positive effects of representative institutions upon those peoples who are prepared for them, in countries where the desired harmony between political freedom and authority, between order and the public good, has been attained. [. . .] There is no doubt that a representative system is not the sole guarantee of justice and of liberty. On the contrary, it can be effective only if there exist other institutions that are close to the people and that affect popular life. An independent, incorruptible, well-organized court system, an appropriate amount of local self-government much more effectively safeguard the individual, property, and the citizens' interests than does citizen participation in the central government. [. . .] But without political liberty, none of the underlying guarantees is safe from violation. (ibid.: 181)

Chicherin replaced Providence, whether in its Christian-messianic or its historical-determinist form, by *phronesis* [practical wisdom]. In doing so, he rejected both legal nihilism (in its religious-moralistic and revolutionary-socialist variants) and the idea of society's jump to perfection:

> Long before the edited volume *Vekhi*, the scholar [Chicherin] summons to reconsider the radical Russian intelligentsia and to engage in a serious effort to create the foundations of a rule-of-law state, instead of advancing maximalist demands to the supreme power. (Osipov in Chicherin 1998a: 7)

Chicherin was a rare defender of a Russian system of checks and balances grafted on local conditions. He defined 'law [*pravo*] as freedom determined (or limited) by rules [*zakonom*]'[2] and as 'the "moral principle on which the state is founded"', but in practice he prioritised 'the absolute value of the law, and obedience to it' over 'the absolute value of the individual as the source of all social unions' (Walicki 1992: 131; Kelly 1998: 235). Increasingly disappointed by the regime's incapacity for systemic reform, he moved to more radical positions, but retained his rejection of socialism and his advocacy of the combination of private property and political liberty. As Igor' Osipov put it: 'This essentially was a theoretical and political programme, that was potentially capable of bringing together all constructive political forces and to become an alternative to both radicalism and reaction in Russia' (Osipov in Chicherin 1998a: 7).

Whether a coalition of centripetal forces might have yielded a political centre with sufficient mass to enforce a transition to a constitutional monarchy strong enough to survive the revolution years and World War I remains an open question. In any case, such a coalition did not establish itself, arguably because Russia's autocracy was beyond the conservative-reformist repair that Chicherin aimed at. Shortly after his death, a new 'transitional period' started, and with hindsight his words, displaying his Hegelian patience to the full, sound prophetic:

> But whether this awareness will arrive by way of correct inner development, or will be bought at the price of bloodshed and the wreck of many generations, the future will show. Perhaps, we will witness the appearance of a statesman like Cavour or Bismarck, who [. . .] is capable of setting Russia on the road indicated to it by history. It also is possible that there will appear a tsar, animated by an elevated sense of morality [. . .]. In any case, to stick with today's myopic despotism that stifles all powers of the people, is not a possibility. In order for Russia to move forward, it is imperative that arbitrary power is replaced by power that is limited by law and surrounded by independent institutions. The edifice erected by Aleksandr II must achieve its completion; the civil liberty he established must be secured and consolidated by political liberty. Sooner or later, and one way or another, it will be achieved without fail, because it is contained in the necessity of things. (Chicherin 1998a: 614–15)

Chicherin's insistence on the distinctions between a metaphysical understanding of freedom (opposed to determination) and a political one (opposed to oppression), between a private sphere of liberty and a public sphere where the common good has priority, and between civil and political rights is a major innovation in the Russian context and makes him the Russian liberal *par excellence*. His 1897 polemics with Solov'ëv make clear why Solov'ëv, who limits free will to the human capacity to do wrong by refusing to be determined by moral law, is not a liberal. Chicherin, in contrast, insists that freedom has meaning because humans can freely do both good and evil, and that submitting oneself to the moral law equally presupposes freedom as diverging from it (Chicherin 2016: 9; Chicherin 1998a: 55; Evlampiev 2013: 17; Malaia 2002). In the Preface to *Pravo i nravstvennost'* [Law and Morality], Solov'ëv had positioned himself between Tolstoy and Chicherin as two extreme positions: while the former rejected law in the name of pure morality, the latter separated them and claimed that law possesses 'its own absolute principle'. Chicherin vehemently protested against this polemical construction, because he considered Tolstoy an amateur in legal matters, while he regarded his own opinion as 'the fruit of many years of studying law'. Moreover, in Chicherin's perception, Tolstoy indeed adhered to morality in pure exclusivity and Solov'ëv, mirroring Tolstoy's moral absolutism, 'wanted to subordinate everything under it', while he himself, in line with his liberal reading of Hegel, claimed relative independence of the legal sphere (Solowjow 1971: 31; Chicherin 2016: 102).

Novgorodtsev has rightly placed Chicherin's mature work, *Filosofiia prava* [Philosophy of Right] (1900), next to Solov'ëv's *Opravdanie dobra* as one of those 'works that would adorn the academic literature of any country' (Osipov in Chicherin 1998a: 14). Crucial differences between the two *magna opera* appear if we first look at similarities, such as a positive appreciation of statehood (which excludes anarchism), an emphasis on legality (which excludes legal nihilism), a recognition of private property over the means of production (which excludes socialism), a central role for the traditional family and household (which excludes communism), and an understanding of the state as a higher-order ethical organic whole (which excludes individualism). Like Hegel, Chicherin embedded his philosophy of politics in the broader framework of a philosophy of right [*pravo*], while Solov'ëv embedded his philosophy of both right and politics in the framework of a theory of the good [*dobro*]. Both, again like Hegel, attempted to contain the political, Chicherin by offering limited space to political liberty and its manifestations while broadening the scope of civil liberties, Solov'ëv by prioritising a reality of concord that would, in theory, reduce the possibility of conflict to manifestations of evil will: that is, crime. Both, finally, were keenly aware of the polemical and political purport of their work: they opposed socialism, which, for them, merely meant egoism in the plural, but while Solov'ëv waged a 'holistic' war against positivism and particularism – for example, in the form of nationalism – Chicherin was fighting a two-front battle against positivism and metaphysics (the ultimate ground of Solov'ëv's position). Close as their positions may effectively come, the Christian-organicist communitarianism of Solov'ëv does not accept division and partition of the social body, seeing those as manifestations of evil, while the realist statism of Chicherin sees morally neutral manifestations of individual and group self-interest contributing to a differentiated whole. For Chicherin, political struggle is a fact of life, and the task is to accommodate it, while for Solov'ëv political struggle as such is a manifestation of imperfection and evil (Solov'ëv 1988: I, 477–8).

A Liberal Revolution?

Chicherin, widely respected as an erudite historian and liberal philosopher of law, remained a 'major but solitary figure', standing 'almost alone for a political position of moderate reform in an intellectual hothouse dominated by revolutionaries and reactionaries' (Gordin 2016: 27). At the same time, he deeply influenced the next generation of political philosophers, who, notwithstanding different political priorities, were one in their rejection of legal nihilism. Most of them had a partly West European education, and many were both academically and politically active. Two major examples are Pavel Ivanovich Novgorodtsev (1866–1924) and Bogdan Aleksandrovich Kistiakovskii (1868–1920), author of *Sotsial'nye nauki i pravo* [Social Sciences and Law] (1916), in which he tried to found 'rule-of-law socialism' on social science, and Max Weber's main associate regarding the Russian Empire. Other renowned liberals included as Pëtr Berngardovich Struve (1870–1944); Pavel Nikolaevich Miliukov (1859–1943), author of the widely acclaimed, multi-volume *Ocherki po istorii russkoi kul'tury* [Essays about Russian Cultural History] (1903–9), a work in which he addressed political history, too; Vasilii Alekseevich Maklakov (1869–1957); and Judge Anatolii Fëdorovich Koni (1844–1927). They were active politically and institutionally, but more important as practicioners than as thinkers.

In his essay, 'The "Russian Sociological School" and the Category of Possibility in the Solution of Social–Ethical Problems', Kistiakovskii addressed a systematic problem of the utmost relevance: the question of how sociology can be related to a specific political programme. The bulk of the article is a critical analysis of the subjective sociology of Mikhailovskii. Echoing Solov'ëv, Kistiakovskii drove home the point that, precisely by insisting on possibility, and by refraining from a normative argument in terms of 'what ought to be [*dolzhenstvuiushchee byt'*]' and 'what ought not to be', normative preferences are deprived of indisputability and become arbitrary preferences. The point is not that *pravda* cannot, as Mikhailovskii believed, be split into truth [*istina*] and justice [*spravedlivost'*], but that it ought not to be; or that, if it has been split, the two '*ought* to united in one great whole, designated by *pravda*, and that science and art *ought* to serve this one integral *pravda*' (Kistiakovskii 2003: 338, 343). Possibility alone is not enough: 'We strive for the realisation of our ideals not because they are possible, but because our conscious duty imperatively demands it of us and everyone around us' (ibid.: 352).

While Marxist historical determinism tended to provoke the question of why political action would be necessary to bring about the inevitable, *narodnik* subjective sociology created an open field of possibilities for political action but failed to develop a cogent normative argument in favour of one possibility over the others. If the former is a question of political ontology, the latter is one of authority: if several possibilities are present, it is never obvious that the authority of science or philosophy should gain the upper hand. Kistiakovskii's critique of Mikhailovskii was that he 'placed the freedom of man above the force of causal necessity thus ending with voluntarism' (Vucinich 1976: 134). Politics, precisely if it presupposes the freedom to choose between at least two alternatives, is neither deductive nor inductive: arguments and ideas are at work in it, but never exclusively and rarely decisively. Many of those arguments and ideas may come from social science or from philosophy, but there are also interests, ideologies, prejudices and psychological factors such as charisma. Those can be studied and analysed scientifically, as in Weber's pioneering political sociology, but that does not in itself have political implications. Opening the political arena means to open it for, in Kistiakovskii's own words, 'the deepest practical contradictions among different *pravdy* [plural of *pravda*]' (Kistiakovskii 2003: 334), and the overcoming of those contradictions is not a matter of theory alone. This points to an intrinsic problem of liberalism as a hegemonic project. Its eventual success undermines its very position because the emergence of free practices and institutions opens the floor for a plurality of hegemonic projects, including non- and anti-liberal ones, reducing the liberal project to the status of one among many or to the status of an overlapping consensus.

A 'general science of society' can, ideally, explain societal phenomena in terms of cause-and-effect relations on the basis of law or law-like regularities, and it can, even more ideally, predict the behaviour of societal groups, but it is at odds with political philosophy in as much as the latter presupposes free agents motivated in their action by reasons and arguments, not determined by economic or other factors. While Weber tackled this conundrum by becoming, as Joachim Radkau put it, *two Max Webers*: a value-free scientist and a value-obsessed, passionate politician' (van der Zweerde 2010: 58–61), Kistiakovskii tried to avoid becoming 'two Kistiakovskiis'. He did distinguish empirical social science from normative political philosophy but, like other Russian idealists, continued the 'unceasing search for a reconciliation of science and ideology, scholarship and politics' (Vucinich 1976: 125), believing it possible to offer a cogent normative argument.

Contrary to the turn to the religious metaphysics and mysticism of other neo-idealists – Struve, Berdiaev, Bulgakov, Frank – Kistiakovskii held that ethical problems 'could be approached (and solved) scientifically, without reliance on metaphysics' (Rampton 2020: 140). He considered 'the desire for justice [. . .] one of the innate and incontrovertible attributes of the human condition', and thought 'law (and political institutions generally) [. . .] a vehicle for social justice', as well as crucially important for guaranteeing rights (ibid.: 138, 143). Among those rights, this social–liberal included not only negative liberties, but also positive social rights such as 'the right to work, to right to receive care in the event of illness, old age and inability to work, the right to develop fully one's capacities, and the right to a proper education' (ibid.: 144). For Kistiakovskii, 'a socialist state represents the best political form to guarantee both negative liberties and the achievement of social and economic equality' (ibid.: 145), not, however, because it yields a conflict-free synthesis of liberty and equality, but because rule of law creates the conditions under which those two potentially conflicting values can be balanced.

Unlike Chicherin, Kistiakovskii held that political rights and democratic participation were not the culmination or the crown, but the basis and precondition of a rule of a law state (Vucinich 1976: 152). This viewpoint was shared by another important liberal from the same period, Novgorodtsev, who embedded his liberalism in a revitalised conception of natural law (Rampton 2020: 137; Nethercott 2010: 250) and affirmed 'the crucial importance of the right to a dignified existence [as] the only concept that "can save us from both despotism and anarchy in Russia"' (Rampton 2020: 150). Novgorodtsev, law professor at Moscow University, had received his philosophical education in Freiburg, Berlin and Paris, and his liberalism was Hegelian rather than Kantian. While

Kant's conception of human freedom was as universal as it was abstract, he believed that the gap between moral life and social well-being could be bridged only 'by empirical beings in the light of real-life circumstances': that is, within the framework of Hegelian 'Ethical Life' [*Sittlichkeit, nravstvennost'*] (ibid.: 147).

Unlike Kistiakovskii and like Chicherin, Novgorodtsev regarded 'religious belief and the ontological implication of idealism' the proper, objective basis of human freedom and dignity, thus developing the metaphysical–religious argument that Kistiakovskii rejected (ibid.: 147–8). Again like Chicherin, he pointed to the progressive historical development leading up to the modern rule-of-law state, and emphasised Hegel's dissatisfaction with the abstract character of Kant's moral and political philosophy (Novgorodtsev 2011: 300–2). Novgorodtsev combined Chicherin's conception of a liberal *Rechtsstaat*, praising the 'unquestionable step forward' of a 'consistent development of the individualistic principle, which was lacking in the Hegelian system' where the individual was ultimately subordinate to the ethical whole, with Solov'ëv's 'right to a dignified existence' (Walicki 1992: 291–2). Social inequalities are at least partly the result of man-made institutions, which implies that the state, as an ethical whole, has an obligation to repair them.

Unlike Chicherin and like Kistiakovskii, Novgorodtsev emphasised the primary importance of political liberty and representative institutions, not, however, as an aim in itself, but as 'merely one means towards a more fully developed political system, a lawful state that can defend both freedom and equality' (Rampton 2020: 153). After the 1905 Revolution and on the basis of direct political experience as a Duma member, he became more sceptical: 'Political institutions and practices, he concluded, are important, but will never be wholly sufficient to resolve liberalism's constant demand for a recalibration between conflicting values, nor constitute "the alpha and omega of political life"' (ibid.: 153). In *Ob obshchestvennom ideale* [On the Social Ideal] (1911–17), Novgorodtsev engaged in such a recalibration, ending up with a 'principle of free universalism [*svobodnyi univerzalizm*]' as a social ideal which articulates the very tension between the conflicting values of freedom and solidarity (Novgorodtsev 1991: 111; Katsapova 2005: 159). While tending, like Berdiaev and Bulgakov, towards the religious–metaphysical notions of *sobornost'* and universal solidarity, he made a clearly liberal choice for liberty over harmony, distancing himself from conservatives like Joseph de Maistre or Konstantin Leont'ev as much as from Fichte or Plekhanov (Novgorodtsev 1991: 97–8, 125–6; Rampton 2020: 158–9).

All members of the *intelligentsia* wanted freedom of thought (at least for themselves), opposed oppression, censorship and arbitrary power, and were in favour of fundamental civil liberties and a free public sphere. Liberalism, as an explicit political philosophy, expresses these priorities, and had its basis in two partly overlapping groups: on the one hand, theoreticians and academics like Granovskii, Chicherin and Novgorodtsev, some of whom also were politically active (Struve, Ostrogorskii, Kistiakovskii), and, on the other hand, practitioners, at *zemstvo* level, in the legal system (Koni) and in the state apparatus (Miliukov and Maklakov), forerunners of what present-day scholars have called 'guild liberals' and 'system liberals' (Cucciolla 2019). They advocated state interference in Russia's rapidly but unevenly developing capitalist economy, in which both the agrarian question (land shortages, famine, poverty, mismanagement) and the social question (education, exploitation of labour, hygiene) remained unresolved. They also advocated cooperation between state and *zemstvo* because the central government dramatically failed to use the expertise developed at *zemstvo* level (Fediashin 2012: 132–3, 137).

What singles out Russian liberalism generally is its emphasis on law and legality, in opposition to the 'legal nihilism' of both Marxists and Christian political philosophers (with the exception of Vladimir Solov'ëv) (Offord 1985: 59; Walicki 1992: 18–104). Liberalism's opponents were not conservative Christians, moderate social-democrats and labour unionists, as was the case in Western Europe, but radical nihilists of the 'Jacobin' tradition, radical Bolsheviks and equally radical 'religious communitarians' like Tolstoy. As a consequence, most Russian liberals adopted a version of idealism that defended the infinite dignity of 'each individual soul and person' against the cynical 'contempt' regarding 'the "bourgeois" notion of the sanctity of human life' (Morson in Chicherin 1998b: xi). Also, liberals in Russia were atypical (or force us to rethink our definition of liberalism), in that they saw the state not simply as a warrant of individual civil liberties and rights, but also as a major 'instrument of justice' (Cucciolla 2019: xxix; cf. 21, 151).

Conclusion

Russian liberalism highlights the fact that, liberalism's overall depoliticising tendency notwithstanding, under circumstances of oppression and authoritarianism it becomes a fighting and even revolutionary creed. Liberalism does entail a philosophy of politics and state: a good state is one which protects its citizens against each other, against external enemies and against the state itself. Politics is there to mediate the *prima facie* legitimate differences of opinion and interest between citizens. The state should be as small as possible, but in the case of Russia liberals agreed that it needed to be big. Liberalism also entails a philosophy of the political. If individuals are free to develop and express themselves, as well as to pursue their personal happiness as they see fit, there will inevitably arise conflicts, which have to be settled on the basis of some type of equality or fairness. Liberals tend to assume optimistically that this is always possible and that the political can, in that sense, be domesticated. Finally, liberalism is very much aware of its own political dimension when it is in actual conflict with the powers that be or with its political opponents, but it also tends to regard itself as the political philosophy that most fits human nature, if not the only one, understood as inherently free individuality.

This chapter has demonstrated the relevance of political arenas and the crucial difference that their presence or absence makes: intellectual debates and edited volumes became political events in part because they replaced a political arena (Schapiro 1967: 73; Offord 1985: 71; Roosevelt 1986: 92). Liberalism, with its emphasis on individual freedom and inalienable rights, can develop into a serious political movement only when there are places where it can be both advocated and tested. This applies to all positions and currents in political philosophy in Russia: if, at times, they strike one as abstract, extreme or maximalist, this is due to the fact that the political centre, where they could have found compromises, was kept empty by authoritarian governments. This constellation started to change in the early twentieth century. If, previously, Marxism, *narodnichestvo* and liberalism had been 'legal' only to the extent to which they remained scholarly and academic, but ran into trouble as soon as they became political, this started to change once the tsarist regime reluctantly accepted the principle of popular representation and allowed the formation of political parties, of which the liberal Kadet [*Konstitutsionnye demokraty*] Party [KD] became a leading example.

For the 'anninilists', revolution was an end in itself and the only possible form of politics. For the anarchists, revolution was a necessary act of liberating destruction, after which communal politics could start, based on *obshchina*, *mir* and *artel'*. For the

Marxist communists, the root of the political was class struggle, and the final victory of the proletariat would signal the withering away of the state and the end of politics as known hitherto. For the Christian political-philosophical visionaries, the political did not have economic roots, but spiritual ones: individualism, egoism and materialism were perceived as forms of turning against the order of creation. Only for the liberals, and for some of the social-revolutionaries and (Menshevik) social-democrats, did politics, including party pluralism, have a positive ring. However, the early experience with electoral–parliamentary democratic politics after 1905 was anything but encouraging. For later Christian thinkers, politics would still be a necessary evil at best, and during the Soviet period there was barely a place for politics. As a consequence, the positions that were elaborated outside Soviet Russia could have an impact only in a much later period. After the breakdown of the USSR, Russia (along with the other ex-Soviet republics) was still facing the same challenge as in the early twentieth century: how to acknowledge the ubiquity of the political and the inevitability of politics, and how to give it shape.

Notes

1. This implies acceptance of conversion from Orthodoxy to other confessions, toleration of *staroobriadtsy* and lifting of 'oppressive restrictions' on the Jewish population, none of which was self-evident in Russia at the time.
2. Bearing in mind the meaning of *pravo* as right rather than law, and of *zakon* as positive law.

Chapter 6

The Long Russian Revolution – Signposts for a Roller Coaster

As revolutions evolve, moderates, Girondins, and Mensheviks lose out to radicals, Jacobins, and Bolsheviks.

Samuel P. Huntington, *The Clash of Civilizations*
(Huntington 1998: 266)

It is impossible to decree communism. It can be created only in the process of practical research, through mistakes, perhaps, but only by the creative powers of the working class itself.

Aleksandra Kollontai, 'The Workers' Opposition', 1921
(Kollontai 1980: 187)

The last decade of the nineteenth century and the first two decades of the twentieth in Russia have been named the Silver Age [*serebri-annyi vek*]. This was a period of unprecedented, perhaps never surpassed, economic, cultural and intellectual blossoming. It also was a period of unbridled political expectation and unparalleled disaster. After the war against Japan (1904–5) was lost and the first revolution (1905) came about, the tsarist regime embarked on a path of cautious constitutional concessions (soon revoked), which created a political landscape populated by a variety of parties – the very word 'party' articulating the dividedness of society. All parties were led by members of the *intelligentsia*, who spoke 'in the name of' a constituency that, in most cases, was not at all present in the party itself (Malia 1996: 71). Not only Struve, but most political leaders were 'revolutionaries without masses', who had yet to create their own constituency (Kolerov 2020: 33). After 1905, it became painfully clear that, 'strictly speaking, not one of the political parties in Russia had a stable, fittingly organised political basis' (Karpovich 1997: 403).

The Constitutional Democrat Party [KD] (f. 1905) prioritised constitutionalism over revolution, while 'all the parties to the left of the Kadets subordinated their commitment to a constituent assembly to social revolution' (Malia 1996: 71). This explains why the liberals could not forge a coalition with reform-minded forces in the government, and why the evolutionary approach of Maklakov lost out to the revolutionary orientation of Miliukov and Struve (Karpovich 1997: 395, 399). Meanwhile, the government, led by reformers like Stolypin and Witte, persisted in an energetic, deliberate and consistent policy of top-down modernisation, international competition and capitalism. It was government for, but neither by nor of, the people. Among the opposition, there was rarely consensus about the course to be taken or even about the state of affairs: 'Almost every event in the period between 1905 and 1917 has a liberal, a Socialist Revolutionary, a Menshevik and a Bolshevik interpretation' (Semyonov 2019: 28). One can safely add three more: tsarist–monarchist, Christian and nationalist.

This chapter is organised around the three revolutions (1905 and, twice, 1917) (van der Zweerde 2019b, 2021a). It thus covers the period that led up to 1917 and that between October 1917 and the establishment of the new, Soviet regime, or, to use Carl Schmitt's phrase, of a new *ordo ordinans* [ordering order]' at the end of the Civil War (Schmitt 1997: 47 / 2003: 78). The 'long Russian Revolution' (1905–22) (Steinberg 2017: 5, 8; Engelstein 2018: 1) was surrounded by philosophical debate, not only among Marxists and revolutionaries, but also among philosophers of broadly liberal and Christian orientation, who gradually moved from a revolutionary mood to a pessimistic, apocalyptic understanding. The edited volume *Problemy idealizma* [Problems of Idealism] (1902) had already marked a move away from Marxism and materialist to idealist positions, and *Vekhi* [Landmarks, Signposts] (1909) called upon the Russian *intelligentsia* to address its own revolutionary mood critically and to adopt a more sober attitude towards politics. It immediately became a bestseller and provoked critical reaction from all sides, including edited volumes from the liberals, *Intelligentsiia v Rossii* [The Intelligentsia in Russia] (1910), and from the social-revolutionaries, *Vekhi kak znamenie vremeni* [*Vekhi* as a Sign of the Times] (1910) (*Problemy idealizma* 2018; *Vekhi* 1991; *Intelligentsia v Rossii* 1991; *Vekhi kak znamenie vremeni* 1910; Sapov 1998). Several of the aforementioned authors returned as contributors to the gloomy *Iz glubiny* [*De Profundis*; Out of the Depths] (1918), which engaged in apocalyptic pessimism (*Iz glubiny* 1990). *Smena vekh* [Shift of Landmarks] (1921/2), finally, was published by emigrated intellectuals who decided to give up their resistance and join the new regime, laying the groundwork for what later became known as 'national Bolshevism' (*Smena vekh* 1922).

Several of these titles contain the word *vekhi*. A *vekha* is a stake (or, in water, a buoy) or a milestone, both literally and metaphorically. Usually translated as 'signposts' or 'landmarks', *vekhi* combines the meaning of an important moment of transition in a trajectory with the notions of direction and orientation, but also of warning and potential danger. This points to a demand for orientation, evaluation criteria and frames of reference, comparable to Lefortian '*repères de la certitude* [markers of certainty]' (Lefort 1986: 29). The background assumption of this chapter is that such *vekhi* are never given or revealed, and therefore cannot be searched for or discovered. Instead, like real *vekhi*, they are always posited and, therefore, already political: the demarcation of a field and the directions indicated are themselves part of an arena of possible conflict and concord. All the aforementioned volumes aimed to intervene not only in intellectual discussions, but also in current affairs, trying to set a course or give a direction. This shows the extent to which this period formed a living laboratory for the direct interplay of political theory, praxis (action) and *poièsis* (many authors being active in existing institutions), especially with respect to a single question: was 'revolution' a historical inevitability, or a political repertoire that depended on the deliberate action of particular individuals or groups? Those who came out victorious, the Bolsheviks, held that it was both, and that the whole question was about seizing the right moment to jump on the bandwagon of history.

The long revolution was a *smutnoe vremia*, a time of both trouble and opportunity. It is difficult not to regard the discussions and deadlocks of this period with the 'disadvantage of hindsight'. Most texts in political philosophy were manifestly future-oriented or even prophetic: apocalyptic nightmares and utopian dreams shared the expectation that things would change dramatically (van der Zweerde 2013: 107). Koselleck observed that while history is written by the victors in the short term, in the long run we learn more from the defeated (Koselleck 2000: 68). While this is generally convincing, things become less clear when victory and defeat are ambivalent. Political events in Russia continue to belong to the category of the ambivalent and contestable: Was the 1905 Revolution indeed a complete failure? Was the February Revolution of

1917 the true Russian Revolution and October a mere Bolshevik takeover? Who won? Who lost (apart from thousands of ordinary people)? Who betrayed whom in which revolution? Are we not still divided, and fundamentally so, over the question of whether political goals can justify the sacrifice of human lives, and whether this is irrespective or not of the number of victims?

Political revolution involves the removal of a regime and the destruction of the existing *ordo ordinans*. However, this in itself does not necessarily imply physical violence, carnage or terror. If revolution means rapid and radical regime change, we should note that, for example, the revolutions in Central and Eastern Europe around 1989 were radical and rapid, but generally peaceful and non-violent. Turning to the 'Russian Revolution', this explains two things. First, there is the fact that the vast majority of political activists and thinkers, from the radical left to the liberal and Christian right, were convinced that a revolution in the Russian Empire was both inevitable and desirable. Second, there is the fact that only tiny factions in the political landscape considered violence a necessary means or even an end in itself – indeed, the Bolsheviks were one of those factions, but even they were divided. Revolutions quickly develop a dynamic of their own that becomes difficult to steer, and inside an accelerated historical situation there is no way to predict how one's actions will interact with those of others. Consequently, revolution is more about tactics than about strategy. Or, to invoke the imagination: once the locomotive has picked up steam, the question becomes how to prevent its derailing, not where the stations and the signposts [*vekhi*] are.

Momentum of Liberation

The first Russian Revolution was primarily liberal. If fully implemented, the 1905 'October Manifesto' by Nikolai II would have yielded rule of law, constitutional monarchy and a limited form of representative government (Williams 2017: 1). It was, however, not implemented: the tsarist government retreated and the First Duma, elected in 1906 and dominated by the KD, stood in opposition to the regime from the outset. The 1905 Revolution, potentially the finest hour of liberalism in Russia (Malia 2006: 266), failed to give conflict a legitimate place, to offer the various political groups the opportunity to gather political experience and expertise, and to win popular support (Pontuso 2004: 51–2, 57). It did, however, liberate Russian society.

A first liberated sphere was politics itself. Political parties were legalised, elections were introduced and previously illegal and underground organisations faced the option of becoming part of an emerging, 'less imperfect' order. Moisei Iakovlevich Ostrogorskii (1854–1921), widely regarded as a founding father of political sociology, was also a practical politician. He left Russia because of the anti-Semitism that spread after the assassination of Tsar Aleksandr II, but returned in 1906 and became a member of the First Duma for the KD. The KD in fact benefited from limited suffrage and indirect elections, which illustrates one of the dilemmas of liberal parties. While defending equal liberty for all and standing up for civil rights and liberties (freedom of speech, religion, organisation and demonstration), along with free enterprise and property rights, the liberals, as the party of a rising bourgeoisie, did not automatically endorse equal political rights. They had every reason to fear a mass of workers and peasants, which explains why they often connected franchise and property.

In fact, democracy can be considered, and was, suspect from various angles. From a liberal perspective, it is a good [bonum] only if enough people support individual rights and liberties as a way to exclude majority tyranny. From a Christian perspective, it is a good only if people are of good will or, ideally, one in Christ, but not if it fosters division. From a socialist perspective, democracy is a good only if it leads to political participation of the majority of the workers, enabling a redistribution of wealth and power. From an anarchist perspective, democracy is a good only if it means self-government at all levels of society, but not if it is limited to parliamentary representation. From a Bolshevik perspective, it is a good if it brings about the dictatorship of the proletariat, perceived as a legitimate majority tyranny. A democratic politeia is, paradoxically, dependent on a willingness to give up the immediate realisation of any maximalist agenda. In Russia, few were willing to do this.

Although the KD participated in all subsequent four Dumas (1906–12), it faced the problem that constitutional reform had only gone halfway and was gradually withdrawn. The liberals refused to take part in the government because Nikolai II's 'October Manifesto' did not incorporate a satisfactory perspective on a constitutional monarchy (Karpovich 1997: 399). After the announcement of a State Duma [gosudarstvennaia duma], they continued to call for a Constituent Assembly [uchreditel'noe sobranie] (ibid.: 400). However, by refusing to cooperate, the liberals effectively blocked the road to further reforms – the result was less, not more, constitutional monarchy. In fact, the Duma was in permanent opposition to a government in which political parties did not participate (the cabinet was still appointed by the tsar). As a consequence, the KD became central to the February 1917 Revolution.

The liberals were not alone with their dilemmas. The Marxist Russian Social-Democratic Labour Party [RSDRP] faced the question of how to 'divide its energies between legal and extra-legal activities' (Sabine 1963: 810). Before 1905, the answer to this question was simple: all parties were banned (Fedorinov 2000: 79) and their members, when not abroad, repeatedly arrested. This became less obvious, however, when the Duma made the existence of political, albeit not revolutionary, parties possible. The RSDRP boycotted the First Duma elections (1906) but participated in those for the Second (1907), and was represented in the Third (1907) and Fourth (1912), too. A split occurred within the RSDRP, resulting into two factions. On the one hand, the Bolsheviks generally opted for the illegal, revolutionary variant, sticking to the 'Leninist' principle of a professional revolutionary party that would use the Duma only as a podium and would continue the model of Nechaev and *Narodnaia Volia*. On the other hand, the Mensheviks, 'without denying that extra-legal action was necessary, tended to see the purpose of the revolutionary movement as the organisation of the working class for legal political actions' (Sabine 1963: 812).

A second liberated sphere was that of religion. In tsarist times, there was an official marker of certainty: the official Orthodox-Christian nature of the Romanov dynasty and its empire. In relation to this, a number of positions were articulated, including the one that reclaimed an autocephalous church, and until 1917 there were strong modernising tendencies within the ROC, of which Solov'ëv is one example (Valliere 2000). After 1917, the Bolshevik regime established a new marker of certainty: the official atheist nature of the new regime – again, other positions were articulated around it. What the two markers share is certainty, a positive or negative reference to God, official status, and exclusion of alternatives. The period in between, by contrast, was one of both uncertainty and revival. The ROC was one of the beneficiaries of the 'long revolution', especially after its formal subordination to the government via the Holy Synod and its *oberprokuror* was ended in early 1917. Previously hidden and suppressed discussions were now played out in the public sphere (Michelson and Kornblatt 2014; Michelson 2017). After the February Revolution, the ROC started to prepare for a national council [*pomestnyi sobor*] in order to elect a new patriarch. The ROC, however, was torn between opposing trends: returning to pre-Petrine arrangements or answering the call for modernisation. At the same time, occult and esoteric movements flourished among high society, Christian sects were mushrooming across the empire, and spiritualist séances, including the hiring of *iurodivye* from the countryside, were widespread.

Furthermore, the personal sphere was liberated. That the political can become personal had been discovered before by thinkers in the nineteenth century who had been exiled (Herzen, Dostoevsky) or officially declared insane (Chaadaev). That the personal can also become political was discovered around the turn of the century, when a host of poets, writers and thinkers addressed the issue of gender and sexuality, theoretically as well as practically, and dissolved one of the markers of certainty in their rejection of both traditional Christian and modern bourgeois family values (Matich 2005; Engelstein 1992). One famous *vekhi*-switch is the conversion of Dmitrii Sergeevich Merezhkovskii (1865–1941), his wife, Zinaida Nikolaevna Gippius (1869–1945), and their friend, Dmitrii Vladimirovich Filosofov (1872–1940), who were living as a *ménage à trois*, from outspoken monarchism to endorsement of the revolutions of 1905 and February 1917. Explicit enemies of Bolshevik communism, they fled their homeland and later even supported Hitler, hoping that he might defeat Stalin's dictatorship.

Finally, women liberated themselves during the Silver Age. The benevolent paternalism of Solov'ëv and others, who had written about the Women's Question [*zhenskii vopros*] and taught courses for young women (who could not access higher education), had partly prepared the ground. However, things started to change in earnest only when audacious women, like the poets Zinaida Gippius and Poliksena 'Allegro' Sergeevna Solov'ëva (1867–1924; the philosopher's sister), and politicians, like Aleksandra Mikhailovna Kollontai (1872–1952) and Anastasiia Alekseevna Verbitskaia (1861–1928), took matters in their own hands. Women played a prominent role in the revolutions of 1905 and 1917, as they had done in the radical movements of the late nineteenth century (Fauré 1978). After the February Revolution of 1917, and after mass protest led by suffragettes Figner and Poliksena Nestorovna Shishkina-Iavein (1875–1947), the Provisional Government introduced equal voting rights for women and men, before the Netherlands (1919), the USA (1920) or the United Kingdom (1928). In fact, the revolution itself was ignited by women who took to the streets to protest against impossible living conditions. The February Revolution, dated 23 February in the Old Style, took place on 8 March, according to the New Style: that is, on International Women's Day; it was initiated by Clara Zetkin and has been celebrated since 1911. Russian suffragettes and feminists of various political orientations entered the political arena with conflicting agendas: equal rights for women on the one hand, proletarian revolution on the other (Zetkin and Kollontai 2014).

The Short Year 1917

Libraries continue to be filled with accounts and analyses of the two revolutions of 1917. It is one of those episodes that has not been settled in humankind's political memory, and probably never will be. Nor should it: contested political events from the past, like the French Revolution, the Paris Commune and, indeed, the Russian Revolutions, continue to facilitate the articulation of present-day antagonisms. The February Revolution was a bourgeois and a proletarian revolution in one, which is interesting from a theoretical perspective but detrimental from a political one. This result was a split government, a diarchy that lacked authority. The Provisional Government and the Petrograd Soviet of Workers' and Soldiers' Deputies were competing with each other, jointly incapable of ruling a huge country in the middle of a war that Russia was dramatically losing (Ulam 1998: x). The fact that more than a few politicians participated in both bodies indicates the absence of a clear power centre, and this 'empty place of power' was neatly symbolised by the absence of a portrait in the Taurid Palace (Hedeler 2017: 14). It took until September 1917 for Russia to be declared a republic, and the overdue elections for a Constituent Assembly took place only in November. After the Bolsheviks lost those elections, they dismantled the assembly. If February 1917 replaced 'divine legitimation by civic legitimation' (Chubais 2016: 32), then October 1917 replaced popular support by terror and the suppression of any opposition.

For Lenin, parliament was never more than a useful means for revolutionary action. Bolshevik political cynicism was mirrored by scepticism on the part of many idealists. The *Vekhi* authors, for example, had been convinced of the inevitability of a political revolution and hence supported February 1917, but they just as clearly opposed a social revolution. Once the *ancien régime* had been removed, reform would set in (Shelokhaev in *Vekhi* 1991: 8–9). During this period of intense unchaining of the political, philosophical texts had political relevance by default, and it has been argued that 'the real political thrust of the book [*Vekhi*, EvdZ] was an attempt to destroy the informal coalition of the liberals with the left' (Shatz and Zimmermann in *Signposts* 1986: xvii). Note that, of the *Vekhi* authors, five were KD members, and Struve one its leaders. *Vekhi*'s anti-polemical emphasis on reconciliation [*smirenie*] becomes, in a politicised context, inescapably polemical: the polemical function of a text never depends on the author's intentions alone. This becomes clear not only from Lenin's venomous attack, but also from the critical commentary by Merezhkovskii, which bore the title 'Sem' smirennykh [Seven Humble Ones]' (Merezhkovskii in Sapov 1998: 103 [orig. 1909]; van der Zweerde 2013).

The Bolsheviks could grasp central power due to their superior party organisation and strategic instrumentalism. Workers' soviets had already come into existence in 1905 in factories that were on strike, yielding a Petrograd Soviet that existed only briefly. Lenin and the Bolsheviks saw the *sovet* as an instrument in political conflict, not as a means to deal with the political (Iarov 2009: 153). The 1917 Petrograd Soviet, which had an Executive Committee [*ispoln'nitel'nyi komitet*] even before the soviet itself came into existence (ibid.: 155), did perform state functions, but failed to develop into an integral part of a new *politeia*. This was due to mistrust on the part of the Provisional Government, the instrumentalisation of the Petrograd Soviet by Lev Davidovich Trotsky (1879–1940; b. Lev Bronshtein), and the fact that 'whole sections of the "working people" were not represented in the City Council [*gorodskoi sovet*]' (ibid.: 157). The soviets to which the Bolsheviks claimed to hand over all power – *Vsia vlast' sovetam!* – quickly became mere instruments in the hands of a new ruling elite, and despite the etymological link between *sovet* and *veche*, they had little in common with the republican and anarchist idea of commons.

While Western liberals often share a negative perception of the state as a cumbersome barrier to change, Russian liberals perceived the state as an important machine for reform. Their 'spontaneous statism' put them in opposition to the anarchists, even if they both departed from an optimistic anthropology that asserts that humans, if left free to do so, can organise themselves in a spirit of, for the liberals, competition and deliberation, and, for the anarchists, cooperation and 'mutual aid'. The February Revolution had been welcomed by most liberals and by all anarchists, but over the October Revolution they split. Liberals rightly perceived it as the end of both liberal and democratic principles, while anarchists, though sceptical about the Bolshevik agenda, thought that a revolution of workers, soldiers and peasants could clear the palate. Perhaps, under more favourable conditions, February 1917 could have been saved, but October seems to have been destined for disaster. It quickly became clear to most participants that, irrespective of their political colour, dictatorship of the proletariat meant dictatorship of the Bolshevik faction of the RSDRP, renamed *Vserossiiskaia Kommunisticheskaia Partiia (b)* [All-Russian Communist Party (Bolshevik), VKP(b)] in 1918.

Setting *Vekhi* for a New Era

In the early twentieth century Russia, revolution travelled by train. Both Lenin and Kropotkin arrived at Petrograd's Finland Station. On 3 (16) April, Lenin was welcomed by a crowd of 60,000 and the Workers' Marseillaise, the national hymn of the new republic with the French revolutionary melody and socialist wording. Kropotkin, who did not believe in a quick proletarian revolution, arrived at the same station on 30 May (14 June) 1917, greeted by an even larger crowd (Merridale 2017: 184). The abdication of Tsar Nikolai II took place in a train carriage, trains were of crucial importance for Bolshevik *agitprop* during the Civil War, and Stalin, the ultimate victor of the revolutionary period, travelled around the USSR in a special carriage. Trains, however, need signals, and it was the Bolsheviks who posited these *vekhi*.

The early Soviet period was an era of both artistic and intellectual flourishing, combined with repression and terror. After they had established political domination – effectively, dictatorship of the VKP(b) – it took the Bolsheviks several years to consolidate their new *ordo ordinans* in opposition to foreign enemies, as well as competing hegemonic projects. This struggle took place simultaneously in the political, military and economic domains, and in that of culture and academia, but the subordination of the latter two attained full speed only after the Civil War had been won. From that point onwards, domination and hegemony went hand in hand in mutual support (Anderson 2017: 21). Of the six initial hegemonic projects, only the militantly socialist Bolshevik project remained. The conservative project of a constitutional monarchy, started in 1905, failed after February. The monarchist–national project (Denikin and colleagues) could have won the Civil War if the Western powers had been supportive. The anarchist project

(Makhno) became important locally during the Civil War but was defeated. The liberal (KD) and social-democratic (Menshevik and right-socialist-revolutionary) projects dominated between February and October, but failed to establish a new order (Kara-Murza 2017: 16–7).

If, prior to 1917, the liberalism of Struve, the anarchism of Kropotkin, the Christian politics of Bulgakov, the agrarian socialism of Chernov and the Bolshevik communism of Lenin could appear as competing hegemonic projects for Russia, this changed radically after October. A new, 'red' order tried to establish itself by literally any means and, after much bloodshed and terror, succeeded. Revolutions are not only *vekhi*-changers. They are also frame-changers, one of the elements of the new frame being *Velikaia Oktiabria* [Grand October] itself; they are name-changers (from RSDRP to VKP(b); and they rely on game-changers. Lenin was a game-changer in that he refused to join the Provisional Government in April 1917, going against the majority opinion of the Bolsheviks, who wanted to adopt the role of legal opposition within, instead of opposition to the new order that had come into existence after February (Merridale 2017: 226). In his April theses, Lenin defended the idea of a socialist revolution based on the Petrograd Soviet against the Provisional Government, a position which, despite its initial isolation, gained momentum in the course of the year (Žižek 2002: 56–61).

Lenin's genius was a combination of rationalism and pragmatism. In line with the orthodoxy of most revolutionary Marxists in Russia, he embodies the 'Platonic' idea that there is a single truth that can be known by all humans. Consequently, there is only one adequate policy, so that, by implication, the implementation of that single true policy not only constitutes a moral demand, but also justifies the means necessary to achieve it, ruthless violence included (Pontuso 2004: 52). This is indeed an ultra-rationalist and, potentially, ultra-violent idea. In Lenin's case, the indubitable goal of socialist revolution legitimised any means that, paradoxically, explain his absolute pragmatism. Lenin was, however, profoundly wrong because he overlooked the possibility of a derailing dictatorship of, first, the proletariat, then the vanguard party and, finally, its leader. He also wrongly expected a Bolshevik victory to be the starting point for world revolution, leading to a free federation of nations rather than an international system of states, and that this would take a matter of months.

October 1917 constitutes a major historical event, but politically it meant the end, not the beginning, of revolutionary change in Russia. With the almost immediate exclusion and disarmament of not only liberal and monarchist competitors, but also anarchist and socialist-revolutionary ones, it marked the start of massive suppression and denial of the political. The VKP(b), never a mass party to begin with, but a conspiratorial organisation of revolutionary *intelligenty*, quickly moved away from its working-class constituency (Holt in Kollontai 1980: 153–4), and dictatorship of the proletariat turned into party and then personal dictatorship. In this respect, October 1917 deserves to stand forever in the political memory of humankind as an important lesson. The suppression of the political by the new regime was not tactical, accidental or circumstantial, but implied by its role as vanguard of the victorious world proletariat. Being on the right side of history, the regime's task was to end class struggle and not allow any relapse. Aristocrats, *kulaks* [self-employed farmers], agents of the bourgeoisie and, later, 'cosmopolitans' had to be rooted out, and the legitimacy of societal conflict had to be denied:

> The theory of democracy in Leninist nations depends on the idea that abolishing class-based society by definition abolishes all important conflicts of interest. With the abolition of classes, different groups will begin to work together in 'deep harmony,' and [. . .] with only one class in the state, there will be no need for institutionalized conflict in the form of political parties or independent unions. (Mansbridge 1983: 293f)

Pace Mansbridge, it is highly questionable whether the population of Soviet Russia should be qualified as a 'Leninist nation': there was massive resistance from the very start, and Lenin's theory was first and foremost the legitimising ideology of a praxis of suppression and exclusion by a minority, even within the VKP(b).

'October' was attacked from the right by monarchists, nationalists, liberals and Orthodox Christians like the *vekhovtsy*. Leftist critique came from four sides: from within the party (Kollontai, later Bukharin, Trotsky and many others), from other social-democrats (Plekhanov, Luxemburg), from social-revolutionaries (Chernov) and from anarchists (Kropotkin, Emma Goldman, Aleksandr Berkman, Vsevolod Ėikhenbaum [Volin]). The argument that central power needed to be established and fortified before society could be left free to self-organise clearly backfired, as the large-scale resistance in the countryside and the 1921 Kronshtadt uprising testify, not to mention the normative question of whether any small group is ever entitled to impose its will on a largely resistant population.

Kropotkin's earlier warnings against a bureaucratic state returned after 1917 in the form of an opposition between those who, like Kollontai, insisted that the socialist government should give maximum space to the workers' initiative and self-organisation, and the VKP(b) leadership, which opted for reinforcement of the state as an instrument for the destruction of the bourgeoisie as a class (Kropotkin 1906: 37–8; Kollontai 1980: 159–200). Kollontai's 'loyal criticism' can be easily connected to a sociological analysis of bureaucratisation and the forming of a party oligarchy along the lines of Max Weber and Robert Michels (Weber 1998a, 1998b; Michels 1925). There is, however, also a different understanding of socialism at stake: implementation by a party versus self-organisation of, by and for the workers. Bureaucracy is not simply a deplorable side-effect of modern statehood, nor, as Lenin thought, a 'neutral' instrument for management and administration. There are no politically neutral instruments, and bureaucracy is key to a modern, law- and rule-based system of governance, executed through offices. Bolshevik dictatorship meant the adoption of this model of statehood, but with decreasing democratic control by the organised workers or even by the party itself.

Kollontai appealed in vain to the Bolshevik leadership to recognise the activities of labour unions, to 'hold back' its own administrative power, and not to replace the construction of socialism by the workers themselves with a bureaucratic state, run by officials largely recruited from the *intelligentsia*, if not the defeated bourgeoisie:

> The party task is to create the conditions [. . .] so that workers can become workers–creators, find new impulses for work, work out a new system to utilise labour power, and discover how to distribute workers in order to reconstruct society, and thus to create a new economic order of things founded on a communist basis. *Only workers can generate in their minds new methods of organising labour as well as running industry.* This is a simple Marxist truth [. . .].
> (Kollontai 1980 [1921]: 184, also 177–9; Sabine 1963: 812f)

The prolonged period of revolution and civil war also created a testing ground for visions of a radically different society. The Red Army, led by Trotsky, aimed at recapture of the Russian lands and was central to the stage of 'military communism [*voennyi kommunizm*, often euphemistically translated as 'war communism']. The scattered White Armies wanted to restore the old order and created short-lived states in the South and in Siberia under commanders like Denikin, Kornilov, Wrangel' and Kolchak. The Black Army, led by Nestor Makhno, aimed at the creation of an anarchist peasant community: the anarchists, active participants in October, had quickly become enemies of the Soviet state. The Blue Army, led by former social-revolutionary Antonov, resisted Bolshevik rule in the Tambov region, and the Green Armies, though politically close to the majoritarian social-revolutionaries, merely tried to resist confiscation of their crops by either Bolsheviks or Whites. The new regime met with resistance from the side of the old order, including the 'new old order' that had developed since February 1917, and from those on the left who aimed for socialism without 'order', or at least without 'cadre'.

Hatred among the revolutionaries of anything bourgeois or religious was deep-seated and the unchaining of this antagonism led to massacres and public executions. As Gorbachëv's aid, Aleksandr Nikolaevich Iakovlev (1923–2005), reported in 2002, on the basis of newly available data:

> priests, monks, and nuns [. . .] were crucified on the central doors of iconostases, thrown into cauldrons of boiling tar, scalped, strangled with priestly stoles, given Communion with melted lead, drowned in holes in the ice [and] nearly three thousand members of the clergy were shot in 1918 alone. (Iakovlev 2002: 156)

Other sources report that 2,691 priests, 1,962 monks and 3,447 nuns were executed after a trial, and 15,000 without one, during Lenin's own rule (van den Bercken 2018: 399). Bolshevik terror was not a return to tsarist repression, which had been much more moderate, but it did continue the lethal repression of the last five years of tsarist rule (Pontuso 2004: 17, 33–4). Under the old regime, during the 1825–1917 period, a total of 6,350 persons were sentenced to death for political reasons, of whom 3,932 were effectively executed; of these executions, 3,741 fell in the period 1906–10.

Lenin is, of course, not the inventor of political opportunism but he is one of its most radical and consistent theoreticians. The notion of hegemony [*gegemoniia*], made famous through the work of Antonio Gramsci, has its roots in Russian Marxism, specifically in Pavel Aksel'rod and Georgii Plekhanov (Anderson 2017: 13–14).

Hegemony is often misunderstood as the 'soft' alternative to 'hard' domination, similar to the distinction of soft and hard power. In reality, they always go hand in hand. The Bolshevik leadership dealt with this issue pragmatically. Hegemony of the proletariat was, for both Lenin and, later, Stalin, of relevance only in the period prior to October: it meant political leadership within a broad anti-tsarist coalition and was aimed at overruling liberal, social-revolutionary and reformist agendas. After October, it was replaced by Party-organised progaganda: '[N]ot the hegemony, but the dictatorship of the proletariat [. . .] defined the emergent Soviet state. Once it was established, the traditional formula no longer appears in Lenin's writing. Events had superseded it' (ibid.: 18). Contrasting dictator-ship as 'rule by force' to hegemony as 'rule by consent' (ibid.: 16), the opportunism of the Bolshevik leaders boils down to a rejection of the 'soft' idea that consent is better than force. The excessively violent character of the Soviet regime is explicable in terms of the instrumentalism of its dominant ideology: the easiest, quickest and most effective means are always preferred.

One way or another, Bolshevik victory put an end to the *smutnoe vremia*. New *vekhi* were set, and while such things as industrialisa-tion, alphabetisation, mass education, and liberation of women and national minorities remained high on the agenda of the new regime, political turmoil, cultural bloom and sexual liberation gradually came to an end or were streamlined. Inner-party politics remained very lively for roughly a decade, also because 'defeated' Mensheviks started to jump on the bandwagon. The New Economic Policy [NÈP] that followed upon economically disastrous military com-munism did offer new opportunities for entrepreneurship. Progres-sive, innovative and experimental writers, artists and intellectuals could benefit from enormous new opportunities, also in rebuilding the devastated country, if they lent their power to the new regime. In all these cases, the new regime demonstrated a tension in the fun-damental Marxist, but also Spinozist and Aristotelian, conviction that society and culture result from the actualisation of the com-bined potential of its participants. This actualisation presupposes their flourishing and, hence, their freedom. However, the need to secure a position of power under both domestic and international threat implied limitations on said freedom and, hence, flourishing.

Against the backdrop of the new, Soviet *vekhi*, the year 1922 also meant the start of reconciliation movements like the Living Church, the *Smenovekhovtsy*, and the Biocosmists–Immortalists movement, led by Aleksandr Fëdorovich Sviatogor [Agienko]

(1899–1937), the latter a group of former anarchists who considered 'immortality to be at once the goal and the prerequisite for a future communist society, since true social solidarity could only reign among immortals: death separates people' (Groys 2018: 9). The same year saw a start in the decline of many artistic and scientific experiments of the Silver Age, which were made subservient to the Soviet regime, such as the *Proletkul't* and Futurist movements, the film industry, constructivist architecture, and the rocket science of Konstantin Ėduardovich Tsiolkovskii (1857–1935), whose Fëdorov-inspired programme of human colonisation of outer space became the basis of the USSR's successful cosmonautics (ibid.: 11–12). The impact of Fëdorov on early Soviet science and ideology is clear and explains much of its 'hidden religious character' (Obolevitch 2019: 145–9). Of course, many of these manifestations of the booming Silver Age did not die immediately, and several continued a more or less underground existence, but the overall trend was unmistakable. In retrospect, *Proletkul't* leader Anatolii Vasil'evich Lunacharskii (1875–1933)'s aim to gather as many forces as possible behind the Red Banner was perhaps politically naïve, but it helps us to understand why many of the positive achievements of the Soviet period – for example, the education and healthcare systems – took shape not by virtue of, but in spite of, the Bolsheviks.

Conclusion

Society cannot be turned into a laboratory without disastrous consequences, especially not when shells enter through the windows, resources are lacking, and experimenters and experimented are of the same, human, kind. The predominance, in the political philosophies at the time, of a transformative anthropology that aims at a supposedly necessary inner – as among the Christian philosophers – or outer – as among the Marxists – transformation of the human material itself can go in three directions: a collapse of utopian schemes, the creation of small experimental communities and the initiation of the large-scale totalitarian project of creating a New Man and a New Society. The period in question offers examples of all three and shows their tragic failure. The ultimate victory went to a system that, while aiming ideologically at the creation of a radically new society, effectively returned to a realistic take on human beings as needing a number of basic goods (food, shelter, security), seeking a number of higher goods (education, culture, purpose) and making rational choices, while at the same time being guided by basic politi-cal passions (fear, hope, hatred). Note, in passing, that many of these projects started from the optimistic assumption that, if allowed to be free, humans would take the road to self-improvement. The political dimension of possible conflict, however, re-emerges as soon as they do not do so spontaneously, or if some turn out to have different ideas about perfection.

According to Carl Schmitt, 'nothing can escape this logical con-clusion of the political': namely, that it ultimately results in the opposition of friends (allies) and enemies: when the friend–enemy opposition, which defines the political, intensifies, there is no middle choice left, and those who opt for a middle path are crushed artisti-cally or intellectually, if not physically (Schmitt 2018: 112 / 2007: 36). Political philosophers faced the same choice, and most of those who joined or accepted the Bolshevik regime were later suppressed and often liquidated, whether Marxists (such as Aleksandr Bogdanov or Nikolai Bukharin) or not (Gustav Shpet, Pavel Florenskii). Only a few managed to find a way through the Stalin period (Aleksei Losev, Mikhail Bakhtin).

By the end of the Civil War, the Bolsheviks had firmly established their power over a territory that covered most of Russia and would soon reintegrate most of the lost territories of the preceding empire. This marks a long-term division that I propose labelling the 'Soviet Split', with a political, philosophical, geographical and material meaning. From 1921/2, you were either in or out, either friend or enemy. The vast majority of philosophers relevant to our topic emi-grated after October 1917, many of them (including Berdiaev, Il'in and Frank) expelled in 1922 on the so-called *Filosofskii parokhod* [Philosophy Steamer]; this was, in fact, two steamers, which trans-ported the cream of the non-Soviet Russian intelligentsia, on Lenin's personal orders, to Szczecin [Stettin at the time] (Horujy 1994: 188–209; Chamberlain 2006: 77–99). Ironically, this took place not so long after the *Soviet Ark* (USAT *Buford*) had shipped 300 expelled leftists from the USA to the Soviet Union in 1920; many of these were among the harshest critics of Bolshevism, and some of them, such as the anarchists Emma Goldman (1869–1940) and Aleksandr Berkman (1870–1936), had emigrated from Russia to the USA. Most importantly, the Silver Age was over, and the spell of a single philosophical culture, an intellectual community of Russian philosophers, was broken. Adversaries in intellectual debate had become enemies in the class war.

Chapter 7

Soviet Marxism–Leninism and Political Philosophy – Never Mind the Gaps!

> From a wider point of view, that is on a longer historical perspective, proletarian coercion in all its forms, from executions to labour service, is [. . .] a method of creating communist mankind from the human material of the capitalist epoch.
>
> Nikolai I. Bukharin, *The Politics and Economics of the Transition Period* (1979: 165)

Few topics in the world history of political philosophy are more paradoxical than that of the present chapter. On the one hand, it is difficult to find a theory that contains the three meanings of political philosophy distinguished in this book more explicitly than the Leninist brand of Marxism. Marxism–Leninism contains a clear, albeit reductionist, theory of the state, as well as an elaborate theory of revolutionary politics and party organisation. It also contains a clear philosophy of the political, explaining it, in the final analysis, in terms of class struggle. Finally, it contains a clear theory of the way in which philosophy can, and indeed must, itself be a political weapon. The truth contained in the Soviet claim that Marxism–Leninism was the only true and fully consistent continuation of the Marxist legacy is that, in order to offer a 'true and fully consistent continuation' of any philosophical legacy, one has to simplify and dogmatise it.

On the other hand, these three meanings of political philosophy all vanished from Marxism(–Leninism) once it became the *Legitimationswissenschaft* of the new regime (Negt 1974: 7–22). The way in which the nascent Soviet order was framed as an application of

Marxist theory excluded legitimate application of the critical potential of Marxist theory on that order itself. A theory of state and politics was rendered obsolete, as a matter of principle, by the dogma of
the 'withering away' of the state that was implied in the long-term
goal of a communist, self-determining society beyond class (Hoffman
1992). Practically, this was effected by the replacement of politics
by bureaucratic public administration in a society guided by the
Kommunisticheskaia Partiia Sovetskogo Soiuza (KPSS, Communist
Party of the Soviet Union).[1] Lenin had rejected the anarchist idea
of destruction of the state as such, following Engels in the idea of
replacement, as part of a proletarian revolution, of the bourgeois
state by a proletarian form of statehood [*gosudarstvennost'*]: 'After
such a revolution, what withers away is the proletarian state or
half-state [*polugosudarstvo*],' which, although 'the most complete
democracy' so far, is still a form of state which can only 'die away
[*otmeret'*]' (Lenin, *PSS*: XXXIII, 18–19). To destroy the proletarian half-state actively would require another revolution or the idea
of 'permanent' revolution, and would go against the idea of the
proletarian–socialist revolution as the revolution-to-end-all-revolu-
tions. It is precisely the optimistic expectation that the proletarian
half-state would die off that 'rendered redundant any discussion
about improving its institutions and procedures, guaranteeing the
accountability of its officers, or subjecting its actions and policies
to judicial review' (Harding 1996: 151). The second meaning, that
of an explanation of the political as ultimately stemming from class
struggle, receded as social classes became a relic from the past and
ceased to be a source of antagonism within a society under way to
communism. The third meaning, finally, that of philosophy as itself
always-also being political (polemical, conflictual, critical), was
annihilated by the transformation of philosophy into a weapon in
the hands of a single political agent, the Party.

Paradoxically, the radical politicisation of Marxism in the hands
of the Bolsheviks, and of Lenin in particular, destroyed it as a political philosophy. The very idea that state and politics are merely an
instrument in the hands of the ruling class explains why, when positions of dominant and dominated class had switched, 'the conventional political *language*, and the conceptual framework in terms
of which its institutions and procedures might have been discussed
and debated, had already been discredited and rejected' (Harding
1996: 152). Both political *poièsis* – that is, the creation and care of
institutions – and political praxis – that is, the complex process of
dealing with the political – had been overruled by a political theory

that deduced its criteria of judgement from a yet-to-be-realised communist future. Obviously, dominant classes and hegemonic groups will, always and everywhere, regard the state and its institutions as a means to foster their own interests, and the politics of any society reflects existing asymmetrical relations of power. This, however, does not warrant a (theoretical) reduction of state and politics to nothing but an instrument and a reflection; nor does it justify a total neglect of the practical and poiètical dimensions of politics. In fact, neglect of these dimensions forced the new, Bolshevik regime to reinvent both political practices and institutions. The result was, in many respects, a ruthless and violent repetition of the tsarist regime, with massive executions, labour camps, and a long series of secret police organisations with far-reaching prerogatives, including non-judicial trial and execution. The first of these was the CheKa [*Vserossiiskaia Chrezvychainaia Kommissiia* – All-Russian Extraordinary Committee], established on Lenin's orders as early as December 1917 and led by 'Iron' Feliks Ėdmundovich Dzerzhinskii (1877–1926).

The first part of this chapter covers the period 1917–31, including the so-called 'Golden Decade [*zolotoe desiatiletie*]' of the 1920s and the 'Grand Turning Point [*velikii perelom*]' (1929–31): a time of very lively, increasingly politicised, discussion that ended with the establishment of 'orthodox' Marxism–Leninism (Zapata 1983; Alekseev 1990). The second part covers the 'dead period', including the authoritative form that Soviet Marxist–Leninist philosophy obtained with the *Kratkii kurs istorii VKP(b)* [Short Course of the History of the VKP(b)], attributed to Iosif Vissarionovich Stalin [Dzhugashvili] (1878–1953) personally. The third period starts with the official revival of philosophy as a discipline in 1947 and discusses the opportunities for and limitations on 'doing' political philosophy until the decomposition of the USSR: after World War II, and increasingly after destalinisation, Soviet philosophers in a number of niches of the academic system started to address, cautiously and indirectly, issues of political-philosophical significance.

Socialism in the Singular (1917–30)

The full name of the USSR, Union of Soviet Socialist Republics, is unique in world history. It was the only country name without any ethnic, national or geographical reference. It also stands as one of the most misleading names. It was not a union, in fact, but a quasi-colonial empire led by the RSFSR [Russian Soviet Federative Socialist Republic], a name that, by contrast, does have a national component. It shared only the word *sovet* with the original councils of workers, peasants and soldiers. The only thing socialist about its pseudo-feudal economy was the absence of privately owned means of production. And there was no connection with any serious concept of republic. Likewise, even the Party was not a party but, to use Lenin's famous phrase, 'a party of a new type' (Lenin, *PSS*: XXI, vii and *passim*). *The Communist Manifesto* had already defined the Communist Party as different from all other parties: namely, as standing for the end of class struggle, and hence of all parties. The USSR not only had just a sole party, the VKP(b) – later KPSS, but also limited its membership. It was a co-optative organisation, never exceeding 10 per cent of the population (ranging from 800,000 members in 1918 to 19 million in 1986). This turned the party into a political and socio-economic elite. Consequently, 'one could be a Communist party member without believing in communism, and vice versa' (Walicki 1995: xi).

While the Bolshevik success in October is explicable by superior organisation and cunning strategy, the future of the Soviet regime was determined not only by the massive resistance the Bolsheviks had to face, but also by the fact that the predicted world revolution did not take place, and indeed by the intrinsic flaws of Marxism(–Leninism). The marriage of a philosophical doctrine to a political regime demonstrated Marxism's ultimate denial of the legitimacy of societal conflict. At the same time, the cynical analysis of the defeated tsarist–bourgeois regime – namely, that its class essence made its actual form, democratic or despotic, liberal or authoritarian, irrelevant – was transposed to the socialist state:

> Socialism, Lenin argued, could cloak itself in a diverse garb. Its *form* of rule and its mode of justification were of no importance so long as the essential class content of its policies remained intact: 'The form of government,' he concluded fatefully, 'has absolutely nothing to do with it.' (Harding 1996: 158, quoting Lenin's *The Proletarian Revolution and the Renegade Kautsky* (1918))

The Bolshevik victory inaugurated an understanding of politics as planning and administration – that is, depoliticised governance – and of the political as something that would ultimately be overcome by a communist, conflict-free unification of humankind. The exclusion of politics outside, but increasingly also within, the party went along with the gradual extermination of nearly all socialists who had participated in the revolutions of 1917. By early 1918, Menshevik authors had already started to speak of a Thermidor as part of their protest against 'la dictature bolchevique' (Kondratieva 2017: 91–4; Brovkin 1991).

Contrary to a received view which holds that, after the exile of the crème de la crème of Russian philosophers in 1922 on the Philosophy Steamer, philosophy came to a stop in the young USSR, the 1920s were a lively period, the *Zolotoe desiatiletie*, despite gradually increasing political and institutional pressure. The creativity of the Silver Age was continued within a broad, and not necessarily dogmatic, Marxist framework. This particularly concerns fields that had been relatively under-researched by earlier Marxism: language, culture, art, folklore, carnival and other superstructure phenomena. One of the most famous cases is that of the 'Bakhtin Circle'. The 'Marxist credentials' of Mikhail Mikhailovich Bakhtin (1895–1975) remain disputed, but his works gradually became more political, irrespective of their orientation (Voloshinov 1986: ix; Brandist 2004 et al.: 19). Bakhtin's dialogism hints at the political, and polyphony does so even more, making Bakhtin a potential theorist of democracy (Hirschkop 1999), while his theory of carnival is potentially subversive (Simons 1996). The more repressive and monologic a culture or regime, the greater the need for safety valves. Like *iurodstvo* on the individual plane, political laughter – cabaret, carnival, caricature – can, depending on context, be subversive, harmless or supportive with respect to the political order. The Soviet regime that sought to contain Bakhtin's controversial conception of laughter during his ultimately successful PhD defence in 1946, at the height of *zhdanovshchina*, was the same regime that organised the political trials during which the *Politburo* laughed at the accused (Sasse 2015: 10–15, 106–18; Žižek 2001: 102–11).

The transition from the 'golden' 1920s to the depressing 1930s is marked by several episodes that, in different ways, can be read as incidents that show how the Bolsheviks annihilated political and intellectual competition. Four of these episodes are linked to the names of Kollontai, Bukharin, Aksel'rod-Ortodoks and Losev. Kollontai, the only woman in the first Soviet government, responsible for social welfare and nicknamed 'Valkyrie of the Revolution', and Bukharin, editor-in-chief of *Pravda* (1917–29) and nicknamed 'Darling of the Party', were prominent hard-liner 'old Bolsheviks': that is, members of the Bolshevik faction before 1917. Aksel'rod-Ortodoks was an authority on Marxist theory, but as a Menshevik could be accused of jumping on the bandwagon for opportunistic reasons. Losev, finally, was a relic from the past: a pre-revolutionary scholar, and one of the few representatives of Silver Age Russian religious philosophy who decided to stay in Soviet Russia.

Kollontai was one of the leading organisers of female participation in the Bolshevik party and the revolution, demanding full recognition of the role of women in both February and October. As co-founder, with Inessa Fëdorovna Armand (1874–1920, born Elisabeth-Inès Stéphane d'Herbenville), and leader of *Zhenotdel* [Women's Department; f. 1919] within the VKP(b), she fostered women's rights in the 1920s. This included the first legalisation of abortion in the world, practical issues such as day-care centres, and a controversial campaign of forced unveiling in Islamic Uzbekistan (Smiet 2017: 186). In 1930, however, *Zhenotdel* was closed because Party leadership had decided that, with the eradication of private property over the means of production, the 'women's question' had been settled.

Moreover, Kollontai is important because of her consistent protest against a dictatorship of the Party and its *apparatchiki*, and defence of the Marxist idea that only the workers themselves can create a socialist and, later, communist mode of production. However, the Party leadership was mostly concerned with the consolidation of its power by propagandistic and military means. Therefore, the countless initiatives of industrial workers, peasants, teachers and others to organise themselves in collectives, and to improve both production methods and living conditions, were a liability and were met with suspicion, control and opposition by Party bureaucrats. Invoking Marx's and Engels's authority, Kollontai, as spokesperson of the Workers' Opposition, insisted that the Party should restrain itself:

> The Workers' Opposition has said what has long ago been printed in *The Communist Manifesto* by Marx and Engels: the building of communism can and must be the work of the toiling masses themselves. The building of communism belongs to the workers. (Kollontai 1980: 199; Marx and Engels, *MEW*: IV, 580, 585–6)

Feminist Marxist Kollontai was one of the very few who supported Lenin in April 1917, when the latter called for a proletarian revolution rather than for political opposition to the Provisional Government (Kollontai 1970: 44 / 2011: 29; Merridale 2017: 226). A decade later, Kollontai's *Autobiography of a Sexually Emancipated Communist Woman* (1926) was so heavily maimed by censorship that it did not appear. The passages where Kollontai emphasised her own role as a personally motivated revolutionary or her closeness to Lenin, as well as places where she implied that in the USSR women's emancipation still had a long way to go, were removed. The 'corrections' demonstrate that the political became personal when Kollontai was removed to the diplomatic service by Stalin personally (Porter 2014: 368). However, the personal – that is, her precarious position as a feminist within the VKP(b) – was not to be made political, not even in an autobiography: 'My theses, my *sexual and moral* views, were bitterly fought *by many Party comrades of both sexes: as were still other differences of opinion in the Party regarding political guiding principles*' (Kollontai 1970: 60–1 / 2011: 38). The italics indicate what the censor crossed out, leaving only 'My theses, my views, were bitterly fought.'

Another old Bolshevik who became a victim was Nikolai Ivanovich Bukharin (1888–1938). He contributed substantially to the establishment of an 'official' Marxist–Leninist philosophy, both theoretically, with his *Theory of Historical Materialism*, and practically, as a leading Soviet politician until his removal to academic posts in 1929 (Hedeler and Stoljarowa in Bukharin 1996: 277). He was also a major populariser of the Bolshevik world-view, which he and Evgenii Alekseevich Preobrazhenskii (1886–1937) expounded in *Azbuka kommunizma* [The ABC of Communism] (1919). Bukharin, against Kollontai, reduced the 'women's question' to wage labour and private property over the means of production (Bukharin and Preobrazhensky 1969: 98–102 [§15]). The book contains a philosophy both of politics (state and party) (Ibid.: 81–8 [§12], 129–37 [§25]) and of the political, which is reduced to class struggle and thus historically limited:

> The class war now swallows up vast quantities of energy and material means. In the new system this energy will be liberated; people will no longer struggle one with another. The liberated energy will be devoted to the work of production. (ibid.: 119–20 [§22])

It also is an explicit political intervention in the struggle for hegemony: 'Every comrade who takes up this book should read it all through, so that he may acquire an idea of the aims and tasks of communism' (ibid.: 57). A trained economist, Bukharin was the architect of subsequent economic policies of the young Soviet state, culminating in *The Economics of the Transition Period* [*Ėkonomika perekhodnogo perioda*] (1920) (Bukharin 1979). Supporting Lenin's New Economic Policy and defending it after his death (Bukharin 1988: 24–33, 122–45), Bukharin opposed Stalin's accelerated industrialisation and collectivisation in 1928 on economic grounds and was side-lined.

A third episode is the side-lining of leading Marxist Aksel'rod-Ortodoks, who taught philosophy at the Institut Krasnoi Professury [Institute of Red Professorship]. In her widely known lecture series dedicated to a materialist understanding of history, she confidently claimed to 'remain on the old position of Orthodox Marxism without any deviations' (Aksel'rod-Ortodoks 2010: 6). In 1930, she was accused of belonging to one such deviation: namely, to the 'mechanistic' school of philosophy of Bogdanov and Bukharin (Negt 1974: 316). She was even accused of 'zionistic leanings' because, of Jewish background herself, she had dared to suggest Jewish elements in the philosophy of Spinoza (Aksel'rod-Ortodoks 1981: 63–5). The crude appropriation of Spinozist philosophy as proto-Marxism by Abram Moiseevich Deborin [Ioffe] (1881–1963), who 'even defined Marxism as "neo-Spinozism"', leading to an image of Spinoza as 'Marx without a beard' (Maidansky 2003: 203), testifies to the mobilisation of philosophy's past for present-day political goals. At the same time, it shows that the actualisation of the political potential of philosophy does not depend on philosophers' intentions, let alone truth. Ironically, the side-lining of Ortodoks coincided with the establishment of an official, Orthodox Marxism–Leninism, of which Deborin, later one of the founders of the Institute of Philosophy of the Academy of Sciences (f. 1936), was a main architect.

Fourth, an end was put to the careers of thinkers who were Orthodox in a diametrically opposed, Christian sense, such as Florenskii and the Neoplatonist Aleksei Fëdorovich Losev (1893–1988). The latter had stayed in Soviet Russia, secretly taking monastic vows in 1929. He published major works in the 1920s, including an eight-volume title on Ancient Greek thought, known as the *vos'miknizhie* (1927–30). The eighth volume, *Dialektika mifa* [The Dialectics of Myth], contained a qualification of dialectical materialism [*diamat*] as 'a screaming absurdity [*vopiiushchaia nelepost'*]' (Losev 1994: 123, 2014: 115). His analysis made it clear that official *diamat* was, in fact, a philosophical idealism – the same point that Ortodoks had made from the other, materialist end, and a view to which any sensible philosopher would subscribe.

The book became a *politicum*: Losev refused censorship and the book was published privately. It was confiscated, and Losev and his wife were accused of 'militant idealism' and convicted to ten and five years of hard labour, respectively. This cost him his eyesight, career and library (Lossev 2014; Losev 1994: xiii; Marchenkov in Losev 2014: 8–9). Released from GULag after two years, Losev was allowed to return to Moscow and rewrote his *vos'miknizhie*. This time, it was destroyed, along with his new library, by German bombs during World War II. After the war, he dictated the book from memory and received recognition much later, with a state prize for his, again eight-volume, *Istoriia antichnoi èstetiki* [History of Ancient Aesthetics] (1963–88), a work into which he 'smuggled' many Neo-Platonic insights. Ironically, the Stalinist utopia – not, of course, its bleak reality – is a perverted realisation of the (Neo-) Platonic collective utopia, and Losev derived part of his later legitimacy from his critique of bourgeois individualism and liberalism.

These four selected episodes illustrate how the establishment of Stalin's personal dictatorship went along with the silencing and side-lining of political and intellectual opposition to the Bolshevik regime and its increasingly official version of Marxism–Leninism. Although opposition and protest continued in various forms, the combination of ideological hegemony and political domination gave the Soviet system an image of stability and invincibility. The balance between the destruction of opposing forces and the construction of a new society inclined to the latter.

Death and Life (1931–47)

The camp [*lager'*] to which Losev was sent was a major product of Soviet political *poièsis*. Much more than belonging to a brutal penal system, it was one of the means of production of a New Society. Already during the decade of 'Red Terror' that started in the summer of 1918, Lenin had demanded that opponents to the freshly established dictatorship of the proletariat be locked up in concentration camps. This was the start of terror and repression as a systemic and, from the start, legally fixated method 'for the solution of many political and even economic objectives' (Applebaum 2003: xvi; Ivanova 2015a: 65–7). Thus, by 1921, there were already eighty-four camps in forty-three provinces, mostly designed to 'rehabilitate these first enemies of the people' (Applebaum 2003: xvi). Corrective labour camp sentences for political opponents existed for the same seventy years as did the USSR, which shows a systemic connection between the two, even if the flourishing of GULag coincided with the period of Stalin's dictatorship. An inevitable logic may seem to lead from October 1917 to GULag and the personal dictatorship of Stalin from 1929 onwards. Yet, while the logic of a concentration of political power in ever fewer hands was certainly at work, historians have pointed to moments when revolt was a serious option. That Stalin managed to suppress all manifestations of the political does not mean that an alternative was not present. There is no fatality in politics, only irreversibility. Also, the many horrors of the Stalin era should not obscure the systemically identical horrors of the 1920s:

> None of this was Stalin – the dates, and his standing at the time, are against it. [. . .] We credit Stalin with the bloody enforcement of collectivisation, but the reprisals after the peasant risings in Tambov (1920–1921) and Siberia (1921) were no less harsh [. . .]. Stalin did perhaps manifestly depart from Lenin [. . .] in the ruthless treatment of his *own party*, which began in 1924 and rose to a climax in 1937. (Solzhenitsyn 1974: 14–5 / 1975: 11)

In fact, Stalin was applying the core principle of Lenin's political strategy: namely, that the goal, revolution and, after it, consolidation of Soviet power justified any means.

The early Soviet period was a period of serial *politicide*: the *politeia* (the overall political form of society) became a mere instrument in the hands of the Party. By 1931, this process was completed. Of course, since the political is ineradicable, there was a lot of politics within the Party but it could not possibly be legitimate. It suffices to read the biographies and autobiographies of Kollontai, Bukharin, Lunacharskii, Trotsky and many others to become convinced not only of the systematic *politicide* engaged in by Stalin and his henchmen, but also of the utter helplessness of those who tried to oppose him. Their powerlessness derives not simply from Stalin's political genius, but from the fact that he applied political principles that his victims adhered to themselves: the priority of Party interests over personal ones, the need for the Bolshevik Party to survive in a hostile and obstinate environment, and the principle that human beings are mere means to practical ends. The substance of Stalinism, as far as political philosophy is concerned, was the creation and codification of Marxism–Leninism (van Ree 2002: 257). The claim that 'Leninism is the Marxism of the era of imperialism and the proletarian revolution' implied not only 'that Marx's writings applied only to the era of capitalism' (White 2019a: 187), but equally that whatever theorem could be plausibly ascribed to Lenin rendered any separate 'Marxism' obsolete. By constructing a distinct 'Leninist' stage in the development of Marxism (ibid.:

193), Stalin and the later KPSS could manipulate both Marx's and Lenin's theoretical legacies. This also rendered *a priori* problematic any attempt to bring in critically Marx, or Lenin for that matter, against the views and priorities of Lenin–Stalin, and it rendered *prima facie* suspect scholarly analysis of their writings. Ideological control was tighter, the closer one came to the theoretical work of the three *klassiki marksizma–leninizma*: Marx, Engels and Lenin.

Bukharin, loyal to, first, Lenin, whom he supported against Kollontai, and then Stalin, whom he supported against Trotsky, was the last leading old Bolshevik to fall victim to the purges of the 1930s. This last remaining Bolshevik theoretician and the last critic of Stalin was executed in 1938 after three show trials (Pirker 1963: 202–51). In prison (1937–8), he wrote two strikingly contrasting texts: *Sotsializm i ego kul'tura* [Socialism and Its Culture] (1937) and *Filosofskie arabeski* [Philosophical Arabesques] (1937–8). The first book is the second part[2] of a work that he finished while he was still hoping to be released as 'not guilty' of charges fabricated against him since 1929 (Hedeler 2015: 471). In this text, 'darling' Bukharin confirmed his 'great, boundless love for you all [plural], the Party and the whole cause' (ibid.: 532–3) and expressed unconditional loyalty to the project of constructing socialism in the USSR as part of 'the unification of all humanity [that] will essentially create a complete, fully integrated human race' (Bukharin 2006: 85). He describes this as

> not only a subjective ideal of thinkers and [. . .] not only the collective subjective goal of the revolutionary masses; it is also an objective [. . .] historical necessity, consciously being expressed and being made into a reality by the Communist movement of the proletariat. (ibid.: 83)

This unification was made materially possible, but not politically real, by bourgeois capitalism. The text reads as 'orthodox' Marxism–Leninism in its general orientation and tone, and one can understand it either as Bukharin's public position as one of the VKP(b)'s leaders, or as part of his ultimate plea to Stalin that he was and remained a loyal Party member, who subscribed to Stalin's notion of 'intensification of class-struggle'. This intensification of class struggle justified terror, collectivisation and purges. It also, according to Bukharin himself, would justify violence against himself, should he counterfactually be found guilty of working secretly for Nazi Germany.

If *Socialism and its Culture* is marked by objectivism, *Philosophical Arabesques* is profoundly subjective, written in a state of isolation and despair. As Hedeler emphasises, 'Not "we" or "our cause" takes centre-stage here, but "I"' (Hedeler 2015: 476). The earlier identity of subject and object in the historical process collapses. In *Philosophical Arabesques*, the word 'we' appears as often as it does in *Socialism and Its Culture*, but it is no longer the 'we' of the constructors of socialism, some of whom develop the theory, while others turn it into praxis and yet others realise the synthesis of theory and praxis in a written text [*poièsis*]. It is the 'we' of an individual author addressing a reader with whom he aims to connect through his text, with phrases like 'we have already had cause to note' and 'let us take our old example' (Bukharin 2005: 270–1).

Stalin, in his own way, was right: the goal of the show trials was the destruction of the revolutionaries 'as a class'. Comparing himself with Ivan IV, the Terrible [*Groznyi*], and reportedly using his first two names, Ivan Vasil'evich, because of the match with his own initials, I. V. (Iosif Vissarionovich), 'created an absolute autocracy through the suppression of the Bolshevik Party', which in effect meant its destruction as the ruling class of the USSR (Tucker 1974: 180). Political agency as such was annihilated in the name of an already victorious proletariat, and with the aim of constructing socialism in a post-political, 'managerial' way. Revolutionaries had been instrumental in February and October 1917 and during the Civil War, but in an era of systematic construction of socialism in one country, they were an independently minded liability. Bukharin was fundamentally wrong when he thought that he had to consider his own execution a measure of which he himself could approve. The point was precisely not to test measures against either somebody's conscience or any theory. Indeed, Bukharin was the victim of his own support for the construction of socialism in one country (Hedeler 2015: 471), and his guilt was, as Slavoj Žižek put it:

[N]ot the guilt of committing the crimes of which he is accused, but the guilt of persisting in the position of subjective autonomy from which one's guilt can be discussed on the level of facts – in the position which openly proclaims the gap between reality and the ritual of confession. (Žižek 2001: 110)

The key text of the Stalin regime was not accidentally called *Kratkii kurs istorii VKP(b)* [Short Course of the *History* of the VKP(b)] (1938). For a long stretch of time, labelled 'the dead period' by Sovietologists, this text was virtually the only authoritative text in political philosophy (Bocheński 1967: 43; Blakeley 1980: 317; Dahm et al. 1988: 1). There is no separate Marxism–Leninism–Stalinism because Stalinism included the creation of Marxism–Leninism. Stalin did not lay claim to theoretical originality but merely applied what he considered Leninist principles (van Ree 2002: 258; Solzhenitsyn 1974: 14 / 1975: 10; Pontuso 2004: 41–2). The philosophical core of Stalinism as a theory, first elaborated in a series of lectures at Sverdlovsk University in 1924 under the title *Ob osnovakh leninizma* [The Foundations of Leninism] (Tucker 1974: 317), was the reduction of Marxist theory to an axiomatic and dogmatic, orthodox Marxism–Leninism which functioned as an anti-political pseudo-religion, or at least as its functional equivalent.

Orthodox Marxism–Leninism is boring intellectually, yet fascinating political-philosophically because it pushes instrumentalism to the limit. Bukharin reportedly said that 'At any given moment he [Lenin] will change his theories in order to get rid of someone,' rightly adding that 'politically speaking, this shows a basic consistency' (Conquest 1991: 69). We have every reason to believe that Stalin was an utterly 'Machiavellian' politician, clinging to power by any means, including the large-scale purges which remain 'Stalin's personal achievement' and led to the destruction of nearly all 'old' Bolsheviks (ibid.: 68–70). We also, however, have every reason to think that Stalin 'was a true believer [and] a convinced adherent to the Bolshevik ideology of murderous class war' (van Ree 2002: 4, 7). He was deeply convinced of his grand historical role: engaging in international class war but also in the construction of socialism in one country, leading, eventually, to world communism but, for the time being, implying the defence of the Soviet fatherland. Van Ree has thus aptly labelled him a 'revolutionary patriot' (van Ree 2002: 230–72).

Among many wishful misconceptions around the Soviet regime is the idea that, though brutal, it was less murderous than the Nazi regime in the 1933–45 period. This is untrue: not only did the Nazis adopt numerous routines from their Soviet predecessors but the Soviet regime was also responsible for millions of victims over a much longer period of time. A conservative estimate stops at 20 million, not counting the victims of World War II (Courtois et al. 2001: 4, 15). Lethal institutions were established in the USSR well before World War II and continued to exist long after. GULag is one of the main self-inflicted disasters that humanity has experienced in the bloodstained twentieth century

(Ivanova 2015b: xx, 2015a; Shlapentokh 1989, 2001; Apple-baum 2011). The sheer numbers are staggering: according to Applebaum, who prefers conservative estimates, some 28 million Soviet subjects passed through the camps and colonies, and about 10 per cent perished there (Applebaum 2003: 291–2, 582–3). In the early 1940s political prisoners made up a minority of around one-third of the GULag population, and in the post-Stalin period the proportion dropped to single-digit percentages (Hardy 2016: 12, 55). Clearly, the GULag was not an extermination system, but a corrective labour system (equally part of the tsarist and the post-Soviet legal code) and, at the same time, a form of ideologically legitimised forced labour. Corrective labour as a re-educational device is not limited to the Soviet case, and the comparison with slavery should not be made too easily (ibid.: 78). However, the 'army of convicts' was continuously 'recruited' not only from among political opponents and professional criminals, but increasingly from among ordinary people who had violated 'socialist property' or engaged in 'parasitism [*tuneiadstvo*]' – felonies that were easily committed. Forced labour was an important factor in the rapid industrialisation of Soviet society, including large infrastructural projects like *Belomorkanal*, the Moscow metro and the BAM railway, which were wholly or partly based on it. This indeed suggests state slavery: 'The only thing the authorities don't do with these people is sell them, and the reason for that is that there is nobody to sell them to and nobody to buy them from' (Zinov'ëv 1985: 242).

If 10 per cent of those who went through GULag died there, this implies that 90 per cent survived and re-entered Soviet society. Hannah Arendt aptly compared the Soviet labour camps to Purgatory, while the Nazi destruction camps represented Hell, and the concentration camps in non-totalitarian countries, like Australia or South Africa, to Hades (Arendt 2017: 583; Stone 2019: 67). The end product of Nazi camps was ash and golden teeth, while the end product of GULag consisted of steeled subjects; if the former were the destruction ovens of Hell, the second were the blast furnaces of Purgatory, aiming at *perekovka* [reforging] and allowing resurrection. The GULag as a whole was not destructive but productive of life: it was a large bio-political factory. The fact that 'redeemability, at least for some segment of the prisoner population, was never totally abandoned' (Barnes 2011: 12) implied that inmates could come out of this penal system as 'good Soviet subjects' or even 'good communists'. If Nazi camps aimed at extermination in order the purify the social body, GULag was oriented on the transformation of human material into self-disciplining builders of socialism. While Nazi bio-politics relied on the logic of racial differentiation and the purification of a qualitatively heterogeneous human material, Soviet bio-politics treated all indifferently and in this sense relied on the logic of quantitative transformation of homogeneous human material. The Soviet state produced fitting human subjects, endowed with the right consciousness, through both its oppressive and its ideological apparatuses, including its educational and academic system. In doing this, it also continued and revived pre-revolutionary practices, including monastic ones that had been transformed by the internationally renowned Soviet pedagogue Anton Semënovich Makarenko (1888–1939), who came to fame with the re-education of the millions of Civil War orphans in 'children's labour colonies'. In these colonies, randomly selected children were organised in relatively small *kollektivy* that would be given a joint task, such as finding food under difficult circumstances. Succeeding in this task generated not only a sense of self-empowerment, but also a structure of horizontal peer control, mutual surveillance (all watching each other, instead of one watching all), public exposure, repentance and working on oneself [*rabota nad soboi*]. The resulting self-correcting group would then be given a 'socially approved goal' that turned the initial 'gang collective' into a Soviet *kollektiv* (Kharkhordin 1999: 102, 114). The *kollektiv* became, in many respects, the fundamental unit of Soviet society, explaining the mutual surveillance that partly also functioned as an early warning system against vertical structures of domination, as well as the tendency to prevent individual competition and excellence (ibid.: 322; Zinov'ev 1985: 141–58).

A key characteristic of what, with hindsight, can be seen as the paradigmatic Soviet period is the transformation and mobilisation of all societal forces into productive factors within the new society. This included philosophical production, which, on the one hand, was reduced to a single, official version of dialectical and historical materialism; on the other hand, it also took the form of translations of classical texts, including authors like Nicholas of Cusa, Hegel and Aristotle, and included the rewriting of the history of philosophy, both West European and Russian, as, essentially, a forerunner of Marxism (van der Zweerde 1997a: 63–5). Contemporary non-Soviet authors, however, were off limits and so was political philosophy. One major task of philosophy in the USSR was to demonstrate that Marxism, as systematised by Plekhanov, Lenin and others, and as continued by Soviet philosophers, was a superior and partisan, as well as scientific, true philosophy. But another of its goals was to demonstrate that philosophy was indeed a production factor by actually guiding the KPSS and the Soviet people in the realisation of a socialist society in the USSR, in preparation for a global communist future. Soviet ideology contained, as one of its elements, the ideologeme of Marxist–Leninist ideology as a guiding world-view (ibid.: 35–40). In reality, it was not leading, but rather following, legitimising whatever decisions and policies the regime considered opportune. After the Great Patriotic War (1941–5), which the Red Army could win only in the name of Mother Russia, not of communism, *Den' Pobedy* [Victory Day, on 9 May] became as important as *Pervaia Maia* [1 May].

Cold War and Destalinisation (1947–68)

With hindsight, the post-war years in Soviet philosophy appear to be a long period of preparation for better times. From the foundation of a new philosophical journal, *Voprosy filosofii* [f. 1947, still in existence], a steady growth, both quantitatively and qualitatively, of Soviet philosophical culture can be observed (ibid.: 40–54). From 1947 on, a growing number of scholars started to engage in professional philosophical research, discussion and publication. They had a Soviet educational background, even if in some cases they were lucky to receive part of their training from pre-Soviet teachers like Losev, Bakhtin, Valentin Ferdinandovich Asmus (1894–1975) and Arsenii Vladimirovich Gulyga (1921–96). Officially, all Soviet philosophers were Marxists–Leninists, though, unofficially, many of them, within the limited and limiting frame of Soviet academia, explored specific issues within the various disciplines into which philosophy in the USSR was divided. These included logic (both dialectical and formal), philosophy of science and history of philosophy, but not political philosophy.

The founding of *Voprosy filosofii* was accompanied by an extensive 'philosophical discussion' that set *vekhi* for the post-war period. It was also a matter of manning the philosophical front as part of the international class struggle. One can distinguish three frontlines here. The first was the that between socialist–proletarian and capitalist–bourgeois philosophy. The former was presented as a unitary system of dialectical and historical materialism, the latter as falling apart into a multitude of idealist, subjectivist, relativist, sceptical and religious philosophical positions. The second frontline was the more flexible division between dogmatic Marxism–Leninism and the creative development of Marxism itself. Here, non-Soviet Marxists could also be taken into consideration. The third frontline, finally, was a complex set of trenches between the philosophical establishment of the KPSS, all the way up to the 'ideologues' in the *Politburo*, and a labyrinth of niches in which a motley crew of professional philosophers was working. The typically East European split between an Academy of Science and the universities – already in place in tsarist Russia and still present in post-Soviet Russia – served as a filter between research and higher education.

The destalinisation inaugurated by Nikita Sergeevich Khrushchëv (1894–1971) at the 20th KPSS Congress in 1956, three years after Stalin's death, meant a reinforcement of the cult of Lenin, of the Party and of communism itself (Zubok 2019: 482). Replacing Stalin's statues with those of Lenin signified three things: continuity, as something else filled the empty place of the statue; superiority, as the KPSS proved capable of repairing its own faults over the dead body of its deceased leader; and eternity, as the Lenin that took Stalin's place was not the historical figure, but the sanctified, 'eternal' Lenin in the mausoleum on Red Square. Destalinisation, as a correction of Stalin's mistakes, was thus in fact an application of a principle of the Stalinist regime itself: no piece of human material, not even the *generalissimus* himself, could escape the logic of Purgatory, while he was redeemed as the leader who defeated Hitler. This is not to ignore release, relief and rehabilitation for millions of people, philosophers included. However, those improvements did not indicate systemic change, but rather demonstrated the system's sophistication, ranging from reform of the GULag system – which increasingly included vocational training instead of hard manual labour, taking its inspiration from Makarenko (Hardy 2016: 79–80), via an ever-diversified educational system yielding a wide range of professionals – to the establishment of a 'welfare state', which, among other things, replaced the *kommunalka* [collectively inhabited apartment] with family apartments that had a minimum number of square meters per person. Soviet society certainly became more liveable, but without becoming less Soviet.

Opportunities for the articulation of antagonism remained marginal. The period after Stalin's death was marked by revolts, both within GULag, where political prisoners were again, as in 1945, excepted from the mass amnesty of 'ordinary' criminals organised by Beria (Barnes 2011: 205; Ivanova 2015a: 253), and in various cities across the USSR in 1961–2 (Krasnodar, Murom, Aleksandrov,

Novocherkassk), where workers no longer accepted their socio-economic conditions (Solzhenitsyn 1995: 85; Iakovlev 2002: 226–9; Kozlov 2015: 181–92, 195–214, 251–87). These articulations of the political were brutally suppressed, most notoriously in the 1962 Novocherkassk Massacre. They were also denied legitimacy by the regime. Since there already was a KPSS in power and trade unions were watching over workers' living conditions, how could there be any valid reason for protest? At the same time, the very fact that the building of socialism could cost the lives of the workers for whom it was being built sent shockwaves through an increasingly politically aware intelligentsia and was one of the roots of the dissident movement.

In the landscape defined by the aforementioned three frontlines, philosophy in the USSR developed a possibly unique dynamics between inner logic of development and fluctuating outer conditions, or what Richard T. De George has called 'the logical pushes and ideological pulls [. . .] operative in Soviet philosophy' (De George 1967: 48). This dynamics explains the growing tension between professionalism and ideology, and was reinforced by the post-Stalin *ottepel'* [thaw]. On the one hand, under conditions of increased liberty, there was the philosophical drive based on the belief that 'if one has taken the decision to do philosophy, one has to go all the way (Jeu 1969: 23). The decision to do philosophy led to the founding of a second philosophical journal, *Filosofskie nauki* [Philosophical Sciences; f. 1958, still in existence] (ibid.: 62). On the other hand, the subordination of philosophy to ideological priorities did not wane, and the least liberated sphere of all was that of social and political thought. An ideological regime is vulnerable in terms of independent thought: 'those who think differently [*Andersdenkende; inakomysliashchii*] are, by the mere fact that they think, moreover as individuals, suspect in the eyes of organised state power' (Goerdt 1995: 100). The result was the need to engage in 'defensive doublethink' as 'a means of enlisting the approbative force of authorised terms [. . .] behind sympathetic attention to the exact opposite of what they stand for officially' (Scanlan 1985: 331f).

In the USSR, the disciplines of scientific communism and historical materialism occupied the niche that otherwise would have been the place of political philosophy. The more interesting texts were those in which a critique of non-Soviet, revisionist Marxism was given, but they were more relevant as reflections of the current course of the KPSS and its various factions than as attempts to engage in political philosophy, Marxist or not. Consequently, philosophy was political only as a potential threat to the existing order. This order was legitimised in the terms of one particular philosophy, Marxism(–Leninism). Philosophy was, in that sense, political by definition. To the extent to which it, potentially or in reality, gnawed at the foundations of Marxism–Leninism, which it inevitably did whenever it approached it with the tools of the unassisted human mind, it presented a threat. This is the main reason why there was no academic political philosophy in the USSR: surveys of Soviet philosophy do not mention a field of that name (László et al. 1967; O'Rourke et al. 1984; Dahm et al. 1988), a rare exception being a discussion of 'Open Questions in Contemporary Soviet Philosophy of Law and State' (Révész 1967).

The key problem for political philosophy in the USSR, however, was not that there was absolutely no space for political-philosophical reflection by 'unassisted minds' or for critical ideas about Marxism. First of all, such reflection and ideas took shape in the 'deterritorialised' places to which the regime's shadow did not reach: that is, as Aleksandr Moiseevich Piatigorskii (1929–2009) put it, until 1947 in the courtyard, between 1947 and 1956 in the smoking room of the Lenin library, and, finally, in the famous Russian kitchen [na kukhne] (Piatigorskii 1992: 97; Horujy 2017: 326). One of the relatively free, safe spaces was, paradoxically, the GULag system. Increasingly, however, at philosophy departments or in sections of the Institut filosofii, philosophers could speak their minds. The problem was that such reflections did not take the shape, other than by exception, of publications that would have nourished academic or public debate, let alone the possibility that they might have had an actual political impact. At this point, we see a remarkable parallel with the nineteenth century. Paradoxical as it may seem, in a polity that claimed to have Marxist philosophy as its ideological foundation, Marxism–Leninism itself rendered political philosophy impossible.

Conclusion

In addressing and assessing the Soviet period from the perspective of political philosophy, several things are important. The first is that the official ideology, Marxism–Leninism, was an integral part of the Soviet system, organising its discourse, legitimising its policies and setting strict limits on the articulation of the political. As in any other society, the possibility of both conflict and concord was ubiquitous and permanent, and, obviously, had to be dealt with. Here, we need to take into account the fact that Marxism–Leninism as a theory was, obviously, connected to a political praxis, and also to political *poièsis*: the establishment and maintenance of a particular type of Party, and the inclusion of writers and artists in 'unions', outside of which there were only underground, *samizdat* and the *kukhnia* [kitchen]. The inevitable imperfection of the system, and the necessity to suppress manifestations of societal antagonism, were facilitated by the postponement of communism (when all conflict would disappear, along with the projected withering away of the state) into an indefinite future. Existing in a hostile world, socialism would logically be imperfect and threatened from the outside, but societal antagonism was essentially a relic from a receding past.

Second, the suggestion that Marxist–Leninist ideology actually did positively shape and determine the thought and action of the Soviet leaders and the policies of Party and state was itself a major ideologeme – not because it was not true, or because all Soviet leaders were pure cynics, but because the extent to which they were 'sincere communists' did not really matter. There were convinced communists and Marxists among the ranks of the KPSS and among the philosophers teaching at universities and doing their research in institutes, but the question of sincerity has the same limited importance as the question how many members of the Inquisition were devout Christians.

Third, the Soviet period demonstrates in all clarity that philosophy itself, as the activity of the unassisted human mind, is political, even if it does not address political issues at all. Well over 200 philosophers have been recorded as victims of the Soviet regime (Emel'ianov 2004). If those who left the USSR were torn apart from their motherland, those who stayed, survived or were born in Soviet times were torn inside. Many of them managed to retain and, after 1956, develop decent standards of philosophical culture (van der Zweerde 1997b, 2018b), but on condition that they remained sufficiently distant from politically sensitive topics.

Notes

1. See also http://constitution.garant.ru/history/ussr-rsfsr/1977/red_
   1977/5478732/, esp. Chapter 1 (last accessed 31 July 2021).
2. The first part, confiscated upon his arrest, has not been found (Hedeler and Stoljarowa in Bukharin 1996: 281f).

Chapter 8

Christian Political Philosophy in Exile – Between *Sobornost'* and Theocracy

> Judge the Russian people not by those nasty things, which it so often does, but by those great and holy things, which it even in its meanness constantly longs for.
>
> *Mat'* Maria Skobtsova, 'Dostoevsky and the Present', 1929
> (Skobtsova 2016: 86)

The yield of philosophy in twentieth-century Russia has been very rich. Mentioning Roman Jakobson, Mikhail Bakhtin, Iurii Lotman and Lev Vygotskii should suffice to substantiate this claim. Important thinkers like Lev Shestov, Gustav Shpet, Aleksei Losev, Mikhail Lifshits, Ėval'd Il'enkov or Merab Mamardashvili are still in the process of being discovered, assessed and translated. The political-philosophical dimension of their thought, for obvious reasons a more politically sensitive field to which they did not relate explicitly, remains under-researched. Quite selectively, this chapter focuses on so-called 'Russian religious philosophy' [*russkaia religioznaia filosofiia*]. It has been received widely and positively, but mostly among theologians and religiously minded people, much less so among professional philosophers, and still less among social and political philosophers. This is regrettable because this current entails both a philosophy of politics, a philosophy of the political and a political awareness of philosophy itself. It is, at the same time, explicable: Christian overtones make it fit badly into twentieth-century political philosophy, particularly since World War II, when (explicitly) religiously inspired positions have been outshone by Marxist, structuralist and analytical positions that are, if not outright atheist, generally 'secular'.

Not accidentally, the reception of this current is largely confined to theological and 'post-secular' circles with scholars like Teresa Obolevitch, Kristina Stoeckl, Paul Valliere and Rowan Williams.

What can be the relevance of an explicitly religious, Christian political philosophy in a world where Christianity has moved to the margins of political-philosophical debate? There are four substantial reasons to highlight this thread. First, in our current, post-secular environment, religious standpoints are returning to the public sphere with renewed energy. Cases in point include the 'radical Orthodoxy' of John Milbank (Milbank 2006), the public discourse of the Vatican, and the participation of Evangelicals, Catholics and Orthodox in a global 'conservative coalition' emphasising traditional family and community values against the onslaught of hyper-liberalism and multiculturalism. Second, there are fascinating parallels with currents in the Islamic, African and other philosophical traditions, which likewise field a notion of communality against 'modern' individualism. Third, many of the key concepts of contemporary political philosophy (sovereignty, community, consensus, universalism, covenant, apocalypse, brotherhood) are 'secularised' political-theological concepts, which prompts investigation of their Orthodox variants. Moreover, if one believes that political theology itself is a 'theologised' articulation of political-philosophical questions, this is an additional reason to take political theology seriously. Finally, the tradition of Orthodox-Christian social and political philosophy has enjoyed a substantial revival in Russia itself since the Soviet ban was lifted.

The Religious-Philosophical Meetings in St Petersburg (1901–3), and the later Religious-Philosophical Societies of Moscow (1905–18) and St Petersburg / Petrograd (1907–17), were part of the flourishing philosophical culture of the *Serebriannyi vek* [Silver Age] (Scherrer 1973; Burchardi 1998). With sometimes over a thousand members, they were home to discussions about the relation between state and church, the role of the *intelligentsia*, marriage, gender, family, freedom of religion and many more areas, and they can be considered the birthplace of Russian religious philosophy. Artists, poets and philosophers addressed a broad range of philosophical issues, from the role of mysticism in art to Russia's political future. Several of its protagonists had made a recent shift from (legal) Marxism to (religious) idealism, as testified by F. Sergei Nikolaevich Bulgakov (1871–1944)'s *Ot marksizma k idealizmu* [From Marxism to Idealism] (Bulgakov 1903), and the edited volumes *Problemy idealizma* [Problems of Idealism] (1902), *Vekhi* [Signposts/Landmarks] (1909) and *Iz glubiny* [Out of the Depths] (1918). In contrast to the Marxist *bogostroiteli* [God-builders] (Bogdanov, Lunacharskii) who aimed at the creation of a 'new God' who could be the centrepiece of a socialist cult, the *bogoiskateli* [God-seekers] (Bulgakov, Berdiaev, Merezhkovskii, Gippius, Vasilii Rozanov) were not seeking a new God, but rather new ways to the God whose existence they did not question (Grillaert 2008; Rosenthal 2002; Zwahlen 2010).

Key to understanding the political philosophers discussed in this chapter is the fact that, after October, the ROC quickly sank into a state of persecution and, after 1942, subordination to and instrumentalisation by the Soviet regime. To a large extent, the ROC, both institutionally and theologically, continued its existence in exile and underground. The Institut de Théologie Orthodoxe Saint-Serge in Paris (f. 1925), St Vladimir's Orthodox Theological Seminary in New York (f. 1938) and the Institut de Théologie Orthodoxe Saint-Denys in Paris (f. 1944) have housed prominent Orthodox theologians like John Meyendorff, Alexander Schmemann, Bulgakov, Georgii Florovskii and Vladimir Losskii. Their journals and publishing houses have long been much more productive, creative and diverse than the few Orthodox institutions[1] and intellectuals[2] that were tolerated in the USSR. Christian political philosophy, as here understood, was thus largely developed abroad, suffering from the involuntary split of Russian philosophical culture into a Soviet half and a diaspora half. These thinkers were exiles, not emigrants (Hufen 2001: 13–14).

One of the key problems of the political philosophy developed within Russian religious philosophy, and of any Christian political philosophy, is the relationship between individual and society. Christianity, like Islam, is often accused of a subordination of individuals and their interests to the common goals of a religious community and church. The thinkers discussed in this chapter were very much aware of this problem, not least because they wanted to avoid any association with communist collectivism. They rejected both individualism and collectivism, and sought a middle way with the help of notions like *lichnost'* [person(ality)] and *sobornost'* [conciliarity / catholicity / communality] (Esaulov 1995; Putnam 1977; Haardt and Plotnikov 2008; Zwahlen 2010; Plotnikov and Haardt 2012; van der Zweerde 2001, 2008a, 2008b, 2013, 2019c).

While Russian religious philosophy continued ideas developed by Khomiakov, Solov'ëv and others, it elaborated and expanded them in response to a radically different and increasingly 'secular' socio-political reality: explicitly atheist in Soviet Russia, largely secular or laic in Western Europe, where the emigrated thinkers ended up. The 1922 'Soviet Split' of Russian philosophy defines their significance. On the one hand, they were largely cut off from the land they aimed to influence. On the other hand, in Western Europe, the explicitly (Orthodox-)Christian foundation of their theories sat badly in a world of both agnostic and atheistic thinkers, and Catholic and Protestant ones who had accepted secularisation, immanentisation and societal differentiation. It is not accidental that their theist and fideist – or at best 'theanthropist' – position was much less influential in political philosophy than the 'anthropotheist' position of Kojève. The structure of this chapter follows a distinction between a theocratic 'right' (Pobedonostsev, Losev, Il'in), transformative 'left' (Berdiaev, Bulgakov, Skobtsova) and 'centrist' (Frank, Stepun) positions. Beyond these differences, Russian religious philosophy as a whole is best understood as an organicist, ultimately anti-political political philosophy that tries to adapt to a modernising, 'secular' society while promoting a Christian world-view (van der Zweerde 2013: 117–18; van Kessel 2020).

Slay the Evil Dragon!

In the Orthodox-Christian thought of the Silver Age generally, there are two main currents: a traditionalist neo-Patristic current and a modernising, 'sophiological' current. For the first, represented by Losev, Florovskii and Florenskii, bourgeois capitalism and Bolshevik socialism were little more than two different sides of the same, (literally) anti-Christian coin. The 'quiet genius', F. Pavel Aleksandrovich Florenskii (1882–1937), hinted that, 'in essence, bolshevism is the logical conclusion of bourgeois culture' (Florenskii 1994–8: III (2), 367; Pyman 2010: 113). Like Losev, Florenskii lamented the vanishing 'ontological reality of the Christian cosmos' and bore the political-philosophical consequences. The field of political-philosophical positions here is triangular: traditional Orthodoxy, bourgeois modernisation and Bolshevik Prometheism. However, the affinity between the latter two brought this triangle close to a dichotomy. Orthodox thinkers like Losev and Florenskii shared the Marxist critique of capitalist, bourgeois society (its individualism in particular), and Marxist historical materialists like Aksel'rod-Ortodoks would accuse both bourgeois and Orthodox thinkers of idealism, while a bourgeois liberal would reject both of the other two because of their dogmatic adherence to a transcendent frame, rather than accepting the world-immanence of political thought.

One prominent philosopher on the right, sticking to traditional Orthodoxy, was Ivan Aleksandrovich Il'in (1883–1954), a student of Edmund Husserl and Novgorodtsev who emphased rule of law, strong statehood and national community. From that perspective, he did not support the revolutions of 1917. An ardent opponent of the Bolshevik regime (Offermans 2018: 15), he was arrested by the Cheka in 1918, but pardoned by Lenin out of respect for his eminent philosophical work (ibid.: 37). Active during the Civil War on the side of the Whites, he was exiled in 1922, moving to increasingly monarchist and nationalist positions. Not unlike Schmitt, whose conservative Catholicism drove him towards Nazism in 1933, Il'in's conservative Orthodoxy made him support fascism, though not Nazism. Although, for both thinkers, lawful order remained the central principle, they prioritised, if pushed, order over law. Also, again not unlike Schmitt, Il'in's anti-Semitist leanings drove him in the same direction: he shared the essentialist 'Semitism' of many Orthodox-Christian thinkers, whether anti-Semite or philo-Semite.

As for most Russian religious philosophers, including a 'Christian socialist' like Bulgakov (Evtuhov 1997: 205–6; Williams 1999: 229–36), the atheist Bolshevik regime in Russia for Il'in was a manifestation of the Antichrist. The difference was that, in his view, it had to be actively resisted by force, as he elaborated in his *Soprotivlenie zlu siloi* [On Resistance to Evil by Force] (1925)], a book with which he tried to give orientation to the scattered remnants of the White Army (Benois in Il'in 2018a: xi-ii). In 1933, Il'in initially continued his work, begun in 1924, at the Russisches Wissenschaftliches Institut in Berlin. However, he was removed in 1934 when he refused to subscribe to the Nazi party programme, was persecuted by the Gestapo and left for Switzerland in 1938 (Budde 2013: 65).

In the triangular scheme of liberalism, socialism (Bolshevism) and fascism (Nazism), each position defines the other two as alternative manifestations of the same evil. Of course, this is a simplification: many conservatives, who were critical of both liberalism and socialism, did not embrace fascism or national socialism, which they perceived as a left-wing rather than a right-wing movement (ibid.: 86). At the same time, any triangular scheme collapses into a dichotomy when the binary logic of the political enforces a division into friends and enemies, not leaving space for a third position: in the 1930s, expelled Russian philosophers became entangled in this binary logic. From the perspective of a thinker like Il'in, liberalism, socialism, communism and fascism share a revolt against tradition and a transcendent, God-given order. In one individualist and two collectivist variants, their joint humanism and radical this-worldliness either move religion to the 'private sphere' or replace it with a secular ideology with its own idols. Il'in's conservative rule-of-law corporatism placed him in the right-wing camp, yet Il'in did not simply identify with twentieth-century fascism. Instead, he distinguished the 'good [*khoroshii*]' fascism of Franco and Salazar from the 'bad [*plokhoi*]' fascism of Mussolini and Hitler (Il'in 1993: I, 89). The contrast between merely pragmatic 'good' versus 'bad' [*khoroshii, plokhoi*] and the morally and metaphysically charged 'good' versus 'evil' [*dobryi, zloi*] is significant here. From Il'in's perspective, fascism was not a good in itself, but a potentially useful instrument in the obligatory fight against the final enemy: (the D)Evil.

Il'in has become notorious for his support of right-wing and even fascist regimes in Europe. Any means, for him, would be acceptable to beat the greater evil that had begotten Russia. Despite militant and aggressive overtones, however, Il'in neither considered violence something good in itself, nor saw good ends as justifying evil means. Instead, he claimed that two 'extreme solutions' can both be shown to be incorrect:

> [T]he first [Tolstoy's, EvdZ], which betrays the primary purpose of struggle in order to avoid unjust means (non-resistance!), and the second [Lenin's, EvdZ], which turns away from the contemplation of perfection in order to implement, in an unfettered and confident manner, the unjust means. The first solution creates *an illusion of righteousness* [*illiuziia pravednosti*] [. . .]. The second creates *an illusion of utility* and *an illusion of the victory of goodness* [. . .]. (Il'in 2017: 342 / 2018a: 187–8 / 2018b: 268–9)

For Il'in, Tolstoy's moralism places morality above religious experience (ibid.: 138 / 81 / 127) and leads to asceticsm, to a simplification of all spheres of life and to 'non-resistance [*neprotivlenie*]' (ibid.: 161 / 95 / 145). Il'in convincingly argues that Tolstoy is not opposed to 'resistance against evil' as such, if only because one ought to fight evil within oneself, but against violent resistance against evil as it exists between people (ibid.: 20 / 11–2 / 41). For Il'in, this is pure escapism that fails to accept the positive role of state and politics in fighting evil by evil means, if necessary. It also is, one should add, a denial of the ubiquity and permanence of the political. As far as Lenin is concerned, from Il'in's perspective both his means and his end were evil.

Il'in's argument that it is necessary to fight evil depends on an absolutely certain positive knowledge of good and evil, not only in general, abstract terms, but in concrete, existential ones, allowing a clear identification of the enemy or, in his words, the 'evil-doer' [*zlodei*]. Il'in's certain knowledge relies on unshakable Orthodox-Christian faith. From this angle, he attacks not only Tolstoy's pacifism and non-resistance, but also 'just war theory' inasmuch as it limits legitimate violence to self-defence. By contrast, Il'in advocates active fighting against evil in the world, rejecting the 'escapist', pure and simple life of the Tolstoyans. At the same time, contrary to Tolstoy, who 'calls all recourse to force in the struggle with evil "violence"' (Lossky 1951: 388 / Losskii 1991: 494), Il'in considers force [*sila*] in all its forms an evil (meanwhile offering an impressive analysis of force in its many forms, from loving spiritual guidance to capital punishment). Yet he holds, like Solov'ëv, that it can be the lesser of two evils. Consequently, it is permitted if non-violent means have been exhausted. In that case, however, it is not only allowed, but obliged, for the simple reason that evil must be resisted and fought:

> This means that the limit beyond which physical force becomes necessary, is set negatively: both the *spiritual bankruptcy* [*dukhovnaia nesostoiatel'nost'*] of the person being corrected and the *spiritually defenceless* nature [*dukhovnaia bezoruzhnost'*; lit.: spiritual disarmedness] of the person who performs the correction. (Il'in 2017: 191–2 / 2018a: 111 / 2018b: 164–7)

This excludes, if evil is manifestly known, the type of arbitrary carnage performed by the Bolsheviks, but it does raise the question of who or what decides whether all other means have been exhausted and who or what determines spiritual bankruptcy and defencelessnes.

One is easily misled by Il'in's polemical style, especially in his later writings, but his battle against the evil Bolshevik dragon should not make us overlook his defence of a constitutional monarchy in a right-Hegelian fashion, bringing him close in some respects to a liberal like Chicherin. Il'in's right-Hegelian position appears most clearly in his evaluation of the legacy of the French Revolution. Il'in opposes both a liberal reading of Hegel that would emphasise equal rights for all [*égaliberté*] and a left-Hegelian position that would identify brotherhood with class solidarity and, ultimately, communism. Instead, he combines an emphasis on legal order with 'true' fraternity: that is, not simply brotherhood between humans but, as in Fëdorov, the brotherhood exemplified by Jesus Christ.

> A correct understanding of political legal consciousness is not only not hostile to an ethically good will, but accepts it and serves its objectives. Political life rests upon a *brotherly disposition* of the souls [*bratskoe nastroenie dush*], and if this disposition disappears, then political life degenerates. Law in practice serves not only 'freedom' [*svoboda*], but also the 'brotherhood' [*bratstvo*] which was so ceremoniously, and at the same time so impotently, proclaimed by the first French revolution. But 'brotherhood' is that mode of relation of human being to human being the deepest interpretation of which was given by Christ. (Il'in 2014: 225–6 / Il'in 2017: 230)

Il'in's rejection of both Bolshevism and liberalism, his right-Hegelian monarchism and his holding on to a transcendent order place him squarely in the conservative camp and explain his popularity among European conservatives today.

Social Christianity

The social Christianity of Nikolai Aleksandrovich Berdiaev (1874–1948) and others is diametrically opposed to the right-wing monarchism of Il'in, but shares his diagnosis in terms of Antichrist and apocalypse. Characteristic of this 'leftist' position is a rejection of democracy in the sense of a representative system based on individual electoral rights, not because of representation or democracy as such, but because of the individualism and liberalism that it confirms. In *Filosofiia neravenstva* [Philosophy of Inequality] (1918), Berdiaev disconnects liberalism and democracy, linking the first with freedom [*svoboda*] and 'aristocracy' (in the sense of 'rule by the best') and the second with equality and 'the masses'. He denounces democracy along with revolution, arguing that 'great revolutions were always moved by the principle of equality, not freedom' (Berdiaev 2004b: 597 / 2015: 140). Berdiaev advocated an 'anarchic monarchism' that he linked to *sobornost'* (Berdiaev 1996: 118–19, 126–7). 'No human being, he claimed, has a right to power [. . .] the right to power is not proper to anybody [*pravo na vlast' ne prinadlezhit nikomu*]' (ibid.: 130).[3] While this position hints at a Lefortian *lieu vide du pouvoir*, it also reformulates the Slavophile ideal of a direct bond between *tsar'* and people, bypassing any kind of state or government. Such monarchism excludes authoritarianism because ruled and ruler are one in the same religious truth, and it is democratic to the extent to which there is a people with a singular shared faith. Writing about Khomiakov, Berdiaev neatly paraphrases his position: 'The Russian people chose [sic!] autocracy [samoderzhavie] because it did not want the kingdoms of this world nor its blessings [blaga], because its forces are oriented on spiritual doing [delan'e]' (ibid.: 121). In this model, the divinely sanctioned tsar', by occupying the place of power, keeps it free from the power claims by either tyrants or a sovereign people. At this point, democracy, as the self-rule of a people that is one in faith and united in a spirit of sobornost', and theocracy, as the singular power of the God this people believes in, coincide (van der Zweerde 2019c: 24–8).

Berdiaev acknowledged a positive kernel in communism. On the one hand, communism is fundamentally wrong, evil and (literally) anti-Christian because of its materialism and atheism or, metaphysically, 'spirit of non-being [dukh nebytiia]' (Berdiaev 2004b: 478 / 2015: 2). Berdiaev also tells his readers that, in Vekhi, he and his colleagues had warned them (ibid.: 479 / 3). On the other hand, communism is fundamentally right in its call for social justice and its rejection of bourgeois capitalism (Berdiaev 1953: 27–30). This ambiguity does not come out of the blue: Christian socialists like Berdiaev distanced themselves equally from both individualist bourgeois liberalism and collectivist atheist socialism, which they understood as cumulative materialist individualism, not as 'real brotherhood' or 'genuine community'. Collectivism is what Berdiaev and others sought to avoid. Berdiaev explicitly contrasted sbornost' [collectivity] and sobornost', qualifying the latter as 'a high kind of brotherhood [bratstvo] of people' (Berdiaev 2004b: 495 / Berdiaev 2015: 23). This is also why, in his polemics, Berdiaev (unlike Il'in or Schmitt), does not speak in exclusive 'we' versus 'them' terms, but in potentially inclusive 'we' versus 'you' ones (Berdiaev 2004b: 478–9 / 2015: 2–3), indicating not enemies, but adversaries who can become allies, highlighting that political controversies contain the possibility of not only conflict, but also concord.

Closely affiliated with Berdiaev, Mat' [mother] Mariia Skobtsova (1891–1945), born Elizaveta Iur'evna Pilenko, was a prominent member of the French résistance during World War II. She died in 1945 in Ravensbrück when she replaced a Jewish woman who was about to be sent to the gas chamber. The first woman in Russia to study theology, she joined the socialist-revolutionaries and supported February 1917, planned to assassinate Trotsky after he closed the

PSR congress, became tangled up in the Civil War, served as elected mayor of the city of Anapa and escaped execution by the Whites. Thus participating in the Russian Revolution, 'she discovered that she loved individual human beings as opposed to humanity. Revolutionaries taught her love of the human race; the revolution showed her that the revolutionaries loved humanity instead of the individual person' (Olivier Clément in Skobtsova 2003: 10). Love and care should be oriented on individual human beings and their suffering, not on abstract notions of humankind that justify human sacrifice. She left Russia in 1922, ending up in France, where she took religious vows in 1932. She demanded, however, to be a nun in the world and among the poor, rather than in a convent. As a rather atypical nun, given 'the state of her monastic habit with its marks of cooking [and] her attachment to Gauloises cigarettes', she engaged in social work among poor immigrants, a worldly vocation most uncommon in the Orthodox tradition (Plekon 2007: 236–7). A scandalous heroine who argued and acted against racism, Nazism and anti-Semitism alike (Benevich 2003: 171–3) and who explicitly placed herself in the tradition of *iurodstvo* (Skobtsova 1930; Skobtsova 2003: 115, 174, 182–3, 186; Benevich 2003: 124), Skobtsova was canonised in 2004 by the Ecumenical Patriarchate of Constantinople. The ROC, by contrast, continues to look on her with mixed feelings.

Skobtsova developed her ideas in dialogue with Khomiakov, Dostoevsky, Solov'ëv and others. Her writings appeared in the emigrant Russian journals *Put'* (1925–40) and *Novyi grad* (1931–9) (Arjakovsky 2002 / 2013). Starting from the notion of Godmanhood [*bogochelovechestvo*] and humankind's task to realise it, she emphasised that 'the human principle never and in no way possesses any firm or precise seal of its appertaining to truth' (Skobtsova 2016: 125). Echoing Solov'ëv's 'Let's not forget [. . .] that universal history is the realisation of utopias,' she argued that humankind lives 'by the flashes of the creative powder-charge of various utopias', each of which 'answers to some sort of pending true need in science, in social life, in philosophy' (ibid.: 126).[4] Tracing the development of humankind generally and of Russia in particular through a long series of utopias, Skobtsova arrives at a diagnosis of Russian Bolshevism in religious terms. What singles out Bolshevism is not that it is 'godless', but that it is actively 'against-God' and sets 'nothing' in explicit 'opposition to God' (ibid.: 137), echoing Berdiaev's *dukh nebytiia* [spirit of non-being] mentioned above. In other words, the problem is not the utopian dream of a Kingdom of God on Earth, which could still be made compatible with the

Christian faith, but what the Bolsheviks labelled 'militant atheism [*voinstvuiushchii ateizm*]'. In Skobtsova's view, this puts an end not only to religion, but also to humanism, given that divinisation [*theōsis*] is humankind's essence and task. Instead of diagnosing Bolshevism as the 'Promethean' child of humanism, Skobtsova perceived it as a 'sinister and terrible punishment for the splintered image in the world of Christ the God-man [*bogochelovek*]' – the two elements, divine and human, conjoined only 'in the walled cellars of the Cheka or the Solovetsk' and personified in the persecuted clergy and monastics (ibid.: 137).[5] There is a twofold pitfall to be avoided here: to omit the religious dimension entirely and fight Bolshevism with a humanism that shares its atheism, and to remain true to religion but retreat from the world and, thereby, from humanity (ibid.: 140). Skobtsova rejected both.

Skobtsova further aimed to escape the dilemma presented by the choice between autonomous self-will, leading to the existential struggle of many of Dostoevsky's protagonists, and the 'comfortable' unification of humankind offered by Dostoevsky's Grand Inquisitor, Solov'ёv's Emperor or Zamiatin's Benefactor. Dostoevsky had shown that 'the fate of mankind, left to itself, is very precise: it is not in its powers to bear the curse of its own self-will and it is not in its powers to live in a meaningless universe' (ibid.: 59). The way out, however, is not the way of the Inquisitor, which is 'wide' and 'the way of ruin', but the 'way of salvation', which is 'a narrow strait [. . .] difficult to distinguish [. . .] and to go along' (ibid.: 2016: 69). This 'Christian path' is a full affirmation of Godmanhood:

> All the branches of human creativity, – science, art, society, and the state, – are creations, searches for new winged utopias, the apperception of a single truth or a thousand truths, the struggle for the emancipation of labour, the affirmation of the right to work, the attempts of overall building up of societal life, – popular rule, – everything where there is a spark of collective or individual creativity, where individually or collectively human freedom is affirmed, and where man is obliged to be free, – all this should be sanctified and blessed. (ibid.: 141)

Developing a leftist understanding of the Slavophile notion of *sobornost'* (Compton 2016: 13), Skobtsova labelled this 'our Russian socialism', a Christian socialism embodied in the suffering Russian people (ibid.: 81–2). She even proposed to combine the symbol of the cross with the hammer and sickle (ibid.: 86f). In her rendering, the notion of *sobornost'*, which connotes gathering, commonality and church [*sobor*], puts the ideas of *otserkovlenie* [churchification] of society and *ozhivlenie* ['enlivining'] of the church on a par (Compton 2016: 30):

> I think that the fullest understanding of Christ's giving Himself to the world, creating the one Body of Christ, Godmanhood, is contained in the Orthodox idea of *sobornost'*. And *sobornost'* is not just some abstraction [. . .], nor is it . . . a higher reality having no inner connection with the individual human persons who constitute it [. . .]. There is an authentic, and truly Orthodox, mysticism not only of communion with God, but also of communion with man. [. . .]. And it seems to me that this mysticism of human communion is the only authentic basis for any external Christian activity, for social Christianity, which in this sense has not been born yet . . . . (Skobtsova 2007: 277–8)

Yet, Skobtsova kept her distance from a fusion of Christianity and socialism into 'Christian socialism' or 'Christian democracy', which would amount to a confusion of the religious and the socio-political planes. Instead, she insisted on the principle that we should 'render therefore unto Caesar the things which are Caesar's; and unto God the things that are God's' [Matthew 22: 21] (Benevich 2003: 94–6). The establishment of a New City, in her perception, would prepare for, but not amount to, the building of a Kingdom of God on Earth. In this, she drew the same line as Solov'ëv or, indeed, Bulgakov. As Paul Valliere has rightly observed, the rich resources in this left-leaning sophiology and society-oriented Christianity for the ongoing projects of liberation theology and feminism are still in the process of being discovered (Valliere in Emerson et al. 2020: 671–2).

Contrary to Russian thinkers who sided with Stalin against Hitler, or with fascism against communism, *Mat'* Mariia consistently perceived communism, Nazism and fascism as 'three idols [*tri kumira*]' and as three heads of a single dragon that demanded 'human sacrifices' in the name of 'class, race, and state' (Benevich 2003: 175). For Skobtsova, both leftist and rightist totalitarianism had, first and foremost, religious significance (ibid.: 175–6). What she, like Berdiaev, clearly perceived was that Marxism, at least in its Soviet form, and Nazism, are forms of idealism. The first, with its proclamation 'that matter rules over spirit', turns around the idea of material determination. The second revolves around the idea of the vital force of race. Both are, however, primarily ideas (Skobtsova 2003: 129).

Centre

Some exiled Russian religious philosophers moved towards an acceptance of bourgeois society and liberal democracy. Of the representatives of Russian religious philosophy, Semën Liudvigovich Frank (1877–1950) is possibly the most appreciative of contemporary Western society with its rule of law, civil society and parliamentary democracy. He is also the most European, comparable to Arendt due to the partly Jewish background that drove him from Russia, via Berlin and Paris, to London, his broad education at the cutting edge of the philosophy of the time, and his direct experience of two totalitarian regimes. Moreover, of the 'big three' most often referred to (Berdiaev, Bulgakov and Frank, who, among other things, participated in all three of the famous edited volumes of the early twentieth century), he developed the most systematic philosophy, comparable only to Solov'ëv in this respect, and is often cited as 'the most outstanding Russian philosopher [*samyi vydaiushchiisia russkii filosof*]' (Zen'kovskii 1989: II, 392; Obolevitch in Mrówczyński-van Allen et al. 2016: 211; Antonov 2015: 40). While Il'in tended towards polemics, Berdiaev towards *publitsistika*, Skobtsova towards social work and Bulgakov towards theology, Frank produced a social and political philosophy of lasting interest. His moderate communitarianism bears resemblance to the thought, from Catholic, Islamic and Akan backgrounds respectively, of Charles Taylor, Tariq Ramadan or Kwame Gyekye.

Frank's communitarianism is a more systematic elaboration of basic intuitions that we also find, in a more general and abstract form, in Solov'ëv. Frank perceived the elaboration of a Christian social philosophy as his main task during the 1920s in emigration, a project that culminated in his *Dukhovnye osnovy obshchestva* [The Spiritual Foundations of Society] of 1930 (Frank 1987; Boobbyer 1995: 141). Frank's conception has, moreover, been informed not only by his Russian predecessors, but also by his early Marxism and by the empirical sociology of Ferdinand Tönnies, Max Weber and Georg Simmel (Frank 1987: 35, 37, 67, n. 4). Frank developed Tönnies's opposition of two types of society, *Gesellschaft* [society] and *Gemeinschaft* [community], one step further. Weber and Simmel had contrasted *Vergesellschaftung* and *Vergemeinschaftung* as two forms of socialisation, while Frank conceptualised *obshchestvennost'* ['societality' or 'commonality'] and *sobornost'* ['conciliarity' or 'communality'] as two dimensions: the first external, the second internal, present in all forms of human coexistence (Frank 1987: 54; Boobbyer 1995: 144; Ehlen 2009: 115–17). This substantiates the idea of a 'background-we' that is presupposed in all forms of conflict and concord, including relations of enmity that point to 'we versus them' oppositions (van der Zweerde 2008a, 2009).

In line with ideas developed by Solov'ëv, Frank's key objective is to reconcile the individual and the collective dimensions of human existence. He aimed to limit the divisive potential of individualism, which is only one form of particularisation [*obosoblenie*], while giving maximum space to individual personhood [*lichnost'*] through civil society, understood as a sphere of free association and parliamentary democracy (Frank 1987: 142–6, 172–5). Ultimately, Frank's conception of society, displaying the dimensions of *obshchestvennost'* and *sobornost'*, is universal. It moves beyond the nation to include all of humankind. For Frank, the political is a regrettable but undeniable fact. Hence politics is an unpleasant but unavoidable evil, and it can be done better or worse. Consequently, Frank is concerned with the question of how best to give shape to the reality of the political by transforming potential conflict into political pluralism, and by creating maximum opportunities for concord against the common background of both concord and conflict which is the shared *sobornost'* of all human beings. This implies acceptance of liberal democracy as the 'lesser evil' that was also expressed by Simmel.[6]

The strength of Frank's position resides, as Solywoda emphasises, in an organic combination of a radical social philosophy oriented on an ideal humanity which, ultimately, is divine [*bogochelovechestvo*], with an explicitly moderate political philosophy that accepts a plural and liberal society (Solywoda 2008: 83–123). Similarly, in 'Beyond Left and Right' [*Po tu storonu pravogo i levogo*] (1931), Frank is not developing an argument in favour of a harmonious third way, but rather against the extreme manifestations of 'red' communism and 'black' fascism (Frank, *Werke*: VII, 286–6). A Christian social and political philosophy then transforms itself into one of the positions, as Christian socialism or as Christian democracy, within a political system of which it remains critical. In Frank, as in Skobtsova (and Bulgakov), we witness Orthodox thinkers engaged in a process of accommodation to a 'secular' environment that resembles developments in the Catholic and Protestant traditions.

With the notions of *lichnost'* and *sobornost'*, Berdiaev, Skobtsova and Frank articulated, in (Orthodox-)Christian vocabulary, what was articulated, half a century later, by communitarians like Jean-Luc Nancy or Roberto Esposito. The liberal (or bourgeois) subject is human material that successfully produces itself as an 'atomic' individual, and the collective counter-subjects of fascism, nationalism and actually existing socialism (people, race, nation, class) are made up of bourgeois individuals glued together. If those collectives are composite individuals, one must indeed start from the individual, working in the direction of an alternative political ontology and of different kinds of political subjectivity. Rightly diagnosing that the political reality of both liberal-democratic and totalitarian regimes relies on a reduced understanding of the human, these Christian philosophers tended to reject politics and to deny the political. This, at first sight, makes perfect sense: if the political can be eradicated, politics becomes obsolete and we enter a 'post-political' situation. The notion of 'we', as elaborated by Frank, offers a starting point for such an endeavour, but this requires the additional move of rejecting the escape into a 'whole', whether Divine, Sophianic or naturalistic. The openness and connectedness of the human is not only transcendent, but also immanent. Consequently, the resistance against the reduction of the human either to the individual atoms of liberalism or to abstract notions of humankind that motivate collectivism has itself an inescapable political dimension. Next to Frank, Fëdor Avgustovich Stepun (1884–1965) developed an early awareness of the religious – or pseudo-religious – dimension of the Soviet regime and of the contrast between the '*national Russian idea* of bolshevism' and the '*internationalist ideology* of communism' (Stepun 2004: 167). While critical of both, Stepun clearly perceived, in 1931, an analogy between Bolshevism and fascism in the emphasis on order that they shared, a diagnosis shared with the left-wing opposition in the Soviet Union itself, as discussed in the previous chapter.

Conclusion

The political-philosophical significance of Christianity that comes to the fore in the works of the philosophers discussed in this chapter lies in the articulation of a dimension or realm that is not of 'this' world. Turned critically, it implies that nothing can ever claim to exhaust our socio-political reality. This ontological difference, which remains no matter how politics shapes our reality at the ontic level, is a primary given, compatible with a monotheistic, a polytheistic and an agnostic political theology, but not with an atheistic one. It excludes, moreover, both individualistic and collectivistic political ideologies. Christianity's tendency to deny the political can go hand in hand with a refusal to conceive any 'worldly kingdom' as the realisation of God's plan for the world. It can further imply a refusal to fill the place of authority. At this point, the thinkers discussed in this chapter differ from their nineteenth-century predecessors in that they did not aim to establish a world in line with their ideas, but rather to present their ideas in a world that could be welcoming, indifferent or hostile to them.

As the cases of Skobtsova and Frank demonstrate, Christian thinkers, irrespective of denomination, can accept pluralist, liberal democracy even if it does not match their sense of community. It may be an overstatement to say that 'Solov'ëv and Bulgakov saw it [liberal democracy, EvdZ] as the necessary precondition for realising divine-human communion,' but they did indeed move towards an accommodation that becomes even more realistic in a post-secular condition (Papanikolaou 2012: 53; Wood 2017: 155–7; van der Zweerde 2013: 121–3, 2019c: 27–9). Solov'ëv advocated liberty but explicitly rejected political parties and electoral democracy, and Bulgakov accepted multi-party democracy, but only as a necessary evil. If twentieth-century Orthodox-Christian thinkers accept liberal democracy as a necessary condition, it is because it has become a fact of life that offers opportunities for a broad variety of 'comprehensive doctrines'. While accepting liberal democracy as a political reality, they will be inclined, within that context, to attack the liberal, not the democratic, component. They attack liberalism (Papanikolaou 2012: 46), but only in part: its egoistic individualism, legitimation of exploitation and depoliticisation of socio-economic issues are, indeed, targets. However, the primacy of ethics over politics and the ultimate non-recognition of the legitimacy of conflict are points that liberalism and Christianity, Orthodox or other, share.

The single most important similarity between the Orthodox-Christian political philosophy discussed in this chapter and the Marxist–Leninist political philosophy addressed in the preceding one is their ultimate denial of the political. Of course, neither of the two denies the possibility, or even the reality, of conflict and concord in the society contemporary to the political philosophy in question. What they do deny is its ineradicability and, consequently, its ubiquity and recurrence. Both aim to contribute actively to a situation in which concord rules and conflict is a thing of the past or a rare aberration: a regime of symphonic *sobornost'* or of harmonious communism. The difference between the two is that, contrary to Marxism–Leninism,

Christian political philosophy sets clear limits on the achievement of this goal: the limits defined by personal human freedom and dignity, and the sometimes thin line that separates these thinkers from the construction of the Kingdom of God.

During the Soviet period, the thinkers discussed in this chapter, with the exception of Losev, were anathema in the USSR but they were not forgotten. In standard Soviet reference sources and histories of philosophy, they would be decried as 'religious idealists' and 'bourgeois renegades', and opposed to Marxism–Leninism, but essential data about their lives and ideas remained accessible (van der Zweerde 2013: 119; entries in Konstantinov et al. 1960–70 and Averintsev et al. 1989). In the West, their works were widely published and translated, especially by publishing houses such as YMCA Press, and they found their underground ways back to Russia. As soon as it became possible, from 1986 onwards, their writings appeared in their country of origin, often for the first time and in huge editions. This led to a 'revival boom' in the early 1990s, when some cherished the illusion of jumping back over the Soviet Split and picking up the threads from where they had been cut off. Whether or not President Vladimir Vladimirovich Putin (b. 1952) had this in mind when he recommended, during the 2013 New Year's reception, reading Solov'ëv, Berdiaev and Il'in while handing out copies of a luxury edition of their work (Eltchaninoff 2015: 7 / 2018: 1), is another question. The ideas of those three authors move in such different directions that none of them can be held to solve any imminent issue. Yet there is a difference between a particular political-philosophical tradition offering ready-made solutions for current problems, and philosophical texts offering food for thought. While the first is a mistaken view anyway, the second is what applies to the authors here discussed. It is impossible not to start thinking for oneself when reading Il'in, Berdiaev, Skobtsova or Frank.

Notes

1. The Moskovskaia Dukhovnaia Akademiia in Zagorsk / Sergiev Posad and a few monasteries.

2. F. Pavel Florenskii [ex. 1937], Aleksei Losev, Sergei Sergeevich Averintsev (1937–2004), F. Aleksandr Vladimirovich Men' (1935–90 [assassinated]).

3. There is an interesting parallel here with the political theorist of the Muslim Brotherhood, Sayyid Qutb, who, in *Ma'ālim fī al-ṭarīq*

[Milestones; معالم في الطريق] (1964), develops an 'anarcho-Islam' that reminds one of Berdiaev's 'anarcho-Orthodoxy'. Precisely because God is the only sovereign, no human being can claim power over another.

4. In *L'Univers* magazine of 18 December 1893, Eugéne Tavernier summarised a speech by V. l. Solov'ëv from 1893 at the Cercle du Luxembourg, and quoted him: 'N'oublions pas, dit hardiment M. Soloviev, que l'histoire universelle est la réalisation des utopies' (Soloviev 1978: xviii, 348); Solov'ëv is playing on Oscar Wilde's 'Progress is the realisation of Utopias' in *The Soul of Man under Socialism* (1891).

5. Solovetsk refers to the labour camp on the Solovetskii Islands, established in a confiscated monastery, that was the starting point of the GULag system.

6. Georg Simmel, *Soziologie* [*Gesamtausgabe* vol. 11] (Frankfurt am Main: Suhrkamp, 1992), 276–7.

Chapter 9

Counter-Soviet Political Philosophy in Emigration – Beyond the Pale

> Now, several voyages of comparison made (between 1948 and 1958) to the United States and the U.S.S.R. gave me the impression that if the Americans give the appearance of rich Sino-Soviets, it is because the Russians and the Chinese are only Americans who are still poor but are rapidly proceeding to get richer.
>
> Alexandre Kojève, *Introduction to the Reading of Hegel*
> (Kojève 1980 [1969]: 161)

Already before the revolutions of 1917, but especially after the 1922 Bolshevik victory in the Civil War, many Russian philosophers left their native land. Some of them found large audiences in the West; others are still in the process of being uncovered. All of them, however, were determined by their Russian background and by their opposition to the Soviet regime as it actually existed. In this sense, they can all be regarded as their determinate negation [*bestimmte Negation*], different in character but partly shaped by what they reject. This chapter focuses on four thinkers who, detached from their place of origin, reattached to it in various ways: first, Dunayevskaya, by developing a humanist Marxism that disqualified the official Soviet variant; second, Berlin, by coupling political philosophy to an investigation of the thinkers that inspired his fatherland, and Rand, by ranting persistently against any kind of 'socialism'; and finally, Kojève, by considering Soviet communism and Western capitalism as alternative ways towards a single future.

After 1922, the Soviet Union was a fact of life, and alternative perspectives on its reality and on the towering figure of Stalin had decisive and divisive effects on political philosophy. Up until World War II, the USSR established itself as one of two systems that were opposed to each other, as well as to the liberal-democratic system. For communists, fascism was the other side of the same bourgeois capitalist coin. For fascists, liberalism and communism were two variants of cosmopolitanism. For liberals, finally, communism and fascism were two variants of totalitarianism. After World War II, this triangle changed into a binary that resulted in the Cold War, in which each of the two sides had to deal with the other.

The common denominator that links the voluntary émigré philosophers discussed in this chapter is their incompatibility with an undeniable Soviet reality. They were all anti-Bolshevik, albeit on different grounds. For Dunayevskaya, Soviet state capitalism is a betrayal of Marxist socialism. For Berlin, communism and fascism are two major negations of freedom, while for Rand, any form of socialism is a denial of human nature. From the perspective of Kojève, finally, the various systems come remarkably close, but even he, who flirted with being a communist, preferred to skip 'the thirty terrible years that the establishment of communism would mean' (Kojève 2007: 58). The thinkers discussed in this chapter can be ranked as left, right and beyond the left–right divide, and are discussed in that order. Contrary to the exiled Christian philosophers discussed in the previous chapter, these thinkers, who left the early Soviet state on their own initiative and hence were long perceived as traitors, have only recently become the object of serious academic attention in post-Soviet Russia (Granovskaia et al. 2021).

Saving the Revolution: Trotsky and Dunayevskaya

On the left, we find, first and foremost, those thinkers who had welcomed or supported the Russian Revolution, sometimes including October, but disagreed with the turns things took. Of the initial broad coalition of social-democrats (Menshevik and Bolshevik), left social-revolutionaries, syndicalists and anarchists, only the Bolsheviks and a few 'converted' Mensheviks remained. Even they were gradually replaced by a new generation of Soviet rather than Russian communists. Leftist positions have always continued to exist, both outside (the Fourth International) and inside Russia (Dam'e 2006–7). In the USSR, by the time World War II had ended and the Cold War had begun, all revolutionary Bolsheviks except Stalin had been replaced by Soviet *apparatchiki*, educated by the system itself. Present-day history textbooks in Russia do not deny the terror and repression that were part of Stalin's harsh rule but they portray him, above all, as 'an effective top-manager, under whose leadership the country achieved unprecedented successes in economy, culture, and education' (Korneeva 2011: 22).

If Stalin betrayed the revolution, according to the present-day narrative, in doing so he saved Russia from further damage than that already inflicted by Lenin and Trotsky. Trotsky joined the Bolshevik faction only late in the day, to become a main organiser of revolution and leader of the Red Army, a few weeks before October. Unlike many Bolsheviks, including even Bukharin, who was rehabilitated in 1988, Trotsky remained a major enemy of the Soviet system and is still regarded almost exclusively negatively. Several conflicting perspectives exist here. One view is indeed to see in Stalinism the betrayal of October, and in Stalin the author of a 'Soviet Thermidor', as Trotsky called it in *Predannaia revoliutsiia* [The Revolution Betrayed] (1937). The truth of this perspective, adopted by anarchists, Trotskyites and many Leninists, is that Stalin indeed annihilated an entire generation of revolutionary Bolsheviks and turned back the achievements of the revolutions of 1917 and 1905, and even the reforms of 1861. A second approach is to see Stalin as one of the great dictators of the twentieth century. The truth of this perspective is that Stalin can, indeed, be held responsible for several of the largest crimes against humanity in history, inflicted mostly on the people he claimed to lead. A third perspective is to see Stalin as a realist leader who, albeit excessively harshly, restored order after a decade of revolution, military communism and civil war, and stabilised the USSR's position in the international field by adopting *Realpolitik*. The truth of this perspective is that Stalin, contrary to Hitler, did lead his country away from revolution and destruction, not towards it. He did rebuild (or at least could be portrayed as having done so) the country after World War II, which had hit the USSR very hard. This also explains part of his lasting popularity in Russia. In this connection, one should bear in mind what the USSR achieved: alphabetisation of a diverse population, electrification of a huge country, realisation of a nation-wide infrastructure, legal gender equality, emancipation of ethnic minorities, establishment of an educational system and the creation of a supranational cultural space – not to mention the conquest of outer space and the best metro system in the world. All of these have come at an unbelievably high cost, but nobody who visits the former USSR can fail to notice the advantages of education, public transport, the effective use of Russian as a *lingua franca*, or the effects of large-scale migration and intermarriage. Just as it is unacceptable to understate the amount of human suffering, it is impossible to ignore the enormous amount of positive human energy and good intentions that were invested into the Soviet project.

Stalin's 'betrayal of the revolution' is best understood as the effect of an exclusive focus on retaining Bolshevik power 'at any cost'. Exiled in 1929, Trotsky in 1936 sketched three possible outcomes: first, overthrow of the state bureaucracy 'by a revolutionary party having all the attributes of the old Bolshevism'; second, overthrow of 'the ruling Soviet caste' by a bourgeois party that would aim at the restoration of private property over the means of production; and third, a continuation of bureaucratic rule, yielding a state capitalism with a new ruling class (Trotsky 2004: 190–2). This last outcome, which is what actually happened, simply repeats history, leading back to the same inevitable choice between capitalism and socialism. Trotsky continued to identify with October, of which he, as organiser of the Red Army and architect of the Red Terror, had been one of the protagonists. At the end of the day, his Bolshevik nostalgia has proved less inspiring than his consistent critique of global imperialist capitalism, which implies the impossibility of constructing socialism in one country propagated by Lenin, Bukharin and Stalin. According to Solzhenitsyn, who rejects Trotsky's analysis, there never was a Thermidor (Solzhenitsyn 2015: 604; Trotsky 2004: 66–86). Paradoxically, both are right: from Trotsky's perspective, a potentially successful world revolution was betrayed by Stalin, while for Solzhenitsyn, Stalinism meant the next stage of an already criminal regime. Meanwhile, it can be argued that the actual Thermidor took place when Lenin and Bukharin reversed many of the early achievements, reintroducing money, the free market, and private property over the means of production. Their NĖP made Soviet Russia much more akin to authoritarian modernising regimes, such as Atatürk's Turkey. The first *piatiletka* [five-year plan], the enforced collectivisation of agriculture and the annihilation of resisting classes marked the beginning of massive crimes against humanity, but they also revived the Petrine tradition of top-down modernisation. *Pace* Solzhenitsyn and others, NĖP means the replacement of ideocracy by ideology, no matter what we think of the leading ideas themselves or of the practices that they legitimise.

Raya Shpigel-Dunayevskaya (1910–87), who emigrated with her family to the USA in 1922, was excluded from the Communist

Party in the USA because of her support for Trotsky. She had indeed worked briefly for Trotsky, but broke with him in 1939 because of his continued defence of the USSR as a 'workers' state' (Gogol 2004: 8, 23). The year 1939 marks the start of Dunayevskaya's independent life as an influential thinker. She joined the movement of Antoinette F. Buchholz-Konikow [Konikova] (1869–1946), also born in the Russian Empire and an expelled Trotskyite who became prominent in US American feminism with *Voluntary Motherhood* (1923). A pupil of Herbert Marcuse, Dunayevskaya developed her Marxist humanism on the basis of Marx's early writings. Yet, contrary to other Marxist humanists, she emphasised the integrity of Marxist theory by including the works of the later Marx, especially *Das Kapital* (ibid.: 14; Kovel in Dunayevskaya 2000: xv-xvi). If official Soviet Marxism–Leninism – for example, in the works of Teodor Il'ich Oizerman (1914–2017) – tended to interpret the early works in view of the mature ones (Oizerman 1986), Dunayevskaya regarded the latter as elaborations on the former.

Dunayevskaya's diagnosis of Soviet socialism as, in fact, state capitalism was more than just a rejection of Stalinism on the basis of a Marxist analysis. She analysed it, mirroring Kojève, as part of a simultaneous global development of which the USA's New Deal, German Nazism and Japanese *Dai Tōa Kyōeiken* [大東亜共栄圏, Greater East Asia Co-Prosperity Sphere] were parts as well. In her dialectical vision, this global development also included the opposition and resistance, particularly of female and non-white workers, to this 'evolving stage of capitalism', both in the USA and in the USSR. Dunayevskaya, who lived her active intellectual life during the Cold War period when the world was divided into two opposing camps and who was a prominent analyst of Soviet affairs (Dunayevskaya 1992), posed the genuinely dialectical question as to what, if two entities are in opposition, is their common ground. From that point onwards, loyalty to the Soviet project no longer is an issue because it becomes the other side of the same coin.

Escape to Liberty: Berlin and Rand

The most widely known emigrant thinker from Russia, after Berdiaev, is probably Isaiah Berlin (b. Jesajah Berlins) (1909–97). The Russian connection of this Latvian Jew, who learned Hebrew earlier than Russian and Latin, runs deep. In 1915, his family fled from German-besieged Riga to Petrograd, where young Isaiah spent an important part of his childhood, witnessing two revolutions in 1917 before the family fled Bolshevik dictatorship, going back to Latvia in 1920 and on to London in 1921 (Ignatieff 2000: 20–31). While too young, obviously, to be regarded as a 'Russian liberal', Berlin's specific and highly influential brand of pluralist liberalism is unthinkable without his childhood at the heart of the Russian Revolution. Berlin's qualities as a specialist in Russian thought, a field in which he founded a school, are indeed beyond dispute, but the suggestion that he traded analytical philosophy for the history of ideas is misleading, if read as implying that the two are unrelated. In fact, his value pluralism and his aversion to teleologies of history resulted specifically from his encounter with Herzen.

Despite his donnish appearance, Berlin never lost his Russian language, nor his commitment to Russia. Contrary to other critics of Soviet totalitarianism, such as Karl Popper, Hannah Arendt or Claude Lefort, Berlin immediately grabbed the opportunity to travel to Moscow and Leningrad after the final defeat of Nazi Germany (ibid.: 134). When, in 1945, he visited Moscow as a civil servant working for the British government, he was lucky to meet a number of Russian artists and writers. They noted with surprise not only that he was fluent in Russian, but also that, as one of them remarked, his 'very form of thinking . . . was "entirely Russian"' (ibid.: 136). This 'entirely Russian form of thinking' may have pointed to Berlin's instinct as to what he could or could not say, when a statement was 'intended for the microphones' or when it was time to leave a situation that grew too embarrassing (ibid.: 142; 145). Berlin had no difficulty enjoying the language, reuniting with his relatives and connecting to the Soviet Russian writers that he met. These included Boris Pasternak (1890–1960), whose *Doktor Zhivago* Berlin smuggled to Great Britain, Kornei Chukovskii (1882–1969) and, most of all, Anna Akhmatova (1889–1966), with whom Berlin fell in deep, mutual love, as Akhmatova's poem *Cinque* (1946) testifies. Contrary to other anti-Soviet intellectuals, Berlin knew what he was talking about. Not only was his liberalism clearly nourished by his direct experience of the Bolshevik takeover, but his works on the history of Russian thought have become classics, not least of all because of his profound knowledge and love of language and country.

Russian had a decisive impact on Berlin's liberalism in three ways: early childhood experience; the confrontation with totalitarianism during World War II and the Cold War, including his personal encounters with Pasternak, Akhmatova and others; and his study of Herzen, Turgenev, Bakunin, Tolstoy and others. Berlin's abhorrence of any attempt to tell other people (himself included) what to do is shaped by the combination of his early Russian years and his later Soviet experiences. The insight that he gained from experiencing first-hand a regime that claimed to know, better than society itself, how society and the people that constitute it should use their positive freedom, was instrumental in his critique of the Soviet system. It also informed his analysis of both Enlightenment rationalism, for which there can be only one good way to use one's positive freedom, and Romantic 'authenticism', for which every human being must realise her or his innermost self. This insight has inspired him to become one of the grand scholars in the field of history of ideas, which, for him, included Russia. It also made him give pride of place to Herzen as one of Russia's greatest thinkers: somebody who, like Berlin, believed neither in historical determinism, in single best solutions and answers, nor in a single fixed hierarchy of values and principles. Berlin's other lasting contribution to political philosophy, value pluralism, is thus not independent of his Russian connection either. It acknowledges the limits of rational choice and the reality of radical choice, offering space for the radical, the passionate and the irrational: if the positions of Bakunin or Tolstoy are rejected, this is not because they are inconsistent, but because they are based on different values (Gray 2013: 180).

His emphasis on negative liberty, understood as absence of barriers that limit one's freedom, has turned Berlin into a key author in mainstream liberalism, albeit without the triumphant optimism of many other liberals. Indeed, liberalism says that this negative liberty should be maximised and, in principle, be limited only by an equal negative liberty of all others. This not only points to the idea that government should be as small as possible. It also makes it possible to place liberal political philosophies on a scale ranging from an absolute minimum (Robert Nozick, Friedrich von Hayek, Ayn Rand), via more 'realistic' liberal philosophies that expect the state to repair unjustifiable inequality (John Rawls, Judith Shklar), to 'leftist' liberal philosophies that ascribe clear political tasks to government, restrained by inalienable individual rights (Michael Walzer, Amartya Sen and most Russian liberals).

If negative liberty points logically in the direction of individual freedom from barriers and interference, positive liberty comes in at least three forms. First, there is the individual human being who realises an individual life plan (heroism, Romantic authenticity, Nietzschean self-transcendence), of which Rand offers the prototypical example. Second, there is collective self-determination (republicanism, Arendtian acting-in-concert), of which the *sobornost'* of a thinker like Berdiaev and the proletarian heroism of *bogostroiteli* like Lunacharskii are cases (Walicki 2010: 324). Lastly, there is totalitarian collective freedom, in which some decide for others what they should do with their lives, classical examples being, from Berlin's perspective, Rousseau, Lenin and Stalin. Berlin's status as one of the classical liberal political philosophers relies both on this insistence on 'negative' freedom as central to the liberal tradition, and on his critique of particular understandings of 'positive' freedom: namely, precisely those on which the USSR prided itself. This is collective self-determination in the name of an inevitable historical *telos*, a calculated and enforced 'leap to freedom' in accordance with a known libretto (Walicki 1995: 25).

Negative liberty is perceived, by Berlin, as an individual form of liberty, but he tends to suspect positive liberty of being almost inevitably collective, or even collectivist. What seems to be decisive, at the end of the day, is not positive liberty as such, but its teleological justifications (Gray 2013: 120–1; Berlin 2013: 331–3). We can read Berlin's ambiguous relation to positive liberty as a reluctance to say farewell to a more 'Russian' type of liberalism. Paradoxically, his great pluralist hero, Herzen, was, himself, an outlier within Russian political thought. This paradox, however, dissolves once we take the argument to a general level, beyond the opposition between Russia and 'the West'. What Herzen teaches us through Berlin is that liberalism goes astray if it becomes either monistic and individualist, or positivist and collectivist. Berlin's retrospective heralding of Herzen as one of the few realists in the history of political thought in Russia carries a meaning that goes well beyond either Russia or the West. Liberation and emancipation, desired by Berlin as much as by Herzen, inevitably led to a situation of indeterminacy because 'negatively freed' humans still have to decide how to determine themselves 'positively'. As Ignatieff puts it: 'To free a man, Isaiah insisted, was to free him from obstacles – prejudice, tyranny, discrimination – to the exercise of his own free choice. It did not mean telling him how to use his freedom' (Ignatieff 2000: 202–3).

An instinctive allergy to anyone telling anybody how to use her freedom motivated the radical liberalism of novelist and philosopher Ayn Rand (1905–82), born in St Petersburg as Alisa Zinov'evna Rozenbaum. Among the many novels inspired by the early Soviet regime, two stand out in particular. One is *My* [We]

(1921), by Evgenii Ivanovich Zamiatin (1884–1937); widely considered the first of its dystopian kind, this book was the inspiration for George Orwell's *1984* (1949), which has enriched our discourse with notions like Newspeak, Big Brother and Ministry of Truth. The other is Rand's *We, the Living* (1936). Zamiatin and Rand did not write about a dreadful totalitarian society from the relative comfort of the 'free world', but from within that totalitarian reality: Zamiatin as somebody trapped in it, Rand as somebody who had escaped it. Rand's *We, the Living* is not dystopian, but a critical-realist depiction of the early USSR during NÉP.

Rand took a strong interest in politics at a young age and supported the February Revolution. After October, her father's business was confiscated and the family lived in poverty. Although a despised bourgeoise, she graduated from Petrograd University, having been one the first women allowed to enrol. On the one hand, she thus doubly 'benefited from the abolition [after February 1917, EvdZ] of educational restrictions on Jews and women students' (Sciabarra 22013: 326–7). On the other hand, however, she witnessed the reintroduction of quotas by the Bolshevik regime: 'Just as the czars had practiced institutional racism, the Bolsheviks attempted to boost the participation of "proletarian" students through [. . .] a mass purge of "bourgeois" scholars and pupils' (ibid.: 327). This experience made her a sworn enemy of any type of 'affirmative action'.

When she went to the USA in 1926 on a private visit, she stayed. For the atheist Rand, the USSR was not a manifestation of the Antichrist, as it was for Berdiaev or Il'in, but an extreme manifestation of a general evil called statehood or, even more generally, collectively organised humankind. Ironically, the long-term effect of the Soviet system has been an atomisation of society that comes close to Rand's neoliberal ideal. Rand's later best-selling 'utopia of greed', *Atlas Shrugged* (1957), demonstrates the utopian nature of neoliberalism (Linssen 2019: 276), while *We, the Living* depicts a very real society modelled after a collectivist utopia, a world in which the idea of a New Man and a New Society were quickly losing ground to the opportunistic pragmatism of a cynical regime – the engineers of the soul replaced by engineers of practices and bodies, while communism became ideo-logy in the sense of idea-talk.

In Rand's political philosophy, the Promethean hero or hero of will, the fearless and ruthless individual ready to risk death and indifferent to the fate of others, takes centre stage. The only legitimate aim of the state is the protection of such heroes' liberty.

These heroes do not do 'good' things because what is good, and what bad or evil, depends on their very deeds: they set the norm rather than fulfilling it. Here, Rand is as provocative as Hobbes or Schmitt in sketching the radical consequences of the idea that politics precedes ethics. Rand's hero is the opposite of the 'social hero' of 'self-sacrifice and kenotic release', whose 'most heroic act' is the 'highest abnegation', and who occupies the central position in Christian political philosophy (Love 2018: 69). There, the role of the state was to facilitate the realisation of a known good by self-transcending individuals. Randean individuals, by contrast, do not transcend; they only elevate themselves.

Rand's overall philosophy is explicitly atheist, with elements of the intuitivism, objectivism, supermoralism and epistemological realism that she had been taught by her main tutor, Nikolai Onufrievich Losskii (1870–1965). The latter was an important Russian religious philosopher, exiled on the Philosophy Steamer in 1922, and one of the most widely read and translated historians of Russian philosophy (Losskii 1991: 320–39 / Lossky 1951: 251–66; Sciabarra 2013: 10, 39–40). Rand adopted Losskii's philosophical views while dropping his religious premises. Without Christian love and without God's Kingdom, we humans are mortal egoists. As a result, we are left with a single, rationally shaped and hence objectively knowable, godless world populated by radically selfish individuals. This, however, is not a cynical anthropology: being immoral egoists defines our task in life, and the effect is an ethics of *'rational selfishness'*.

> Just as man cannot survive by any random means, but must discover and practice the principles which his survival requires, so man's self-interest cannot be determined by blind desires or random whims, but must be discovered and achieved by the guidance of rational principles. (Rand 1964: xi)

Rand's biggest opponents are collectivism and 'altruism', the latter being a vision which 'permits no view of men except as sacrificial animals and profiteers-on-sacrifice, as victims and parasites', and that 'permits no concept of a benevolent co-existence among men – [. . .] no concept of *justice*' (ibid.: ix). Justice, for Rand, means that we should 'never seek or grant the unearned and undeserved, neither in matter nor in spirit' (ibid.: 28). While there is a parallel here with Nietzsche, Rand distances herself from him, and from the Russian symbolist poets and artists

(Merezhkovskii, Gippius and others) that she knew well, with a strongly rationalist 'Apollonian' opposition to 'Dionysian' irrationalism, symbolists or the New Left of the 1960s (Sciabarra 2013: 31), and she explicitly equates rationality with psychological health: 'For the rational, psychologically healthy man, the desire for pleasure is the desire to celebrate his control over reality. For the neurotic, the desire for pleasure is the desire to escape from reality' (Rand 1964: 74–5).

Through her novels and essays, Rand has been highly influential outside academic circles: on the basis of a strictly rationalist and atheist philosophy called objectivism, she propagated a rational egoism that resembles many neoliberal ideas, making Ludwig von Mises one of her admirers. For Rand, capitalism 'is the only *moral* social system' since it alone gives virtue free play, and as a side effect, it also serves the public good (Peikoff 1991: 380, 392). Direct influence is hard to prove but *We the Living* predates Friedrich von Hayek's *The Road to Serfdom* (1944) by eight years, and *Atlas Shrugged* appeared three years before *The Constitution of Liberty* (1960). The safest assessment is that both Rand's ideas and those of the neoliberal economists fell on the same fertile soil. Academic recognition came much later: for example, in the form of the *Journal of Ayn Rand Studies*, published by Penn State University since 1999.

Rand's political philosophy, a radical 'negative' liberalism that weds the idea of a minimal 'night-watch state' to a rejection of democracy as majority tyranny, is and remains highly controversial. Her explicit atheism made it even more controversial in the USA, while her objectivism and moral absolutism distanced her from other libertarians. Rand opposed every other political philosophy, and her polemics, in a truly Schmittian vein, yielded many enemies and very few friends. Her individualist rationalism also implies a rejection of any form of racism and nationalism, of which, from her perspective, both Nazism and Soviet-Russian patriotism were examples, and which, in the final analysis, boiled down to tribalism (Sciabarra 2013: 326–7). Also, she expresses with provocative candour the spontaneous philosophy of substantial segments of the world's political and economic elites. In a way, she is expressing, in the clearest possible way, the 'atomist–individualist' philosophy that accompanies the 'exploded' civil society Hegelians feared and Marxists decried. This brings her surprisingly close to another important atheist political philosopher with Russian roots: Kojève.

Towards a Universal State: Kojève

Alexandre Kojève was born in Moscow as Aleksandr Vladimirovich Kozhevnikov (1902–68). He lived through World War I and the revolution as a teenager, tried to build a career in the early Soviet years, failing because of his bourgeois background, was arrested, and fled the country in 1920 (Auffret 1990: 86–93). He only returned to the USSR on what he himself described as a 'comparative voyage' (Kojève 1979: 436 / 1980: 161). Kozhevnikov was one of the 'torn' and 'chased' philosophers of the twentieth century, but unlike many of them (Arendt, Strauss, Benjamin, Frank, Dunayevskaya, Berlin, Levinas, Stepun, Rand, Koyré), he was not of Jewish descent and suffered 'only' as a bourgeois. Like Rand, Kojève was a self-declared atheist, but an atheist of a different kind. He offered an 'atheist' alternative to the conception of Solov'ëv, who had strongly influenced him (Groys 2012b: 148). Most precisely, Kojève can be read as a pan(en)atheist who replaced Solov'ëv's *bogochelovechestvo* [Godmanhood] by *theanthropism*, which is hard to understand as anything other than as *chelovekobozhestvo* [Deified Humankind].

Anybody who takes an interest in West European philosophy in the twentieth century, especially in France, knows the name of Kojève. Anybody engaged in Hegel scholarship knows the fame Kojève achieved with his *Introduction à la lecture de Hegel*, which saved his many students the trouble of reading Hegel in the original (Dunayevskaya 2002: 165–6). Equally many are aware of the lasting effect of his mistranslation of Hegel's '*Herrschaft und Knechtschaft*' with 'master and slave' instead of 'lordship and bondage' – a mistranslation that does injustice to Hegel, dialectics and actually enslaved people (Kojève 1979: 170–84 / 1980: 41–57; Kistner and Van Haute 2020: 53). Anybody familiar with late twentieth-century political philosophy knows that Francis Fukuyama derived his thesis of 'the end of history' explicitly from Kojève (Fukuyama 1992: 65–7; Kojève 1979: 434–7, n. 1 / 1980: 158–62, n. 6). Anybody well versed in the study of Russian philosophy, finally, knows Kojève's pioneering study on Solov'ëv, in which he emphasised the crucial importance of the Sophia-figure (Kojève 2018; Love 2018: 6).

However, the habitual perception of Kojève as a Frenchman introducing Hegel disregards his Russian background, also in the intellectual sense of his philosophical roots. Kojève grew up in a Russia that was a self-evident part of European philosophical culture and whose great thinkers were obsessed with the question of Russia's role in world history, which, for many of them, was connected to questions of *theōsis* and *bogochelovechestvo*. When he unpreparedly took over a course on Hegel from Alexandre Koyré, the Russian émigré philosopher Aleksandr Vol'fovich Koira [Koiranskii] (1882–1964), Kojève was not a Hegel scholar, but a specialist in Russian religious philosophy, especially with regard to Solov'ëv, on whom he had written his German dissertation.

Just as every political philosophy presupposes a political anthropology, it presupposes a political theology: that is, a discourse about the positive, negative or neutral relation between God (or gods) and religion on the one hand, and society and politics on the other. Kojève's atheism guided him to an absolutisation of what in Hegel, whom he reads as a pantheist, is objective, not absolute spirit. This leads both to the idea of an 'end' of history and to the subordination of political subjectivity to objective historical processes. Ignoring the gap that exists – even for an agnostic but certainly for Hegel – between objective and absolute spirit, Kojève becomes the author and actor of 'politicide' in the sense of a murdering of political subjectivity. It is Kojève's atheistic political theology that entitles him to claim that 'obviously, absolute Authority in the strong sense of the word is never realised in practice. Only God is *held* to possess (or more precisely, God *should have* possessed it)' (Kojève 2014: 31 / Kojève 2004: 91–2). If there is no God, there also is no Authority, and the Absolute becomes radically world-immanent. Kojève's atheism is a mono-atheism, which makes him the antipode of the Russian religious philosophers, and brings his universal homogeneous state close to the empire of Dostoevsky's Grand Inquisitor, Solov'ëv's Emperor or Zamiatin's Benefactor. Kojève is most famous for his 'end of history' thesis, part of which is a replacement of politics by administration and of government by governance. Even if the impact of Kojève's *politicide* can be exaggerated, his influence has been enormous (van Middelaar 1999; Derrida 1993: 123; Groys 2012b: 145). In France, it was only with Claude Lefort that political philosophy re-entered the scene.

Influential as it may have been, Kojève's interpretation of Hegel is highly problematic, and can be read as a right-Marxist vulgarisation. Indeed, Kojève's 'homogeneous and universal world state' resembles Marx's vision of a free, classless society beyond mediation much more than Hegel's conception of a constitutional state based on, precisely, mediating institutions (Pöggeler 1995: 25). Moreover, Kojève's suggestion that such a free society, projected in a distant future by Marx, had already been attained in the USA, where 'practically [*sic!*], all the members of a "classless society" can from now on appropriate for themselves everything that seems good to them, without thereby working any more than their heart dictates' (Kojève 1980: 161 / 1979: 436; *MEW*: XXV, 828), was rightly criticised by Soviet scholars as an 'exaltation [*voskhvalenie*] of "the American way of life" that even its most zealous official pro-pogandists would not permit themselves' (Kuznetsov 1982: 113). In fact, a brief look into any of Dunayevskaya's writings would suffice to highlight an intersection of class, race and gender that points to the exact opposite of what Kojève suggested. Meanwhile, Soviet authors who demonstrated Kojève's distortion of Hegel's position, Marx's critique of that position and Marx' own position on any 'end of history' barely mentioned Kojève's Russian roots (ibid.: 108–11, and 52, n. 1).

Kojève based his conception on the *Phänomenologie des Geistes* [Phenomenology of Mind] (Kojève 2007: 59), which was Hegel's trajectory towards Absolute Knowledge [*absolutes Wissen*]: not his philosophical system, but the point from which such a system would be possible. In fact, Kojève barely touches upon Hegel's system, thus ignoring, among other things, the latter's *Rechtsphilosophie* [Philosophy of Right] (1821). The *Phänomenologie des Geistes* is where Hegel began, and it is where Kojève stopped (Butler 2012: 77–8; Pöggeler 1995: 24–5). Hegel published his book in 1807, a year after the precise moment when, in Jena 1806, history ended for Kojève:

> Observing what was taking place around me and reflecting on what had taken place in the world since the Battle of Jena, I understood that Hegel was right to see in this battle the end of History properly so-called. In and by this battle the vanguard of humanity virtually attained the limit and the aim, that is, the *end*, of Man's historical evolution. (Kojève 1980: 160 / 1979: 436)

This immediately raises many questions: did Hegel actually consider Jena 1806 the 'end of history'? In a famous letter, he claimed to have seen the *Weltseele* [World Soul] riding out on horseback: that is, Napoleon Bonaparte, who had just taken the city and was inspecting his army.[1] In that letter, there is no suggestion of any 'end' of history, but ought he have made that claim, as Kojève suggests? Indeed, should we, or can we, distinguish between 'history properly speaking' and 'history improper', as Kojève claims to have 'understood' Hegel? Did history come to an end in 1806 with Napoleon and Hegel? Hegel certainly did not make that claim, but instead argued that philosophy cannot predict the future and, more specifically, that it was unpredictable, in the early nineteenth century, what historical role Russia would play – a statement that organised the debate between 'Slavophiles' and 'Westernisers'. The suggestions that 'according to Hegel history definitively comes to a close [*okonchatel'no zamykaetsia*] at the establishment of burgher-bureaucratic conditions in Prussia' and that his philosophy of history did not leave 'any place at all for socialism, nor for the national movements of the present century, nor for Russia and the Slavonic nation [*slaviansto*] as historical forces' can be found in Solov'ëv's encyclopaedia entry on Hegel (Solov'ëv 1997: 79). Boris Groys has argued that Kojève repeated not Hegel's but Solov'ëv's move, replacing Sophia by Hegel and the Christian Revelation by Hegel's philosophy (Groys 2012b: 151–7). Koyré and, in particular, Kojève interpret his philosophy of history in such a way that history has ended. Kojève writes, in plain absurdity and without reference, that 'Hegel says that the "absolute" State that he has in mind (Napoleon's Empire) is the *realisation* of the Christian Kingdom of heaven' (Kojève 1979: 193 / 1980: 67; Rutkevich 2009). In fact, Kojève is doing what Solov'ëv wrongly accused Hegel of: namely, transforming an eschatological end of history into a historical one (Jubara 2001: 149–50).

If history has ended, history since 1806 becomes the gradual implementation of this 'absolute State'. Marx's thesis of a transition from humanity's pre-history to history proper looks like the inverse of this but follows the same scheme, especially if we bear in mind that in both cases the political has been dealt with in a manner that is here to stay: equal rights and liberties for all on the basis of mutual recognition in one case, a communist society in the other, combined with bureaucratic administration in both. This would imply that Hegel's reference to America as the land of the future, and to Russia as not yet having shown the world what it would yield,[2] pointed to a global extension of the principles articulated between 1776 and 1815. Transposed to the twentieth century, this reduces the Cold War to a minor conflict within a single development, rather than a struggle between fundamentally opposed ideas, as both parties in that conflict framed it. History, then, is not history, but implementation, and politics not Politics, but administration – as Lenin indeed suggested.

Kojève depicted himself as 'Stalin's consciousness' in the Hegelian sense of consciousness: that is, expressing what was true about him

(Auffret 1990: 405). This points to an important shift: for thinkers like Solov'ëv and Dostoevsky, it was crucially important to be able to distinguish between Christ and Antichrist (Groys 2012b: 166), but also difficult to do so. Zamiatin's *Blagodetel'* [Benefactor], Dostoevsky's Grand Inquisitor, who leaves to Jesus Christ a ridiculously pathetic role (almost that of a *iurodivyi*), and Solov'ëv's Emperor are very difficult to distinguish from a genuine Messiah because they do satisfy most of people's desires. Interpreting Stalin as the leader who restored order after the years of revolution, and who had to use harsh measures to do so, who saved Russia and rebuilt the USSR after World War II, bridges this distance. The remaining difference is that between a human Well-Doer and the Son of God, but this difference makes sense only from a theistic point of view – which is the point of view that Kojève rejected. For Kojève, what matters was the final outcome, and not the means or the ideology. According to Kojève, the USSR was not an anti-modern system, let alone a pre-modern one, but an attempt to realise the ideals of the French Revolution on East European soil, albeit in a brutal way, and to create a modern industrial society based, politically, on *égaliberté* [equaliberty]. If the Atlantic and the Soviet paths are alternative ways towards the single goal of a universal homogeneous state based on mutual recognition and equal rights, we move beyond the opposition of left and right that was of crucial importance for the ideological self-legitimisation of both the Soviet and the Western blocs. From this angle, it is not surprising that the End of History thesis resurfaced around the time that the USSR fell apart.

Conclusion

Most Russian philosophers who emigrated and made a career outside Soviet Russia can be gathered under the label *bestimmte Negation*: their thought was, in key points, negatively determined by their Soviet experience. Trotsky and Dunayevskaya have gained prominence in Marxist circles and, obviously, October and Bolshevism remained a constitutive other for them and their followers. Berlin and Rand have gained their place in Western academia in such a way that their demonstrable Russian background is sometimes barely mentioned or even completely overlooked (Peikoff 1991). Kojève, who cunningly concealed his Russian roots, remains an influential and controversial figure. In all these cases, their rootedness in Russian culture and the traumatic uprooting that marks their early Soviet experience remain indispensable for seriously understanding their thought. At the same time, the pitfall of cultural reductionism must be avoided: all these thinkers related actively to their background and thereby liberated themselves from its determining force.

In the universal and homogeneous state sketched by Kojève, political relations have been replaced by juridical ones against the backdrop of an *a priori* accepted hegemonic order: all obey the universal command; all are, in that sense, slaves of 'a rather Stalinist (a)theocracy' (Love 2018: 253). What is the difference between this Kojèvian universal end-state and the European welfare state that he helped to build after World War II, or with an (ideal-theoretical) state of complete mutual recognition of all by all? The latter would be the kind of state Rand abhorred and it has been demolished by a few decades of neoliberal hegemony. That development has not, however, yielded a universal state of the type Rand would approve of, if only because a strong government must serve the market. It has yielded the convergence of a plurality of states in which business and politics are decreasingly distinguishable and in which everybody is expected, however briefly, to be a hero of will, or, alternatively, to become a loser. The entrepreneurial self combines calculated self-interest (Berlin's Enlightenment rationalism) with heroic manifestation of the self (Berlin's Romantic authenticism and Rand's genius) against the background of a universal legal and procedural state (Kojève's project) in which all recognise all, on the basis of *égaliberté*, as long as they relate indifferently to each other. What remains is a scattered left-socialist opposition (including Dunayevskaya's humanist Marxism). Both 'brotherhood' and the 'souls' of nations have become elements of electoral speeches and of commodified religiosity yielding 'spiritual salvation' in the private sphere. Paradoxically, the 'brutal' Soviet way of realising a universal state generated, in post-Soviet Russia, a profound longing for spiritual renaissance, national identity and humanity that was confronted harshly with the cynicism of a 'free world', to which Kojève contributed both theoretically and practically. The difference between any such total state, whether Randian or Kojèvian, and the societies we actually live in is the remaining possibility of conflict and concord that relies on the ontological difference: the never-closing gap between being and existence. A universal and homogeneous state based on all-round mutual recognition is no more a reality in Kabul in 2021 than it was in Petrograd in 1921 or, indeed, in Berlin in 1821.

Notes

1. 'An Niethammer [13 October 1806]', in G. W. F. Hegel (1982), *Weltgeist zwischen Jena und Berlin: Briefe*, ed. Hartmut Zinser. Frankfurt am Main: Ullstein, 58.
2. Note that Hegel wrote this after Russia had, in the second half of the eighteenth century, defeated Prussia and, in the early nineteenth, defeated Napoleon: Russia had appeared on the scene of world history most visibly, yet its agenda was unknown.

Chapter 10

Late Soviet and Early Post-Soviet Political Philosophy – Licking the Wounds

Communist society is highly stable, except when it is not.
> Michael Kirkwood, *Alexander Zinoviev:*
> *An Introduction to his Work* (Kirkwood 1993: 229)

No one will blame God himself, when after a murder, the murderer is found to carry a Bible.
> Anatolii Butenko, 'Vinoven li Karl Marks v
> "kazarmennom sotsializme"?' (Butenko 1989: 24)

However spectacular the period of *glasnost'* and *perestroika* may have been, there are pertinent reasons to take a broader time-frame and include developments in the mature Soviet period. The collapse of the Soviet system combined socio-economic stagnation with ideological bankruptcy and increasing dissent (Shlapentokh 1990: 174–80; Zubok 2011: 259–69). Between 1965 and 1968, the relatively liberal period of 'thaw [*ottepel'*]' ended. Frost set in with the trial against writers Iulii Daniel' and Andrei Siniavskii in 1965. On 5 December (Constitution Day), 200 people joined the *miting glasnosti* [*glasnost'* meeting], and the 1968 suppression of the Prague Spring in Czechoslovakia provoked protests in Moscow, too (Vaissié 1999: 56–72; Berglund 2012: 48–50; Horvath 2005: 18–20). Those who engaged in an explicit critique of Soviet society landed in the broad category of 'dissidents'. Exchange between Soviet and West European philosophers was suppressed. However, while repressive domination was effective, ideological hegemony became increasingly hollow, credibility being replaced by calculation. Anthologies of dissident publications, in *samizdat* and *tamizdat*, demonstrate both the sustained critique by Trotskyists, neo-Leninists and neo-Bolsheviks, often linked to workers' protest, and the call for cautious democratisation and liberalisation which, from 1968 until the late 1980s, formed the political agenda of many scientists and intellectuals, including a substantial part of the KPSS elite (Saunders 1974: 19–34, 399–401).

This explains why the USSR changed so quickly in the late 1980s: release of political prisoners, quasi-unlimited freedom of conscience, speech, discussion and publication, and the chance to establish independent organisations and associations share a sense of liberation and relief (Savranskaya 2019: 77; Zubok 2019: 57). Mikhail Sergeevich Gorbachëv (b. 1931), whose grandfathers had served GULag time, allowed a nation-wide self-critique. Organisations like *Memorial* became vocal and monuments to the victims of GULag were erected. Soviet statues were removed on a large scale but also left untouched in many places (today, every town still has a central square with a Lenin statue). In the early twentieth century, the tsarist regime had been bound to disappear after the war lost against Japan and the failed revolution of 1905. Similarly, the 'stagnated' Soviet gerontocracy was doomed to collapse. What is striking in both cases is the speed with which the old regime crumbled, leading to a *smutnoe vremia* which is also a time 'of opportunity and hope for positive change' (Obolonsky 2019: 125). Every political regime is subject to a process of generation and corruption, and regimes can respond to this with a capacity to adapt and regenerate. Liberal-democratic regimes owe their stability to this capacity, but even a one-party system like the USSR's offered opportunities for the articulation of the perceived necessity for reform: Gorbachëv's programme of *perestroika* and *glasnost'* originated in the KPSS. After the fair and competitive 1989 elections to the Congress of People's Deputies of the Soviet Union, most delegates were still KPSS members, but the party was nevertheless splitting up (Zubok 2019: 85).

People left the KPSS, the Komsomol and other organisations in large numbers (Kramer 2019: 101; Kirkwood 1993: 227) and there were numerous rehabilitations, but no purges or persecutions. Most bureaucrats retained their positions:

Unlike the treatment of former Nazi officials in Germany, no professional ban was ever instated for former leaders of the Communist Party of the Soviet Union, let alone its rank-and-file members. Only negligible compensation has been provided to those victims who have been officially 'rehabilitated' [. . .]; and there has been no serious philosophical debate in Russia, secular or religious, over problems of collective guilt, memory, and identity. (Etkind 2013: 10 / 2018: 21)

This verdict is not entirely accurate, however, as many attempts were undertaken to 'digest' the Soviet period, open the archives and confront uneasy questions (Solzhenitsyn 1995; Pecherskaia 1997; Iakovlev 2002; Tolstaja 2013, 2020, 2013; Chubais 2017).

Contrary to other former Soviet republics, post-Soviet Russia could not point to foreign invasion or occupation. Nor was there any external pressure to engage in self-searching; it could not seriously blame anybody except itself, and a 'clean break' had proved impossible. Theories about a world-wide conspiracy of Jews and freemasons against the Russian people were hardly taken seriously outside obscurantist and reactionary circles. After Boris Nikolaevich El'tsin (1931–2007) withstood an attempted military coup in August 1991, he forced Gorbachëv to resign and allied himself with the presidents of Ukraine and Belarus' to divide the Russian lands into, roughly, Great, Little and White Russia. Of the three, the Russian Federation declared itself the heir of the USSR in foreign politics, and El'tsin emerged as a Russian Augusto Pinochet, imposing neoliberal shock therapy. It was also El'tsin who strangled electoral democracy in post-Soviet Russia. In 1996, Gennadii Ziuganov, leader of the Kommunisticheskaia Partiia Rossiiskoi Federatsii (KPRF), successor to the militantly atheist KPSS), would have won the presidential elections, had not both Russian oligarchs and the West heavily supported El'tsin for a second term (Reddaway and Glinski 2001; Freeland 2005; Klein 2007: 224, 232). Even if the transition from Soviet to post-Soviet Russia was politically smooth and relatively non-violent, socio-economically it was very violent and went squarely against the will of the majority of Russians:

> It would be wrong to assert that Russians turned away from Gorbachev's liberal-democratic project because of some innate authoritarianism. It was, rather, the sharp pain of losing the entire social safety net and the established communal identity while elites shamelessly enriched themselves that turned people away from the liberal program that promised but did not deliver. (Savranskaya 2019: 87)

Since the failure of the liberal-democratic project, both *'liberal'* and *'demokrat'* have become words of abuse in everyday Russian.

The Soviet Union fell apart in December 1991. Contrary to the former countries of the 'Eastern bloc' and the non-Russian ex-Soviet republics, 'Russia lacked a myth of national liberation capable of explaining the essence of the post-communist transition' (Solovey 2019: 160). Post-Soviet Russia could only engage in self-critique and soul-searching, and while these did take place massively and at high debate temperature, the need to create a new Russia with, largely, the same geographical, human and economic material as the RSFSR became a priority and, along with it came the demand for a new 'idea'. The intellectual debate was dominated by positions that had taken shape during the 1968–86 period.

In philosophy, too, there was no 'de-sovietisation' (DeBlasio 2014: 155–6; Scherrer 2003: 8; Evlampiev 2014: 13). Three different strands had crystallised in political-philosophical thought, all three suppressed and denied legitimacy by the handmaid of the regime: official Marxist–Leninist philosophy. These were non-official Marxism, liberalism and Christian thinking, each a continuation of pre-Soviet currents (Meerson-Aksënov and Shragin 1977: 14–15). Once the covering lid of official philosophy had been lifted, these currents came to the fore more clearly, each with its internal opposition: dogmatic Marxism versus revisionism, classical liberalism versus neoliberalism and traditional religious philosophy versus religious nationalism. This chapter discusses them in that order. To these three post-Soviet continuations, we can add early enemies of the Bolsheviks, such as anarchism and syndicalism (Dam'e 2009: 203), previously decried 'bourgeois' currents departing from Foucault (Podoroga 1993) and many others (Ackermann et al. 1995). In the long run, the 1990s will be remembered important as a period of mindboggling pluralism of positions and outlets (van der Zweerde 1997a).

The Baby and the Bathwater: Coming to Terms with Marxism–Leninism

When it comes to the fate of the official philosophy of the Soviet regime, a distinction must be made between the liberation from this hegemonic philosophical system, and the attempts to liberate that system itself by undoing dogmatism. Philosophical culture in the USSR after 'destalinisation' consisted of a complex network of niches inhabited by a few pre-revolutionary philosophers such as Losev, a number of unorthodox 'creative' Marxists, scholars working in fields like mathematical logic or semiotics, a few more or less explicitly religious thinkers, and large numbers of historians of philosophy. Absent from this list is 'political philosophy' in any explicit sense – which means that we have to look for its implicit manifestations. The fact that explicitly political philosophy was off limits reflects how philosophy as such was politically sensitive. All philosophy was political philosophy in the third sense distinguished in this study, while political philosophy in the first sense was non-existent, and philosophy in the second sense could be found in unexpected places like history of philosophy (Ryklin 2019: 10; van der Zweerde 2021b: 86–8).

Borders between professional philosophy and dissident thought were fluid and permeable. Three ideal-typical dissident positions are exemplified by Aleksandr Aleksandrovich Zinov'ev (1922–2006), Aleksandr Isaevich Solzhenitsyn (1918–2008) and Andrei Dmitrievich Sakharov (1921–89). For Zinov'ev, the Soviet system was essentially a perverted bourgeois society that, instead of a New Man, had created the pitiable *homo sovieticus* (Zinov'ev 1986). For the conservative *neopochvennik* and Russian nationalist Solzhenitsyn, a former GULag inmate, the system was intrinsically wrong on moral and spiritual grounds with its enforced collectivism, militant atheism and fake internationalism. For Sakharov and other 'liberal-democratic' opponents, the USSR could be a liveable society if only it functioned according to its own rules, in particular its constitution, which, on paper, granted full political, civil and socio-economic rights.

Zinov'ev qualified his 1978 exile as 'a punishment for a crime that we had not committed' (Zinov'ev 2019: 380). He engaged in a minute analysis of the workings of power and ideology in the USSR, paying equal attention to theory, praxis and *poièsis*: 'He regards ideology (including the ideological *apparat*) as having four main functions' (Kirkwood 1993: 162). The first was 'to acquaint citizens with the officially recognised ideological doctrine, to force them [. . .] to accept it. [. . .] This [. . .] acceptance must be regularly and publicly exhibited.' The second function is 'to monitor everything which goes on in the cultural sphere'. The third is 'to interpret everything that happens in the world [. . .] in the light of the fundamental principles of the ideology'. And fourth, 'perhaps its most important function is to coerce citizens into being [. . .] active, creative participants in all sorts of ideological spectacles at all levels of society' (ibid.: 162). The point was not sincere conviction: 'We note again that *belief* in the ideology is not required' (ibid.: 162). Not unlike Orthodox Christianity, Soviet ideology was more about orthopraxis – doing and saying the right things at the right moment – than about orthodoxy – having the right conviction.

In a contribution to *Iz-pod glyb* [From Under Rubble] (1974), Solzhenitsyn made 'national rebirth' dependent on a process of repentance and self-limitation [*raskaianie i samoogranichenie*] of the Russian nation. In passing, he referred, with a whiff of wishful thinking, to other nations, such as 'the British, French and Dutch peoples [who] as a whole bear the guilt [*vina*] (and marks on their souls [*v dushe svoei sled*]) for the colonial policies of their governments' (Solzhenitsyn 1974: 121/ 1975: 111). Reminiscent of Solov'ëv, Solzhenitsyn's claim was not limited to Russia: 'Mystically welded together in a community of guilt, a nation is also [like an individual, EvdZ] inescapably directed towards the inescapability of common repentance' (ibid.: 123 / 113; Mahoney 2001: 53). Twenty-four years after its publication, in 1998, he considered this as 'one of his most important articles, expressing one of his key thoughts' (Mahoney 2001: 100). Solzhenitsyn's key objective, the recovery of the nation's soul, assumes that nations exist and have souls that must be balanced with the body politic. This is, essentially, a depoliticising move typical of many dissidents: the 'element of "spiritualism" or "angelism" in Solzhenitsyn's political reflection' is comparable to '[Vaclav] Havel's expectation that the "apolitical politics" of the dissident experience can define the functioning political life of a modern commercial republic' (ibid.: 55).

The positions of dissidents often went in opposite directions, reviving oppositions like that between 'Westernisers' and 'Slavophiles', as the debate between Sakharov and Solzhenitsyn in the 1970s testifies. After Sakharov, in his 1971 *Memorandum*, had called upon the Soviet leadership to engage in a policy of liberalisation and democratisation along 'Western' lines, Solzhenitsyn, in his 1973 *Letter to the Soviet Leaders*, pointed out the crisis of the liberal West and called for a primarily spiritual renaissance of Russia (Vaissié 1999: 224–36). The liberal Sakharov and the anti-liberal Solzhenitsyn demonstrate that, indeed, 'not all who struggle against illiberal regimes are themselves liberals' because they are 'men and women who simply love freedom and know more about it than we could understand' (Nathans 2019: 65). Official Soviet ideology 'recognised no space for "non-political" ideas or activities' (ibid.: 67), and Soviet reality did not have a legitimate arena for the articulation of the political anyway. This is why the insistence by *pravozashchitniki* [right / law defenders, often mistranslated as 'human rights activists' (Horvath 2005: 84)] 'that their activities were out-side of politics' (Nathans 2019: 67) is precisely what made them political. The joint strategy of not violating Soviet laws and calling upon the regime to respect its own Constitution was, indeed, a 'méthode infaillible' invented by the dissidents (Eltchaninoff 2016: 16; Nathans 2019: 64), but it was far from non-political. The prin-ciple of rule of law is a political principle, and the manifest con-tradiction between the Soviet Constitution and the policies of the regime is a political contradiction. The dissidents who confronted an oppressive regime that they perceived in terms of the opposi-tions of evil and good, lie and truth, tended towards a moral con-ception in which political conflict is identified with evil and lie, not with difference between *prima facie* legitimate positions, priorities and interests. The shared political philosophy of the dissidents was not limited to claiming constitutionally granted rights such as free-dom of speech or demonstration. It also entailed the notion of a moral responsibility of both politicians and intellectuals, a legacy which, of course, has not lost any of its relevance and is, obviously, not limited to Russia (Osipov 2014: 243–4, 259).

Meanwhile, official Marxist–Leninist ideology, hollow and mouldy, still dominated discursive space, filling thousands of pages, demanding enormous amounts of intellectual energy and perpetu-ating the form of a single, all-encompassing true doctrine. In the late 1980s, however, this constellation imploded: the system acted as the constitutive other for public opinion, and while opinions with respect to the future differed, the rejection of the past was quasi-universal (Kabakov 1988). Arguably, Gorbachëv and his ideologues could not have done it right: 'The introduction of *glas-nost'* and the fragmentation of the monolithic power system [. . .] turned out to be highly potent forces for destruction of the Com-munist order' (Kirkwood 1993: 229). To use Marx's metaphor, Soviet-style socialism had both dug its own grave and yielded its own gravediggers. These came in three groups – dissidents, *maf-fiosi* and reformers – and the forces set free to reform the system turned out to be destructive ones (Shlapentokh 2001: 179–80).

Reformers disagreed about whether the system was actually dead: Gorbachëv's programme of, first, acceleration [*uskorenie*] and democratisation, and then *perestroika* [reconstruction], *glasnost'* and new thinking [*novoe myshlenie*] aimed at profound reconstruc-tion of the system in order to preserve it (Gorbachëv 1987; Sauvé 2019: 146–50). A key figure in the attempt to give socialism a restart was Ivan Timofeevich Frolov (1929–99), a philosopher of science who focused on complex global problems, approaching them in a spirit of science-based humanism oriented on the realisation of what he called 'the global triad of present and future: the human being, humankind, humanity [*chelovek, chelovechestvo, chelovechnost'*]' (Frolov 1989: 29–30). Unfolding a grand vision for Russia and the world, taking along ecological and global interdependency and inviting the cooperation of others, Frolov remained silent in the field of political philosophy. Instead, the call to engage in 'new thinking' placed full emphasis on the cognitive side of politics (good governance, management, expertise, technocracy and so on) at the expense of the properly political: that is, potentially conflictual dimensions. A philosophical conception of politics was lacking, as was an understanding of why, if humankind could know which way to go, it was not already going there.

Apart from the publications by Frolov and other *perestroika* ideologues, the late Soviet period yielded a bulky collection of essays under the exemplary title *Inogo ne dano* (Afanas'ev 1988), translatable as *Nothing Else is Given*, but also as *There Is No Alternative* (TINA). In fact, there was an alternative: namely, the end of KPSS rule and the breakdown of the Soviet system. The realisation of that alternative in 1991 put an end to the marriage of the existing regime and the Marxist–Leninist ideology by which it claimed to be guided. While this divorce meant the sudden death of Marxism–Leninism, it also implied the unemployment of thousands of teachers of Marxist–Leninist philosophy, as well as the emancipation of Marxism from its role as handmaid of the official ideology. The ensuing Marxism debate contained many questions: could Marxism be identified with Marx? Was Marxism–Leninism the only true form of Marxism? Should Marx(ism) be held responsible for 'real existing socialism' in the USSR (Butenko 1989)? Was Soviet socialism the application of Marxism (Iakovlev 1993)? Could Marxism outlive *perestroika* (Nikiforov 1990)?

Obviously, Marx was not a Marxist (Mezhuev 2007), any more than Plato was a Platonist or Arendt an Arendtian: the thought of a philosopher contains more possibilities than any -ism can capture. Marx himself claimed to offer hypotheses, was open to criticism, and showed his readiness to revise his theory, including the possibility of socialism on an agrarian basis. Application of the basic Marxist scheme of socio-economic basis, juridical–political superstructure and corresponding societal forms of consciousness yields the following picture of a *perestroika* that, in Zinov'ev's famous words, ended in a *katastroika* (Kirkwood 1993: 196–220). First, a run-down economy was fragmentised and privatised at dazzling speed, a process that Russians at the time called '*prikvatizatsiia* [grabbing]'. Second, the new political system combined an 'imported model' of liberal democracy, with its multi-party system and rule of law [*gospodstvo zakona*], with the authoritarianism of El'tsin's neoliberal shock-therapists. Third, a broad range of opinions and ideologies pointed to an equally broad range of possible roads to salvation.

During this period, a soft-Gramscian notion of civil society, conceived as a sphere of voluntary association separate from both state and market, gained prominence in the 1980s and 1990s, thanks to authors like Ernest Gellner, and Jean L. Cohen and Andrew Arato (Gellner 1994; Cohen and Arato 1992). This notion of civil society [*grazhdanskoe obshchestvo*] was enthusiastically received in Russia and became a major organiser of philosophical debate (Khoros et al. 1998; Kharkhordin 1998; van der Zweerde 1996, 1998, 1999). Key to this debate, within a post-Marxist framework, was the rehabilitation of civil [*grazhdanskoe*] over bourgeois [*burzhuaznoe*] society, splitting up what Hegel and Marx had conflated into the single notion of *bürgerliche Gesellschaft*.[1] Next to the idealisation of civil society, part of the Soviet legacy was the politically naïve idea that the bureaucratic state could be a neutral instrument of a ruling elite (repeating the Bolshevik position of 1917), as well as the concept that ideology could change from being a set of 'responsive' forms of consciousness into a guiding light for the realisation of a new programme. If Gorbachëv had wrongly assumed that his 'new thinking' would become a material force by 'capturing the masses', the neoliberal reformers of the early 1990s wrongly believed that they could bypass the state's apparatuses. Common to both is an underestimation of the importance of political *poièsis*: making good laws and functioning institutions.

One major hurdle in the process of coming to terms with Marxism–Leninism was its alleged materialist character. Soviet ideology relied on an idealism that suggested that the 'right' ideas – historically right and confirmed by science – would guide the Soviet people and the rest of humanity to a bright communist future. The smooth replacement, in curricula and departments, of disciplines like Marxist–Leninist philosophy or scientific communism with so-called *kul'turologiia* [cultural studies] was not a matter of turning a Marxist paradigm upside down, but of substituting a 'cultural-civilisational determinism [*kulturell-zivilisatorischer Determinismus*]' for the economic determinism of historical materialism (Scherrer 2003: 9). Marxian historical materialism, claiming to put Hegelian idealism 'back on its feet', had already been 'turned on its head' by Marxism–Leninism in its prospective, future-oriented role. *Kul'turologiia* was one of the candidates for filling the perceived 'ideological vacuum'. Key concepts, like nation, culture, civilisation, identity, modernisation, globalisation and so on, had to be redefined once their habitual interpretations had lost their credibility (ibid.: 8–20). Profoundly idealistic Soviet ideology was replaced by various forms of *kul'turologiia*: their task was to set new *vekhi* for a post-Soviet Russia.

The aforementioned edited volume *Inogo ne dano* of 1988 received a reply in 1995 in the form of *Inoe* [Something Else], three edited volumes plus a guide [*Putevoditel'*] of 1,400 pages in total (Chernyshev 1995: *Putevoditel'*, 24). If *Inogo ne dano* had been looking for a single alternative, *Inoe* rejected this very idea: 'An ideology in the traditional understanding of the term is the last thing that Russia needs today' (ibid.: 8). In 1988, plurality was seen as a potential problem; in 1995, it was celebrated in a spirit of pluralism. Gone was the sense that intellectuals had the responsibility of 'showing their nation the way' – the spectre traditionally haunting the Russian *intelligenty* (Novikova and Sizemskaia 1993). Such pluralism, however, contrasted with a perceived 'ideological vacuum'.

Metaphors can mislead: there cannot be an ideological 'vacuum' because symbolic-discursive space, contrary to physical space, does not have a fixed size that can be filled or not filled. It expands and shrinks with the content that fills it. The fact that Marxist–Leninist ideology had been massively present as the constitutive other of various counter-ideologies led to a widely felt need for a new 'Russian idea'. In 1992, a conference was organised by the Gorbachëv Foundation around 'the Russian idea and Russia's new statehood [*novaia rossiiskaia gosudarstvennost*]' (Gulyga 1995: 11; Maslin et al. 1992; Piskunov et al. 1994). In 1996, the El'tsin administration launched a call 'for a more balanced proposal' and a national newspaper organised a contest (Helleman et al. 2004: 19; Smith 2002: 158–72). Unsurprisingly, the result was neither 'what a nation thinks about itself in time', nor 'what God thinks about it in eternity' (Soloviev 1978: 83; Solov'ëv 1989: II, 220; Maslin et al. 1992: 187), but a multitude of opinions about what the single unifying idea should be.

The discussion around a 'Russian idea' touched upon a painful question: should such an idea be a *russkaia* or a *rossiiskaia ideia*? The first refers to an ethnic-national Russian identity that might exclude others; the second refers, more realistically, to the multi-ethnic and multi-religious Russian Federation in which roughly 80 per cent of the population is ethnically Russian (against a little over 50 per cent in the USSR), a figure that includes the many people of 'mixed' background as a result of intermarriage (Chubais 2017: 24). The second option, however, would not do justice to the widespread sentiment that ethnic Russians were the main victims of Soviet-style socialism. This sentiment was already articulated in 1974 by the prominent dissident Igor' Rostislavovich Shafarevich (1923–2017):

> In fact, *the basic features of national life in the USSR are a direct result of the hegemony in our country of socialist ideology. This ideology is the enemy of every nation, just as it is hostile to individual human personality.* [. . .] *The Russians no less than others are its victims; indeed, they were the first to come under fire.* (Shafarevich in *Iz-pod glyb* / *From Under the Rubble* 1974: 106 / 1975: 97; all italics in the original)

Twenty years later, Shaferevich's friend Solzhenitsyn wrote: 'It is old news today, and has been published many times, that the chief burden of the Soviet economic system was borne by the RSFSR' (Solzhenitsyn 1995: 83). With respect to both the Russian and the Soviet Empires, one cannot understand them, as Pierre-André Taguieff put it, 'if one does not take into account that Russia has "thought of itself as simultaneously colonised by the West and as a colonising power"' (Taguieff in Laruelle 2005: 11). Indeed, one of the paradoxical effects of ethnic-Russian prominence in the former USSR was that, contrary to Estonians, Ukrainians or Uzbeks, Russians did not 'have' a nominal republic; nor was there a Russian Communist Party, with its own Central Committee, apart from the CPSU (Alekseeva in Gay and Alekseeva 1994: 202–3). Apart from blaming 'the West', dissidents like Solzhenitsyn and especially Shafarevich tended to point to 'the Jews' as guilty standard-bearers of socialism, internationalism and cosmopolitanism. While Solzhenitsyn's *Dvesti let vmeste* [Two Hundred Years Together] does engage in essentialist 'Semitism' alongside an equally essentialist understanding of the Russian nation, he seeks nuance and ambivalently balances Judeophilia and anti-Semitism (Solzhenitsyn

2001–2; Larson 2005: 129–39). By contrast, Shafarevich's 1982 *Russofobiia* has been qualified as 'arguably the most influential anti-Semitic text since the *Protocols of the Elders of Zion*' (Horvath 2005: 6) and his 2002 *Trëkhtysiacheletniaia zagadka; tainaia istoriia evreistva* [A Three-Thousand Year Mystery: The Secret History of Jewry] did nothing to improve his reputation (Shafarevich 2019a, 2019b).

Liberalisms

In his preface to the two-volume *Rossiiskii liberalizm: idei i liudi* [Russian Liberalism: Ideas and People], liberal philosopher Aleksei Alekseevich Kara-Murza (b. 1956) proudly noted that in nearly forty regions of Russia, commemorative signs had been established for outstanding liberals who lived there (Kara-Murza 2018: I, 9). While this number will be outdone, for a long time to come, by the number of plaques commemorating the brief presence of Lenin in a particular building, it indeed points to a broad acceptance of the many representatives of liberalism in Russia: 'At the end of the 1980s, [. . .] for the first time in Soviet history [. . .], [L]iberal-minded people began to feel pride in their own country instead of the previous feelings of shame' (Obolonsky 2019: 131). However, liberalism was as equivocal as it had been in the past. It had a positive ring for all those post-Soviet Russians who shared 'the intention to become as independent from the state as possible' (ibid.: 137). It also had a positive but more republican ring for those who wanted Russia to become a 'normal' liberal-democratic country and for whom Gorbachëv's *perestroika* programme, though a welcome break with the Soviet past, did not go far enough. Finally, it had a positive ring for those who wanted to privatise the economy. At the same time, it had a negative ring for those who anticipated a breakdown of traditional norms and values, opposed the rise of 'Western' individualism and libertarianism, or feared becoming victims of liberalisation and privatisation.

We witness a return of patterns known from the heyday of liberalism in Russia, with three main groups of liberals. First, there are those who, like Grigorii Iavlinskii (b. 1952) of the Iabloko Party, adhere to a liberal political ideology and who have the sympathy of parts of the critical intelligentsia. Second, there are the 'system liberals', a group within the Russian political and economic elite who are the main opponents of both the *siloviki* [literally: power-persons]: that is, the representatives of army, police and secret service, and the ideological hard-liners (Sauvé 2019: 151; Solovey 2019: 156–8; Melville 2019: 216–19). System liberals aim at legal and political reform, mostly using economic arguments; inviolable property rights, fair civil law, freedom to move and invest, absence of corruption, political reform, media pluralism and academic freedom are the logical next steps. Leaving details to the 'kremlin-ologists', it seems fair to suggest that the post-Soviet situation in Russia, marked by restricted political rights combined with high degrees of personal and 'consumer' freedom, reflects a balance between these two forces.

Third, and most relevant in the longer run, there is what Barabashev and Prokof'ev have labelled 'guild liberalism', the *philosophie spontanée* of professionals that is comparable with the liberalism of the *zemstvo* employees of the nineteenth century. The constituency of this type of liberalism is the professional networks and expert communities in governance, public administration, management, education, health care and so on. 'Guild liberals' are people who cannot do what they are supposed to do unless they have a considerable degree of freedom to share their experiences and concerns with their colleagues' (Barabashev and Prokofiev 2019: 166–9, 185–8). This trend also fits Solzhenitsyn's advocacy of a 'democracy of small areas', calling for a revival of the *zemstvo* as the traditional Russian form of local self-government (Solzhenitsyn 1991: 71, 75–80). While liberals traditionally were more committed to top-down liberalisation, following the Petrine model, it was the conservative nationalist Solzhenitsyn who emphasised the importance of local self-government (Fediashin 2012: 203; Mahoney 2001: 179–80).

Russia's short-lived liberal-democratic euphoria coincided, not accidentally, with a return of the idea of a global liberal-democratic hegemony. As the Soviet bloc fell apart, Francis Fukuyama revitalised Kojève's thesis about the 'end of history' by suggesting that 'the current worldwide liberal revolution' (Fukuyama 1992: 208; Fukuyama 1990), combining economic liberalism, equal rights for all and universal mutual recognition, might yield a universal and homogeneous state of the type Kojève had projected and towards which state-run socialism was just an alternative route: 'Though the Bolshevik and Chinese revolutions seemed like monumental events at the time, their only lasting effect would be to spread the already established principles of liberty and equality to formerly backward and oppressed peoples' (ibid.: 66). Fukuyama's position, which he later abandoned, was challenged by Russian thinkers (Migranian and Fukuyama 1992; Zamoshkin 1990).

One of them, Tat'iana Aleksandrovna Alekseeva (b. 1947), connected to mainstream Western political philosophy in an attempt to move beyond Cold War oppositions as well as liberal triumphalism. While the Soviet system had, allegedly, been determined by philosophy in the shape of dogmatic Marxism–Leninism, post-Soviet Russia tended to disregard, according to Alekseeva, political theory and philosophy altogether. Invoking, of all people, Lenin's arch-enemy Plato as saying that neglect of philosophy by politicians signified 'complacent ignorance [*samodovol'noe nevezhestvo*]', she sided with John Rawls in claiming that, in order to 'enter world civilisation', Russia would need three combined perspectives: that of the politician who looks ahead to the next elections, that of the statesman who looks as far as the next generation, and that of the philosopher who looks at the indeterminate future [*neopredelënnoe budushchee*] (Alekseeva 2000: 3, 15). Prolonged cooperation with William Gay yielded an advocacy of 'capitalism with a human face' as an alternative to the failed humanist socialism of the *perestroika* ideologues (Gay and Alekseeva 1995).

Dismantlement of the common cultural and socio-economic space urged those who had initially supported *perestroika* and democratisation to shift from the Fukuyamean 'end of history' paradigm to schemes that resembled the Huntingtonian paradigm of clashing civilisations. This paradigm also offered new constitutive others. Erstwhile liberal Aleksandr Sergeevich Panarin (1940–2003), a political philosopher of fame (Il'in and Panarin 1994), revitalised the idea of a continuity between Russian Empire, Soviet Union and a new Eurasian block largely covering the same territory (Laruelle 2012: 86–101). Panarin developed this idea in a number of articles collected as '*Vtoraia Evropa' ili 'Tretii Rim'?* [Second(ary) Europe or Third Rome?], answering the question with a clear 'neither of the two' (Panarin 1996: 130–3, 136–7):

> There is an alternative. It is connected to the Eurasian idea. The paradox of that idea is that, while it comes forward as tougher with regard to the West [. . .], it averts a clash of Russia with the West, directing it [Russia, EvdZ] to the East, to its habitual civilisational niche. (ibid.: 138)

Countering Fukuyama with *Revansh istorii* [History's Revenge] (Panarin 1998), Panarin detected a 'spirit of Enlightenment (or more deeply – Christian) universalism' in both the Kojèvian idea of a universal homogeneous state and the idea of a convergence towards a 'single industrial society' (ibid.: 131). An identification of Russia with its position as 'Third Rome' would only lead to a confrontation, while an identification with Eurasia would allow Russia to retain its own 'Enlightenment tradition' without 'Byzantine revision' (ibid.: 138–9). Eurasianism and an identification with what Huntington, around the same time, identified as an 'Orthodox civilisation' (Huntington 1998: 26–7, 162–8, 270–2) are at odds with the universalism of both liberalism and Christianity. The latter points to an ambiguity in Orthodox Christianity.

Russian Religious-Philosophical Revivalism

Marx's famous qualification of religion as the 'opium of the people [*Opium des Volkes*]' is often misread as 'opium for the people [*Opium für das Volk*]' (*MEW*: I, 378). The suggestion of a 'conspiracy' of priests as an integral part of bourgeois-capitalist society, meant to keep the exploited and oppressed voluntarily obedient in this valley of tears by promising an after-life of equality and justice, has suited the anti-religious agendas of Bakunin and the Bolsheviks. Rather than mocking a long history of wishful misreading, it is fruitful to develop the idea further. In any society marked by domination and exploitation (that is, all societies thus far), there is a systemic demand for 'opium' and religion is one of the providers. Arguably, Marxism itself played the role of 'opium of the intellectuals' with, like any *pharmakon*, the double function of poison and medicine. The fact that religion generally, and Christianity in particular, has much to offer on this front implies neither that religion is the only 'pusher' in this respect, nor that this is all there is to say about religion. Christian political philosophy with its revolutionary and reconciliatory potential is a major case in point.

During Soviet times, organised religion had been suppressed with varying degrees of intensity but it was never fully eradicated, and it retained its function as a spiritual escape from the hardships of everyday life and as a refuge of conscience. Under extreme conditions, such as GULag or the Leningrad blockade, religion quickly regained relevance and respect, and a substantial part of camp, underground and dissident culture in the USSR was of a religious orientation (Meerson-Aksënov 1977: 505–81; Ellis 1986: 287–454; Goricheva 1985: 42–3; Horvath 2005; Boobbyer 2005). While religion was connected to moral and political resistance against the regime, the ROC as an institution was, simultaneously, closely linked to Soviet power. Its rehabilitation in 1943 was not only profoundly instrumental in nature, but it also went along with renewed suppression, infiltration and surveillance: 'The number of Russian Orthodox clergymen repressed in 1943 totalled more than 1,000, and half of them were shot. From 1944 to 1946, more than 100 executions took place each year' (Iakovlev 2002: 165). The ROC's KGB-infiltrated 'Golden Cage [*zolotaia kletka*]' was a privileged prison: privileged in relation to other religions, and especially to other Christian denominations, but imprisoned by its imposed service to state and party (Ellis 1986: 250–81). The popular perception of Stalin as a 'saviour' of the ROC has to be taken with a big pinch of salt (Kostriukov 2017: 225; Iakovlev 2002: 168).

One effect of *perestroika* was the liberation of religion generally, and of the ROC in particular. The protagonists of a reformed, humanist socialism were not themselves religious but they were not 'militantly atheist' like their predecessors. The millennial year 1988, a thousand years after the baptism of Kievan Rus', marked a fundamental change. Not only did the authorities facilitate the celebration itself, but church property was returned, and the Gorbachëv administration passed a law on Freedom of Conscience in 1990 which liberated the entire religious field. Since the dissolution of the USSR in 1991, the Russian Federation has been a secular state with constitutionally warranted freedom of religion. However, a 1997 'Law on Freedom of Conscience and Religious Organisations' pinpointed four traditional religions in Russia: Judaism, Islam, Buddhism and Christianity, ascribing special significance to Orthodoxy as a defining factor in Russia's cultural heritage.[2] While the ROC shuns state church status, it does opt for a 'neo-symphonic' division of labour between powers ecclesiastical and civil. If the church is a main voice in the fields of morality and spirituality, while the state takes care of public order and security, then together they stand for a strong and united Russia (Papkova 2011; Richters 2014). Moreover, the state protects the traditional religions against propaganda, proselytism and evangelisation by other than traditional denominations, 'new religious movements' and (neo)paganism.

In line with this religious revival, the 1990s witnessed a striking popularity of the notion of *sobornost'*, the 'harmonious spiritual community', as Sergei Sergeevich Horujy (1941–2020) called it (Horujy 2017: 349). Much of *sobornost'* discourse was distinctively nostalgic and infatuated, referring either to a better version of

Soviet collectivism or to a transformation of society into a religious community. These are two perspectives which equally disregard the ontological distance between societal actuality and spiritual potential, the first by denying it, the second by stepping over it in real time. Arguably, both communism and *sobornost'* should remain what they essentially are: ideas, not blueprints; concepts, not ideologies. Still, Christian political philosophy organised around the notion of *sobornost'* has found many serious advocates, both in Russian Orthodox circles and in Orthodox Christianity globally (Papanikolaou 2012; Stoeckl 2008; Roudometoff et al. 2005; Demacopoulos and Papanikolaou 2017: 1–58).

There is, in opposition to the official position of the ROC, which seeks state protection in order not to end up as 'one among many voices in a pluralistic public space' (Papanikolaou 2012: 94; *Osnovy* I.4 / Thesing and Uertz 2001: 14–15), a strong current within Orthodox Christianity that moves out of an imperial and authoritarian paradigm towards a communitarian one that often includes partial acceptance of pluralist liberal democracy. Its communitarian orientation, theorised as a reformulation of *sobornost'*, often sees individualist liberalism as its main opponent while fully appreciating the opportunities that a 'post-secular' environment offers public religion. This breaks through the Huntingtonian exclusion of Orthodoxy, along with Islam, from Western civilisation, and invites a new confrontation between tradition and modernity (Leustean 2014: 98–9; Roudometoff et al. 2005). However, like liberalism and Christianity (and Islam) generally, Orthodox Christianity prioritises the moral over the political. Any 'ethics first' approach tends towards limited recognition of the political as something to be overcome in principle, even if in practice this will never happen. It tends to regard the political community either as a realisation of social harmony, or as a necessary compensation for humans' sinful, fallen nature, or it combines those two perspectives by regarding the second as a pre-condition of the first, thus giving new currency to the concepts of 'deification [*theōsis*]' and 'theanthropy [*bogochelovechestvo*]': 'The political community is not the antithesis to the desert but one of the many deserts in which the Christian must combat the demons that attempt to block the learning of love' (Papanikolaou 2012: 4). This perspective can indeed imply acceptance of liberal democracy but precludes a positive appreciation of politics generally (ibid.: 56).

The revival of Russian religious philosophy in the 1990s posed two questions: can philosophy as such be 'religious', given the traditional opposition of philosophy and theology, and can Christian thought be 'Russian' in any significant sense of the word (DeBlasio 2014: 84–104)? One possible answer is that philosophy can be done within a religious or national context without losing its philosophical character, its being rooted in the unassisted human mind, as long as it addresses and then transcends its very own embeddedness. Interestingly, the revitalisation of modernising positions like those of Solov'ëv, Berdiaev or Bulgakov gradually gave way to more contemporary positions like that of Horujy, who engaged in dialogue with Michel Foucault, Gilles Deleuze and others, to rethink the human condition in a post-modern and post-Soviet reality (Scanlan 1994: 41–4; Stoeckl 2008: 137–50; Horujy 2015b). Horujy, like Merab Konstantinovich Mamardashvili (1930–90), the 'filmmaker's philosopher' (DeBlasio 2019), and Vladimir Veniaminovich Bibikhin (1938–2004), had kept a distance from both official Soviet philosophy and the dissident movement. Philosophers like these three are now among the most widely published and read. Paradoxically, their relevance for political philosophy is defined by their outsider position, in relation to both Marxism–Leninism and to the fashionable currents of the 1990s.

Conclusion

One clear effect of the Soviet period was the reduction of political arenas. Ideologically, the Soviet system relied on a projected future disappearance of societal conflict and politics alike, and it allowed for articulations of the political to a very limited extent only: discussions within the KPSS and in the margins of the academic system. The notions of political party, which suggests that different parts of society have different agendas, and of labour union, which presupposes possible conflict between employers and employees, had been neutralised and depoliticised by allowing only one. Other than that, there was only the private sphere, including the *kukhnia*, and isolated strikes and protests. Conflict exists in any society and it existed within the Party (between reformers, humanists, pragmatists, nationalists and so on), but it was, by default, illegitimate. The breakdown of the Soviet system thus signalled a liberation of the political. Since 1988, many antagonisms have come to the fore in post-Soviet Russian society but the political arena where they can be 'fought out' remains restricted. When Russians took to the streets, sometimes in unprecedentedly high numbers, they showed not only their opposition to the government, but also the absence of suitable political arenas apart from streets and squares. The rise of a neoliberal oligarchy, including business and media tycoons, has aggravated this situation.

The search for a 'new Russian idea' must be seen against this backdrop. It is tempting to ridicule deliberate 'identifications' and compare them with the pathetic attempts of the European Union at around the same time to forge a 'European identity'. During the El'tsin era, however, the search was for something to keep together a society that quickly fell apart under the impact of economic shock therapy. The 1990s in Russia are now generally framed as a period of crisis and chaos, including a perceived crisis of direction and identity. The choice, in this book, of the year 2000 as a point of transition is not meant to suggest that everything changed when Vladimir Putin rose to power, if only because his rise was orchestrated by El'tsin. However, if the 1990s were characterised by a plurality of answers to the question of Russia's place in the world and its identity, the 2000s saw the emergence of a clear perspective.

The forward perspective offered by the Putin and Medvedev administrations alleviated guilt issues and victim questions by presenting a new Russia with regained self-confidence, identified as European but not as Western. It reclaimed its position as a regional power, it identified with Russia's history, including the Soviet period, and acknowledged tragedies and mistakes (terror, deportations, GULag), but also emphasised its achievements (education, cosmonautics and the victory over Nazi Germany in the Great Patriotic War [*velikaia otechestvennaia voina*]). The newly forged Russian identity is more state-centred – *rossiiskii* – than ethnically Russian – *russkii* –, and multi-ethnic, yet with ethnic Russians as the dominant group. It also is multi-religious but identifies Orthodox Christianity as a major defining factor. The 1990s were, for the majority of Russians, a decade of uncertainty and of sometimes desperate searching for markers of certainty and identity: in other words, a search for *vekhi*. The year 2000, when Putin first became president, marks the transition to a situation in which a new *ordo ordinans*, made up of a neoliberal market economy dominated by oligarchs and a strong state with a heavily presidential system, proved itself stable for at least the next two decades. It is also the year when the ROC defined its relation to society and state in its *Social Doctrine* [*Osnovy sotsial'noi doktriny RPTs*] (*Osnovy* 2000 / Thesing and Uertz 2001). New *vekhi* were set.

Two decades under Presidents Putin, Medvedev and Putin again have changed the picture. They have turned Russia into a more affluent and more modern, but also more consumerist society than it has ever been; indeed, it is much more akin to its earlier opponent, the Western capitalist world. At the same time, those two decades have generated new markers of certainty. Russia knows its place in the world, knows its national interests and where it is going. It is aware that it has a great past, certainly including a number of black pages but without it being one big, black book. Political power is centralised and vertical, the country is run from the Kremlin, and the authorities are not there to be ridiculed. This Russia is ready to receive ideas from any corner of the world, including post-'68 French political philosophy, but it is not going to let anybody tell the Russian Federation, or its inhabitants, where to go, how to act or what to think. This 'new' and self-confident Russia, setting its own *vekhi*, is home to new developments in political philosophy, too.

Notes

1. In German, for the same reasons, *Zivilgesellschaft* was distinguished from *bürgerliche Gesellschaft*.
2. See http://pravo.gov.ru/proxy/ips/?docbody=&nd=102049359 (last accessed 7 July 2019]

Chapter 11

Political Philosophy for a New Russia – New Wine in Old Bottles?

Jailing punks and merry students for singing a little song breeds hatred and heroes. The punks and students become revolutionaries and philosophers.

Maksim Shevchenko, Russian state TV, 2012[1]

In early 2014, President Putin distributed as New Year presents editions of three books: Solov'ëv's *Opravdanie dobra* [Justification of the Good (1899) [Solovyov 1988 / 2005]], Berdiaev's *Filosofiia neravenstva* [The Philosophy of Inequality (1923) [Berdiaev 2004b / 2015]] and Il'in's *Nashi zadachi* [Our Tasks (1948–54) [Il'in 1993]] (Eltchaninoff 2015: 7; Laqueur 2015: 177). All along Russia's border, Europeans were eager to know what motivated the actions of the President of the Russian Federation. Michel Eltchaninoff's *Dans la tête de Vladimir Poutine* tried to meet this demand. Eltchaninoff saw continuity: 'The USSR was not a country, but a concept. In Putin's hands, Russia is once again the name of an idea' (Eltchaninoff 2015: 171 / 2018: 169). If this is true, then the quest for a new Russian idea that haunted Russian political philosophy in the 1990s has been answered by the current administration. In fact, the Russian government has several ideological constructions at its disposal: the *Realpolitik* framework of a regional power with global ambitions, the vision of a pan-Orthodox or pan-Slavonic world under Russian leadership that defends traditional values against Western liberalism, materialism and individualism, and the vision of a large Eurasian block between Europe, the Middle East and East Asia that acts as successor to the Russian Empire and Soviet Union.

Having, in the 1990s, licked its post-Soviet wounds, but also feeling betrayed by an at first welcoming but then excluding West, Russia entered a new era around 2000. Politically, this was the beginning of the Putin(–Medvedev) presidency. Socio-economically, it meant a rapid increase in the standard of living and the development of a consumers' society. Societally, it marked an improvement in services and public safety. Religiously, finally, it started with the ROC's affirmation of its position with a *Social Conception* (*Osnovy* 2000 / Thesing and Uertz 2001). Russia's current regime links an increasingly 'vertical' government, 'managed' civil society and 'sovereign' democracy with an economic oligarchy that fully participates in neoliberal global capitalism. The regime is authoritarian, not totalitarian: it does not pretend to transform Russian society. While it controls the mass media and suppresses serious political opposition, it tolerates a limited political pluralism, considerable academic freedom, an uncontrollable internet and marginal independent journalism (Slavtcheva-Petkova 2018). As a result, Russian citizens, less than half of whom remember the Soviet period, may rightly fear the strong arm of power, yet they feel free to speak and have become accustomed to unprecedented levels of personal freedom. Channels for the political articulation of societal antagonism are, however, lacking, which leads to political violence, at times massive demonstrations, and a broad range of forms of non-violent protest.

While liberalism is present in Russia in the form of neoliberal policies (privatisation, low flat-rate tax, unprotected labour market), the political environment is illiberal. Liberalism discredited itself in the 1990s and is no longer prominent as a political philosophy. If it ever existed, the hegemony of liberalism was short-lived, and Russia 'faced the phenomenon of "selective liberalism", where political liberalism was disjoined from economic liberalism' (Obolonsky 2019: 131). Liberalism is an equivocal term, but even Russian liberalism's traditional emphasis on positive liberty did not meet the demand for political and moral orientation. As a political current, liberalism is waiting for better times in two variants: the social liberalism of the politically marginal Iabloko Party, and the suppressed national liberalism of Aleksei Naval'nyi (b. 1976) and others (Laruelle 2019: 175–84). 'National' here means *russkii*, not *rossiiskii*, which Naval'nyi considers 'a "chimera" inherited from the El'tsin years' (ibid.: 183).

Rapid diversification of the fields of academic research, education and publication has occurred against the backdrop of combined institutional stability and socio-economic precarity. In this field, too, Russia has quickly overtaken developments elsewhere. As a separate discipline, political philosophy existed briefly at universities and at the Institute of Philosophy of the Russian Academy of Sciences [IF RAN] (with over 250 researchers probably the largest institution of its kind world-wide). The major philosophical journals, *Voprosy filosofii* (f. 1947), *Filosofskie nauki* (f. 1958) and *Logos* (f. 1991), frequently contain articles, reviews and 'round tables' in the field of political philosophy, and the bilingual St Petersburg-based journal *Stasis* (f. 2013) is largely dedicated to it. Besides these, the journals *Russian Studies in Philosophy* (f. 1962 as *Soviet Studies in Philosophy*, renamed 1992) and *Studies in East European Thought* (f. 1961 as *Studies in Soviet Thought*, renamed 1992) remain invaluable sources of both (translated) primary and secondary literature.

Additionally, the three post-Soviet decades have yielded a rich textual basis. Russian authors that were anathema during the Soviet period have been republished in enormous numbers since 1988, and much of twentieth- and twenty-first-century political philosophy is available in translation. It is easy to obtain major works by such authors as (following the Russian alphabet) Arendt, Butler, Virno, Hessen [Gessen], Dahl, Ellinek [Jellinek], Žižek, Zinov'ev, von Hayek [Khaek], Il'in, Collingwood, Lefort, Maritain, Novgorodtsev, Ostrogorskii, Popper, Rawls, Sloterdijk, Trubetskoi, Foucault [Fuko], Huntington [Khantington], Chicherin, Schmitt, Iurkevich and Jaspers. Soviet categories like 'for official use only [DSP: *dlia sluzhebnogo pol'zovniia*]' or '*spetskhran* [*otdel spetsial'nogo khraneniia*, the limited access part of library collections]' have disappeared, and censorship of books has been non-existent for thirty years.

This chapter cannot possibly aim at comprehensiveness. Instead, it selectively addresses a few cases, chosen on the basis of, on the one hand, the availability of translations and, on the other, the extent to which they demonstrate the continuation, in new forms, of earlier patterns. The cases are: the political-philosophical reception of Heidegger, the tension between religion and the political, the development of radical protest, and the revival of more distanced but not uncommitted political philosophy.

Much Ado About Heidegger

The reception of Heidegger in post-Soviet Russia highlights a watershed in political philosophy between attempts to provide Russia with a grand civilisational scheme in the tradition of

Danilevskii, Kojève, Fukuyama and Huntington, and the endeavour to contribute to contemporary philosophical debates generally and develop an independent position as a philosopher. At one end, the right-wing ideologist Aleksandr Gel'evich Dugin (b. 1962) developed a 'Fourth Political Theory', after the alleged failure of three earlier theories – namely, communism, fascism and liberalism – and integrating 'the closely related ideologies of National Bolshevism and Eurasianism' (Dugin 2012: 13, 33). For this 'Fourth Political Theory', based on a right-Schmittian understanding of the political and of politics, Dugin mobilised Heidegger by framing 'Dasein' as a free, self-determining historical subject (ibid.: 52–4; Dugin 2004). At the other end, Horujy and Bibikhin engaged with Heidegger in order to address key issues in social and political philosophy. As in Western academia, the 'dark' sides of Heidegger were addressed in Russia in the wake of Victor Farías's well-known book,[2] and the publication of the *Schwarze Hefte* [*Chërnye tetrady*] (Laruelle and Faye 2018). Nelli Vasil'evna Motroshilova (1934–2021), in 1989, rightly expanded 'the most important question of the "Heidegger case": what led him to Nazism, and how?' into the 'more general question: if the alliance of a talented person, a genius even, with totalitarian power and with a misanthropic [*chelovekonenavistnicheskoi*], racist ideology proves possible, then how and why does such an alliance [. . .] arise and exist?' (Motroshilova 2013: 463).

Martin Heidegger, arguably the philosophically most apolitical and politically most controversial of all twentieth-century European philosophers, provoked profound controversy in Russia. While his double guilt (persistent anti-Semitism and support for the Nazi regime) merges for Western observers, it confronts Russian philosophers in a complicated way. Nazism was the arch-enemy of the USSR, which it defeated in 1945, but anti-Semitism is a recurrent problem in Russian history (Ehrenburg and Grossman 2009: v–xii) and Russia struggles with its own totalitarian past. In Soviet times, Heidegger was portrayed as a Nazi supporter and bourgeois subjective idealist in encyclopaedia entries by specialist Piama Pavlovna Gaidenko (1934–2021) (Gaidenko in Konstantinov et al. 1960–70: V, 426–8; Averintsev et al. 1989: 721–2). At the same time, Heidegger's thought was a forbidden fruit, circulating in unofficial translations.

Dugin's map of a 'multi-polar world' matches Huntington's map of a 'world of civilisations' (Dugin: 2014a: 57–8; Huntington 1998: 26–7). Additionally, Dugin links a Heideggerian 'liberation of Dasein' to a future 'trajectory of the approaching *Ereignis* (the "Event"), which will embody the triumphant return of Being' (Dugin 2012: 29). Such immediacy excludes mediation, which explains Dugin's lashing out against Hegel, the champion of mediation (ibid.: 38). This distinguishes Dugin from Il'in, who also advocated 'a "return" to Being [*"vozvrashcheniia" k bytiiu*]' (Evlampiev 2014: 69), but whose right-Hegelian position implied the idea of a strong, sovereign state that embodies the inevitability of mediation.

Politics, for Il'in, was about limiting violence, a contrast with Dugin's infamous 'I believe that one should kill, kill, and kill. I am saying this as a professor' (Leggewie 2016: 62). Violence is needed to break Western hegemony, which in turn is needed to allow Russia to manifest itself. Here, Dugin attacks Putin, arguing that he sticks to the formal, 'European' dimension of statehood and avoids engaging with 'any level of substance':

> The primary, formal characteristic of a government is its sovereignty. Putin is ready to defend it, but the idea that Russia should have some sort of mission or purpose aside from its technical effectiveness [. . .] has not yet taken root. (Dugin 2014c: 251)

Such a 'mission or purpose' would both answer Hegel's question about Russia's world-historical role and finish the Heideggerian job that Nazi Germany had failed to accomplish: the liberation of Being. Heidegger's own statements concerning Russia's future inspired Dugin:

> The History of the future of the earth is contained in the essence of Russianness [*Russentum*], which has not yet been freed to itself. [. . .] Russia – that we [*sic!*] may [. . .] free it to its essence and open it to the breadth of its suffering as to the essentiality of an essential salvation of the earth. (Love 2017: 258)[3]

Heidegger's 'requiem for Western philosophy' ended in nihilism (Dugin 2014b: 31). This may be a trauma for Western philosophy, but for Russia it means a liberation and an opportunity 'not only for confronting but also for overcoming the impact of Hegel and Marx', opening up 'possibilities for thinking in different ways that seem foreclosed to Western thinkers far too entrenched in their own tradition to see clearly outside of it' (Love 2017: 256, 268).

Of course, such a liberation does not necessarily point to a 'global' conception like Dugin's. If the metaphysical idea of a Russian idea, introduced by Dostoevsky in 1862 (Chubais 2017: 25), was of Western origin, then Heidegger's 'metaphysicide' puts an end to the very idea that each nation or civilisation embodies an idea, that these ideas manifest themselves one after another in human history, and that Russia must yet find, determine and express its own idea (DeBlasio 2014: 105–16).

The opposite of a monological 'ideology' à la Dugin is the possibility of an 'event of truth' in the plural: that is, of 'free philosophical speech' or *parrhèsia* (Pavlov 2019: 143–4). Entitled almost identically, Dugin's *Martin Khaidegger: filosofiia drugogo nachala* [Martin Heidegger: The Philosophy of Another Beginning] (2010 / 2014) and Bibikhin's *Drugoe nachalo* [Another Beginning] (2017b / 2020) discuss Heidegger at length but move in opposite directions (Laruelle et al. 2018: 7–8). Bibikhin, translator of *Sein und Zeit* into Russian, highlights Heidegger's analysis of human being-in-the-world [*in-der-Welt-sein*] as always-already a being-(there-)with-others [*Mit(da)sein*] (Bibikhin 2017a: 299). With Bibikhin, we enter the field of being-in-communion as one possibility among others, limited not to fellow human beings but, more generally, to 'fellow forms of being-(t/)here' including other than human forms, linking it to the notion of Sophia in one of his major works, *Les (hulè)* [Wood (Matter)] (Bibikhin 2011 / 2021; Magun in Bibikhin 2021: x).

For Horujy, like Bibikhin a pupil of Losev, Heidegger was a contrast, rather than a direct influence (Horujy 2017: 325–7). He linked a post-modern argument from Heidegger to a pre-modern argument derived from the hesychast thinker Gregory of Palamas (Laruelle et al. 2018: 7, n. 2; Horujy 2015a). Generally, Horujy distinguished two trends in 'the current philosophical situation' (which, for him, is not restricted to Russia): namely, 'de-ontologisation and re-ontologisation', corresponding to denial or acceptance of ontological difference – which is another way of rejecting Dugin's immediacy (Horujy 2017).

Both Horujy and Bibikhin leave behind Dugin's Russocentric obsession with historical and geopolitical development. With Horujy, the primary political question is not how to shape Russia's future, but how to give a place to human '*expérience-limite*' (Horujy 2017: 330). This 'extreme human experience' comes in three 'extreme anthropological manifestations [*predel'nye antropologicheskie proiavleniia*]', which share the notion of 'unlocking [*razmykanie*]' that Horujy links to Heidegger's *Erschliessung* in *Sein und Zeit* (Horujy 2015b: 123 / 2010: 627; Horujy 2017: 331). The first manifestation, the 'Ontological Human (constituted in the ontological unlocking)', derives from the hesychast tradition, where it signifies the synergic encounter of human and divine energy opening 'the way to their perfect union, *theosis*' (Horujy 2017: 330).

Although Horujy himself never emphasises the political dimension, it is easy to see the link with the traditional role of hesychasm as a critical undercurrent in Orthodoxy that rejects the divine imprimatur of worldly authorities. This becomes even clearer if we look at the other two manifestations, the 'Ontic Human (constituted in the unlocking of some ontic Other, for example, the unconscious)' and the 'Virtual Human (constituted in virtual anthropological practices)' (ibid.: 331–2). Heidegger's exclusive focus on the ontological dimension made him blind to harsh ontic reality. Horujy links Heidegger's ignorance of any other than 'ontological experience', his 'hard and uncompromising ontologism; hyper- or over-ontologism, if you will', directly to his blindness to the 'anthropological practices of Nazism' and the *'anthropological catastrophe'* of the Nazi mass murders (ibid.: 348–51). Highlighting Heidegger's claim that 'the Germans [. . .] represent a kind of anthropological avant-garde', Horujy quotes from his *Heraclitus* (1943–4): 'there is only the future, which is not decided yet, and we, the Germans, are the first and, very likely, the only ones for the long time to come, who can and must think towards it' (ibid.: 350). He ends with a harsh condemnation:

'I first saw Auschwitz a few years ago, when I was studying *Heraclitus* [Heidegger's, EvdZ]. And when I was standing in front of the famous gate with the slogan *Arbeit macht frei*, I had suddenly a clear impression that something was missing there. The Soviet past has firmly imprinted stereotypes of the totalitarian landscape in my consciousness, and I quickly realised that on either side of the gate there should be beautiful streamers with the words about the Noble Mission of the Germans. With Heidegger's words quoted above. (ibid.: 351)

Horujy and Bibikhin both seek a place within society for philosophy proper, Horujy reviving the centuries-old hesychast tradition of detached intellectual endeavour, Bibikhin tapping into the eternal dialectical opposition of philosophy and ideology. Dugin, by contrast, seeks to provide Russia with a positive ideology, thus marking a watershed in political philosophy that, in this case, is occasioned by the reception of a thinker like Heidegger. The 'event of truth' sought by philosophy is, at the same time, what ideology seeks to use as its basis, While ideology is always 'parasitic' in that respect, 'the driving motive of Bibikhin's thought [is] the desire to overcome ideology' (Pavlov 2019: 142).

Religion and Protest

In the course of history, the Russian Orthodox-Christian tradition has had an uneasy relationship with the powers-that-be: on the one hand, institutional subordination during the tsarist period, persecution and instrumentalisation during the Soviet period; on the other, brief periods of freedom (1917–18 and since 1988) and elements of protest like *iurodstvo* and political hesychasm, which stand for a distance between church and state. Elements of political hesychasm can be found in the ROC's official *Social Doctrine* (Petrunin 2009: 9; Payne 2011: 103). It emphasises the distinction between the Kingdom of God, for which the church stands and in which evil has been defeated, and 'this world', for which the secular state is responsible and in which it can do wrong:

> Since the state is part of 'this world', it does not participate in God's Kingdom, because there, where Christ is 'all and in all [*vsë i vo vsem*]' (Col. 3:11), there is no coercion and no opposition between the human and the Divine, and consequently, there also is no state. (*Osnovy* 2000: III.3 / Thesing and Uertz 2001: 24)

This implies the principle of disobedience [*nepovinovenie*]:

> If state power forces the Orthodox believers to deviate from Christ and His Church, and to engage in sinful, soul-harming [*dushevrednye*] deeds, the Church must refuse to obey the state [. . . and] appeal to its children [*chadam*] with a call for peaceful civil disobedience. (*Osnovy* 2000: III.5 / Thesing and Uertz 2001: 31)

Yet, the church reserves this disobedience as a right and duty to the church as a whole. By not granting it to individual believers, let alone clergy, the ROC combines acceptance of the actual political state of society with a ban on political participation of Orthodox clergy. Also, it mirrors the 'vertical' structure of the state rather than applying to itself a 'horizontal' principle of *sobornost'* (*Osnovy* 2000: III.4–7, IV.2–4; Hoppe-Kondrikova et al. 2013: 209–15).

In practice, there is little conflict between church and state. The ROC, led by Patriarch Kirill [Gundiaev] (b. 1946), and the government, led by President Putin (baptised secretly by the Patriarch's father), both occupy a pragmatic, intermediate position. In the case of the state, the extremes are nationalists, (neo)fascists and populists on the one hand, who focus on 'substance' and the Russian idea, and the liberal-democratic and (radical) left opposition on the other, who focus on 'form' and 'negative' liberty. In the case of the church, the excluded extremes are the obscurantist, chauvinistic and anti-Semitic wings and the liberal, ecumenical and universalist wings. Excluding the right implies rejection of xenophobia, ethnic hatred and aggressive nationalism, while exclusion of the liberal wing underpins the ROC's patriotism that relates both 'to the nation as an ethnic community and to the community of citizens' (*Osnovy* 2000: II.4 / Thesing and Uertz 2001: 19).

State and church today are not a single symphonic whole; nor is one subordinate to the other. Caesaropapism and tsarist autocracy, theocracy and ideocracy are repeated lessons from the past. State and church are distant from the explicitly 'symphonic' ideology of the KPRF, which claims to uphold Christian values and calls Jesus Christ the first communist in history. Keen on constructing a national-patriotic front, the KPRF rejects the 'myth that the communist ideology contradicts Christianity and demands the propagation of atheism' and claims their essential identity:

> The [. . .] values of a genuine [*nastoiashchee*] communist movement wholly coincide with the social values of Christianity, since the teaching of Christ from the very beginning rejected exploitation and private property: the first communes appeared precisely among the ancient Christians.[4]

The price for this sublation of the contrasting *Wahrheit und Lüge* [Truth and Lie] of communism that Berdiaev had highlighted is the denial of seven decades of persecution, suppression and subordination of the ROC by the KPSS (Grammatchikov 2017).

The politically dominant state–church alliance suppresses both serious political opposition and the critical political potential of religious traditions. In this context, a revival of *iurodstvo* can be noted. In one of her prison letters to Slavoj Žižek, trained philosopher Nadezhda Andreevna Tolokonnikova (b. 1989) explicitly referred to the holy fool Vasilios Blazhennyi: 'In the beating, political heart of civil Russia's capital city, at the site of Pussy Riot's January 2012 performance, at the base of Red Square, stands St. Basil's Cathedral, named after Russia's beloved Basil Fool for Christ' (Tolokonnikova and Žižek 2014: 42), to which Žižek replied: 'We should not be ashamed to evoke here, as you do, the tradition of the "fools for Christ"' (ibid.: 46). Whether their appeal to religion is 'genuine' or 'an intentional form of blasphemy and hooliganism' is impossible to judge (Gabowitsch 2017: 169) but, politically, this evocation means carving out a niche in a field of legitimate positions. The religious references of Pussy Riot are among the least understood among Western audiences. Paradoxically, many of those sympathetic to Pussy Riot's political protest share the ROC's diagnosis of their performance as being blasphemous, except that, from a post-Christian perspective, such 'blasphemy' directed against an allegedly archaic and reactionary institution is applauded.

Pussy Riot did not mock Orthodoxy but instead appealed to true religion, joining a long list of Russian religious philosophers and activists in unchaining the political potential of the Orthodox-Christian tradition. Pussy Riot's punk prayer used the symbol-heavy melody of Sergei Rakhmaninov's *Ave Maria* (Gabowitsch 2017: 165). As such, this points neither to seriousness nor to mockery, which is precisely the stance of the Holy Fool. The political question then becomes who decides about the status and authority that a Holy Fool embodies. At the end of the day, it matters little whether Tolokonnikova rightly claims a *iurodstvo* pedigree, nor whether *iurodstvo* is a genuine form of Christian piety or a remnant of paganism. What does matter is that Pussy Riot participates in a tradition that, from Avvakum to Mariia Vladimirovna Alëkhina (b. 1988), claims the positive liberty 'to speak truth to power'. The point, moreover, is not whether what they say is actually true or not, but that they articulate the political. In matters political, the primary distinction is not between truth and falsity, but between truths and lies. A plurality of outspoken truths points to the legitimacy of conflict between different points of view, priorities, visions, utopias and even interests.

Political Radicals

Russia appears to have a clear centre of political gravity, the Kremlin, around which other agents position themselves. Radical opponents, however, have understood Foucault and they know that power is present at the micro-level, too. The Soviet period, with its systemic and often excessive state violence, has made political protest culture in Russia largely non-violent (Gabowitsch 2013: 268–9, 2017: xi). Often, it is outright funny, engaging in 'laughtivism' by staging, for example, LEGO-figurine demonstrations (Popović 2015: 118–21). Peaceful protest is perceived as legitimate by many people, particularly when it is about concrete and local issues in, for example, the economic or environmental sphere (Arkhipova and Alekseevskii 2014: 291–326).

The massive protest waves in Russia in the early 2010s display two contrasts. One is that between the national and the global dimensions. The year 2011 saw massive non-violent protest in many places and over a great number of issues, from rigged elections to mushrooming bread prices. On the one hand, we must 'not throw together [. . .] and homogenise these very heterogeneous movements' (Mouffe 2013: 107), yet neither should we deny their many interrelations. We can relate them to global issues like migration, ecology, neoliberal economics and austerity measures. Moreover, contemporary media facilitate the adoption and adaptation of practices and repertoires across the globe, allowing the means of protest to travel along with their goals. As elsewhere, Russian protests manifested a combination of local and global topics and sentiments. Tolokonnikova explicitly takes her protest to the global level. Her 'think globally, act locally' points to glocality (Tolokonnikova 2018: 236; Roudometoff 2016). It is impossible to think truly globally because one always thinks from a specific conjuncture. However, it is also impossible to address political issues in local isolation, not only because every issue is connected to issues elsewhere, but also because the world is always watching and activism without a 'media strategy' has never existed – even *iurodivye* have always known about their audience.

A second, equally important, contrast is that between liberal and radical opposition. Richard Pipes already noted, referring to the nineteenth and early twentieth centuries, three positions, apart from those who directly support the regime: the liberal conservatives who aim at reform by the regime without changing it (Chicherin), the oppositional liberals who aim at replacing the administration, but not the regime (Struve) and the radicals (Lenin) who aim at fundamental regime change (Pipes 2005: xv). In contemporary Russia, the 'system liberals' who work within the state's institutions belong to the first group, Aleksei Naval'nyi to the second, and Pussy Riot to the third. Pussy Riot falls within the category of what Chicherin in 1862 labelled 'street liberalism [*ulichnyi liberalizm*]': 'The street liberal does not want to know anything except his own self-will [*svoevoliia*]' and 'cannot stand authority' (Chicherin 1998a: 464–5). When Tolokonnikova advocates 'floating by in a barrel, accepting nobody's authority' (Tolokonnikova and Žižek 2014: 40), one may add: except that of her own conscience and reason – as in the case of Bakunin. Today's opposition in Russia also refers to the dissidents of the

1970s and 1980s, including their non-violence, individualism, transparency and appeal to the authorities to respect their own law (Eltchaninoff 2016: 18, 22–3, 29–37; Vaissié 1999: 103; Chubais 2017).

Contrary to liberals, radicals will always politicise. Pussy Riot's Tolokonnikova rhetorically asked: 'Is what Pussy Riot does art or politics? For us it's one and the same – art and politics are insepa- rable. We try to make art political and at the same time enrich politics with developments from art' (Tolokonnikova 2018: 77). The point of political protest is not whether it 'works': it is about keeping alive the idea of alternatives and an awareness of the con- tingency and fragility of political order, and about speaking truth to power. This also applies to Pëtr Andreevich Pavlenskii (b. 1984). His *aktsiia 'svoboda* [freedom]' against the tension between Russia and Ukraine in 2014 was performed on the highly symbolic Malo- Koniushennyi bridge, where, in 1881, *Narodnaia Volia* [People's Will] had assassinated Aleksandr II. Pavlenskii was obviously in control of the legal procedure that followed (Pavlenskii 2016b: 55; Pavlenskii 2016b: 169, n. 44). Smart political art remains 'in com- mand of the situation' (Popović 2015: 142; Velminski in Pavlenskii 2016b: 121) and forces the representatives of political order to become an active part of the art work itself: for example, when they have to liberate the artist from barbed wire or pull nails out of his scrotum (Pavlenski 2016a: 52).

Other radical traditions have also survived the Soviet period. As capitalism has morphed into global financial capitalism and lib- eralism into hegemonic neoliberalism, the two major nineteenth- century radical critiques of that constellation, Marxism and anar- chism, have retained their relevance. Indeed, it is impossible to understand Russia without taking into account the profound streak of anarchy that runs through all levels of everyday life – the land where, as frequent visitors know, everything that is forbidden is possible. At the same time, it is impossible to understand Russia's political reality without its *avtoritarizm*, as fear, as habit and as reflex (Korneeva 2011: 66–7). The tension between authority and anarchy still defines Russia. The anarchists and syndicalists, who were among the most outspoken critics of Bolshevism, have retained their connection of theory and practice, even if they face difficulties in establishing themselves politically and retreat to the level of theory: for example, in the tradition of colloquia and pub- lications centred on Bakunin's former estate, Priamukhino (Dam'e 2009: 203–5; Kornilov et al. 2011–18).

Time to Think Aloud Again

In Russia in 2005 and 2011–12, unprecedented mass protest erupted; it labelled itself *Snezhnaia revoliutsiia* [Snow Revolution], thus adding white to the colour revolution repertoire (Alëkhina 2017; Lur'e 2012; Arkhipova and Alekseevskii 2014; van der Zweerde 2015, 2018a). The Russian government succeeded in averting the 'spectre of a "Moscow Maidan"' with a strategy of 'authoritarian resistance' that alternatingly aimed to 'insulate, redefine, accuse, bolster, subvert and cooperate' (Ambrosio 2010: 137; Horvath 2013: 47–84). Russia fits global trends of growing authoritarianism and illiberal democracy that go along with neoliberal capitalism, and in Russian academia, too, precarity and competition have become the norm.

In spite of these trends, political philosophy in Russia is more diverse than it has ever been and Russian political philosophers contribute to a wide range of disciplines, bringing Russian elements and perspectives into the international academic debate. This includes contributions to gender studies by Veronika Sharova (b. 1981) (Sharova 2013), critical analysis of public discourse by Tat'iana Vaizer (b. 1980) (Vaizer 2020), studies of migration and racism by Vladimir Malakhov (b. 1958) (Malakhov 2007, 2014), environmental philosophy by Oksana Timofeeva (b. 1978) (Timofeeva 2018), explorations of republicanism in Russia by Oleg Kharkhordin (b. 1964) and of American radicalism by Rodion Belkovich (b. 1984) (Kharkhordin 2009, 2018; Belkovich 2020), and the philosophy of (political) humour – a subject that feeds back to topics like carnival (Bakhtin), 'world of laughter [*smekhovoi mir*]' (Likhachëv and Panchenko 1991), laughtivism (Popović 2015) and the figure of the trickster / trickstar (Lipovetsky 2015). Laughter, mockery and ridicule contribute to political-philosophical discussions about public language (Vakhtin and Firsov 2019), speech, silence and agency. Emigrated philosophers like Mikhail Épstein (b. 1950, em. 1990) and Boris Groys (b. 1947, em. 1981) have established themselves as important contemporary thinkers in the fields of (trans)cultural philosophy and aesthetics, both with a clear political sensitivity (Epstein 2011, 2019; Berry and Epstein 1999; Groys 1998 / 2011, 2012a, 2018). Long-time residents of the USA and Germany, they continue to build bridges between Western and Russian philosophical traditions. Dealing with Russia's atypical colonial post, finally, are Aleksandr Étkind (b. 1955) and Madina Tlostanova (b. 1970) (Etkind 2011 / 2018; Tlostanova 2015).

The harshness of political reality in Russia, past and present, offers important correctives to the complacent character of much of Western political philosophy. The dimension of 'hard power', whether as physical or economic violence, must not be replaced by an exclusive focus on 'soft power' and hegemony. The fact of the matter is that hegemony, including ideology, and domination, including violence, always supplement each other. The legitimate question of violence versus non-violence typically does not address the issue of physical, symbolic and structural violence. On such points, Russian scholars can, due to their political experience, correct the discursivism and constructivism, not to mention the comfortable smugness, of many of their Western colleagues (Iakovlev 2002; Kapustin 2010: 215–55; Kovrizhnykh and Butyl'skaia 2015).

Russia's recent political history supports the original theory of 'negative' revolution propounded by Artemii Magun (b. 1974) (Magun 2008 / 2013). Magun sees the core of the negative revolution of the late Soviet and early post-Soviet periods in the destruction of the political subject, a destruction prepared for by the Soviet regime with its cooptative elite party and largely dependent labour unions, neither of which could act as an independent political agent. In the post-Soviet period, independent labour unions emerged, and strikes and protests have become numerous (Kagarlitsky 1995: 137–47).[5] Many political parties were founded, but most of them quickly turned into electoral platforms rather than political subjects, again mirroring global trends. From this angle, it is more adequate to speak of the preclusion of political subjectivity, despite the booming of civil society. Nevertheless, Russian citizens are more critical and ready to stand up for their rights than in the 1990s, even if their civic independence does not translate into political activity (Chebankova 2015: 140–63).

Was the 'Snow Revolution' of 2011 still part of the negative revolution of 1985–99 (Magun 2013: 15–30) or is it a reaction against it? Is it part of a revolt of the young against their fathers, for whom, as old dissident Vladimir Konstantinovich Bukovskii (1942–2019) put it in 2012, 'everything was indifferent except making money' (Eltchaninoff 2016: 31)? The revolutions in Eastern Europe were hijacked by neoliberalism but this 'in no way undermines their revolutionary character, the degree of dethroning of authority that they accomplished' (Magun 2013: 29). If, when advocating 'electoral democracy and a business-friendly rule of law' yet passing 'decision-making into the hands of large corporations and non-elected experts', the neoliberal regime has authoritarian tendencies, it tolerates demonstrations 'as long as they demonstrate the relative weakness of the anarchically minded movements of the "multitude"' (ibid.: 29). The very fact that the 'new wave of mobilisation' of the early 2010s 'meets a much more serious resistance' than the negative revolution that demolished Soviet structures is a sign of its strength and opens the door 'to an adequate political self-understanding' (ibid.: 30). To put it in the terms of this study: the replacement of one, Soviet authority by the next, neoliberal one invites resistance, but also reflection. A neoliberal regime accelerates the atomisation of society that resulted from the Soviet system, but it also invites the articulation of a counter-hegemony with a moral agenda that yet has to become political. The relevance of these observations far exceeds the boundaries of Russian reality.

The 'negative' character of political philosophy, then, becomes of particular relevance: it does not positively state what is true or just; it critically, *ex negativo*, out of their denial and suppression, indicates what truth and justice are. Here, Boris Gur'evich Kapustin (b. 1951) can be placed in the category of truly politically thinking philosophers like Hannah Arendt, Michael Walzer and Judith Shklar. Like them, he highlights a key feature of human existence: namely, the possibility of conflict and concord even if, in a particular time and place, there seems to be consensus about where to draw the line between what is and what is not 'political' (Kapustin 2004: 202–5). Kapustin radically opposes the position of the 'philosopher-king', which he rightly identifies as a 'euphemism for the unity of Reason and Force [*Razuma i Sily*]' and as 'a trap both for the politically engaged *and* for the critically thinking intellectual' (Kapustin 2010: 419). The philosopher-king can be approached as the philosopher occupying the position of king, called to implement politically a true vision of a just society, or as the king being adequately raised and instructed by the philosopher. The second, Platonic and neo-Platonic variant is typical of pre-modern times. The first, Jacobin variant is key to understanding modern politics – with Russia as one of its testing grounds.

A fresh start, finally, with a (neo-)Marxist analysis of present-day socio-economic and political reality was made by Andrei Koriakovtsev and Sergei Viskunov, departing from the revival of Marxism after its *samokritika* [self-critique] of the 1990s (Oizerman 2003; Mezhuev 2007). They make full use of Marx's *Paris Manuscripts*, which had inspired the *shestidesiatniki*, and of a 'dissident' like Zinov'ev, one of the very few 'to attempt a large-scale investigation of the specific, objective, inner laws and logic of development of "real communism/socialism"' (Koria-kovtsev and Viskunov: 609; Zinov'ev 1985). Given the fact that capitalism is more global and interconnected than ever, we have every reason to expect Russian neo-Marxists and post-Marxists to apply their intellectual legacy, freed from Soviet ideologisa-tion but nourished by its experience, to contemporary realities (Kagarlitskii 2013).

All these Russian political philosophers cross national, linguistic and cultural borders, taking part of their inspiration from 'indig-enous' Russian traditions, including independent and dissident thinkers from the Soviet period like Bibikhin or Zinov'ev. Their 'Russianness' is hard to pin down, but not harder than the equally unmistakable 'Americanness' of John Rawls and Bonnie Honig, the 'Africanness' of Kwame Gyekye and Achille Mbembe, or the 'Frenchness' of Catherine Malabou and Jacques Rancière – not to mention the 'Dutchness' of the present author. Political philosophy is, by default, connected to particular places and times, and phi-losophers, if they seek to have political impact, relate to the specific conjuncture in which they find themselves.

Conclusion

It is impossible to make conclusive claims with respect to history-in-the-making. Riding the glocal surf of authoritarianism, the cur-rent Russian regime appears stable for the foreseeable future. At the same time, political reality seems more volatile and less predict-able than ever. If, for domestic or international reasons, the incum-bent regime tightens its grip on society, this will affect academia. However, as long as neoliberal and neopatrimonial order prevails over neototalitarian projects to reshape Russian society, the pres-ent constellation, with its numerous niches, is likely to persist. The existing plurality of creative and critical positions has little direct connection to serious political opposition or protest, but ample opportunity to connect Russia's rich and torn political history, at the level of philosophical reflection, with humankind's collective and plural political memory and awareness.

The three post-Soviet decades have made clear at least two things. One is that the short Soviet century has acted as a refrig-erator when it comes to political philosophy: in many respects, the constellation of positions that took shape after 1990 resembles earlier, pre-Soviet times. This microwave oven effect has, how-ever, outlived itself, and political philosophy in Russia has become much less post-Soviet, while remaining recognisably Russian. This suggests that lasting geographical and historical factors act as a selectively determining force with respect to the rich plethora of ideas: 'ideocracy', like theocracy, is not an alternative regime type, but an ideologeme that serves to conceal partocracy and hierocracy. The 'sobering up' that Russian intellectuals went through once their high hopes of inclusion in a liberal-democratic Europe (Gorbachëv's 'common home [*obshchii dom*]') were crushed, entails the broader lesson that the separation of the world into blocs is not determined by political ideologies.

The second point is that the gap between the critical, deconstructive and post-modern spirit that prevails in academic political philosophy, and the demand for unquestioned identities and grand geopolitical schemes, is a global one. A modernity that fails to convince is forced to outshout itself: the anti-Western and anti-modern rhetoric of someone like Dugin is the constitutive other of identitarian defences of 'Western liberal democracy'. Both repeat the 'Schmittian' pattern of transposing the political to the plane of international and inter-civilisational relations in order to suppress or deny the political in the domestic sphere. Political philosophers who, motivated by the perceived urgency of a national crisis, try to contribute to a better future for their country by supporting particular political platforms are bound not only to be disappointed by the *Realpolitik* of their protagonists, but also to do their discipline a bad service. The alternative is always there: thinking from within the context of one's political reality while transcending it in the direction of shared glocal issues.

Notes

1. Quoted in Gabowitsch 2017: 191.
2. Victor Farías, *Heidegger and Nazism* (Philadelphia: Temple University Press, 1989) [Fr. orig. 1987].
3. Martin Heidegger, *Gesamtausgabe* (Frankfurt: Klostermann, 2012), LXIX, *Die Geschichte des Seyns*: 108, 119.
4. See https://kprf.ru/activity/culture/120314.html (last accessed 18 July 2019) and https://www.bbc.com/russian/society/2016/04/160427_tr_kprf_orthodox_church_symbiosis (last accessed 16 May 2021).
5. See https://newlaborforum.cuny.edu/2016/12/08/labor-under-putin-the-state-of-the-russian-working-class (last accessed 23 May 2020).

Conclusion – Mediation Beyond Duality and Immediacy

> Oh, all our Slavophilism and Westernising is no more than one great misunderstanding between us, although it was historically necessary.
> Fyodor Dostoevsky, *A Writer's Diary* (Dostoevsky 1994: 1294 / 2017: 732)

From a Western perspective, Russian political reality often strikes us as harsh, and this harshness also tends to dominate news coverage. This perception has a long history. Examples easily trigger the imagination, from Dostoevsky, who was nearly executed for reading a letter aloud, via large-scale terror authorised by class-war criminals like Lenin and Stalin, to the heavy crackdown on political opposition in the present century. Oppositional activity, from attempts at the tsar's life to the political art of Pavlenskii, appears equally radical. Looking at these events from a global perspective, however, makes them much less exceptional. Besides, there is no shortage of political violence in 'the West' either. Moreover, major causes of political violence in Russia, such as autocracy, serfdom and capitalism, are of Western origin, not to mention imported philosophies like Enlightenment rationalism or Marxist socialism. This suggests that we are dealing more with images of Self and Other than with historical and empirical fact. For long stretches of time, Russia has oscillated between two forms of 'otherness': either as the Other Europe or as Europe's Other, and in both cases as part of the same divided Christendom. Russia has been Western Europe's constitutive other as much as the other way around, and both sides are uncertain whether the other is an outside or an inside other.

For Russian political philosophers, too, 'Europe' has often acted as a major inner yardstick, even though alternative voices have been articulated, from Danilevskii to Dugin. More broadly, Russians expressing the hope that their country might one day become 'normal' are referring, as a rule, to the assumed 'normality' of Western countries, however much they may simultaneously loathe its hedonistic liberalism. Many categories and topics of political philosophy in Russia are, indeed, of West European provenance, and the different conclusions arrived at by Russian thinkers can, in the majority of cases, be read as the effect, not of different philosophy, but of different circumstances and, hence, different premises. If, however, as many would argue, we are currently living in a world no longer dominated exclusively by European Christianity, this picture may change quickly, and the resurgence of the opposition between *zapadniki* and *slavophiles* in the 1990s may turn out to be the last one. In that respect, this book can, provisionally, be seen as addressing an era that has come to an end. General conclusions, then, must be read against this hypothetical backdrop.

Russian political philosophy has shown us a number of alternative possible developments of ideas that are familiar to Western readers: a liberalism with a focus on positive instead of negative liberty, a Marxism turned into a legitimising ideology instead of a critical theory, and Christian political philosophy turned into a theory about universal resurrection and true brotherhood. At the same time, Russia has yielded a rich anarchist tradition and a current of communitarian *sobornost'*-thinking, of which the resources have not yet been exhausted. Also, important notions like *simfoniia* and *bogochelovechestvo* [Divine Humanity / Godmanhood], which have their roots in the Byzantine and Orthodox-Christian tradition, offer alternatives to predominant concepts in the Western political-philosophical tradition, and the dual concepts of truth – *pravda* versus *istina*- and freedom – *svoboda* versus *volia* – complicate matters in a productive way. The overall interest of these developments lies in their widening of the space of political philosophy, something urgently needed in the present-day world.

Russian political philosophy, both part of a Christian-European civilisation and clearly distinct from it many respects, occupies a peculiar position as a possible object of two present-day endeavours in academic political philosophy: comparative philosophy and intercultural philosophy. While the first highlights similarities and differences between various traditions that have arisen largely independently of each other, the second aims at dialogue between them, in an interesting parallel with ecumenical and cosmopolitan movements. Russian political philosophy sits uneasily in this field precisely as a consequence of its 'half-otherness' and Russian philosophers have, not accidentally, often oscillated between stressing the connection, if not identity, with Western philosophy, and emphasising the *samobytnost'* [originality, uniqueness] of their own tradition. This half-otherness complicates comparison as well as dialogue but, at the same time, it can assist in breaking through the idea of a plurality of independent, equally original traditions, each identified with allegedly separate parts of the world. Potentially, Russian political philosophy can undermine civilisational essentialism. From that angle, emphasis on *samobytnost'* then appears as wishful compensation for the lack of essential otherness. But then, by the same token, it also serves to undermine Western suprematism, as if political philosophy in Russia should always be measured by a yardstick that does not question itself.

One of the things that is likely to have struck the reader is the stark contrast, among and even within Russian political philosophers, between wishful, even utopian idealism and a strong sense of the 'life and death' harshness of political reality. Sober realism, from Herzen via Il'in to Kapustin, does not lead thinkers to give up their idealism, but forms a valuable antidote against facile idealism. But even Solov'ëv, arguably the most idealist of all, combines his utopian vision of a free theocracy with full awareness of the everyday material dimension. Radicals like Bakunin or Lenin justify the use of means that might be needed to reach the highest possible goal: the creation of a free and just society. Nothing of this is uniquely Russian, of course, but the predominance of this contrast is indeed striking.

Merab Mamardashvili linked this contrast to a major difference between Western and Eastern Christianity: 'Western Christianity assumes that humans' task, whenever they give something concrete form, consists in making that thing the imperfect, finite carrier of the infinite' (Mamardachvili 1991: 60). If, as a consequence, West European culture is based on the idea of giving imperfect form to everything, 'Orthodox culture is *obsessed by ideality*. [. . .] Hence, if it is not the ideal, it is nothing at all' (ibid.: 61; translations mine, EvdZ). What seems to dominate, in the Orthodox tradition, and by extension in Russian political philosophy, is a binary opposition of ideality and reality, and what seems to be lacking is a concept of mediating concreteness.

In the flow of actual life, any binary opposition is always overcome by a mediating third, so that Mamardashvili's diagnosis can, in fact, be read as an instance of what he diagnoses: a binary opposition between Latin and Byzantine Christianity with, in his case, a clear preference for the European variant. Hence his pessimistic conclusion: 'One wants the whole, or nothing. And since the whole clearly is not there, obviously, one ends up with nothing' (ibid.). The truth of this diagnosis, if we limit ourselves to Russian political philosophy, is that the mediating third tends to come last, while in Western political philosophy it has tended to take centre stage. We see this, among other things, in a relative absence of notions like social contract and in a general abhorrence of compromise.

To phrase it in historical terms: if, in the Western tradition, Aristotle has gained the upper hand over Plato, in the Eastern tradition it is mostly the other way around. If Plato is most of all known for the notion of the philosopher-king who would implement a just society, in Aristotle the perfect monarch is rather an exceptional possibility, while the default is the free interaction of citizens.[1] This 'Platonising' tendency comes to the fore in the Russian case in the figure of the *Belyi tsar'* [White Tsar] (Dobrokhotov 2001). The 'Slavophile' idea of a good and just Christian ruler who, combined with good-natured faithful flock, indeed makes mediating institutions and mechanisms superfluous, or even harmful. If the anarchy of the multitude is tamed by a shared Christian faith, the autocracy of the *tsar'* becomes the authority of *pravda*. One step further, one can strip this model of the figure of the *tsar'* and focus on the *obshchina*, as did the agrarian socialists, and also on the *artel'*, a shift that yields the optimistic anarchism of Bakunin and Kropotkin, for whom only the authority of reason and argument counts. Anarchism is not, to be sure, the advocacy of anarchy, but rather its self-sublation to universal self-organisation.

Christian political philosophers like Solov'ëv, Berdiaev or Skobtsova typically hesitate to adopt this model, accepting mediation as a necessary evil but ultimately preferring immediacy, offering *sobornost'* as a possible way out. This is connected to an ambivalent anthropology that defines humanity as fallen, but at the same time as potentially good, or even divine. A major counterforce at this point relies on the more pessimistic anthropology of, moderately, Chicherin or, radically, Il'in: strong, if necessary authoritarian, power is needed to steer people away from anarchy and in the direction of a well-ordered society. It may also be needed to keep the Antichrist, in Bolshevik or other disguise, at bay.

Whether framed in a political–theological terminology that turns around Kingdom of God, Apocalypse and Prometheus, or in a 'secular' terminology that focuses on rationality, class struggle and a future kingdom of freedom, the dilemmas and choices are the same. A decision must be taken as to whether or not to clear the field for the establishment of a just society, whether or not to pretend to read the libretto of history and draw practical consequences from it, whether or not to define opponents and adversaries as enemies who must be disarmed or destroyed, whether or not to aim at the creation of political institutions, from parties to constitutions, that can channel political energy but at the cost that the outcomes are, by default, unpredictable and uncertain. The canalisation of political antagonism, as an alternative to the authoritarian suppression of the political, offers a second way out between, on the one hand, denial of the political and, on the other, its unchaining in revolution and civil war. Such canalisation, however, critically depends on the acceptance of the ineradicability of the political: the recurrent presence of societal antagonism and the necessity of its transformation into preferably non-violent politics.

The republican undercurrent, rooted in the pre-Muscovite *veche*, resurfaced in the advocacy of the *zemstvo* by liberals like Chicherin, but also by a conservative nationalist like Solzhenitsyn. It is, arguably, the most realistic position, in the sense that it pays due attention to the poiètical dimension of politics. If Western political philosophy often lacks a focus on institutions and tends to take them for granted, Russian political philosophy displays a tendency to treat institutions as neutral instruments for any preferred policy. Hence the expectation that an autocratic regime would install a liberal constitution or that a one-party dictatorship might yield socialism in one country. Explicable as it may be, there is a fatal dynamics at play between the instrumentalism of the ruling and the legal nihilism of the ruled, even if those two groups coincide, as in the case of the direct democracy that, at least on paper, existed in the initial Petrograd Soviet. This is why exceptions to legal nihilism like Chicherin and Solov'ëv continue to be relevant, precisely because they had to resist this dynamic.

It is not accidental, from this perspective, that only exiled thinkers like Frank and Stepun embraced, albeit reluctantly, the idea of liberal-democratic rule of law, or that the emigrant Kojève exalted it to the level of a universal and homogeneous state which, rather than being our political reality after the convergence of different trajectories, should be a permanent warning-sign against the illusion of a post-political situation. There is little difference, from that angle, between present-day benevolent patrimonialism and the dystopias of Dostoevsky's Grand Inquisitor, Solov'ëv's Emperor or Zamiatin's Benefactor. The problem here is not that post-politics is our reality, but rather that its illusion continues to seduce all over the world. In reality, tsars are neither White nor Black, they only come in different shades of grey.

Highlighting these red threads that have gradually been weaved from the texts and authors discussed in this book is one way of concluding it. The other is to look back at this motley crew of philosophers as a rich reservoir of ideas and theories, often strikingly similar to what readers may be familiar with, but at other times dazzlingly distant from it: the Jacobinism of socialists who ended as professional terrorists, the radicalism that made Tolstoy and Solov'ëv take Fëdorov seriously in the first place, the unhampered instrumentalism of Bolsheviks who turned even themselves into mere means for the realisation of a sacred end. For better or for worse, such examples demonstrate a key motif of philosophy: namely, to follow an argument, once started, to its logical conclusion. The distance from real politics is what makes many of those theories abstract, but it also is what makes them disastrous once the gap from theory to praxis is bridged. This is what not only can, but must, provide food for thought, and not just in Russia.

What unites the political philosophers that populate the pages of this book is the fact that they attempted to wedge the authority of argument into the space between the binary opposition of autocratic unity and anarchic plurality, including the plurality of political philosophy itself. Many of them were squeezed in that narrow space. Their importance, however, does not lie in the extent to which they succeeded in their endeavour. Nor does it lie merely in the fact that, when the authority of the better argument appears to fail, philosophy itself tends to become apodictic and dogmatic, developing its own form of authoritarianism. The importance lies in what their adventures can tell us about, first, Russia, including its Soviet period; second, political philosophy generally; and third, the way in which the latter relates to the political and to politics. These adventures include, of course, exile, emigration and execution. They include censorship, *samizdat* and *tamizdat*. And they include the consultation of *philosophes* by an enlightened tsarina who decided not to introduce the constitutional reforms that she deemed rationally superior, the marriage of political philosophy to a regime that proclaimed unity in its ideology and union in its very name, and the recent recommendation by President Putin to read Berdiaev, Solov'ëv and Il'in.

Many lessons can be taken from the content of this book and different readers may draw different conclusions. If I limit myself to three positive points of broader importance, the first is about the importance of mediation in general, and of mediating institutions in particular. Not allowing space for plurality and interaction means to ignite 'irrational' forms of protest such as *iurodstvo*: historical *iurodstvo*, as well as its twentieth- and twenty-first-century avatars, can be read as symptoms of the absence of a political arena. Suppression of the political invokes uprisings and it invites conspiratorial political organisations. Limiting or controlling academic freedom when it comes to philosophy generally, and to political philosophy in particular, precludes the emergence of a 'laboratory of ideas' in which theories can be tested before trying to put them into practice. The repeated combination of failed reforms and failing reformist political philosophy is not accidental, but testifies to an incapacity to deal with the political other than by suppressing or denying it. In such cases, the insiders' perspective cannot be replaced with external analysis: we must read Kollontai, Zinov'ev and Magun if we want to learn anything. The result is, on the one hand, a tendency to escape in the direction of anti-political, a-political or post-political conceptions and, on the other, a tendency towards overall rejection of the existing order or of political order as such. While these two tendencies differ in their quietist, as opposed to violent, approaches, what they share is a denial of the political, and especially of the political character of their own position.

A second lesson is that a lot of truth is contained in the age-old distinction between theory, praxis and *poièsis*. Among Russian political philosophers, awareness of the importance of all three is the exception rather than the rule: Chicherin, Frank and Berlin are among the few who emphasise the importance not only of making good laws and institutions, but also of understanding and treating them as more than mere instruments for the achievement of political ends. However, this neglect of the poiètical dimension of politics is also widespread in political philosophy outside Russia. In the Russian case, this lapsus may be due to the actual predominance of instrumentalism. In the case of mainstream Western philosophy, it may well be due to the presence of institutions that permit a focus on theory and praxis, including action, but then seduces philosophers to overlook the fragility of the very pre-conditions of their activity. At the same time, the advantages of clearly distinguishing theory, praxis and *poièsis* quickly evaporate when they are synthesised in a grand, organicist schema, as is the case with Solov'ëv. Arguably, if political philosophy wants to remain political, it has to balance these three and even to avoid constructing a system.

The third lesson concerns the necessary distance between political philosophy and political reality. Direct political control over philosophy, or even a ban, annihilates philosophy's potential for the political life of a society, leaving no other option than to go underground or abroad. Nineteenth-century Russia is a shining example of this, though not the only one by far. Conversely, direct integration of political philosophy in a political regime turns ideals of equality and freedom into cornerstones of an ideology that can legitimise a totalitarian system with lethal consequences. The Soviet system is an example of this, but a one-to-one correspondence of a liberal political philosophy claiming to combine *égaliberté* with a globalising neoliberal capitalism (which has absorbed Russia, too), while letting *fraternité*, in whatever form, fall off the table, can be just as lethal. Moreover, both impede the articulation of societal antagonism in such a way that a mediating dynamic becomes possible. For this reason, attempts to fill the perceived ideological vacuum after the decomposition of the Soviet system by discovering, inventing or regauging a unifying national idea contain the same fatality. The point is not whether such proposed 'Russian ideas' are peaceful or aggressive, cosmopolitan or jingoistic, nor that they tend to become as hollow as an 'American dream' or a 'European community of values'. The problem is the very idea of such an idea. Here, for example, Dugin's fourth political theory aims to close the gap between political philosophy and political reality, while Horujy's and Bibikhin's resistance keeps it open. The fact that they all partly base themselves on Heidegger, elaborating different possibilities of development, strongly suggests that this distance does not maintain itself, but must be actively established and maintained by political philosophers. Likewise, the opposition between the political–theological legitimisation of tsarist autocracy and the politically distanced tradition of hesychasm points to the necessity to actively keep a distance.

Finally, to end on a negative note, we must unlearn the idea that mistaken philosophies have disastrous effects. It is more than obvious that the long Soviet episode includes some of the major political crimes in the history of humankind, comparable to the Shoah or the European colonisation of Africa. It is equally clear that Soviet

Marxism(–Leninism) has played a key role in the self-legitimisation
of the system, and that many philosophers have engaged in excus-
ing for too long what they wrongly saw as the only alternative to
the despised bourgeois capitalism of the West. However, to ascribe
Soviet tragedies to the political philosophy of Lenin, Plekhanov
or indeed Marx would be to fall into the trap of Soviet ideology:
namely, that real existing socialism was, indeed, a more or less
direct application of those philosophies. Those who feel inspired
by Marx's eleventh Feuerbach thesis easily overlook the fact that
Marx was not saying that it was philosophers who should change
the world. Rather than seeing historical reality as an effect of flawed
philosophical theories, one should pose the question as to which of
their elements facilitated the instrumentalisation of those theories.
What happened around and after October 1917 must remain an
object of philosophical reflection, but not of paralysing auto-flag-
ellation. During the Soviet period, the numerous attempts to apply
Marxist categories critically to Soviet reality were suppressed not
philosophically, but politically. At the end of the day, Lenin's politically motivated instrumentalisation of philosophy and of his own
person for the sacred goal of the proletarian revolution is a lesson
about ends and means, and about the dependence of political philosophy on the conditions of its possibility: free, unassisted minds,
free, uninhibited discussion and free, unrestricted public spaces.

   For the above reasons, the rich and diverse tradition of political
philosophy in Russia must, according to the present author, become
part of political philosophy world-wide, to enrich the discipline, to
understand Russia better and to assess the impact of Russian thinkers. As Russian scholars have been studying non-Russian political
philosophy for centuries, non-Russian scholars should mirror this
endeavour in their own way, not on moral grounds but on intellectual ones. Paradoxically, this means the construction of an object,
'Russian political philosophy', which, at the end of the day, does
not exist separately. This paradox is present in the very title of this
book which, in that precise manner, is self-deconstructive. For me
personally, reading Herzen, Chicherin, Solov'ëv, Kropotkin, Skobtsova, Berlin, Rand, Frank, Horujy, Bibikhin, Kapustin or Magun
means opening different windows not just on Russia, but also,
and more importantly, on political philosophy. As is the case with
'Western' political philosophy, where those philosophers are of
lasting interest whose ideas and theories transcend the specific situation in which they were first articulated, the Russian philosophers
that give most food for thought are those who cannot be simply
tied down as 'typically Russian'. Luckily, there are plenty of them.

Note

1. Plato, *Politeia*, V.xviii [473d]; Aristotle, *Politika*, III.xi.13 [1288a, 27–8].

Afterword

Since this book was finished, a major episode started, the result of which remains unclear. The army of the Russian Federation invaded Ukraine, a 'brother-nation' with which it has a lot in common, including a shared origin in Kievan Rus'. On the Russian side, this 'special military operation' is presented as a legitimate intervention to defend its geopolitical interests and to protect its Russian compatriots on the other side of the border. At the same time, it fits a narrative on the restoration of the political and economic space that once was the USSR and, before that, the tsarist Russian empire. Also, it is accompanied by discourses about Russia's mission to protect true, Orthodox Christianity, of which the Moscow Patriarchate continues to understand itself as guardian. The question how 'ordinary' territorial and economic interests relate to ideas of a Great Russia is, as always, difficult to decide.

Readers of this book will recognise motifs and patters connected to names like Dostoevsky, Il'in, Solzhenitsyn and Dugin. They will also notice the prominence of a 'Russian idea'. Hopefully, however, they will not overlook the many critical elements in the currents and positions discussed in this book, connected to the names of Herzen, Skobtsova, Bibikhin and others; elements that can be easily transposed to the present situation. If that situation demonstrates one thing, it is that there never is a one-to-one correspondence between the actual domestic and foreign politics of a particular country and political philosophy as it exists in that country. In 2022, political opposition and protest in Russia are under even heavier pressure than they already were, and this also affects the academic world. Many people inside and outside Russia today feel as if three decades of intellectual effort have been lost and Russia returns to Soviet, or even Stalinist times. While this sentiment is understandable, it is also inaccurate: much of the yield of those 30 years has found a place in the minds of thousands of young Russians who have no experience with the long Soviet period. Whatever the final outcome of the current situation, two generations of Russians have learned to think critically and independently. And, as in earlier periods, we may consider the importance of a material basis of intellectual work: thousands of uncensored books that, contrary to the internet, cannot be simply closed.

Bibliography

Where confusion over authors' names is likely, the spellings as they appear on the publication's cover have been added between brackets: for example, Iakovlev [Yakovlev] and Chubais [Tschubais]. It is assumed that readers will generally be able to identify Aleksey and Alexei, Liubov and Liubov', Soloviev and Solovyov, and so on. The abbreviation 'izd.' indicates a university press.

Abramov, M. A. (ed.) (1997), *Opyt russkogo liberalizma: antologiia*. Moscow: Kanon+

Ackermann, Arne, Harry Raiser, Dirk Uffelmann (eds) (1995), *Orte des Denkens: neue russische Philosophie*. Vienna: Passagen

Afanas'ev, Iurii N. (ed.) (1988), *Inogo ne dano: perestroika: glasnost', demokratiia, sotsializm*. Moscow: Progress

Aksel'rod-Ortodoks, Liubov I. (1981), 'Spinoza and Materialism', in George L. Kline (ed.) *Spinoza in Soviet Philosophy*, 2nd edn. Westport, CT: Hyperion Press, 61–89 [Russian orig.: 1925; English orig.: London: Routledge and Kegan Paul and New York: Humanities Press, 1952]

Aksel'rod-Ortodoks, Liubov' I. (2010 [1924]), *Kritika osnov burzhuaznogo obshchestvovedeniia i materialisticheskoe ponimanie istorii*. Moscow: Librokom

Alëkhina, Mariia (2017), *Riot Days*. St Petersburg: (*samizdat*) [English: Maria Alyokhina, *Riot Days*. New York: Metropolitan Books, 2017]

Alekseev, Pëtr V. (ed.) (1990), *Na perelome: filosofskie diskussii 20-kh godov: filosofiia i mirovozzrenie*. Moscow: Politizdat

Alekseev, Pëtr V. (ed.) (1995), *Filosofy Rossii XIX–XX stoletii: biografii, idei, Trudy*, 2nd edn. Moscow: Kniga i biznes

Alekseeva, Tat'iana A. (2000), *Nuzhna li filosofiia politike?* Moscow: Éditorial URSS

Alexander, John T. (2003), *Bubonic Plague in Early Modern Russia: Public Health and Urban Disaster*. Oxford: Oxford University Press

Ambrosio, Thomas (2010), 'Russia', in Donnacha Ó Beacháin and Abel Polese (eds), *The Colour Revolutions in the Former Soviet Republics: Successes and Failures*. London and New York: Routledge, 136–55

Anderson, Perry (2017), *The H-Word: The Peripeteia of Hegemony*. London and New York: Verso

Anderson, Thornton (1967), *Russian Political Thought: An Introduction*. Ithaca, NY: Cornell University Press

Antonov, Konstantin M. (ed.) (2015), *'Samyi vydaiushchiisia russkii filosof': filosofiia religii i politiki S.L. Franka*. Moscow: izd. PSTGU

Antonov, Mikhail V. (2012), *Istoriia pravovoi mysli Rossii*. St Petersburg: Vysshaia Shkola Ėkonomiki

Antonov, Mikhail V. (2019), *Formalism, Realism and Conservatism in Russian Law*. PhD, Leiden

Applebaum, Anne (2003), *GULAG: A History*. New York: Random Books [Russian: Ėnn Ėpplbaum, *GULAG*. Moscow: Ast, 2017]

Applebaum, Anne (ed.) (2011), *Gulag Voices: An Anthology*. New Haven, CT, and London: Yale University Press

Arendt, Hannah (2017 [1951]), *The Origins of Totalitarianism*. London: Penguin

Arjakovsky, Antoine (2002), *La Génération des penseurs religieux de l'émigration russe: la revue* La Voie (Put'), *1925–1940*. Kiev and Paris: L'Esprit et la Lettre [English: *The Way: Religious Thinkers of the Russian Emigration in Paris and their Journal, 1925–1940*, ed. John J. Jillions and Michael Plekon, transl. Jerry Ryan. Notre Dame, IN: Notre Dame University Press, 2013]

Arkhipova, Aleksandra S., Mikhail D. Alekseevskii (eds) (2014), *'My ne nemy': antropologiia pretesta v Rossii 2011–2012 godov*. Tartu: Nauchnoe izdatel'stvo ĖLM

Arndt, Andreas (2012 [1985]), *Karl Marx: Versuch über den Zusammenhang seiner Theorie*, 2nd edn. Berlin: Akademieverlag

Auffret, Dominique (1990), *Alexandre Kojève: la philosophie, l'état, la fin de l'histoire*. Paris: Grasset & Fasquelle

Averintsev, Sergei S., Ė. A. Arab-Ogly, L. F. Il'ichëv, S. M. Kovalëv, I. M. Landa, V. G. Papov, et al. (eds) (1989 [1983]), *Filosofskii ėntsiklopedicheskii slovar'*, 2nd edn. Moscow: Sovetskaia Ėntsiklopediia

Avrich, Paul (1972), *Russian Rebels 1600–1800*. New York and London: W. W. Norton

Avrich, Paul (1988), *Anarchist Portraits*. Princeton: Princeton University Press

Avrich, Paul (2005 [1967]), *The Russian Anarchists*. Edinburgh and Oakland, CA: AK Press

Avvakum [Avvakuum] Petrov (Kondrat'ev) (2001), *Het leven van aartspriester Avvakuum, door hemzelf geschreven*. Antwerp: Benerus

Bakounine, Michel (2009), *Catéchisme révolutionnaire*. Paris: L'Herne [orig. 1865]

Bakunin, Michael (1990), *Statism and Anarchy*, ed. M. Shatz. Cambridge: Cambridge University Press

Bakunin, Mikhail (1977 [1851]), *The Confession of Mikhail Bakunin*, transl. Robert C. Howes, intro. Lawrence D. Orton. Ithaca, NY: Cornell University Press

Bakunin, Mikhail [Michael] (1973), *Selected Writings*, ed. Arthur Lehning. New York: Grove Press

Bakunin, Mikhail A. (2014), *Gosudarstvennost' i anarkhiia*. Moscow: Knizhnyi Klub Knigovek [German: *Staatlichkeit und Anarchie, und andere Schriften*. Frankfurt: Ullstein, 1972]

Balibar, Étienne (2012), *La Proposition de l'égaliberté*. Paris: PUF [English: *Equaliberty*. Durham, NC, and London: Duke University Press, 2014]

Baluev, Boris P. (1995), *Liberal'noe narodnichestvo na rubezhe XIX–XX vekov*. Moscow: Nauka

Barabashev, Aleksei, Vadim Prokof'ev [Prokofiev] (2019), 'Why Reforms of Public Service in Russia are Cyclic: An Institutional Explanation from a Liberal Perspective', in Cucciolla (ed.), 165–88

Barnes, Steven A. (2011), *Death and Redemption: The Gulag and the Shaping of Soviet Society*. Princeton: Princeton University Press

Beales, Derek (2016), 'Philosophical Kingship and Enlightened Despotism', in Goldie and Wokler (eds), 497–524

Beecher, Jonathan (2013), 'Early European Socialism', in Klosko (ed.), 369–92

Belinsky, V. G., N. G. Chernyshevsky, N. A. Dobrolyubov (1976 [1962]), *Essential Writings by the Founders of Russian Literary and Social Criticism*. Bloomington and London: Indiana University Press

Belkovich, Rodion Iu. (2020), *Krov' patriotov: vvedenie v intellektual'nuiu istoriiu amerikanskogo radikalizma*. St Petersburg: izd. Vladimir Dal'

Benevich, Grigorii (2003), *Mat' Mariia (1891–1945): dukhovnaia biografiia i tvorchestvo*. St Petersburg: Vysshaia religiozno-filosofskaia shkola

Bercken, Wil van den (2018), 'De Orthodoxe Kerk van Rusland', in Herman Teule, Alfons Brüning (eds), *Handboek Oosters Christendom*. Leuven: Peeters, 381–410

Berdiaev [Berdiajew], Nikolai A. (1953), *Wahrheit und Lüge des Kommunismus*. Darmstadt and Geneva: Holle [Russian orig.: 1930]

Berdiaev, Nikolai A. (1996 [1912]), *Aleksei Stepanovich Khomiakov*. Tomsk: Volodei

Berdiaev, Nikolai A. (2004a), *Russkaia ideia*. Moscow: Ast [English: Nikolai Berdiaev, *The Russian Idea*. Hudson, NY: Lindisfarne Press, 1992; Russian orig.: Paris: YMCA Press, 1946]

Berdiaev, Nikolai A. (2004b), *Filosofiia neravenstva*. Moscow: Ast [Russian orig.: Berlin, 1923; English: N. Berdyaev, *The Philosophy of Inequality*, transl. Fr. S. Janos. Mohrsville, PA: FRSJ, 2015]

Berglund, Krista (2012), *The Vexing Case of Igor Shafarevich, a Russian Political Thinker*. Basel: Birkhäuser / Springer

Bergman, Jay (1983), *Vera Zasulich: A Biography*. Stanford, CA: Stanford University Press

Berlin, Isaiah (1978 [1948]), *Russian Thinkers*. Harmondsworth: Penguin

Berlin, Isaiah (2013), *Concepts and Categories*. Princeton: Princeton University Press

Berry, Ellen E., Mikhail N. Epstein (1999), *Transcultural Experiments: Russian and American Models of Creative Communication*. New York: St Martin's Press

Beyme, Klaus von (2001), *Politische Theorien in Russland 1789–1945*. Wiesbaden: Springer Fachmedien

Bibikhin, Vladimir V. (2011), *Les (hulè)*. Moscow: Nauka [English: *Woods*. Cambridge: Polity Press, 2021; partly in *Stasis* 3, 2015, no. 1 as 'The Wood(s)']

Bibikhin, Vladimir V. (2017a), 'From *Being and Time* to the *Beiträge*', in Love (ed.), 295–323

Bibikhin, Vladimir V. (2017b), *Drugoe nachalo*. St Petersburg: Nauka [German (selection): Vladimir Bibichin, *Der andere Anfang*. Berlin: Matthes & Seitz, 2020]

Billington, James H. (1970 [1966]), *The Icon and the Axe: An Interpretative History of Russian Culture*. New York: Vintage Books

Blakeley, Thomas J. (1980), 'Union of Soviet Socialist Republics', in J. R. Burr (ed.), *Handbook of World Philosophy: Contemporary Developments since 1945*. London: Aldwych Press, 317–26

Bocheński, J. M. (1967 [1950]), *Der sowjetrussische dialektische Materialismus (Diamat)*, 5th edn. Bern and Munich: Franke

Boer, Roland (2019), *Red Theology: On the Christian Communist Tradition*. Chicago: Haymarket

Bogdanov (Malinovskii), Aleksandr A. (1989 [1913–22]), *Tektologiia: vseobshchaia organizatsionnaia nauka*, 2 vols. Moscow: Ėkonomika [German: *Allgemeine Organisationslehre: Tektologie*, Regensburg: EOD, 2020 [Berlin: 1926]]

Bogdanov (Malinovskii), Aleksandr A. (2003 [1906–8]), *Ėmpiriomonizm: stat'i po filosofii*. Moscow: Respublika [English: *Empiriomonism: Essays in Philosophy, Books 1–3*, ed. and transl. David G. Rowley. Chicago: Haymarket, 2021]

Boobbyer, Philip (1995), *S. L. Frank: The Life and Work of a Russian Philosopher 1877–1950*. Athens: Ohio University Press

Boobbyer, Philip (2005), *Conscience, Dissent and Reform in Soviet Russia*. London and New York: Routledge

Bowring, Bill (2013), *Law, Rights and Ideology in Russia: Landmarks in the Destiny of a Great Power*. Abingdon and New York: Routledge

Braibant, Sylvie (1993), *Élisabeth Dmitrieff, aristocrate & pétroleuse*. Paris: Belfond

Brandist, Craig, David Shepherd, Galin Tihanov (eds) (2004), *The Bakhtin Circle: In the Master's Absence*. Manchester: Manchester University Press

Breckner, Katharina (1996), *Die Sozialismusidee als Konstante der neueren russischen Ideengeschichte*. PhD, Hamburg

Brovkin, Vladimir N. (ed.) (1991), *Dear Comrades; Menshevik Reports on the Bolshevik Revolution and the Civil War*. Stanford, CA: Hoover Institution Press

Budde, Dirk (2013), 'Ivan A. Ilin – Vom Wesen der Rechtgläubigkeit', in Daniel Führing (ed.), *Gegen die Krise der Zeit: Konservative Denker im Porträt*. Graz: ARES

Bukharin, Nikolai (1979), *The Politics and Economics of the Transition Period*. London and New York: Routledge [Russian orig. 1920]

Bukharin, Nikolai I. (1988), *Izbrannye proizvedeniia*. Moscow: Politizdat

Bukharin, Nikolai I. (2005 [1937–8]), *Philosophical Arabesques*. New York: Monthly Review Press [German: *Philosophische Arabesken [Gefängnisschriften 2]*. Berlin: Karl Dietz, 2005]

Bukharin, Nikolai I. (2006 [1937–8]), *Socialism and its Culture [The Prison Manuscripts]*. London: Seagull Books [German: *Der Sozialismus und seine Kultur [Gefängnisschriften 1]*. Berlin: BasisDruck, 1996]

Bukharin, Nikolai I., Evgenii A. Preobrazhensky (1969 [1922]), *The ABC of Communism*. London: Penguin [Russian orig.: 1919]

Bulgakov, F. Sergei Nikolaevich (1903) *Ot marksizma k idealizmu*. St Petersburg: Obshchestvennaia Pol'za

Burchardi, Kristiane (1998), *Die Moskauer 'Religiös-Philosophische Vladimir-Solov'ev-Gesellschaft' (1905–1918)*. Wiesbaden: Harrassowitz

Butenko, Anatolii P. (1989), 'Vinoven li Karl Marks v "kazarmennom sotsializme"?', *Filosofskie nauki*, 4: 17–26

Butler, Judith (2012 [1987]), *Subjects of Desire: Hegelian Reflections in Twentieth-Century France*. New York: Columbia University Press

Bykova, Marina F., Michael N. Forster, L. Steiner (eds) (2021), *The Palgrave Handbook of Russian Thought*. Cham: Palgrave Macmillan

Carpi, Guido (2015), 'Il marxismo russo e sovietico fino a Stalin', in Stefano Petrucciani (ed.), *Storia des marxismo*, 3 vols, vol. I: *Socialdemocrazia, revisionismo, rivoluzione*. Rome: Carrocci, 101–45

Carrère d'Encausse, Hélène (1988), *Le Malheur russe: essai sur le meurtre politique*. Paris: Fayard [English: *The Russian Syndrome: One Thousand Years of Political Murder*. New York: Holmes & Meier, 1993]

Carter, Stephen K. (2015 [1991]), *The Political and Social Thought of F. M. Dostoevsky*. London and New York: Routledge

Cassin, Barbara (ed.) (2004), *Vocabulaire européen des philosophies: dictionnaire des intraduisibles*. Paris: Seuil / Le Robert [English: *Dictionary of Untranslatables: A Philosophical Lexicon*. Princeton: Princeton University Press, 2014]

Chaadaev, Pëtr Ia. (1991), *Polnoe sobranie sochinenii i izbrannye pis'ma*, 2 vols. Moscow: Nauka

Chamberlain, Lesley (2006), *Lenin's Private War: The Voyage of the Philosophy Steamer and the Exile of the Intelligentsia*. New York: St Martin's Press

Chebankova, Elena (2015), *Civil Society in Putin's Russia*. London and New York: Routledge

Chernov, Viktor M. (1997), *Konstruktivnyi sotsializm*. Moscow: Rosspèn [orig.: Prague, 1925]

Chernyshev, Sergei B. (ed.) (1995), *Inoe*, 3 vols + guide [*Putevoditel'*]. Moscow: Argus

Chernyshevskii, Nikolai [Chernyshevsky] (1989), *What is to Be Done?*, intro., ed. and transl. M. R. Katz and W. W. Wagner. Ithaca, NY, and London: Cornell University Press [Russian orig.: 1863]

Chicherin, Boris N. (1998a), *Filosofiia prava*. St Petersburg: Nauka

Chicherin, Boris N. (1998b), *Liberty, Equality, and the Market: Essays by B. N. Chicherin*. New Haven, CT, and London: Yale University Press

Chicherin, Boris N. (2016), *O nachalakh ètiki: otzyv na knigi Vladimira Solov'èva* Opravdanie dobra *i* Pravo i nravstvennost': *s otvetami V. S. Solov'èva*. Moscow: Lenand

Chizhkov, Sergei L. (2013), 'Gertsen i Chicherin: drama razmezhivaniia politicheskikh techenii', in A. A. Guseinov, A. A. Kara-Murza, A. F. Iakovleva, V. L. Sharova (eds), *Aleksandr Gertsen i istoricheskie sud'by Rossii*. Moscow: Kanon+, 95–108

Christoyannopoulos, Alexandre (2020), *Tolstoy's Political Thought: Christian Anarcho-Pacifist Iconoclasm Then and Now*. London and New York: Routledge

Chubais [Tschubais], Igor (2016), *Wie wir unser Land verstehen sollen: russische Idee und russländische Identität: Vergangenheit, Gegenwart, Zukunft*. Aachen: Shaker Media [Russian orig.: 2014]

Chubais [Tschubais], Igor (2017), *Das andere Russland: Gedanken eines Moskauer Dissidenten*. Aachen: Shaker Media

Claeys, Gregory, Christine Lattek (2013), 'Radicalism, Republicanism and Revolutionism', in Gareth S. Jones, Gregory Claeys (eds), *The Cambridge History of Nineteenth-Century Political Thought*. Cambridge: Cambridge University Press, 200–53

Cohen, Jean, Andrew Arato (1992), *Civil Society and Political Theory*. Cambridge, MA: MIT Press

Compton, Madonna Sophia (2016), *Mother Maria Skobtsova and Matrona Popova: Russian Women of Wisdom and Courage*. Berkeley and Kansas City: The Raphael Group

Conquest, Robert (1991 [1990]), *The Great Terror: A Reassessment*. Oxford: Oxford University Press

Courten, Manon de (2004), *History, Sophia and the Russian Nation*. Bern: Peter Lang

Courtois, Stéphane, Nicholas Werth, Jean-Louis Panné, Andrzej Paczkowski, Karel Bartošek, Jean-Louis Margolin (2001), *The Black Book of Communism: Crimes, Terror, Repression*. [French orig.: *Le Livre noir du communisme: crimes, terreur, repression*. Paris: Robert Laffont, 1997]

Cucciolla, Riccardo Mario (ed.) (2019), *Dimensions and Challenges of Russian Liberalism: Historical Drama and New Prospects*. Cham: Springer

Custine, Adolphe Marquis de (1975 [1839]), *Lettres de Russie*. Paris: Gallimard

Dahm, Helmut, Thomas J. Blakeley, George L. Kline (eds) (1988), *Philosophical Sovietology: The Pursuit of a Science*. Dordrecht: Reidel

Dam'e, Vadim V. (2006–7), *Zabytyi internatsional: mezhdunarodnoe anarkho-sindikalistskoe dvizhenie mezhdu dvumia mirovymi voinami*, 2 vols. Moscow: Novoe Literaturnoe Obozrenie

Dam'e [Damier], Vadim (2009), *Anarcho-Syndicalism in the 20th Century*, transl. Malcolm Archibald. Edmonton: Black Cat Press [Russian orig.: Vadim V. Dam'e, *Anarkho-sindikalizm v XX veke*, Moscow: izd. IVI RAN]

Danilevskii, Nikolai Ia. (1995 [1895]), *Rossiia i Evropa*. St Petersburg: Glagol' [English: *Russia and Europe*, transl. Stephen M. Woodburn. Bloomington, ID: Slavica, 2013]

De George, Richard T. (1967), 'Philosophy', in G. Fischer (ed.), *Science and Ideology in Soviet Society*. New York: Atherton Press, 47–81

DeBlasio, Alyssa (2014), *The End of Russian Philosophy: Tradition and Transition at the Turn of the 21st Century*. Basingstoke: Macmillan

DeBlasio, Alyssa (2019), *The Filmmaker's Philosopher: Merab Mamardashvili and Russian Cinema*. Edinburgh: Edinburgh University Press

Demacopoulos, George E., Aristotle Papanikolaou (eds) (2013), *Orthodox Constructions of the West*. New York: Fordham University Press

Demacopoulos, George E., Aristotle Papanikolaou (eds) (2017), *Christianity, Democracy, and the Shadow of Constantine*. New York: Fordham University Press

Dennes, Maryse (1987), *Le Baptême de la Russie: mille ans de foi chrétienne*. Paris: Nouvelle Cité

Derrida, Jacques (1993), *Spectres de Marx*. Paris: Galilée

Dmitriev, S. S. (1987), 'Granovskii i russkaia obshchestvennost'', in Timofei N. Granovskii (ed.), *Lektsii po istorii srednevekov'ia* [1849/50]. Moscow: Nauka, 317–35

Dobrokhotov, Aleksandr L. (ed.) (2001), *Belyi tsar': metafizika vlasti v russkoi mysli [khrestomatiia]*. Moscow: Maks Press

Dostoevskii, Fëdor M. (2017), *Sila i pravda Rossii* [selection from *Dnevnik pisatelia*]. Moscow: Ripol klassik. [English: Fyodor Dostoevsky, *A Writer's Diary*, 2 vols, transl. Kenneth Lantz, intro. Gary Saul Morson. Evanston, IL: Northwestern University Press, 1994]

Dugin, Aleksandr G. (2004), *Filosofiia politiki*. Moscow: Arktogeia

Dugin, Alexander (2012), *The Fourth Political Theory*. Mumbai and Budapest: Arktos

Dugin, Alexander (2014a), *Eurasian Mission*. Mumbai and Budapest: Arktos

Dugin, Alexander (2014b), *Martin Heidegger: The Philosophy of Another Beginning*. Arlington, VA: Radix [Russian orig.: *Martin Khaidegger: filosofiia drugogo nachala*. Moscow: Akademicheskii Proekt, 2010]

Dugin, Alexander (2014c), *Putin vs Putin: Vladimir Putin Viewed From the Right*. Mumbai / Budapest: Arktos

Dunayevskaya, Raya (1992), *The Marxist–Humanist Theory of State Capitalism: Selected Writings*. Chicago: News & Letters

Dunayevskaya, Raya (2000 [1957]), *Marxism and Freedom: From 1776 until Today*. New York: Humanity Books

Dunayevskaya, Raya (2002), *The Power of Negativity: Selected Writings on the Dialectic in Hegel and Marx*, ed. Peter Hudis and Kevin B. Anderson. Lanham, MD: Lexington Books

Edie, James M., James P. Scanlan, Mary-Barbara Zeldin, George L. Kline (eds) (1976 [1965]), *Russian Philosophy*, 3 vols. Knoxville: University of Tennessee Press

Ehlen, Peter (2009), *Russische Religionsphilosophie im 20. Jahrhundert: Simon L. Frank*. Munich: Karl Alber

Ehrenburg, Ilya, Vasily Grossmann (2009 [2002]), *The Complete Black Book of Russian Jewry*, ed. and transl. David Patterson. New Brunswick, NJ, and London: Transaction

Ellis, Jane (1986), *The Russian Orthodox Church: A Contemporary History*. London and New York: Routledge

Eltchaninoff, Michel (2015), *Dans la tête de Vladimir Poutine*. Arles: Actes Sud [English: *Inside the Mind of Vladimir Putin*. London: Hurst & Co., 2018; German: *In Putins Kopf*. Stuttgart: Cotta, 2016]

Eltchaninoff, Michel (2016), *Les Nouveaux Dissidents*. Paris: Stock

Ely, Christopher (2010), 'Street Space and Political Culture in St. Petersburg under Alexandr II', in Mark Bassin, Christopher Ely, Melissa K. Stockdale (eds) (2010), *Space, Place, and Power in Modern Russia: Essays in the New Spatial History*. DeKalb: Northern Illinois University Press, 167–94

Emel'ianov, Boris V. (2004), *'Zheleznyi vek' russkoi mysli: pamiati repressirovannykh*, Ekaterinburg: izd. Ural'skogo Universiteta

Emerson, Caryl, George Pattison, Randall A. Poole (eds) (2020), *The Oxford Handbook of Russian Religious Thought*. Oxford: Oxford University Press

Engelstein, Laura (1992), *The Keys to Happiness: Sex and the Search for Modernity in Fin-de-Siècle Russia*. Ithaca, NY, and London: Cornell University Press

Engelstein, Laura (2018), *Russia in Flames: War, Revolution, Civil War 1914–1921*. Oxford: Oxford University Press

Epstein, Mikhail (2011), *Russian Spirituality and the Secularization of Culture*. Monee, IL: Franc-Tireur

Epstein [Ėpshtein], Mikhail (2019), *The Phoenix of Philosophy: Russian Thought of the Late Soviet Period (1953–1991)*. New York: Bloomsbury

Esaulov, Ivan A. (1995), *Kategoriia sobornosti v russkoi literature*. Petrozavodsk: izd. Petrozavodskogo un-ta

Etkind [Ėtkind], Aleksandr (2011), *Internal Colonization: Russia's Imperial Experience*. Cambridge: Polity Press [Russian: *Vnutrenniaia kolonizatsiia: imperskii opyt Rossii*. Moscow: NLO, 2018]

Etkind [Ėtkind], Aleksandr (2013), *Warped Mourning: Stories of the Undead in the Land of the Unburied*. Stanford, CA: Stanford University Press [Russian: *Krivoe gore: pamiat' o nepogrebënnykh*. Moscow: NLO, 2018]

Evlampiev, Igor' I. (2013), *Politicheskaia filosofiia B.N. Chicherina*. St Petersburg: izd. SPbGU

Evlampiev, Igor' I. (ed.) (2014), *Ivan Aleksandrovich Il'in*. Moscow: Rosspėn

Evlampiev, Igor' I. (2018), 'Lev Tolstoi i poiski istinnogo khristianstva v russkoi filosofii', *Filosofskie nauki*, 8, 90–106

Evtuhov, Catherine (1997), *The Cross and The Sickle: Sergei Bulgakov and the Fate of Russian Religious Philosophy, 1890–1920*. Ithaca, NY, and London: Cornell University Press

Farías, Victor (1989), *Heidegger and Nazism*. Philadelphia: Temple University Press [Fr. orig. 1987]

Fauré, Christine (ed.) (1978), *Quatre femmes terroristes contre le tsar: Vera Zassoulitch, Olga Loubatovich, Elisabeth Kovalskaïa, Vera Figner: textes réunis et présentés par Christine Fauré*, transl. Hélène Châtelain. Paris: Maspéro

Fediashin, Anton A. (2012), *Liberals Under Autocracy: Modernization and Civil Society in Russia, 1866–1904*. Madison: University of Wisconsin Press

Fedorinov, Vadim E. (2000), *Obshchestvenno-politicheskaia mysl' Rossii kontsa XIX–nachala XX veka o kontseptsii politicheskoi partii*. Moscow: izd. Rossiiskogo un-ta druzhby narodov

Fëdorov, Nikolai F. (1982), *Sochineniia*. Moscow: Mysl'

Fedotov, George P. (1965–6 [1946]), *The Russian Religious Mind*, 2 vols. New York: Harper & Row

Fetscher, Iring (2016), 'Republicanism and Popular Sovereignty', in Goldie and Wokler (eds), 573–97

Figner, Vera (1991 [1927]), *Memoirs of a Revolutionist*. DeKalb: Northern Illinois University Press

Fischer, George (1969 [1958]), *Russian Liberalism: From Gentry to Intelligentsia*, 2nd edn. Cambridge, MA: Harvard University Press

Fitzpatrick, Sheila A. (2002 [1970]), *The Commissariat of Enlightenment: Soviet Organization of Education and the Arts under Lunacharsky*. Cambridge: Cambridge University Press

Florenskii, Pavel A. (1994–8), *Sochineniia*, 4 vols. Moscow: Mysl'

Frank, Semen L. (1987 [1930]), *The Spiritual Foundations of Society*. Athens and London: Ohio University Press [Russian: *Dukhovnye osnovy obshchestva*, Moscow: Respublika, 1992; German: *Werke*, vol. 3]

Frank, Simon L. (2000–13), *Werke*, 8 vols. Freiburg and Munich: Karl Alber

Freeland, Chrystia (2005 [2000]), *Sale of the Century: The Inside Story of the Second Russian Revolution*. London: Abacus

Frolov, Ivan T. (1989), *O cheloveke i gumanizme: raboty raznykh let*. Moscow: Izdatel'stvo politicheskoi literatury

Fukuyama, Francis (1990), 'Konets istorii', *Voprosy filosofii*, 3: 134–48

Fukuyama, Francis (1992), *The End of History and the Last Man*. London: Penguin

Gabowitsch, Mischa (2017), *Protest in Putin's Russia*. Cambridge: Polity Press [German orig.: *Putin kaputt!?* Berlin: Suhrkamp, 2013]

Gay, William C., Tat'iana A. Alekseeva (eds) (1994), *On The Eve of the 21st Century: Perspectives of Russian and American Philosophers*. Lanham, MD: Rowman & Littlefield

Gay, William C., Tat'iana A. Alekseeva (1995), *Capitalism with a Human Face*. Lanham, MD: Rowman & Littlefield

Gellner, Ernest (1994), *Conditions of Liberty: Civil Society and its Rivals*. London: Penguin

Goerdt, Wilhelm (1995 [1984]), *Russische Philosophie: Grundlagen*, 2nd edn. Freiburg and Munich: Karl Alber

Gogol, Eugene (2004), *Raya Dunayevskaya: Philosopher of Marxist-Humanism*. Eugene, OR: Wipf & Stock

Goldie, Mark, Robert Wokler (eds) (2016 [2006]), *The Cambridge History of Eighteenth-Century Political Thought*. Cambridge: Cambridge University Press

Good, James Allan (2006), *A Search for Unity in Diversity; The 'Permanent Hegelian Deposit' in the Philosophy of John Dewey*. Lanham, MD: Lexington Books.

Gorbachëv, Mikhail S. (1987), *Perestroika i novoe myshlenie dlia nashei strany i dlia vsego mira*. Moscow: Politizdat

Gordin, Michael D. (2016), '"What a Go-a-Head People They Are!": The Hostile Appropriation of Herbert Spencer in Imperial Russia', in Bernard Lightman (ed.), *Global Spencerism: The Communication and Appropriation of a British Evolutionist*. Leiden and Boston: Brill, 13–34

Goricheva [Goritschewa], Tatjana (1985), *Die Kraft christlicher Torheit: Meine Erfahrungen*. Freiburg im Breisgau: Herder

Grammatchikov, K. B. (ed.) (2017 [2016]), 'Pravoslavnyi' stalinizm, 2nd edn. Moscow: Simvolik

Granovskaia, O. L., D. N. Drozdova, A. M. Rutkevich (eds) (2021), *Perekrëstki kul'tur: Aleksandr Koire, Aleksandr Kozhev, Isaiia Berlin*. Moscow: Rosspèn

Granovskii, Timofei N. (2010), *Publichnye chteniia, stat'i, pis'ma*. Moscow: Rosspèn

Gray, John (2013 [1996]), *Isaiah Berlin: An Interpretation of his Thought*. Princeton: Princeton University Press

Grillaert, Nel (2008), *What the God-Seekers Found in Nietzsche.* Amsterdam and New York: Rodopi

Groys, Boris (1988), *Gesamtkunstwerk Stalin: Die gespaltene Kultur in der Sowjetunion*, transl. from Russian by Gabriele Leupold. Munich and Vienna: Carl Hanser [English: *The Total Art of Stalinism*. London and New York: Verso, 2011]

Groys, Boris (2012a) (ed.), *Moscow Symposium: Conceptualism Revisited.* Berlin: Sternberg Press

Groys, Boris (2012b), *Introduction to Antiphilosophy*, transl. David Fernbach. London and New York: Verso

Groys, Boris (2018), *Russian Cosmists*. Cambridge, MA, and London: MIT Press

Gulyga, Arsenii V. (1995), *Russkaia ideia i eë tvortsy*. Moscow: Soratnik

Haardt, Alexander (2008), 'Personalität in Recht und Moral: Vl. Solov'ëvs Begegnung mit Kant', in Haardt and Plotnikov (eds), 171–90

Haardt, Alexander, Nikolaj Plotnikov (eds) (2008), *Diskurse der Person-alität: die Begriffsgeschichte der 'Person' aus deutscher und russischer Perspektive*. Munich: Wilhelm Fink [Russian: *Personal'nost': iazyk filosofii v russko-nemetskom dialoge*. Moscow: Modest Kolerov, 2007]

Hagemeister, Michael (1989), *Nikolaj Fedorov: Studien zu Leben, Werk und Wirkung*. Munich: Otto Sagner

Halperin, Charles J. (1985), *Russia and the Golden Horde: The Mongol Impact on Medieval Russian History*. Bloomington and Indianapolis: Indiana University Press

Hamburg, Gary M. (1992), *Boris Chicherin and Early Russian Liberalism, 1828–1866*. Stanford, CA: Stanford University Press

Hamburg, Gary M., Randall A. Poole (eds) (2010), *A History of Russian Philosophy 1830–1930*. Cambridge: Cambridge University Press

Harding, Neil (1996), *Leninism*. Houndmills: Macmillan

Hardy, Jeffrey S. (2016), *The Gulag After Stalin: Redefining Punishment in Khrushchev's Soviet Union, 1963–1964*. Ithaca, NY, and London: Cornell University Press

Hare, Richard (1951), *Pioneers of Russian Social Thought*. Oxford: Oxford University Press

Hartnett, Lynne A. (2014), *The Defiant Life of Vera Figner*. Bloomington: Indianapolis University Press

Hedeler, Wladislaw (2015), *Nikolai Bucharin – Stalins tragischer Opponent*. Berlin: Matthes & Seitz

Hedeler, Wladislaw (ed.) (2017), *Die russische Linke zwischen März und November 2017*. Berlin: Karl Dietz

Hegel, Georg W. F. (1971), *Werke*, 20 vols. + Register. Frankfurt am Main: Suhrkamp

Hegel, Georg W. F. (1982), ‚An Niethammer', in *Weltgeist zwischen Jena und Berlin: Briefe*, ed. Hartmut Zinser. Frankfurt am Main: Ullstein

Heidegger Martin (2012), *Gesamtausgabe*. Frankfurt: Klostermann

Helleman, Wendy (ed.) (2004), *The Russian Idea: In Search of a New Identity*. Bloomington: Slavica

Herzen, Aleksandr I. (1954–63), *Byloe i dumy*, in *Polnoe sobranie sochinenii [PSS]*, 30 vols. Moscow: izd. AN SSSR, vols 8–11 [English: *My Past and Thoughts*. London: Chatto & Windus, 1968]

Herzen, Aleksandr I. (2003 [1956]), *Selected Philosophical Works*. Hawaii: University Press of the Pacific

Hingley, Ronald (1967), *Nihilists: Russian Radicals and Revolutionaries in the Reign of Alexander II (1855–81)*. London: Weidenfeld and Nicolson

Hirschkop, Ken (1999), *Mikhail Bakhtin: An Aesthetic for Democracy*. Oxford: Oxford University Press

Hoffman, John (1992), 'Has the "Withering Away" Thesis Finally Withered Away?', in Ronald J. Hill (ed.), *Beyond Stalinism: Communist Political Evolution*. London: Frank Cas, 84–106

Hoppe-Kondrikova, Olga, Josephien van Kessel, Evert van der Zweerde (2013), 'Christian Social Doctrine East and West: The Russian Orthodox Social Concept and the Roman Catholic Compendium Compared', *Religion, State & Society*, 41.2: 199–224

Horujy, Sergei S. (1994), *Posle pereryva: puti russkoi filosofii*. St Petersburg: Aleteiia

Horujy, Sergey S. (2010), 'Slavophiles, Westernizers, and the Birth of Russian Philosophical Humanism', in Hamburg and Poole (eds), 27–51

Horujy, Sergei S. (2015a), 'Bibikhin, Heidegger, and Palamas on the Problem of Energy ', *Stasis*, 3.1: 54–81 [Russian: ibid., 82–109]

Horujy, Sergey S. (2015b), *Practices of the Self and Spiritual Practices: Michel Foucault and the Eastern Christian Discourse*, ed. Kristina Stoeckl, transl. Boris Jakim. Grand Rapids, MI: Wim B. Eerdmans [Russian orig.: *Fonar' Diogena*. Moscow: Institut filosofii, teologii i istorii sv. Fomy, 2010, 492–684]

Horujy, Sergei S. (2017), 'Heidegger, Synergic Anthropology, and the Problem of Anthropological Pluralism', in Love (2017), 325–53

Horvath, Robert (2005), *The Legacy of Soviet Dissent: Dissidents, Democratisation and Radical Nationalism in Russia*. London and New York: Routledge

Horvath, Robert (2013), *Putin's Preventive Counter-Revolution: Post-Soviet Authoritarianism and the Spectre of Velvet Revolution*. London and New York: Routledge

Hufen, Christian (2001), *Fedor Stepun, ein politischer Intellektueller aus Rußland in Europa: die Jahre 1884–1945*. Berlin: Lukas

Huntington, Samuel P. (1998), *The Clash of Civilizations and the Remaking of World Order*. London: Touchstone Books

Huret, Jules (2007), *Enquête sur la question sociale en Europe*. Elibron Classics. Boston, MA: Adamant Media Corporation [orig.: Paris: Perrin et Cie, 1897]

Hussain, Athar, Keith Tribe (1983), *Marxism and the Agrarian Question*. London: Macmillan

Iakovlev [Yakovlev], Alexander N. (1993), *The Fate of Marxism in Russia*. New Haven, CT, and London: Yale University Press

Iakovlev [Yakovlev], Alexander N. (2002), *A Century of Violence in Soviet Russia*. New Haven, CT, and London: Yale University Press

Iarov, Sergei V. (2009), 'Sovety: organy respubliki ili instrumenty kontrolia nad respublikoi', in Kharkhordin (ed.), 153–162

Ignatieff, Michael (2000), *Isaiah Berlin: A Life*. London: Vintage

Il'in, Ivan A. (1993), *Nashi zadachi: stat'I 1948–1954 gg.*, 2 vols. Moscow: Russkaia kniga

Il'in, Ivan A. (2014), *On the Essence of Legal Consciousness*, ed., intro. and transl. William E. Butler, Philip T. Grier and Vladimir Tomsinov. London: Wildy, Simmonds & Hill [Russian orig.: *O sushchnosti pravosoznaniia*, written 1916–19, first publ. 1956; also in I. A. Il'in (2017), *Sil'naia vlast', russkaia ideia: illustrirovannoe izdanie*. Moscow: izd. Ė, 145–318

Il'in, Ivan A. (2017 [1925]), *O soprotivlenii zlu siloi*, 6th edn. Moscow: izd. Dar" [English: Ivan Alexandrovich Ilyin, *On Resistance to Evil by Force*. Zloven and London: Taxiarch Press, 2018a; German: Iwan Iljin, *Über den gewaltsamen Widerstand gegen das Böse*. Wachtendonk: Hagia Sophia, 2018b]

Il'in, Mikhail V. (2004), 'Words and Meanings: On the Rule of Destiny. The Russian Idea', in Helleman (ed.), 33–55 [Russian orig. 1996]

Il'in, Viktor V., Aleksandr S. Panarin (1994), *Filosofiia politiki*. Moscow: izd. MGU

Immonen, Khannu [Hannu] (2015), *Mechty o novoi Rossii: Viktor Chernov (1873–1952)*, transl. E. Shragi. St Petersburg: izd. EUSPb

Intelligentsiia v Rossii (1991 [1910]), ed. N. Kazakova. Moscow: Molodaia gvardiia

Israel, Jonathan I. (2001), *Radical Enlightenment: Philosophy and the Making of Modernity 1650–1750*. Oxford: Oxford University Press

Ivanov, Sergei A. (2005), *Blazhennye pokhaby: kul'turnaia istoriia Iurodstva*. Moscow: Iazyki slav'ianskikh kul'tur

Ivanova, Galina M. (2015a), *Istoriia GULAGa*. Moscow: Politicheskaia Ėntsiklopediia

Ivanova, Galina M. (2015b [2000]), *Labor Camp Socialism: The Gulag in the Soviet Totalitarian System*, ed. Donald J. Raleigh, transl. Carol Flath. London and New York: Routledge

Iz glubiny: sbornik statei o russkoi revoliutsii (1990 [1918]). Moscow: izd. MGU [English: *Out of the Depths (De profundis)*, transl. and ed. William F. Woehrlin. Irvine, CA: Charles Schlacks Jr, 1986; German: *De profundis: vom Scheitern der russischen Revolution*, ed. Ulrich Schmid. Berlin: Suhrkamp, 2017]

Iz-pod glyb: sbornik statei (1974). Paris: YMCA Press [English: *From Under the Rubble*. London: Collins & Harvill Press, 1975]

Jensen, Kenneth Martin (1978), *Beyond Marx and Mach: Aleksandr Bogdanov's* Philosophy of Living Experience. Dordrecht: Reidel

Jeu, Bernard (1969), *La Philosophie soviétique et l'Occident: essai sur les tendances et sur la signification de la philosophie soviétique contemporaine (1959–1969)*. Paris: Mercure de France

Jubara, Annett (2000), *Die Philosophie des Mythos von Aleksej Losev im Kontext 'Russischer Philosophie'*. Wiesbaden: Harrassowitz

Jubara, Annett (2001), 'Vom Reich des Antichristen zum Homogenen Weltstaat: Das "Ende der Geschichte" bei Vladimir Solov'ev und Alexandre Kojève', in Annett Jubara, David Benseler (eds), *Dialektik und Differenz: Festschrift für Milan Prucha*. Wiesbaden: Harrassowitz, 149–62

Kabakov, Viacheslav T. (1988), *Zavisit ot nas: perestroika v zerkale pressy*. Moscow: Knizhnaia palata

Kaehne, Axel (2007), *Political and Social Thought in Post-Soviet Russia*. London and New York: Routledge

Kagarlitskii, Boris Iu. (2013), *Neoliberalizm i revoliutsiia*. St Petersburg: Poligraf

Kagarlitsky, Boris (1989), *The Thinking Reed: Intellectuals and the Soviet State from 1917 to the Present*, transl. Brian Pearce. London and New York: Verso

Kagarlitsky, Boris (1995), *Restoration in Russia: Why Capitalism Failed*. London and New York: Verso

Kaldellis, Anthony (2011), 'Aristotle's *Politics* in Byzantium', in Vasileios Syros (ed.), *Well Begun is Only Half Done: Tracing Aristotle's Political Ideas in Medieval Arabic, Syriac, Byzantine, and Jewish Sources*. Tempe, AZ: ACMRS, 121–43

Kapustin, Boris G. (2004), *Moral'nyi vybor v politike*. Moscow: izd. MGU

Kapustin, Boris G. (2010), *Kritika politicheskoi filosofii: izbrannye èsse*. Moscow: Territoriia budushchego

Kara-Murza, Aleksei A. (ed.) (2018), *Rossiiskie liberal: idei i liudi*, 2 vols. Moscow: Novoe izdatel'stvo

Kara-Murza, Aleksey, Olga Zhukova (2019), 'The Political Philosophy of Russian Liberalism', in Cucciolla (ed.), 3–14

Kara-Murza, Sergei G. (2017), *1917: dve revolIutsii – dva proekta*. Moscow: Algoritm

Karenovics, Ilja (2015), *Weisheitsfreunde: Der Kreis der 'Ljubomudry' 1820–1830 und die Entstehung der russischen Philosophie*. Berlin: Ripperger und Kremers

Karpovich, Mikhail M. (1997), 'Dva tipa russkogo liberalizma', in Abramov (ed.), 387–407

Katsapova, Irina A. (2005), *Filosofiia prava P .I. Novgorodtseva*. Moscow: IF RAN

Katz, Michael R. (ed.) (2014), *The Kreutzer Sonata Variations: Lev Tolstoy's Novella and Counterstories by Sofiya Tolstaya and Lev Lvovich Tolstoy*. New Haven, CT, and London: Yale University Press

Kelly, Aileen M. (1998), *Toward Another Shore: Russian Thinkers Between Necessity and Chance*. New Haven, CT, and London: Yale University Press

Kelly, Aileen M. (1999), *Views from the Other Shore: Essays on Herzen, Chekhov, and Bakhtin*. New Haven, CT, and London: Yale University Press

Kelly, Aileen M. (2016), *The Discovery of Chance: The Life and Thought of Alexander Herzen*. New Haven, CT: Harvard University Press

Kessel, Josephien van (2020), *Sophiology and Modern Society: Sergei Bulgakov's Conceptualization of an Alternative Modern Society*. PhD, Radboud University, Nijmegen

Kharkhordin, Oleg (1998), 'Civil Society and Orthodox Christianity', *Russia–Asia Studies*, 50.6: 949–68

Kharkhordin, Oleg (1999), *The Collective and the Individual in Russia: A Study of Practices*. Berkeley: University of California Press

Kharkhordin, Oleg (ed.) (2009), *Chto takoe respublikanskaia traditsiia*. St Petersburg: izd. EUSPb

Kharkhordin, Oleg (2018), *Republicanism in Russia*. New Haven, CT: Harvard University Press

Khomiakov, Aleksei S. (1994), *Sochineniia*, 2 vols. Moscow: Medium

Khoros, V.G., K. L. Maidanik, V. V. Sumskii, A. G. Volodin, T. E. Vorozheikina, A. V. Zagorskii, et al. (1998), *Grazhdanskoe obshchestvo: mirovoi opyt i problemy Rossii*. Moscow: Êditorial URSS

Kirkwood, Michael (1993), *Alexander Zinoviev: An Introduction to his Work*. Basingstoke: Macmillan

Kistiakovskii, Bogdan A. (2003), 'The "Russian Sociological School" and the Category of Possibility in the Solution of Social–Ethical Problems', in Poole (ed.), *Problems of Idealism*, 325–55 [Russian orig.: *Problemy idealizma*: 343–450]

Kistner, Ulrike and Philippe Van Haute (eds) (2020), *Violence, Slavery and Freedom between Hegel and Fanon*. Johannesburg: Wits University Press

Klein, Naomi (2007), *The Shock Doctrine: The Rise of Disaster Capitalism*. London: Penguin

Kline, George L. (1974), 'Hegel and Solovyov', in Joseph O'Malley, Keith W. Algozin, Frederick G. Weiss (eds), *Hegel and the History of Philosophy*. The Hague: Martinus Nijhoff, 159–70

Klosko, George (ed.) (2013 [2011]), *The Oxford Handbook of the History of Political Philosophy*. Oxford: Oxford University Press

Kojève, Alexandre (1979 [1947]), *Introduction à la lecture de Hegel: leçons sur la* Phénomenologie de l'Esprit, ed. Raymond Queneau.

Paris: Gallimard [English: *Introduction to the Reading of Hegel*, ed. Alan Bloom, transl. James H. Nichols. Ithaca, NY, and London: Cornell University Press, 1980 [1969]; Russian: *Vvedenie v chtenie Gegelia*. Moscow: 1998; St Petersburg: Nauka, 2003]

Kojève, Alexandre (2004 [1942]), *La Notion de l'autorité*. Paris: Gallimard [English: *The Notion of Authority*. London and New York: 2014; Russian: *Poniatie vlasti*. Moscow: 2007]

Kojève, Alexandre (2007), *Überlebensformen*. Berlin: Merwe

Kojève, Alexandre (2018 [1934]), *The Religious Metaphysics of Vladimir Solovyov*, Cham: Palgrave Macmillan [French orig.: 'La Métaphysique religieuse de Vladimir Soloviev', *Revue d'Histoire et de Philosophie Religieuses*]

Kokorev, Aleksandr S. (2012), 'B. N. Chicherin i A. I. Gertsen o putiakh razvitiia rossiiskogo obshchestva', *Vestnik TGU*, 7: 249–52

Kołakowski, Leszek (2005 [1978]), *Main Currents of Marxism*. New York and London: W. W. Norton [Polish orig.: *Główne nurty markiszmu*. Paris: Instytut literacki, 1976–8]

Kolerov, Modest A. (2020), *Pëtr Struve: revoliutsionner bez mass 1870–1918*. Moscow: Tsiolkovskii

Kollontai, Alexandra (1970), *Autobiographie einer sexuell emanzipierten Kommunistin*, ed. Iring Fetscher. Munich: Rogner & Bernhard. [English: Alexandra Kollontai, *The Autobiography of a Sexually Emancipated Communist Woman*. New York: Prism Key Press, 2011; censored Russian orig.: 1926]

Kollontai, Alexandra (1980 [1977]), *Selected Writings*, transl. and intro. Alix Holt. New York and London: W. W. Norton

Kondratieva, Tamara (2017 [1989]), *Bolcheviks et Jacobins: itinéraire des analogies*. Paris: Les Belles Lettres

Koni, Anatolii F. (2015 [1933]), *Delo Very Zasulich*. Moscow: Knizhnyi klub knigovek [orig.: 1933]

Konstantinov, Fëdor V., V. F. Asmus, L. F. Denisova, B. È. Bykhovskii, M. T. Iovchuk, B. M. Kedrov, et al. (eds) (1960–70), *Filosofskaia èntsiklopediia*, 5 vols. Moscow: Sovetskaia Èntsiklopediia

Koriakovtsev, Andrei A., Sergei Viskunov (2016), *Marksizm i polifoniia razumov*. Moscow and Ekaterinburg: Kabinetnyi uchënyi / Armchair Scientist

Korneeva, Elena A. (2011), *Tsarstvo Putina: neostalinizm pros'bam naroda*. St Petersburg: Piter

Kornilov, S. G., A. P. Lavrent'eva, P. V. Riabov, I. S. Sidorov, S. I. Sidorov (2011), *Samoorganizatsiia i samoupravlenie naseleniia v Rossii: istoricheskii opyt i sovremenne problemy: mestnoe samoupravlenie* [Priamukhinskie chteniia 2009 goda]. Moscow: Futuris

Kornilov, S. G., A. M. Kornilova, P. V. Riabov, I. S. Sidorov, S. I. Sidorov (2012a), *Anarkhisty 'protiv' anarkhii i anarkhizma* [Priamukhinskie chteniia 2011 goda]. Moscow: Futuris

Kornilov, S. G., A. M. Kornilova, P. V. Riabov, I. S. Sidorov, S. I. Sidorov (2012b), *Anarkhizm i mirovaia kul'tura* [Priamukhinskie chteniia 2010 goda]. Moscow: Futuris

Kornilov, S. G., A. M. Kornilova, P. V. Riabov, I. S. Sidorov, S. I. Sidorov (2013), *Anarkhizm: ot teorii k dvizheniiu, ot dvizheniia k obshchestvu* [Priamukhinskie chteniia 2012 goda]. Moscow: Futuris

Kornilov, S. G., A. M. Kornilova, P. V. Riabov, I. S. Sidorov, S. I. Sidorov (2016), *Anarkhizm – uchenie radosti* [Priamukhinskie chteniia 2015 goda]. Moscow: Regtaim

Kornilov, S. G., A. M. Kornilova, E. I. Kondrakhina, N. V. Malinin, K. S. Podlipaeva, P. V. Riabov, et al. (2018), *Velikaia rossiiskaia revoliutsiia 1917–1921: libertarnyi vzgliad* [Priamukhinskie chteniia 2017 goda]. Moscow: Regtaim

Koselleck, Reinhart (2000), 'Erfahrungswandel und Methodenwechsel: eine historisch-anthropologische Skizze', in *Zeitschichten: Studien zur Historik*. Frankfurt am Main: Suhrkamp

Kostriukov, Andrei A. (2017), 'Kul't Stalina: obnovlenchestvo ili iazychestvo?', in Grammatchikov (ed.), 220–30

Kovrizhnykh, Olesia A., Larisa V. Butyl'skaia (2015), *Politicheskoe nasilie: iazykovoe manipulirovanie obshchestvennym soznaniem*. Moscow: Kanon+

Koyré, Alexandre (1976 [1929]), *La Philosophie et le problème national en Russie au début du XIXe siècle*. Paris: Gallimard

Kozlov, Vladimir A. (2015 [2002]), *Mass Uprisings in the USSR: Protest and Rebellion in the Post-Stalin Years*, transl. and ed. Elaine McClarnand MacKinnon. London and New York: Routledge

Kramer, Mark (2019), 'Autocratic Ideology as an Obstacle to Liberal Democratic Thought in Post-Soviet Russia', in Cucciolla (ed.), 89–106

Krasikov, Vladimir I. (2011), *Sotsial'nye seti russkoi filosofii*. Moscow: Volodeĭ

Kropotkin, Peter (2002 [1970]), *Anarchism: A Collection of Revolutionary Essays*, ed. Roger N. Baldwin. Mineola, NY: Dover

Kropotkin, Pëtr A. (1906), *L'État: son rôle historique*. Paris: Temps nouveaux [reprint Paris: Hachette Livre]

Kudiukin, P. M. (2013), 'Gertsen mezhdu libertarnym i liberal'nym sotsializmom', in Kornilov (ed.), 191–4

Kuznetsov, Vitalii N. (1982), *Frantsuzskoe neogegelianstvo*. Moscow: izd. MGU

Laqueur, Walter (2015), *Putinism: Russia and its Future with the West*. New York: St Martin's Press

Larson, Nathan D. (2005), *Aleksandr Solzhenitsyn and the Modern Russo-Jewish Question*. Stuttgart: ibidem

Laruelle, Marlène (2005), *Mythe aryen et rêve impérial dans la Russie du XIXe siècle*. Paris: CNRS Éditions

Laruelle, Marlène (2012 [2008]), *Russian Eurasianism: An Ideology of Empire*. Baltimore: Johns Hopkins University Press [French orig.: *La*

Quête d'une identité impériale: le néo-eurasisme dans la Russie contemporaine. Paris: Éditions PETRA, 2007]

Laruelle, Marlène (2019), *Russian Nationalism: Imaginaries, Doctrines, and Political Battlefields*. London and New York: Routledge.

Laruelle [Lariuėl'], Marlène, Emmanuel Faye [Ėmmaniuėl' Fai] (eds) (2018), *Khaidegger, 'Chernye tetradi' i Rossiia*, transl. Mikhail Maiatskii. Moscow: izd. dom Delo

László, Ervin (ed.) (1967), *Philosophy in the Soviet Union: A Survey of the Mid-Sixties*. Dordrecht: Reidel

Lausberg, Michael (2017), *Bakunins Philosophie des kollektiven Anarchismus*. Münster: Unrast

Lefort, Claude (1986), *Essais sur le politique XIXe–XXe siècles*. Paris: Seuil [Russian: Klod Lefor, *Politicheskie ocherki (XIX–XX veka)*, ed. E. A. Samarskaia. Moscow: Rosspėn]

Leggewie, Claus (2016), *Anti-Europäer: Breivik, Dugin, al-Suri & Co.* Berlin: Suhrkamp

Lenin, Vladimir I. (1971–5), *Polnoe Sobranie Sochinenii [PSS]*. Moscow: izd. Politicheskoi Literatury

Leustean, Lucian N. (2014), 'Review of Papanikolaou 2012', *Religion, State & Society*, 42: 98–100

Levandovskii, Andrei A. (2010), 'Timofei Nikolaevich Granovskii', in Granovskii 2010, 7–66

Likhachëv [Lichačev], Dmitrij S., Aleksandr M. Panchenko [Pančenko] (1991), *Die Lachwelt des alten Rußland*. Munich: Wilhelm Fink [Russian orig.: '*Smekhovoi mir' Drevnei Rusi*, 1976]

Linssen, Jeroen (2019), *Hebzucht: een filosofische geschiedenis van de inhaligheid*. Nijmegen: Vantilt

Lipovetsky, Mark (2015), 'Pussy Riot as the Trickstar', *Apparatus: Film, Media and Digital Cultures of Central and Eastern Europe*, <http://www.apparatusjournal.net/index.php/apparatus/article/view/5/70> (last accessed 13 October 2021)

Losev, Aleksei F. (1994 [1930]), *Dialektika mifa*. Moscow: Mysl' [English: *The Dialectics of Myth*, transl. Vladimir Marchenkov. London and New York: Routledge, 2014 [2003]]

Losev [Lossev], Alexei [Alekseï] and Valentina (2014), '*La Joie pour l'éternité': correspondence du Goulag (1931–1933)*. Geneva: Éditions des Syrtes

Lossky, Nikolai O. (1951), *History of Russian Philosophy*. New York: International Universities Press [Russian: N. O. Losskii, *Istoriia russkoi filosofii*. Moscow: Vysshaia Shkola, 1991]

Love, Jeff (ed.) (2017), *Heidegger in Russia and Eastern Europe*. London and New York: Rowman & Littlefield

Love, Jeff (2018), *The Black Circle: A Life of Alexandre Kojève*. Columbia, NY: Columbia University Press

Luk'ianov, S. M. (1990), *O Vl. S. Solov'ëve v ego molodye gody: materialy k biografii*. 3 vols. Moscow: Kniga [orig.: St Petersburg: 2-aia gosudarstvennaia tipografiia, 1916–21 (3 vols)]

Lur'e, Vadim F. (ed.) (2012), *Azbuka protesta*. Moscow: OGI

McDaniel, Tim (1996), *The Agony of the Russian Idea*. Princeton: Princeton University Press

Magun, Artemy (2013), *Negative Revolution: Modern Political Subject and its Fate After the Cold War*. New York: Bloomsbury [Russian orig.: *Otritsatel'naia revoliutsiia: k dekonstruktsii politicheskogo sub"ekta*, St Petersburg: izd. EUSPb, 2008); French: *La Révolution négative: déconstruction du sujet politique*. Paris: L'Harmattan, 2009]

Mahoney, Daniel J. (2001), *Aleksandr Solzhenitsyn: The Ascent from Ideology*. Lanham, MD: Rowman & Littlefield

Maidansky, Andrey (2003), 'The Russian Spinozists', *Studies in East European Thought*, 55: 199–216

Malaia, Vera G. (2002), 'B. N. Chicherin i V. S. Solov'ëv: sut' filosofskoi polemiki', *Solov'ëvskie issledovaniia*, 5: 152–70

Malakhov, Vladimir (2007), *Ponaekhali tut . . . ocherki o natsional-izme, rasizme i kul'turnom pliuralizme*. Moscow: Novoe literaturnoe obozrenie

Malakhov, Vladimir (2014), *Kul'turnye razlichiia i politicheskie granitsy v ėpokhu global'nykh migratsii*. Moscow: Novoe literaturnoe obozrenie

Malia, Martin (1996 [1994]), *The Soviet Tragedy: A History of Socialism in Russia, 1917–1991*. New York: Free Press

Malia, Martin (2006), *History's Locomotives: Revolutions and the Making of the Modern World*. New Haven, CT, and London: Yale University Press

Mamardachvili, Merab (1991), *La Pensée empêchée: entretiens avec Annie Epelboin*. La Tour d'Aigues: Éditions de l'Aube

Mandelbaum, Michael (2002), *The Ideas that Conquered the World*. New York: Public Affairs

Mansbridge, Jane J. (1983 [1980]), *Beyond Adversary Democracy*. Chicago: University Press of Chicago

Marks, Steven G. (2003), *How Russia Shaped the Modern World: From Art to Anti-Semitism, Ballet to Bolshevism*. Princeton: Princeton University Press

Marx, Karl, Friedrich Engels (1956–), *Werke* [*MEW*], 39 vols + suppl. vol. Berlin (DDR): Dietz

Masaryk, Tomáš Garrigue (1992 [1913]), *Russische Geistes- und Religionsgeschichte*, 2 vols. Frankfurt am Main: Eichborn

Masing-Delic, Irene (1992), *Abolishing Death: A Salvation Myth of Russian Twentieth Literature*. Stanford, CA: Stanford University Press

Maslin, Mikhail A. (ed.) (1992), *Russkaia ideia*. Moscow: Respublika

Matich, Olga (2005), *Erotic Utopia: The Decadent Imagination in Russia's Fin de Siècle*. Madison: University of Wisconsin Press

Medushevsky, Andrey N. (2006), *Russian Constitutionalism: Historical and Contemporary Development*. London and New York: Routledge

Meerson-Aksënov [Aksenov], Mikhail, Boris Shragin (eds) (1977), *The Political, Social and Religious Thought of Russian 'Samizdat': An Anthology*. Belmont, MA: Nordland

Melville, Andrei (2019), 'The Illiberal World Order and Russian Liberals', in Cucciolla (ed.), 205–21

Mendel, Arthur P. (2014 [1961]), *Dilemmas of Progress in Tsarist Russia: Legal Marxism and Legal Populism*. Cambridge, MA: Harvard University Press

Merridale, Catherine (2017), *Lenin on the Train*. Harmondsworth: Penguin

Mezhuev, Vadim M. (2007), *Marks protiv marksizma*. Moscow: Kul'turnaia revoliutsiia

Michels, Robert (1925), *Soziologie des Parteiwesens*. Stuttgart: Kröner

Michelson, Patrick L. (2017), *Beyond the Monastery Walls: The Ascetic Revolution in Russian Orthodox Thought 1814–1914*. Madison: University of Wisconsin Press

Michelson, Patrick L., Judith D. Kornblatt (eds) (2014), *Thinking Orthodox in Modern Russia*. Madison: University of Wisconsin Press

Middelaar, Luuk van (1999), *Politicide*. Amsterdam: Van Gennep.

Migranian, Andranik M., Francis Fukuyama (1992), 'Dialog o kontse istorii', *Put'*, 1: 234–41

Milbank, John (2006), *Theology and Social Theory: Beyond Secular Reason*. Oxford: Blackwell

Miller, Martin A. (1986), *The Russian Revolutionary Émigrés, 1825–1870*. Baltimore and London: Johns Hopkins University Press

Monas, Sidney (1991), 'The Twilit Middle Class of Nineteenth-Century Russia', in Edith W. Clowes, Samuel D. Kassow and James L. West (eds), *Between Tsar and People*. Princeton: Princeton University Press, 28–37

Motroshilova, Nelli V. (2013), *Martin Khaidegger i Khanna Arendt: bytie – vremia – liubov'*. Moscow: Gaudeamus / Akademicheskii Proekt

Mouffe, Chantal (2000), *The Democratic Paradox*. London and New York: Verso

Mouffe, Chantal (2013), *Agonistics: Thinking the World Politically*. London and New York: Verso

Mrówczyński-Van Allen, Artur, Teresa Obolevitch, Paweł Rojek (eds) (2016), *Beyond Modernity: Russian Religious Philosophy and Post-Secularism*. Eugene, OR: Pickwick Publications

Mrówczyński-Van Allen, Artur, Teresa Obolevitch, Paweł Rojek (eds) (2018), *Peter Chaadaev: Between the Lover of Fatherland and the Love of Truth*. Eugene, OR: Pickwick Publications

Mrówczyński-Van Allen, Artur, Teresa Obolevitch, Paweł Rojek (eds) (2019), *Alexei Khomiakov: The Mystery of Sobornost'*. Eugene OR: Pickwick Publications

Murray-Miller, Gavin (2020), *Revolutionary Europe: Politics, Community and Culture in Transnational Context, 1775–1922*. London: Bloomsbury

Nathans, Benjamin (2019), 'Human Rights Defenders Within Russian Politics', in Cucciolla (ed.), 63–72

Nechaev, Sergei G. (1871), *Katekhizis revoliutsionera*, <https://www.marxists.org/subject/anarchism/nechayev/catechism.htm> (last accessed 13 October 2021)

Negt, Oskar (ed.) (1974 [1969]), *Nikolai Bucharin, Abram Deborin: Kontroversen über dialektischen und historischen Materialismus*. Frankfurt am Main: Suhrkamp

Nethercott, Frances (2007), *Russian Legal Culture Before and After Communism: Criminal Justice, Politics, and the Public Sphere*. London and New York: Routledge

Nethercott, Frances (2010), 'Russian Liberalism and the Philosophy of Law', in Hamburg and Poole (eds), 248–65

Nikiforov, Aleksandr L. (1990), 'Perezhivët li marksizm perestroiku?', *Obshchestvennye nauki*, 3: 115–28 [German: 'Wird der Marxismus die Perestrojka überleben?', in Alexander Litschev, Dietrich Kegler (eds) (1992), *Abschied vom Marxismus: Sowjetische Philosophie im Umbruch*. Reinbek bei Hamburg: Rowohlt, 31–48]

Nikol'skii, Aleksandr A. (2000), *Russkii Origen XIX veka: Vl. S. Solov'ëv*. St Petersburg: Nauka [orig.: Kharkov, 1902]

Novakshonoff, Bishop Varlaam (2017), *God's Fools: The Lives of the Holy 'Fools for Christ'*. Dewdney: Synaxis Press

Novgorodtsev, Pavel (1991), *Ob obshchestvennom ideale*. Moscow: izd. Pressa [orig. 1911–17]

Novgorodtsev, Pavel I. (2011), *Lektsii po istorii filosofii prava: ucheniia novogo vremeni XVI-XIX vv.* Moscow: Krasand

Novikova, L. I., I. N. Sizemskaia (eds) (1993), *Intelligentsiia, vlast', narod: antologiia*. Moscow: Nauka

O'Meara, Dominic J. (2003), *Platonopolis: Platonic Political Philosophy in Late Antiquity*. Oxford: Clarendon Press

O'Rourke, James J., Thomas J. Blakeley, Friedrich J. Rapp (eds) (1984), *Contemporary Marxism: Essays in Honor of J. M. Bocheński*. Dordrecht: Reidel

Obolevitch, Teresa (2014), *La Philosophie religieuse russe*. Paris: Les Éditions du Cerf

Obolevitch, Teresa (2019), *Faith and Science in Russian Thought*. Oxford: Oxford University Press

Obolonsky, Alexander V. (2019), 'Ethical Liberal Values vs. the Soviet Political and Administrative Heritage from the 1980s to the Present', in Cucciolla (ed.), 123–38

Offermans, Wolfgang (2018 [1979]), *Mensch werde wesentlich: das Lebenswerk des russischen religiösen Denkers Iwan Iljin für die*

Erneuerung der geistigen Grundlagen der Menschheit, 2nd edn. Wachtendonk: Hagia Sophia

Offord, Derek (1985), *Portraits of Early Russian Liberals*. Cambridge: Cambridge University Press

Oittinen, Vesa (ed.) (2009), *Aleksandr Bogdanov Revisited*. Helsinki: Aleksanteri Institute

Oizerman, Teodor I. (2003), *Marksizm i utopizm*. Moscow: Progress-Traditsiia

Oizerman, Teodor I. (1986 [1962]), *Formirovanie filosofii marksizma*, 3rd edn. Moscow: Mysl' [German: *Die Entstehung der marxistischen Philosophie*. Berlin (DDR): Dietz, 1980]

Okenfuss, Max J. (1995), *The Rise and Fall of Latin Humanism in Early-Modern Russia*. Leiden, New York and Cologne: E. J. Brill

Osipov, Igor' D. (2014), *Filosofiia politiki i prava v Rossii*. St Petersburg: izd. SPbGU

Osnovy sotsial'noi doktriny RPTs (2000), <https://mospat.ru/ru/documents/social-concepts/> or <http://www.patriarchia.ru/db/text/419128.html> (both last accessed 13 October 2021) [German: Josef Thesing, Rudolf Uertz (eds) (2001), *Die Grundlagen der Sozialdoktrin der Russisch-Orthodoxen Kirche*. Sankt-Augustin: Konrad Adenauer Stiftung]

Panarin, Aleksandr S. (1996), '*Vtoraia Evropa' ili 'tretii Rim'? Izbrannaia sotsial'no-filosofskaia publtsistika*. Moscow: IF RAN

Panarin, Aleksandr S. (1998), *Revansh istorii: rossiiskaia strategicheskaia initsiativa v XXI veke*. Moscow: Russii put'

Papanikolaou, Aristotle (2012), *The Mystical as Political: Democracy and Non-Radical Orthodoxy*. Notre Dame, IN: Notre Dame University Press

Papkova, Irina (2011), *The Orthodox Church and Russian Politics*. Oxford: Oxford University Press

Pavlenskii [Pavlenski], Pëtr (2016a), *Le Cas Pavlenski: la politique comme art*. Paris: Louison Éditions

Pavlenskii [Pawlenski], Pëtr (2016b), *Der bürokratische Kampf und die neue Ökonomie politischer Kunst*. Berlin: Merwe

Pavlov, Ilya (2019), 'Perestroika and the Nineties in Vladimir Bibikhin's Hermeneutics', *Social Sciences [Russian Academy of Sciences]*, 50.3: 135–46

Payne, Daniel P. (2011), *The Revival of Political Hesychasm in Contemporary Orthodox Thought*. Lanham, MD: Lexington Books

Pecherskaia, Natalia (ed.) (1997), *Theology after Auschwitz and the GULag and the Relation to Jews and Judaism in the Orthodox Church in Communist Russia*. St Petersburg: St Petersburg School of Religion and Philosophy

Peikoff, Leonard (1993 [1991]), *Objectivism: The Philosophy of Ayn Rand*. New York: Meridian

Petrunin, Vladimir (2009), *Politicheskii isikhazm i ego traditsii v sotsial'noi kontseptsii moskovskogo patriarkhata*. St Petersburg: Aleteiia

Philippot, Robert (1991), *Les Zemstvos: société civile et état bureaucratique dans la Russie tsariste*. Paris: Institut d'Études Slaves

Piatigorskii, Aleksandr M. (1992 [1989]), *Filosofiia odnogo pereulka*. Moscow: Progress

Piatigorskii, Aleksandr M. (2007), *Chto takoe politicheskaia filosofiia: razmyshleniia i soobrazheniia*. Moscow: Evropa

Pipes, Richard (1964), 'Narodnichestvo: A Semantic Inquiry', *Slavic Review*, 23.3: 441–58

Pipes, Richard (1966 [1959]), *Karamzin's Memoir on Ancient and Modern Russia: A Translation and Analysis*. New York: AtheneumKaramzin

Pipes, Richard (2005), *Russian Conservatism and Its Critics*. New Haven, CT, and London: Yale University Press

Pirker, Theo (ed.) (1963), *Die Moskauer Schauprozesse 1936–1938*. Munich: DTV

Piskunov, V. M., N. B. Zlobina (eds) (1994), *Russkaia ideia v krugu pisatelei i myslitelei russkogo zarubezh'ia*, 2 vols. Moscow: Iskusstvo

Plaggenborg, Stefan, Maja Soboleva (eds) (2008), *Alexander Bogdanov: Theoretiker für das 20. Jahrhundert*. Munich: Otto Sagner

Planty-Bonjour, Guy (1974), *Hegel et la pensée philosophique en Russie 1830–1917*. The Hague: Martinus Nijhoff

Platonov, Sergei F. (1985 [1970]), *The Time of Troubles*. Lawrence: University Press of Kansas [Russian orig.: Prague, 1923]

Plekhanov, Georgi V. (2004 [1960]), *Selected Philosophical Works*, 5 vols. Honolulu: University Press of the Pacific

Plekon, Michael (2007), 'Mother Maria Skobtsova (1891–1945): Commentary', in Witte and Alexander (eds), 233–70

Plotnikov, Nikolaj, Alexander Haardt (eds) (2012), *Gesicht statt Maske: Philosophie der Person in Russland*. Münster: LIT

Podoroga, Valerii A. (1993), 'Fenomen vlasti', *Filosofskie nauki*, 1–3: 44–55

Pöggeler, Otto (1995), *Ein Ende der Geschichte? Von Hegel zu Fukuyama*. Opladen: Westdeutscher

Pontuso, James F. (2004 [1990]), *Assault on Ideology: Alexander Solzhenitsyn's Political Thought*, 2nd edn. Lanham, MD: Lexington Books

Popović, Srđa (2015), *Blueprint for Revolution*. Melbourne and London: Scribe

Porter, Cathy (2014 [1980]), *Alexandra Kollontai: A Biography*, 2nd edn. Chicago: Haymarket

Povest' vremennykh let [*Nestor's Chronicle*] (1997). St Petersburg: Azbuka [orig. 1118]

Pribytkova, Elena A. (2011), *Nesvoevremennyi sovremennik: filosofiia prava V. S. Solov'ëva*. Moscow: Modest Kolerov

Problemy idealizma (2018 [1902]), ed. Modest Kolerov. Moscow: Modest Kolerov [English: *Problems of Idealism: Essays in Russian Social*

Philosophy, transl. and ed. Randall Poole. New Haven, CT, and London: Yale University Press, 2003]

Pustarnakov, Vladimir F. (2003), *Universitetskaia filosofiia v Rossii.* St Petersburg: izd. RKhGI

Putnam, George F. (1977), *Russian Alternatives to Marxism: Christian Socialism and Idealistic Liberalism in Twentieth-Century Russia.* Knoxville: University of Tennessee Press

Pyman, Avril (2010), *Pavel Florensky: A Quiet Genius.* New York and London: Bloomsbury

Radishchev, Aleksandr N. (1994 [1790]), *Puteshestvie iz Peterburga v Moskvu.* Paris: Bookking International [Dutch: Aleksandr Radisjtsjev, *Reis van Petersburg naar Moskou.* Antwerpen: Benerus, 2018]

Raeff, Marc (1966), *Origins of the Russian Intelligentsia: The Eighteenth-Century Nobility.* New York: Harbinger

Rampton, Vanessa (2020), *Liberal Ideas in Tsarist Context: From Catherine the Great to the Russian Revolution.* Cambridge: Cambridge University Press

Rand, Ayn (1964 [1961]), *The Virtue of Selfishness.* New York: Signet

Reddaway, Peter, Dmitri Glinski (2001), *The Tragedy of Russia's Reforms: Market Bolshevism Against Democracy.* Washington, DC: United States Institute of Peace Press

Ree, Erik van (2002), *The Political Thought of Joseph Stalin.* London and New York: Routledge Curzon

Révész, László (1967), 'Open Questions in Contemporary Soviet Philosophy of Law and State', in László 1967, 127–48

Riasanovsky, Nicholas V. (1993 [1963]), *A History of Russia*, 5th edn. Oxford: Oxford University Press

Richters, Katja (2014), *The Post-Soviet Russian Orthodox Church.* London and New York: Routledge

Rimscha, Hans von (1983), *Geschichte Rußlands.* Darmstadt: Wissenschaftliche Buchgesellschaft

Ronin, Vladimir (2001), '". . . Tot de dood erop volgt!" De Russische herinnering aan Avvakoem', in Avvakuum, 163–96

Roosevelt, Priscilla R. (1986), *Apostle of Russian Liberalism: Timofei Granovsky.* Newtonville, MS: Oriental Research Partners

Rosenthal, Bernice Glatzer (2002), *New Myth, New World: From Nietzsche to Stalinism.* University Park, PA: Pennsylvania State University Press

Ross, Kristin (2016), *Communal Luxury; The Political Imaginary of the Paris Commune.* London and New York: Verso

Roudometoff, Victor (2016) *Glocalization: A Critical Introduction.* London and New York: Routledge

Roudometoff, Victor, Alexander Agadjanian, Jerry Pankhurst (eds) (2005), *Eastern Orthodoxy in a Global Age: Tradition Faces the Twenty-First Century.* Lanham, MD: AltaMira Press

Runciman, Steven (2003 [1977]), *The Byzantine Theocracy*. Cambridge: Cambridge University Press

Rutkevich, Aleksei M. (2009), 'Koyre o Gegele', in M. A. Solopova, M. F. Bykova (eds), *Sushchnost' i slovo: sbornik nauchnykh statei k Iubileiu professora N.V. Motroshilovoi*. Moscow: Fenomenologiia-Germenevtika, 457–75

Ruttenburg, Nancy (2008), *Dostoevsky's Democracy*. Princeton: Princeton University Press

Ryklin, Mikhail [Michail] (2019), *Leben, ins Feuer geworfen: die Generation des Großen Oktobers*. Berlin: Suhrkamp [Russian orig.: *Obrechennyi mir*, Moscow: Novoe literaturnoe obozrenie, 2017]

Sabine, George H. (1963 [1937]), *A History of Political Theory*, 3rd edn. London: George G. Harrap

Sapov, V. V. (ed.) (1998), *Vekhi: pro et contra*. St Petersburg: izd. RKHGI

Sasse, Sylvia (ed.) (2015), *'Das Lachen ist ein großer Revolutionär': Michail M. Bachtins Dissertationsverteidigung im Jahr 1946*. Zürich: Edition Schublade

Saunders, George (ed.) (1974), *Samizdat: Voices of the Soviet Opposition*. New York: Monad Press

Sauvé, Guillaume (2019), 'The Lessons from Perestroika and the Evolution of Russian Liberalism', in Cucciolla (ed.), 139–51

Savranskaya, Svetlana (2019), 'Gorbachev's "New Thinking": A Proto-Liberal Program for the Soviet Union', in Cucciolla (ed.), 73–87

Saward, John (2014), *Perfect Fools*. Oxford: Oxford University Press

Scanlan, James P. (1985), *Marxism in the USSR: A Critical Survey of Current Soviet Thought*. Ithaca, NY, and London: Cornell University Press

Scanlan, James P. (ed.) (1994), *Russian Thought after Communism: The Recovery of a Philosophical Heritage*. Armonk, NY, and London: M. E. Sharpe

Schapiro, Leonard (1967), *Rationalism and Nationalism in Russian Nineteenth-Century Political Thought*. New Haven, CT, and London: Yale University Press

Scheidegger, Gabriele (1993), *Perverses Abendland – barbarisches Russland: Begegnungen des 16. und 17. Jahrhunderts im Schatten kultureller Missverständnisse*. Zürich: Chronos

Scherrer, Jutta (1973), *Die Petersburger Religiös-Philosophischen Vereinigungen*. Wiesbaden: Harrassowitz

Scherrer, Jutta (2003), *Kulturologie: Rußland auf der Suche nach einer zivilisatorischen Identität*. Göttingen: Wallstein

Schmitt, Carl (1997 [1950]), *Nomos der Erde*. Berlin: Duncker & Humblot [English: *Nomos of the Earth*. Candor, NY: Telos, 2003]

Schmitt, Carl (2018 [1927 / 1932 / 1933 / 1963]), *Der Begriff des Politischen*. Berlin: Duncker & Humblot [English: *The Concept of the Political*, 2nd edn. Chicago: University Press of Chicago, 2007 [1996]]

Schrooyen, Pauline (2006), *Vladimir Solov'ëv in the Rising Public Sphere*. PhD, Nijmegen

Sciabarra, Chris Matthew (2013), *Ayn Rand, the Russian Radical*, 2nd edn. University Park, PA: Pennsylvania State University Press

Semyonov, Alexander (2019), 'Whither Russian Liberalism?', in Cucciolla (ed.), 27–42

Shafarevich, Igor' R. (2019a [1982]), *Russofobiia*. Moscow: Rodina

Shafarevich, Igor' R. (2019b [2002]), *Trëkhtysiacheletniaia zagadka: tainaia istoriia evreistva*. Moscow: Rodina

Shanin, Teodor (ed.) (2018 [1983]), *Late Marx and the Russian Road: Marx and 'the Peripheries of Capitalism'*, 2nd edn. London and New York: Verso

Sharova, Veronika L. (2013), 'Gender Aspects of the Modern Left-Wing Politics: The Specifics of Russia', in *Philosophy: Theory and Practice*, Moscow: IF RAN, 179–84

Shchukin, Vasilii (2001), *Russkoe zapadnichestvo: genezis, sushchnost', istoricheskaia rol'*. Łódź: ibidem

Shlapentokh, Vladimir (1989), *Public and Private Life of the Soviet People: Changing Values in Post-Stalin Russia*. Oxford: Oxford University Press

Shlapentokh, Vladimir (1990), *Soviet Intellectuals and Political Power: The Post-Stalin Era*. London and New York: I. B. Tauris

Shlapentokh, Vladimir (2001), *A Normal Totalitarian Society: How the Soviet Union Functioned and How It Collapsed*. Armonk, NY, and London: M. E. Sharpe

Simons, Anton (1996), *Carnaval en terreur*. PhD, Utrecht

Skobtsova, Elizaveta [Mother Maria] (1930), 'O iurodivikh', *Vestnik Russogo Studencheskogo Khristianskogo Dvizheniia / Le Messager*, 8–9: 3–13

Skobtsova, Elizaveta [Mother Maria] (2003), *Essential Writings*. Maryknoll, NY: Orbis Books

Skobtsova, Elizaveta [Mother Maria] (2007), 'The Mysticism of Human Communion', in Witte and Alexander (eds), 276–8

Skobtsova, Elizaveta [Mother Maria] (2016), *The Crucible of Doubts*. Mohrsville, PA: frsj Publications

Slavtcheva-Petkova, Vera (2018), *Russia's Liberal Media: Handcuffed but Free*. London and New York: Routledge

Smart, Ninian (2000 [1999]), *World Philosophies*. London and New York: Routledge

Smena vekh: sbornik statei (1922). Smolensk: Zavodoupravlenie Poligraficheskoi Promyslennosti gor. Smolenska [orig.: Prague, 1921]

Smiet, Katrien (2017), *Travelling Truths: Sojourner Truth, Intersectionality, and Feminist Scholarship*. PhD, Radboud University, Nijmegen

Smith, Kathleen E. (2002), *Mythmaking in the New Russia: Politics and Memory during the Yeltsin Era*. Ithaca, NY, and London: Cornell University Press

Smith, Oliver (2011), *Vladimir Soloviev and the Spiritualization of Matter*. Boston: Academic Studies Press

Snyder, Timothy (2011), *Bloodlands: Europe between Hitler and Stalin*. London: Vintage Books

Soboleva, Maja (2007), *Aleksandr Bogdanov und der philosophische Diskurs in Russland zu Beginn des 20. Jahrhunderts*. Hildesheim: Georg Olms

Sochor, Zenovia A. (1988), *Revolution and Culture: The Bogdanov–Lenin Controversy*. Ithaca, NY, and London: Cornell University Press

Solov'ëv, Vladimir S. (1988), *Sochineniia*, 2 vols, ed. A. V. Gulyga. Moscow: Mysl'

Solov'ëv, Vladimir S. (1989), *Sochineniia*, 2 vols, ed. N. Kotrelëv and E. Rashkovskii. Moscow: Pravda

Solov'ëv, Vladimir S. (1997), *Filosofskii slovar' Vladimira Solov'ëva*, ed. G. V. Beliaev. Rostov-na-Donu: Feniks [German in: Wladimir Sołowjew, *Deutsche Gesamtausgabe der Werke*. Freiburg im Breisgau: Erich Wewel, vol. VI]

Solovey, Valeriy (2019), 'Liberals or Technocrats? Liberal Ideas and Values in the Mindset of the Russian Political Elite', in Cucciolla (ed.), 155–64

Soloviev, Vladimir (1978), *La Sophia et les autres écrits français*, ed. François Rouleau. Lausanne: L'Age d'Homme

Soloviev, Vladimir S. (2000), *Politics, Law, and Morality: Essays by V. S. Soloviev*, transl. and ed. Vladimir Wozniuk. New Haven, CT, and London: Yale University Press

Soloviev, Vladimir S. (2003), *The Heart of Reality: Essays on Beauty, Love, and Ethics*, transl. and ed. Vladimir Wozniuk. Notre Dame, IN: Notre Dame University Press

Soloviev, Vladimir S. (2007), *Enemies from the East? V. S. Soloviev on Paganism, Asian Civilizations, and Islam*, transl. and ed. Vladimir Wozniuk. Evanston, IL: Northwestern University Press

Solovyov, Vladimir (1985 [1892–4]), *The Meaning of Love*, transl. Thomas R. Beyer, Jr. Hudson, NY: Lindisfarne Press

Solovyov, Vladimir (1990), *War, Progress and the End of History: Three Conversations Including a Short Story of the Anti-Christ*, transl. Alexander Bakshy. Hudson, NY: Lindisfarne Press

Solovyov, Vladimir (2001 [1950]), *A Solovyov Anthology*, ed. S. L. Frank. London: Saint Austin Press

Solovyov, Vladimir S. (2005 [1918]), *The Justification of the Good: An Essay on Moral Philosophy*, transl. Nathalie Duddington, ed. Boris Jakim. Grand Rapids: Willem B. Eerdmans. Also: *Vladimir Solov'ëv's Justification of the Moral Good*, transl. and ed. Thomas Nemeth. Cham: Springer, 2016 [orig. (1897) in Solov'ëv (1988), I]

Solowjow, Vladimir S. (1971), *Recht und Sittlichkeit*, ed. H. H. Gäntzel. Frankfurt am Main: Vittorio Klostermann

Solywoda, Stephanie (2008), *The Life and Work of Semën L. Frank.* Stuttgart: ibidem

Solzhenitsyn, Aleksandr I. (1974), 'Na vozvrate dykhaniia i soznaniia', in *Iz-pod glyb*, 7–28 [Eng.: 1975, 3–25]

Solzhenitsyn, Alexander (1991), *Rebuilding Russia: Reflections and Tentative Proposals.* London: Harvill [Russian orig.: 1990]

Solzhenitsyn, Aleksandr I. (1995), *'The Russian Question' at the End of the Twentieth Century.* New York: Farrar, Straus and Giroux

Solzhenitsyn, Aleksandr I. (2001–2), *Dvesti let vmeste (1795–1995)*, 2 vols. Moscow: Russkii put'

Solzhenitsyn, Alexander (2015), *The Solzhenitsyn Reader: New and Essential Writings 1947–2005*, ed. Edward E. Ericsson, Daniel J. Mahoney. Wilmington, DE: ISI Books

Stahl, Henrieke (2019), *Sophia im Denken Vladimir Solov'evs: eine ästhetische Rekonstruktion.* Münster: Aschendorff

Steila, Daniela (1991), *Genesis and Development of Plekhanov's Theory of Knowledge.* Dordrecht: Kluwer

Steinberg, Mark (2017), *The Russian Revolution, 1905–1921.* Oxford: Oxford University Press

Steiner, George (1996), *Tolstoy or Dostoevsky: An Essay in the Old Criticism*, 2nd edn. New Haven, CT, and London: Yale University Press

Stepun, Fëdor A. (2004), *Russische Demokratie als Projekt: Schriften im Exil 1924–1936.* Berlin: BasisDruck

Stoeckl, Kristina (2008), *Community after Totalitarianism: The Russian Orthodox Intellectual Tradition and the Philosophical Discourse of Political Modernity.* Frankfurt am Main: Peter Lang

Stone, Dan (2019), *Concentration Camps: A Very Short Introduction.* Oxford: Oxford University Press

Stoyanov, Tzvetan (2000), *Le Génie et son maître: Fiodor Dostoïevski et Konstantin Pobedonostsev.* Paris: L'Esprit des Péninsules [Bulgarian orig. 1978]

Strauss, Leo (1988 [1959]), *What is Political Philosophy? And Other Studies.* Chicago: University Press of Chicago

Stroev, Alexandre (ed.) (2006), *Voltaire – Catherine II: correspondance 1763–1778.* Paris: Non Lieu

Thompson, Ewa M. (1987), *Understanding Russia: The Holy Fool in Russian Culture.* Lanham, MD: University Press of America

Timofeeva, Oksana V. (2018), *The History of Animals: A Philosophy.* London: Bloomsbury [Russian orig.: *Istoriia zhivotnykh.* Moscow: Novoe literaturnoe obozrenie, 2017]

Tlostanova, Madina (2015), 'Between the Russian / Soviet Dependencies, Neoliberal Delusions, Dewesternizing Options, and Decolonial Drives', *Cultural Dynamics*, 27.2: 267–83

Tolokonnikova, Nadezhda, Slavoj Žižek (2014), *Comradely Greetings: The Prison Letters of Nadya and Slavoj.* London and New York: Verso

Tolokonnikova, Nadya (2018), *Read and Riot: A Pussy Riot Guide to Activism*. San Francisco: HarperOne

Tolstaja, Katja (2013), 'Theology and Theosis after Gulag. Varlam Shalamov's Challenge to Theological Reflection in Postcommunist Russia', in Fernando Enns, Annette Mosher (eds), *Just Peace: Ecumenical, Intercultural, and Interdisciplinary Perspectives*, Eugene, OR: Wipf and Stock, 50–69

Tolstaja, Katja (2020), *Theology after the Gulag: Conditions for Reflection on the Soviet Past and Post-Soviet Present*. Oxford: Oxford University Press (forthcoming)

Tolstoï, Léon (2003), *Écrits politiques*, transl. Éric Lozowy. Montréal: Éditions Écosociété

Tolstoy, Leo (1987), *Writings on Civil Disobedience and Nonviolence*. Philadelphia, PA, and Santa Cruz, CA: New Society

Trepanier, Lee (2010 [2007]), *Political Symbols in Russian History: Church, State, and the Quest for Order and Justice*. Lanham, MD: Lexington Books

Trotsky, Leon (2004 [1937]), *The Revolution Betrayed*. Mineola, NY: Dover Publications

Tschižewskij [Chizhevskii], Dmitrij (1974), *Russische Geistesgeschichte*. Munich: Wilhelm Fink

Tucker, Robert C. (1974), *Stalin as Revolutionary 1879–1929*. London: Chatto & Windus

Ulam, Adam B. (1998 [1977]), *Prophets and Conspirators in Prerevolutionary Russia*. London and New York: Routledge

Utechin, S. V. (1963), *Russian Political Thought*. London: J. M. Dent & Sons

Vaissié, Cécile (1999), *Pour votre liberté et pour la nôtre: le combat des dissidents de Russie*. Paris: Robert Laffont

Vaizer [Weiser], Tat'iana (2020), 'Speaking Without Listening: Imitating Dissensus in the Agonistic Public Debates in Russian Political Talk-Shows in the 2010s', *Javnost – The Public*, 27.1, 80–96

Vakhtin, Nikolai, Boris Firsov (eds) (2019), *Public Debate in Russia: Matters of (Dis)order*. Edinburgh: Edinburgh University Press

Valliere, Paul (2000), *Modern Russian Theology: Bukharev, Soloviev, Bulgakov*. Grand Rapids, MI: Eerdmans

Vekhi (1991 [1909]), ed. N. Kazakova. Moscow: Molodaia gvardiia [English: *Signposts*, transl. and ed. Marshall S. Shatz and Judith E. Zimmerman. Irvine, CA: Charles Schlacks Jr, 1986; German: *Wegzeichen*, transl. and ed. Karl Schlögel. Frankfurt am Main: Eichborn, 1990]

Vekhi kak znamenie vremeni: sbornik statei (1910). Moscow: Zveno

Venturi, Franco (2001), *Roots of Revolution: A History of Populist and Socialist Movements in 19th Century Russia*. London: Phoenix Press [Italian orig. 1952]

Volodin, Aleksandr I. (1973), *Gegel' i russkaia sotsalisticheskaia mysl' XIX veka*. Moscow: Mysl'

Volodin, Aleksandr I., B. M. Shakhmatov (eds) (1985), *Utopicheskii sotsializm v Rossii: khrestomatiia*. Moscow: Politizdat

Voloshinov [Vološinov], V. N. (1986), *Marxism and the Philosophy of Language*, transl. Ladislav Matejka and I. R. Titunik. Cambridge, MA: Harvard University Press [Russian orig. 1929]

Vucinich, Alexander (1976), *Social Thought in Tsarist Russia: The Quest for a General Science of Society, 1861–1917*. Chicago: University Press of Chicago

Walicki, Andrzej (1989 [1969]), *The Controversy over Capitalism*. Notre Dame, IN: Notre Dame University Press

Walicki, Andrzej (1989 [1975]), *The Slavophile Controversy: History of a Conservative Utopia in Nineteenth-Century Russian Thought*, 2nd edn. Notre Dame, IN: Notre Dame University Press

Walicki, Andrzej (1992 [1967]), *Legal Philosophies of Russian Liberalism*, 2nd edn. Notre Dame, IN: Notre Dame University Press

Walicki, Andrzej (1995), *Marxism and the Leap to the Kingdom of Freedom: The Rise and Fall of the Communist Utopia*. Stanford, CA: Stanford University Press

Walicki, Andrzej (2010), 'Russian Marxism', in Hamburg and Poole (eds), 305–25

Walsh, David (2013), 'Dostoevsky's Discovery of the Christian Foundation of Politics', in Richard Avramenko and Lee Trepanier (eds), *Dostoevsky's Political Thought*. Lanham, MD: Lexington Books, 9–30

Walzer, Michael (2012 [1994]), *Thick and Thin: Moral Argument at Home and Abroad*. Notre Dame, IN: Notre Dame University Press

Weber, Max (1998a [1906]), *Rußlands Übergang zum Scheinkonstitutionalismus* [Rußlandbericht 2]. Koblenz: Fölbach [orig.: Archiv für Sozialwissenschaft und Sozialpolitik]

Weber, Max (1998b [1906]), *Zur Lage der bürgerlichen Demokratie in Rußland* [Rußlandbericht 1]. Koblenz: Fölbach [orig.: Archiv für Sozialwissenschaft und Sozialpolitik]

Whatmore, Richard (2013), 'Enlightenment Political Philosophy', in Klosko (ed.), 296–318

White, James D. (1996), *Karl Marx and the Intellectual Origins of Dialectical Materialism*. Basingstoke and London: Macmillan

White, James D. (2019a), *Marx and Russia: the Fate of a Doctrine*. London: Bloomsbury

White, James D. (2019b), *Red Hamlet: The Life and Ideas of Alexander Bogdanov*. Chicago: Haymarket

Williams, Rowan (ed.) (1999), *Sergii Bulgakov: Towards a Russian Political Theology*. Edinburgh: T&T Clark

Williams, Stephen F. (2017), *The Reformer: How One Liberal Fought to Preempt the Russian Revolution.* New York and London: Encounter Books

Wirtschaftler, Elise K. (2008), *Russia's Age of Serfdom 1649–1861.* Malden, MA, and Oxford: Blackwell

Witte, John, Jr, Frank S. Alexander (eds) (2007), *The Teachings of Modern Orthodox Christianity on Law, Politics, and Human Nature.* New York: Columbia University Press

Wolff, Larry (1994), *Inventing Eastern Europe: The Map of Civilization on the Mind of the Enlightenment.* Stanford, CA: Stanford University Press

Wood, Nathaniel (2017), '"I Have Overcome the World": The Church, The Liberal State, and Christ's Two Natures in the Russian Politics of *Theosis*', in Demacopoulos and Papanikolaou (eds), 155–71

Zamaleev, A. F. (1987), *Filosofskaia mysl' v srednevekovoi Rusi.* Leningrad: Nauka

Zamoshkin, Iurii A. (1990), '"Konets istorii": ideologizm i realizm', *Voprosy filosofii,* 3: 148–55

Zapata, René (1983), *Luttes philosophiques en U.R.S.S. 1922–1931.* Paris: PUF

Zaretsky, Robert (2019), *Catherine and Diderot: The Empress, the Philosopher, and the Fate of the Enlightenment.* Cambridge, MA: Harvard University Press

Zen'kovskii, Vasilii V. (1989 [1948]) *Istoriia russkoi filosofii,* 2nd edn, 2 vols. Paris: YMCA Press

Zetkin [Tsetkin], Klara, Aleksandra Kollontai (2014), *Chego khotiat zhenshchiny?* Moscow: Algoritm

Zinov'ev [Zinoviev], Alexander (1985), *The Reality of Communism.* London: Paladin [Russian orig. 1981]

Zinov'ev [Zinoviev], Alexander (1986), *Homo Sovieticus.* London: Paladin [Russian orig.: Lausanne: L'Age d'Homme, 1982]

Zinov'ev, Aleksandr A. (2019), *Sovetskaia Ėpokha: ispoved' otshchepentsa.* Moscow: Rodina

Žižek, Slavoj (2001), *Did Somebody Say Totalitarianism?* London and New York: Verso

Žižek, Slavoj (ed.) (2002), *Revolution at the Gates: Selected Writings of Lenin from 1917.* London and New York: Verso.

Zubok, Vladislav (2011 [2009]), *Zhivago's Children: The Last Russian Intelligentsia.* Cambridge, MA: Harvard University Press

Zubok, Vladislav (2019), 'Intelligentsia as a Liberal Concept in Soviet History, 1945–1991', in Cucciolla (ed.), 45–62

Zwahlen, Regula M. (2010), *Das revolutionäre Ebenbild Gottes: Anthropologien der Menschenwürde bei Nikolaj A. Berdjaev und Sergej N. Bulgakov.* Vienna and Berlin: LIT

Zweerde, Evert van der (1996), 'Civil Society and Ideology: A Matter of Freedom', *Studies in East European Thought,* 48, 171–205

Zweerde, Evert van der (1997a), 'Philosophical Periodicals in Russia Today (Mid-1995)', *Studies in East European Thought*, 49, 35–46

Zweerde, Evert van der (1997b), *Soviet Historiography of Philosophy: Istoriko-Filosofskaja Nauka*. Dordrecht: Kluwer Academic

Zweerde, Evert van der (1998), 'Die "bürgerliche Gesellschaft" in den Diskussionen russischer Philosophen heute', in Maria Deppermann (ed.), *Russisches Denken im europäischen Dialog*. Innsbruck and Vienna: StudienVerlag, 278–310

Zweerde, Evert van der (1999), '"Civil Society" and "Orthodox Christianity" in Russia: A Double Test-Case', *Religion, State & Society*, 27.1: 23–45

Zweerde, Evert van der (2001), '"Sobornost'" als Gesellschaftsideal by Vladimir Solov'ev und Pavel Florenskij', in Norbert Franz, Michael Hagemeister, Frank Haney (eds), *Pavel Florenskij – Tradition und Moderne*. Frankfurt am Main: Peter Lang, 225–46

Zweerde, Evert van der (2003), 'Vladimir Solov'ëv and the Russian–Christian Jewish Question', *Journal of Eastern Christian Studies*, 55.3–4: 211–44

Zweerde, Evert van der (2007), 'Beyond Occidentism and Philosophic Geography: Reflections on Europe's Eastern Border', in Małgorzata Kowalska (ed.), *The New Europe: Uncertain Identity and Borders* (Białystok: Uniwersitet v Białymstoku, 47–62

Zweerde, Evert van der (2008a), 'Gesellschaft, Gemeinschaft, Politik: zur Aktualität der Sozialphilosophie Semen Franks', in Holger Kuße (ed.), *Kultur als Dialog und Meinung*. Munich: Otto Sagner, 113–39

Zweerde, Evert van der (2008b), '"Subjektivismus neuen Typs" oder: Wie die Versellschaftung des Subjekts zur Idealisierung der Persönlichkeit führte', in Haardt and Plotnikov (eds), 251–63

Zweerde, Evert van der (2009), 'Gemeinschaft nach der Gemeinschaft', in Wilhelm Guggenberger, Dietmar Regensburger, Kristina Stöckl (eds), *Politik, Religion, Markt: Die Rückkehr der Religion als Anfrage an den politisch-philosophischen Diskurs der Moderne*. Innsbruck: Innsbruck University Press, 157–83

Zweerde, Evert van der (2010), 'Social Scientist or Cynical Citizen? Max Weber as a Political Philosopher', in Vesa Oittinen (ed.), *Max Weber and Russia*. Helsinki: Aleksanteri Institute, 38–62

Zweerde, Evert van der (2013), 'The Rise of the People and the Political Philosophy of the *Vekhi* Authors', in Robin Aizlewood and Ruth Coates (eds), *Landmarks Revisited: The* Vekhi *Symposium 100 Years On*. Boston: Academic Studies Press, 104–27

Zweerde, Evert van der (2015), 'Democratic Repertoires: The South Caucasus Case(s)', in Alexander Agadjanian, Ansgar Jödicke and Evert van der Zweerde, *Religion, Nation and Democracy in the South Caucasus*. London and New York: Routledge, 38–56

Zweerde, Evert van der (2018a), 'Democratic Repertoires of Political Legitimization: Russian Echoes and European Realities', in Thomas Hoffmann and Andrey Makarychev (eds), *Russia and the EU: Spaces of Interaction*. London and New York: Routledge, 9–26

Zweerde, Evert van der (2018b), 'Soviet Theory of the History of Philosophy as Capstone of Soviet Philosophical Culture', *Rivista di storia della filosofia*, LXXIII, 2: 357–71

Zweerde, Evert van der (2019a), 'Between Mysticism and Politics: The Continuity in and Basic Pattern of Vladimir Solov'ëv's Thought', *Interdisciplinary Journal for Religion and Transformation in Contemporary Society*, 5.1: 136–64

Zweerde [Zveirde], Evert van der (2019b), 'Stoletie, kotoroe budorazhit dushu . . . Oktriabrskaia revoliutsiia kak sakral'nyi ob"ekt', *Gosudarstvo, Religiia, Tserkov' v Rossii i za rubezhom*, 1–2.37: 643–69

Zweerde, Evert van der (2019c), 'Theocracy, *Sobornost'*, and Democracy: Reflections on Vladimir Putin's Philosophers', in Christoph Schneider (ed.), *Theology and Philosophy in Eastern Orthodoxy*. Eugene, OR: Wipf and Stock, 11–31

Zweerde, Evert van der (2020), 'Vladimir Solov'yov on Terror, Love and Violence', in Mahmoud Masaeli, Rico Sneller (eds), *Responses of Mysticism to Religious Terrorism*. Oud-Turnhout and 's-Hertogenbosch: Gompel and Svacina, 177–97

Zweerde, Evert van der (2021a), 'A Hundred Years That Shook The Mind . . . Philosophical Effects of the Russian Revolution', in Nikolaj Plotnikov (ed.), *Die Philosophie der russischen Revolution*. Berlin: LIT (forthcoming)

Zweerde, Evert van der (2021b), 'Russian Political Philosophy: Between Autocracy and Revolution', in Bykova et al. (eds), 73–94

Index

absolutism, absolutist, absolute,
    3, 6, 7–10, 12, 14, 21, 80, 84,
    157, 159–61
    absolute Authority [Kojève], 159
    absolute autocracy, 120
    absolute State, 161
    moral absolutism, 84, 157
absolute monarchy *see* monarchy
agency, agent(s), ix, 19–20, 45,
    55, 78, 87, 103, 110, 120,
    194, 197–8
agrarian question, 89
Akhmatova, A., 152
Aksel'rod, P., 48, 105
Aksel'rod-Ortodoks, L. I., 50, 53,
    113, 116, 132
aktsiia, 196
Alëkhina, M. V., 194
Aleksandr I, 20, 80
Aleksandr II, 8, 19–20, 30,
    33, 38, 61, 71, 79–80, 83, 96,
    196
Aleksandr III, 8, 19, 34,
    38, 71
Alekseeva, T. A., 175, 178
anarchic monarchism *see*
    monarchism

anarchism, anarchist(s), x, xii, 17,
    43–4, 47, 59, 64, 80, 84, 90,
    96, 100–3, 105, 107–8, 110,
    148–9, 168, 196, 203, 205
anarchist communism *see*
    communism
anarchy, anarchic, 2, 13, 16, 77,
    87, 196, 199, 205, 207
ancien régime see old regime
annihilism, annihilist(s), 27
antagonism, 6, 53, 60, 67, 99,
    105, 110, 125, 128, 182, 186,
    206, 209
Antichrist, Anti-Christian, viii, 72,
    132–3, 136–7, 155, 162, 205
anti-political, 6, 58–9, 72, 121,
    132, 208
anti-Semitism, anti-Semitic,
    'Semitism', 57, 96, 133, 138,
    175–6, 188, 193
Apocalypse, apocalyptic, 72–3,
    93–4, 130, 136, 206
a-political, 208
Arendt, H., 122, 141, 152, 154,
    158, 172, 187, 199
aristocracy, aristocratic, 3, 70,
    136

Aristotle, Aristotelian 4, 9, 23,
    106, 123, 205
artel', 45, 48, 90, 205
asceticism, 59, 67
Asmus, V. F., 124
assassination, 15, 33–4, 38, 41, 96
atheism, atheist, 57, 73, 97, 129,
    131, 137, 139, 157–9, 193
  militant, 139, 169
atomisation, 155, 199
authority, authorities, vii, ix,
    4–11, 13–14, 19, 27, 46,
    49–50, 57, 59, 70, 77, 79,
    81–2, 86, 99, 113–14, 122,
    144, 159, 180, 184, 191,
    194–6, 198–9, 205, 207
authoritarianism, authoritarian, 3,
    33, 90, 112, 136, 150, 167, 173,
    181, 186, 197–8, 200, 205–7
autocephalous, 5, 97
autocracy, autocratic *see*
    samoderzhavie
Averintsev, S. S., 145n
Avvakum [Petrov], 11, 194

Bakhtin, M. M., 108, 113, 124,
    129, 197
Bakunin, M. A., 19, 26–7, 29–32,
    35, 38–9, 42–3, 47, 71,
    152–3, 179, 195–6, 204–5
basileus, 4; *see also* tsar'
Beccaria, C., 13
Belinskii, V. G., xii, 61, 79
Belkovich, R. Iu., 197
Belyi tsar' [White Tsar], 11, 39,
    61, 205
Benefactor [Zamiatin], 72, 139,
    159, 162, 207
Berdiaev, N. A., 15, 18, 23, 28,
    62, 87–8, 108, 131–2, 136–8,
    140–2, 145, 151, 154–5, 182,
    185, 193, 205, 208

Berkman, A., 103, 108
Berlin, I., 25, 30, 73n, 76–7,
    147–8, 151–4, 158, 162–3,
    208, 210
Bibikhin, V. V., xii, 182, 188,
    190–1, 200, 209–10
Bible, 61, 165
Biocosmists–Immortalists, 106
bio-politics, bio-political, 122–3
Blanc, L., 19, 39
Bogdanov [Malinovskii], A. A.,
    xii, 51–3, 108, 116, 131
bogochelovechestvo
    [Godmanhood, Divine
    Humanity, Theantropy], 57,
    68, 138, 142, 158–9, 181,
    203
Bogochelovek [God-Man], 68, 139
bogoiskateli [God-Seekers], 131
bogostroiteli [God-Builders], 131
Bolshevism, Bolshevik(s), 32, 41,
    45, 50, 52, 89, 93–102, 104–8,
    110–15, 117–21, 132–3,
    135–6, 138–9, 143, 147–50,
    152–3, 155, 162, 168, 173,
    177, 179, 196, 205
  Bolshevik dictatorship, 104,
    152
  Bolshevik regime, 32, 97, 108,
    111, 117, 133, 155
  Bolshevik takeover, xi, 41, 95,
    152
  National Bolshevism, 94, 188
  Old Bolsheviks, 113, 115, 119,
    121
  Bolshevik Revolution *see*
    revolution
bottom-up, 13, 38
bourgeois, 16, 24, 42, 45, 52–3,
    77, 89, 98, 105, 110, 112,
    117, 124, 132, 141, 143, 150,
    155, 158, 168–9, 173

anti-bourgeois, 59

bourgeoisie, 23, 35, 40, 51, 77,
96, 103–4

capitalism, 53, 119, 132, 137,
148, 210

renegades, 145

society [burzhuaznoe
obshchestvo], 24, 42, 77,
132, 141, 169, 173

bourgeois revolution see
revolution

boyars see gentry

brotherhood [fraternité, bratstvo],
63, 65–7, 78, 130, 135–7,
163, 203, 209

Büchner, L., 19

Buddhism, 180

Bukharin, N. I., 37, 52, 103,
108–9, 113, 115–16, 118–21,
149–50

Bukovskii, V. K., 198

Bulgakov, f. S. N., xii, 87–8, 102,
130–3, 140–2, 144, 182

bureaucracy, bureaucratic
state, bureaucratisation,
bureaucrat(s), 11, 23, 28,
104, 110, 114, 150, 161,
166, 173

Byzantium, Byzantine, x, 2, 4–5,
9, 16, 179, 203, 205

Caesaropapism, Caesaropapist, 4,
6, 193

canalisation of the political, viii,
20, 206

capitalism, capitalist epoch, 38,
41, 43–7, 49–50, 53, 93,
118–19, 132, 137, 147–8,
150–1, 157, 186, 196–7, 200,
202, 209–210

with a human face [Alekseeva],
178

categorical imperative [Kant],
70–1

censorship, 13, 18, 21, 57, 89,
114, 116, 187, 207

centralisation, 9, 23

Chaadaev, P. Ia., 22, 98

Chaikovskii, N. V., 40

chelovekobozhestvo [Deified
Humanity], 158

Chernov, V. M., 41, 45,
102–3

Chërnyi Peredel [Black
Repartition], 41, 49

Chernyshevskii, N. G., xiii,
18, 24, 27–30, 35, 39,
46, 51

Chicherin, B. N., 70, 76–8, 80–5,
87–9, 135, 187, 195, 205–6,
208, 210

Christendom, 202

Christian Kingdom see God's
Kingdom

Christian monarch see monarchy

Christian political philosophy, x,
23, 35, 55–6, 58–9, 63, 68,
73, 77, 89, 91, 130–1,
141–2, 144–5, 156, 179, 181,
203, 205

Christian politics [khristianskaia
politika], 58, 72, 102

Christianity, 2–4, 11, 23, 55,
57, 60, 62–3, 65–6, 68, 73,
130–1, 136, 140, 143–4,
179–81, 193, 203–5

Orthodox Christianity see
Orthodoxy

Chukovskii, K. I., 152

circles [kruzhki], 15, 21–2, 25,
43, 49

civil disobedience, 63, 192

civil rights and liberties, 38, 76,
81, 84, 89, 96

civil society [*grazhdanskoe obshchestvo*], 77
civil war, 60, 104, 149, 206
Civil War [Russia], 93, 101–2, 108, 120, 123, 133, 138, 147
class solidarity, 135
class struggle, class war, 45–6, 53, 91, 103, 108–10, 112, 115, 121, 124, 202, 206
  intensification of class struggle [Stalin], 119
classless society, 53–4, 159–60
clergy, 13, 15, 28, 56, 105, 139, 180, 192
Cold War, 124, 148, 151–2, 161, 178
collectivisation, 53, 116, 118–19, 150
collectivism, collectivist, 131, 134, 137, 143, 154–6, 169, 181
colour revolution, 197
communality, 23, 130–1, 141
commune *see obshchina*
communism, communist(s), vii, 53, 67, 80, 84, 91–2, 98, 102, 104, 107, 109–12, 114–15, 119, 121–2, 124–6, 128, 131, 134–5, 137, 140, 142–4, 147–50, 155, 161, 171, 173, 181, 188, 193, 200
  anarchist communism [Kropotkin], 46–8
Communist Party, 53, 101, 110, 112, 166, 175
  KPRF, 167, 193
  KPSS, 110, 112, 119, 124–6, 128, 166–7, 172, 182, 193
  VKP(b), 101–4, 111–12, 114–15, 119–20

communitarianism, communitarian(s), community, 58, 61, 63, 73, 76, 80, 85, 89, 141, 143–4, 180–1, 203
Comte, A., 19, 29
concentration camps, ix, 117, 122
concord, viii, 46–7, 54, 60, 84, 94, 127, 137, 142, 144, 163, 199
conflict, viii, 33, 39, 46, 53–4, 57–8, 60–1, 63, 65, 84, 87, 94–5, 100, 103, 108, 112, 127–8, 137, 142, 144, 161, 163, 171, 182, 192, 194, 199
conservatism, conservative, 8, 19–20, 22, 24, 27, 30, 33–4, 38, 46, 55–7, 59–61, 70, 73, 83, 89, 101, 130, 133–4, 136, 169, 177, 206
  conservative liberalism [Chicherin], 77, 81
conspiracy, conspiratorial, 15, 18, 25, 29–31, 51, 103, 167, 179, 208
Constant, B., 76
Constantinople *see* Rome: Second [Constantinople]
Constituent Assembly, 41, 93, 96, 99
constitution, constitutional, 4, 8, 12, 20, 77, 159, 169, 171, 206
  monarchy, 20, 24, 77, 81, 83, 95–7, 101, 135
  reform, 20–1, 34, 92, 96, 207
constitutionalism, 76, 93
constitutive other [Mouffe], viii–ix, 7, 22–3, 28, 162, 171, 174, 178, 201–2
construction of socialism in one country, 120–1, 150, 206
corporatism, 134
cosmopolitanism, 148, 175

counter-hegemony, 199
critical (political) potential, 42,
    45, 55–7, 73, 110, 116, 179,
    193–4

Daniel', Iu. M., 165
Daniel'son, N. F., 43, 45
Danilevskii, N. Ia., 1, 29,
    188, 203
Darwin, Ch., 19
Deborin [Ioffe], A. M., 116,
Decembrist(s), 15–16, 19–20
Deleuze, G., 182
democracy, 3, 12, 61, 96, 103,
    110–13, 136–7, 140–2, 144,
    157, 167, 173, 177, 181, 186,
    197–8, 201, 206
  democratisation, 166, 170–1,
    178
denial of the political, 35, 55, 58,
    103, 134, 144, 206, 208
depoliticisation, 112, 144, 182
Desnitskii, S. E., 14, 78
despotism, 12–14, 33, 80, 83, 87
destalinisation, 111, 124–5, 169
determinate negation [bestimmte
    Negation], ix, 147, 162
determinism (historical), 25, 35,
    44, 76, 87, 153, 173
dialectical materialism see
    materialism
dialectics, dialectical, 26, 46, 51,
    124, 151, 158
  method, 24, 47
dictatorship of the proletariat
    see proletariat
Diderot, D., 13–14
dissident(s), 4, 126, 165, 169–70,
    175, 179, 182, 198–200
Divine Humanity see
    bogochelovechestvo
Divine Plan, 72

divinisation, deification, théōsis,
    57, 69, 139, 159, 181, 191
Dmitrieff see Tomanovskaia
Dobrokhotov, A. L., 11, 205
domination, 5, 10, 27, 48, 72,
    101, 106, 117, 123, 165,
    179, 198
Dostoevsky, F. M., xiii, 31, 55,
    56–63, 66, 68–9, 72, 98,
    138–9, 159, 162, 189, 202, 207
Dugin, A. G., xii, 24, 188–91,
    201, 203, 209
dukhobory [Spirit Wrestlers], 63
Duma, 88, 95–7
Dunayevskaya [Shpigel], R.,
    xii–xiii, 147–8, 150–1, 158,
    160, 162–3
dystopia, dystopian, 72, 155, 207

égaliberté [equaliberty] [Balibar],
    66, 79, 135, 162–3, 209
egoism, 46, 84, 91, 157
Ekaterina II, 8, 10, 12–14
El'tsin, B. N., xi, 167, 173–4, 183,
    186
elections, electoral democracy, 41,
    91, 96–7, 99, 136, 144, 163,
    166–7, 178, 195, 198
Eltchaninoff, M., 185
emigration, émigré, 30, 42–3, 63,
    141, 147–63, 207
Emperor [Solov'ëv], 139, 159,
    162, 207
empress, emperor, caesar,
    imperator, khan, 4–5, 13–14,
    140
End of History [Kojève], 69,
    158–62, 177–8
Engels, F., 40, 42, 45–6, 50, 110,
    114, 119
Enlightened monarch see
    monarchy

Enlightenment, 2, 12–14, 16, 29, 53, 153, 163, 178–9, 202

equality, equal rights, 75, 78, 87–8, 90, 99, 135–6, 149, 161–2, 177, 179, 209

eschatology, eschatological, 59, 161

Esposito, R., 143

Eurasianism, 179, 188

excommunication, 57, 63, 73n

exile, xi, 14–15, 21, 26, 30–1, 41–2, 44, 61, 113, 129–46, 169, 207

existentialism, 59–60

fascism, 133–4, 140, 142–3, 148, 188, 192

February 1917 Revolution *see* revolution

Fëdorov, N. F., 30, 56–9, 62–9, 72, 73n, 107, 136, 207

feminism, feminist, 99, 114–15, 140, 151

Ferguson, A., 14

Feuerbach, L., 19, 28, 50, 210

Fichte, J. G., 19, 88

Figner, V. N., 33–4, 36n, 98

Filosofov, D. V., 98

Florenskii, f. P. A., 108, 116, 132, 145n

Florovskii, G. V., 131–2

Foucault, M., 168, 182, 187, 194

Fourier, Ch., 19

Franco, F., 134

Frank, S. L., xii, 60, 87, 108, 132, 141–5, 158, 206, 208, 210

freedom *see* liberty

freedom of religion, 70, 130, 180

French Revolution *see* revolution

Frolov, I. T., 171–2

Fukuyama, F., 158, 177–8, 188

Gaidenko, P. P., 188

Gellner, E., 173

gender, 98, 130, 149, 160, 197

gentry, nobility, boyars, 5, 8–9, 11, 13, 16, 21–2, 28, 30, 37, 40, 77

gerontocracy, 166

Gippius, Z. N., 98, 131, 157

Girondin(s), 79, 92

glasnost', 165–6, 171

Gnosticism, Gnostic, 32, 35, 63

God's Kingdom (on Earth), Kingdom of God, Christian Kingdom, 6, 57, 60, 65, 69–70, 138, 140, 145, 156, 161, 192, 206

God-Man *see Bogochelovek*

Godmanhood *see bogochelovechestvo*

Gogol', N. V., 61

Golden Cage [*zolotaia kletka*], 180

Golden Decade [*zolotoe desiatiletie*], 111

Golden Horde, Tatar Golden Horde, 2, 5

Goldman, E., 103, 108

Gorbachëv, M. S., 13, 105, 166–7, 171, 173, 176, 180, 201

Gospel, 63

Gramsci, A., 105, 173

Grand Inquisitor [Dostoevsky], 69, 72, 139, 159, 162, 207

Grand Turning Point [*velikii perelom*], 111

Granovskii, T. N., 77–80, 89

Great Patriotic War, 124, 183

Gregory of Palamas, 6, 190

Groys, B., 161, 197

guild liberals *see* liberalism

GULag, 117, 121–3, 125, 127, 146n, 166, 169, 179, 183

Gulyga, A. V., 124, 174
Gyekye, K., 141, 200

Hades, 122
hard power, 106, 198
harmony, harmonious, ix, 4, 47,
    57–8, 66, 71, 82, 88, 103,
    142, 144, 181–2
Hayek, F. von, 153, 157, 187
Heaven, 65–6, 72, 161
Hegel, G. W. F., Hegelianism,
    Hegelian(s), 19, 22, 24, 26,
    28–9, 35, 50, 69, 76, 78–9,
    81, 83–4, 87–8, 123, 135–6,
    157–61, 164n, 173–4, 189
hegemony [gegemoniia],
    hegemonic project(s), 6, 27,
    29, 77, 86, 101–2, 105–6,
    111, 115, 117, 163, 165, 168,
    175, 177, 186, 189, 196, 198
Heidegger, M., Heideggerian(s)
    24, 187–91, 209
Hell, 70, 122
heresy, heretic, heretical, 6, 52, 57
Herzen [Gertsen], A. I., xii, 15,
    18–19, 22, 24–6, 28–30, 35,
    39, 41–2, 45, 76, 78, 80–1,
    98, 152–4, 204, 210
hesychasm, hesychast, political
    hesychasm, 6–7, 56,
    190–2, 209
Hinduism, 63
historical determinism see
    determinism
historical materialism see
    materialism
Hitler, A., 98, 125, 134, 140, 149
Hobbes, Th., 9, 156
Holy Synod, 8–9, 57, 97
homo sovieticus [Zinov'ev], 169
homogenous, homogenise, 12,
    123, 195

homogenous state see universal
    homogenous state
Honig, B., 200
Horujy, S. S., xii, 180, 182, 188,
    190–1, 209–10
human material, 107, 109, 123,
    125, 143
humanism, humanists, 9, 134,
    139, 151, 172, 182
humanist socialism see socialism
humanity, 57, 67–9, 71, 78, 119,
    121, 138–9, 142, 149–50,
    160, 163, 172–3, 205
Humanity, Deified see
    chelovekobozhestvo
Humanity, Divine see
    bogochelovechestvo
humankind, xii, 47, 50, 60, 65,
    67, 103, 112, 138–9, 142–3,
    155, 158, 172, 209
Huntington, S., 92, 178–9, 181,
    187–8
Huxley, Th., 48

Iakovlev, A. N., 105
Iavlinskii, G. A., 176
identity, viii, 9, 22–3, 80, 120, 163,
    167, 174–5, 183, 193, 204
ideocracy, 150, 193, 201
ideology, viii, xiii, 12, 21, 23,
    40, 47, 49–50, 59, 87, 103,
    106–7, 121, 126–8, 134, 140,
    150, 162, 169–70, 173–6,
    188, 190–1, 198, 203, 207,
    209–10
    ideologeme, 4, 6, 124, 128, 201
    ideological hegemony, 117, 165
    ideological vacuum, 174, 209
    ideologues, 125, 171–2, 178
    ideo-logy, 155
    Marxist–Leninist ideology,
        124, 171–4

Il'enkov, È. V., 129
Il'in, I. A., xii, 71, 108, 132–7,
  141, 145, 155, 186–7, 189,
  204–5, 208
immediacy, 189, 190, 205
immortality, immortalisation,
  immortalists, 65, 67, 69,
  106–7
individualism, individualist,
  individualistic, 41, 46, 48,
  57, 59, 73, 77, 84, 88, 91,
  117, 130–2, 134, 136–7,
  142–4, 154, 157, 176, 181,
  185, 196
industrialisation, 40, 45, 55, 106,
  116, 122
instrumentalism, 100, 106, 121,
  206–8
intelligentsia, intelligent(y), 9,
  15–16, 20, 22, 28–9, 31,
  35, 42, 50, 61, 78, 82, 89,
  92–3, 103–4, 108, 126, 130,
  174, 176
internationalism, 20, 169,
  175
Iskra [The Spark], 34
Islam, Islamic, 5, 56, 63,
  114, 130–1, 141, 146n,
  180–1
istina, xi, 44, 86, 203
Iurkevich, P. D., 187
iurodstvo, iurodivyi, iurodivye,
  7–8, 15–16, 113, 138, 162,
  192–4, 208
Ivan IV, 5, 7–8, 120

Jacobinism, Jacobin(s), 15, 32, 38,
  79–80, 89, 199, 207
Jadidism, 56
Jesus Christ, 17n, 63, 68–9, 136,
  162, 193
Jewish question, 56

Judaism, 180
just war (theory), 68, 71, 135

Kagarlitskii, B. Iu., xiii,
Kapustin, B. G., 199, 204, 210
Kara-Murza, A. A., 176
Kazan' Conspiracy, 30
KD, Kadet, 90, 93, 95–7, 100, 102
Kharkhordin, O. V., 197
Khomiakov, A. S., 23, 131,
  137–8
Khrushchëv, N. S., 125
Kiev, Kievan, 2–3, 7, 180
Kirill [Gundiaev], Patriarch, 192
Kistiakovskii, B. A., xiii, 77, 85–9
Kojève [Kozhevnikov], A.,
  Kojévian, xii, 132, 147–8,
  151, 157–63, 177, 188, 206
kollektiv, 123
Kollontai, A. M., xii, 92, 98,
  103–4, 113–15, 118–19, 208
Kolokol [The Bell], 19, 26
Koni, A. F., 34, 85, 89
Konikova [Buchholz–Konikow],
  A. F., 151
Koriakovtsev, A., 199
Kovalevskii, M. M., 39
Koyré [Koira(nskii)], A., 158–9,
  161
Kronshtadt uprising (1921), 104
Kropotkin, P. A., xii, 39–40, 42,
  46–9, 101–4, 205, 210
kukhnia, 128, 182
kul'turologiia, 173–4

labour camps, 111, 122
labour union(s), labour
  unionist(s), 89, 104, 198
Lassalle, F., 39
laughtivism [Popović], 113,
  194, 197
Lavrov, P. L., 24, 30, 39–42, 70

Lefort, Cl., ix, xi, 94, 136, 152, 159, 187
legal consciousness, 136
legal liberals *see* liberalism
legal Marxism *see* Marxism
legal *narodniki see narodism*
legal nihilism, 75, 82, 84–5, 89, 206
legitimacy of conflict, ix, 103, 112, 144, 194
Legitimationswissenschaft, 109
Leibniz, G. W., 14
Lenin [Ul'ianov], V. I., xii, 18, 23, 37, 44, 50–3, 99–106, 110–12, 114–15, 117–19, 121, 123, 125, 133–4, 149–50, 154, 161, 166, 176, 195, 202, 204, 210
Leningrad *see* Sankt Peterburg, Petrograd, Leningrad,
Leninism, Leninist(s), 50, 97, 109, 118
Leont'ev, K. N., 29, 88
liberal democracy, liberal-democratic, 141–4, 148, 166–7, 169, 173, 176–7, 181, 192, 201, 206
liberalisation, 20, 77, 166, 170, 176–7
liberalism, liberal(s), 103, 117, 133, 136, 143, 148, 153, 170, 176–7, 181, 186, 195–6
  guild liberals, 89, 177
  legal liberals, 76
  national liberalism, 186
  neoliberalism, 48, 155–7, 163, 167–8, 173, 183, 186, 195–200, 209
  social liberalism, 76–7, 87, 186
  system liberals, 89, 176–7, 195
liberation of Being [Dugin], 189

liberation of women, women's rights, 56, 99, 106, 114–15
libertarian(s), 48, 76, 157, 176
liberty, 47–8, 75–6, 80–4, 87–8, 96, 126, 144, 155, 177
  negative [Berlin], 77, 87, 153–4, 193, 203
  positive [Berlin], 76–7, 153–4, 186, 194, 203
libretto (of history) [Herzen], 25–6, 35, 45, 49, 78, 154, 206
lichnost', 131, 142
lieu vide du pouvoir [Lefort], 136
Lifshits, M. A., 129
Living Church, 106
logic of the political [Schmitt], 133
Lomonosov, M. V., 12
Lopatin, G. A., 43
Loris-Melikov, M. T., 33–4
Losev, A. F., 108, 113, 116–17, 124, 129, 132, 145, 168, 190
Losskii, N. O., 65, 156,
Losskii, V. N., 131
Lotman, Iu. M., 129
love, 58, 60–8, 71, 119, 138, 156, 181
Lunacharskii, A. V., 107, 118, 131, 154

Magun, A. V., 198, 208, 210
Maistre, J. de, 88
Makarenko, A. S., 123, 125
Makhno, N., 102, 105
Maklakov, V. A., 85, 89, 93
Malabou, C., 200
Malakhov, V. S., 197
Malthus, Th., 29
Mamardashvili, M. K., 129, 182, 204–5
Marx, K., 26, 29, 37, 39–46, 48–50, 52, 58, 70, 114, 116, 119, 151, 160, 172–3, 189, 210

Marxism, Marxist(s), x, 34–5,
    37–54, 59, 75, 86, 89–91, 93,
    97, 104–10, 112–14, 116,
    118, 121, 123, 125–9, 131–2,
    140–1, 147–8, 151, 162,
    172–3, 179, 196, 199,
    202–3, 210
  legal, 44, 130
  Marxist humanism
    [Dunayevskaya], 147, 151, 163
  non-official Marxism, 168
  orthodox Marxism, 116
  right-Marxist, 159
Marxism–Leninism, Marxist–
    Leninist, 50, 53, 109–28,
    144–5, 168, 171–4, 182, 210
  Marxist–Leninist ideology, 124,
    171–4
  Marxist–Leninist philosophy,
    111, 115, 144, 168, 172–3
  official Marxism–Leninism, 151
  orthodox Marxism–Leninism,
    xi, 116, 119, 121
mass protest, 98, 197
materialism, 27, 67, 91, 137, 185
  dialectical materialism [*diamat*],
    37, 50, 52, 116, 123–4
  historical materialism [*istmat*],
    37, 50, 52, 115, 123–4,
    126, 174
Mbembe, A., 200
mediation, 159, 189, 205, 208
Memorial, 166
Men', f. A. V., 145n
Menshevik(s), 35, 50, 91–3,
    97, 102, 106, 112–13,
    148
Merezhkovskii, D. S., 98, 100,
    131, 157
messianism, messianic, 61, 82
Meyendorff, J., 131
Mikhailov, A. D., 33

Mikhailovskii, N. K., 30, 39, 41,
    44–5, 79, 85–6
Milbank, J., 130
militant atheism *see* atheism
military communism [*voennyi
    kommunizm*], 105–6, 149
Miliukov, P. N., 85, 89, 93
Mill, J. S., 19, 28–9
minorities, 12, 106, 149
mir, 3, 17, 38, 90
Mises, L. von, 157
misogyny, 67
modernisation, 2, 8, 10, 12–13,
    19, 21, 23, 28, 38, 55–6, 59,
    93, 98, 132, 150, 174
monarchy, monarch, monarchic,
    9–10, 13, 70, 80, 205
  absolute, 8–10, 12, 14
  Christian, 10, 34, 59, 71
  constitutional, 20, 24, 77, 81,
    83, 95–7, 101, 135
  Enlightened, 10, 12–13, 207
monarchism, monarchist, 59, 93,
    98, 101, 103, 133, 136
  anarchic [Berdiaev], 136
Montesquieu, Ch., 13, 23
moralism, 134
morality, 56, 64, 66, 70, 72, 75,
    81, 83–4, 134, 180
Muscovy, 3, 5–6, 8–9, 12
Moscow, xiii, 2–3, 5–6, 12, 14,
    67, 80, 87, 117, 122, 130,
    152, 158, 165
Moscow Maidan, 197
Motroshilova, N. V., 188
Mouffe, Ch., viii, 60, 76
multi-party democracy, 144, 173
Mussolini, B., 134

Nancy, J.-L., 143
Napoleon Bonaparte, 2, 21,
    160–1

narod, 13, 16, 22, 28–9, 35, 38, 40–1, 61, 66
narodism, narodnichestvo, narodnik(i), x, 17, 31, 40–1, 43–6, 49–50, 59, 70, 76, 79, 86, 90
  legal *narodniki*, 43, 45, 76
  liberal *narodniki*, 43, 45, 79
Narodnaia Volia [People's Will], 19, 32–4, 41, 49, 51, 71, 97, 196
narodnost', 23, 38
national community, 133
national liberalism *see* liberalism
nationalism, nationalist(s), 20, 27, 60, 62, 77, 84, 93, 103, 133, 143, 157, 168–9, 177, 182, 192–3, 206
natural law, 10, 87
Naval'nyi, A. A., 186, 195
Nazism, Nazi(s), 119, 121–3, 133, 138, 140, 151–2, 157, 166, 183, 188–9, 191
Nechaev, S. G., 31–2, 38, 40, 51, 97
neoliberalism, neoliberal *see* liberalism
neo-Patristic, 132
Neoplatonism, neo-Platonic, 4, 117, 199
NĖP, 106, 150, 155
New Man, 57, 107, 155, 169
new mankind [Fëdorov], 67
New Society, 57, 107, 155
Nicholas of Cusa, 123
Nietzsche, F., 153, 156
nihilism, nihilist(s), 27, 31, 38, 60, 89, 189
Nikolai I, 8, 19–20, 61, 79
Nikolai II, 8, 34, 95–6, 101
Nikon, Patriarch, 9
nobility *see* gentry

non-official Marxism *see* Marxism
non-resistance, 64, 134–5
non-violence, non-violent, 63, 95, 167, 186, 194, 196, 198, 206
Novgorod, 3, 5, 48
Novgorodtsev, P. I., 76–7, 84–5, 87–9, 133, 187
Novocherkassk Massacre [1962], 126
Nozhin, N. D., 46
Nozick, R., 48, 76, 153

oberprokuror, 34, 57, 97
objectivism [Rand], 156–7
obozhestvlenie, 69
obshchee delo see Fëdorov
obshchestvennost' [Frank], 141–2
obshchina, 3, 27, 37–41, 44–6, 48–9, 90, 205
October 1917 Revolution *see* revolution
October Manifesto, 95–6
official philosophy, 168
Ogarëv, N. P., 30
Oizerman, T. I., 151
old regime, *ancien régime*, 99, 105, 166
oligarchy, 3, 104, 183, 186
opium of the people [Marx], 179
ordo ordinans [Schmitt], 93, 95, 101, 183
Orthodoxy, Orthodox-Christian, Orthodox Christianity, vii, 3, 6, 19, 23–4, 38, 56, 61, 91n, 97, 130, 132–3, 135, 144, 169, 179–81, 183, 191–2, 194, 203
Osipov, I. D., 83
Ostrogorskii, M. Ia., 89, 96, 187
Osvobozhedenie Truda [Liberation of Labour], 34
ottepel' [thaw], 126

pacifism, 63, 68, 135
Panarin, A. S., 178
Paris Commune, 99
parliamentary democracy, 141–2
Pasternak, B., 152
paternalism, benevolent, 98
patriarch, patriarchate, 4–5, 8–9,
    98, 192
patrimonialism, 207
patriotism, 22, 64, 157, 193
Pavlenskii, P. A., 196, 202
peace, 58, 71
peasant commune *see obshchina*
peasantry, peasants, 3, 9, 11,
    15–16, 37, 40, 42, 45, 51, 61,
    64, 96, 101, 112, 114
penal justice, criminal justice, 71
perestroika, 165–6, 171–2, 176,
    178, 180
Pestel', P. I., 15–16
Pëtr I, 2–3, 5, 8–10, 23, 79
Petrograd *see* Sankt Peterburg
Petrograd Soviet, 99–100,
    102, 206
philosopher-king [Plato], 14,
    199, 205
philosophical culture, xiv, 108,
    124, 128, 130–1, 158, 168
philosophy of politics, 12, 53, 72,
    84, 90, 129
philosophy of the political, 90,
    109, 129
Philosophy Steamer [*Filosofskii
    parokhod*], 108, 113, 156
Piatigorskii, A. M., vii, 127
Plague Riot [*chumnoi bunt*], 11
Plato, Platonic, Platonist, 4,
    23, 69, 102, 117, 172, 178,
    199, 205
Plekhanov, G. V., 37, 40–2, 45,
    48–50, 52–3, 89, 103, 105,
    123, 210

pluralism, 82, 91, 142, 152–3,
    168, 174, 177, 186
Pobedonostsev, K. P., 34, 57, 132
poièsis, ix, 26, 49, 69, 94, 110,
    117, 120, 128, 169, 173,
    208–9
Politburo, 113, 125
politeia, viii, 96, 100, 118
political agency, 19, 120
political anthropology, 159
political arena(s), 8, 86, 90, 99,
    182–3, 208
political economy, 37–8, 43
political hesychasm *see* hesychasm
political laughter *see* laughtivism
political liberty, 81–4, 88
political party, parties, ix, 49, 90,
    92, 96–7, 103, 144, 182, 198
political rights, 11, 70, 75, 81, 83,
    87, 96, 177
political subject(ivity), 143,
    159, 198
political theology, political–
    theological, vii–viii, 4, 6,
    9, 16, 73, 130, 143, 159,
    206, 209
politicide [van Middelaar], 60,
    118, 159
Popper, K. R., 152, 187
popular sovereignty *see*
    sovereignty
positive law, 70, 72, 91n
positivism, positivist, 19, 53,
    84, 154
post-political, 120, 143, 207–8
post-secular, 130, 181
Prague Spring, xiii, 165
pravda, xi, 44, 86, 203, 205
pravo, 70, 82, 84, 91n
pravoslavie see Orthodoxy,
    Orthodox-Christian,
    Orthodox Christianity,

praxis, ix, 26, 49, 69, 94, 103, 110, 120, 128, 169, 207–8
Preobrazhenskii, A. E., 115
pre-revolutionary philosophers, 113, 168
private property, 26, 70, 77, 79, 81–2, 84, 96, 114–15, 150, 177, 193
proletariat, proletarian, 31, 39–42, 45, 51–4, 91, 103, 106, 117, 119–20, 124, 154–5
  dictatorship of the proletariat, 96, 101–4, 106, 117
  proletarian half-state [Lenin], 110
  proletarian revolution see revolution
Proletkul't, 52–3, 107
Prometheus, Promethean, Prometheism, 57–8, 132, 139, 155, 206
Prosveshchenie see Enlightenment
Proudhon, P.-J., 19, 39
Provisional Government, 98–100, 102, 114
Pskov, 3, 5, 48
PSR, 41, 138
publitsistika, 68, 72, 141
Pugachëv, E., 11
Purgatory, purge(s), 119, 121–2, 125, 155, 166
Pussy Riot, 193–6
Putin, V. V., 145, 183–6, 189, 192, 208

Qutb, Sayyid, 145n

racism, 138, 155, 157, 197
radicalism, radical, radicalisation, 16, 31, 35, 60, 73, 83, 194–7, 207

Radishchev, A. N., 12–15
Ramadan, T., 141
Rancière, J., 200
Rand [Rozenbaum], A., Randian, 48, 76, 147–8, 151, 153–8, 162–3, 210
raskol, raskol'nik(i) see starovertsy, staroobriadtsy
Rawls, J., 76, 153, 178, 187, 200
Razin, S., 11
raznochinets, raznochintsy, 28, 30
reactionary, -ies, 8, 19, 46, 85, 167, 194
Red Army, 104, 124, 149–50
Red Terror, 32, 117, 150
reform(s), reformist(s), 8, 13, 20, 29, 33, 35, 43, 48, 61, 77–9, 81, 83, 85, 93, 99, 100, 106, 208
  Church, 9, 11
  constitutional, 21, 96
  GULag, 125
  legal, 30, 34, 177
  political, 13, 16, 177
  radical, 15
  reformer(s), 9, 19–20, 93, 171, 173, 182
  religious, 56
  system, 78, 82, 171
Reformation, 23, 27
regime change, 15, 95, 195
rehabilitation(s), rehabilitated, 125, 149, 166, 173, 180
religious community, 131, 181
representation, representative government, 13, 15, 76–7, 82, 88, 90, 95–6, 136
repressive domination, 165
republicanism, republican(s), 2–3, 13, 16–17, 48, 76, 100, 154, 176, 197, 206
resurrection, 63, 65–7, 122, 203

revolt *see* uprising(s)

revolution, 15–16, 19–20, 23, 26–7, 29, 31–3, 35, 37, 40, 43, 46–7, 77–8, 80, 90, 93–5, 99, 102, 104, 118, 136, 149, 162, 206

American, 15

anarchist, 47

Bolshevik, 50, 177

bourgeois, 42, 66, 79, 99

Chinese, 177

colour, 197

cultural, 53

European [1848], 20

French [1789], 15, 78, 99, 101, 135–6, 162

liberal, 79, 85–9, 95, 177

negative [Magun], 198–9

proletarian, 99, 101, 110, 114, 118, 210

Russian [1905], 16, 88, 92–5, 97–8, 149, 166

Russian [1917], 34, 93, 95, 97–8, 99, 112, 114, 133, 138, 147–8, 152, 155, 158

Russian, 10, 40, 92–108

Russian, February 1917, 94, 97–100, 138, 155

Russian, October 1917, 35, 41, 72, 94, 100, 103, 120

snow, 197–8

socialist, 40–1, 45, 102, 110

world, 102, 112, 150

revolution to end all revolutions, 110

revolutionary democrat(s), 15, 25

Ricardo, D., 28

ROC [Russian Orthodox Church], 8–10, 23, 34, 56–7, 63, 97–8, 131, 138, 180–1, 183, 186, 192–4

Romanov [dynasty], 2, 97

Rome, First [Rome], 6

Second [Constantinople], 5–6, 23, 138

Third [Moscow], 6, 178–9

rossiiskii, 61, 183, 186

Rousseau, J.-J., 10, 76, 154

RSDRP, 34, 51–2, 56, 97, 101–2

RSFSR, 111, 168, 175

rule of law, 13, 76–7, 80, 82, 85, 87, 95, 133–4, 141, 171, 173, 198, 206

Russian idea, 62, 143, 174–5, 183, 185, 189, 192, 211

Russian religious philosophy, philosophers, 72, 114, 129–33, 141, 156, 159, 181, 194

Russian Revolution(s) *see* revolution

russification, 38

russkii, 61, 183, 186

Saint Petersburg *see* Sankt Peterburg

Saint-Simon, Cl. H. de, 19

Sakharov, A. D., 169–70

Salazar, A. de, 134

samizdat, 15, 128, 165, 207

samobytnyi, samobytnost', 24, 204

samoderzhavie, autocracy, autocratic, 3, 8, 10, 12–16, 19, 21, 23, 28, 42, 33, 38, 56, 75, 77, 80, 83, 120, 137, 193, 202, 205–7, 209

samokritika [self-critique], 199

Sankt Peterburg, Petrograd, Leningrad, 14, 28, 33–4, 99–102, 130, 151–2, 154–5, 163, 179, 187, 206

sbornost', 137

Schelling, F. W. J., 19, 22–3, 28
schism, schismatics *see starovertsy*
Schmemann, A., 131
Schmitt, C., vii, 58, 93, 108, 133,
    137, 156–7, 187–8, 201
scientific communism, 126, 173
Second Coming, 57, 72
secret police, 15, 34, 111
secular, secularisation, secularised,
    vii, 55–6, 73, 129–32, 142,
    167, 180–1, 192, 206
self-determination, self-
    government, self-organisation,
    self-rule, 3, 13, 20, 56, 76–7,
    82, 104, 137, 177, 205
Semitism, anti-Semitism,
    Judeophilia, 96, 133, 138,
    175, 188
Sen, A., 153
serfdom, serf(s), 6, 8, 11, 15,
    20–2, 37–8, 42, 61, 81, 202
sexual question, sexual love,
    sexuality, 64–5, 67, 98
Shafarevich, I. R., 175–6
Sharova, V. L., 197
shestidesiatniki, 199
Shestov [Schwarzmann], L. I., 129
Shklar, J., 153, 199
shock therapy, neoliberal shock
    therapy [Klein], 167, 173,
    183
Shpet, G. G., 108, 129
Silver Age [*serebriannyi vek*], 92,
    98, 107–8, 113–14, 130, 132
simfoniia 2, 4, 6, 203
Simmel, G., 141–2
Siniavskii, A. D., 165
Skobtsova [Pilenko, Kuz'mina–
    Karavaeva], m. M., 129, 132,
    137–42, 144–5, 205, 210
slavianofil'stvo, slavianofil(y), 19,
    22–3, 25, 27, 59

Slavophile(s) *see slavianofil'stvo*
Smith, A., 14, 28
smutnoe vremia [*smutnye
    vremena*], 8, 10, 94, 106, 166
Snow Revolution *see* revolution
sobor, 3, 8, 98, 140
sobornost', xi, 23, 39, 61, 72,
    88, 131, 136–7, 139–42,
    144, 154, 180–1, 192,
    203, 205
social Christianity, 136, 140
social Darwinism, 46, 48
social democracy, social
    democrat(s), 39, 45, 48, 89,
    91, 97, 102
social justice, 59, 67, 75–6,
    87, 137
social liberalism *see* liberalism,
    liberal(s)
social question, 56, 70, 89
socialism, 16, 27, 37–54, 57–8,
    60–1, 66–7, 73, 81–2, 84,
    104–5, 111–12, 120, 123,
    126, 128, 137, 140, 143,
    147–8, 150, 161, 171, 175,
    177, 210
    agrarian, 25, 38–41, 43, 46,
        102, 172
    anarchist, 39, 63
    Bolshevik, 132–3
    Christian, 71, 136, 139–40,
        142
    democratic state, 39
    French, 19
    humanist, 178, 180
    Marxist, 39, 46, 148, 202
    narodnik, 46, 50
    revolutionary, 64, 80
    rule-of-law, 77, 85
    scientific, 41, 46, 48
    Soviet, 151, 171–3
    utopian, 41, 59, 70

socialist revolutionaries, SR, 41,
    93, 102–3, 106, 137
soft power, 106, 198
Solov'ëv, V. S., xii–xiii, 19, 29–30,
    34, 57–60, 62–4, 66, 68–72,
    74n, 75, 77, 83–5, 88–9,
    97–8, 131, 135, 138–42,
    144–5, 146n, 158–9, 161–2,
    170, 174, 182, 185, 204–10
  free theocracy, 58, 69–70, 204
  free theosophy, 69
  free theurgy, 69
Solov'ëva, P. S., 98
Solzhenitsyn, A. I., 118, 150,
    169–70, 175, 177, 206
Sophia, Sophianic, 6, 69, 143,
    158, 161, 190
sophiology, sophiological, 132,
    140
Sorskii, N., 6
sovereignty, vii, 130, 189
  popular, 15, 139
sovet, 100, 112
Soviet regime, 93, 106–7, 112–13,
    121, 128, 131, 143, 147, 154,
    168, 198
Soviet Split, 108, 132
Spencer, H., 19, 29
spetskhran, 187
Spinoza, Spinozist, 106, 116,
Spiridonova, M. A., 41
spravedlivost', 44, 86
Stalin [Dzhugashvili], I. V.,
    Stalinism, Stalinist(s), xi, 98,
    101, 106, 108, 111, 115–22,
    125–6, 140, 147–51, 154,
    161–3, 180, 202
starovertsy, staroobriadtsy, 9, 11,
    91n
startsy, 6
state and church, 4–6, 11, 35,
    130, 193

state capitalism, 148, 150–1
statehood [gosudarstvennost'], 23,
    84, 104, 110, 133, 155,
    174, 189
statism, statist(s), 24, 78, 85, 100
Stepun, F. A., 132, 143, 158, 206
Straus, L., 14, 158
street liberalism [Chicherin], 81,
    195
Struve, P. B., 45, 76–7, 85, 87, 89,
    92–3, 100, 102, 195
supermoralism [Losskii], 67, 156
suffrage, 15, 82, 96
suffragettes, 98–9
suppression of the political, 19,
    103, 206, 208
Sviatogor [Agienko], A. F., 106
svoboda, 136, 196, 203
syndicalism, syndicalist(s), 148,
    168, 196
Synodal Church see Holy Synod
system liberals see liberalism

tamizdat, 18, 165, 207
Taylor, Ch., 141
teleology, teleological, 50, 76, 154
terror, terrorism, terrorist(s), 20,
    31–2, 34–5, 38, 40–1, 49–50,
    64, 71, 99, 101–2, 105, 117,
    119, 149, 183, 202
textual basis, 187
theanthropism see
    chelovekobozhestvo
theantropy see
    bogochelovechestvo
theocracy, 58, 69–70, 129, 137,
    163, 201, 204
theosis, theōsis see divinisation,
    deification, theōsis
Thermidor, Soviet Thermidor,
    113, 149–50
Timofeeva, O. V., 197

Tkachëv, P. N., 31, 38, 40, 42
Tolokonnikova, N. A., 193–6
Tolstoy, L. N., xiii, 18, 34, 56–9, 62–4, 67–8, 70, 72, 84, 89, 134–5, 152–3, 207
Tolstoyans, 135
Tomanovskaia, E. L. [Élisabeth Dmitrieff], 46
Tönnies, F., 141
top-down, 3, 12–13, 28, 38, 93, 177
totalitarianism, totalitarian, 15, 107, 140–1, 143, 148, 152, 154–5, 186, 188, 209
transformative anthropology, 107, 132
Trepov, D. F., 34, 40
Trotsky [Bronshtein], L. D., 37, 42, 100, 103–4, 118–19, 137, 148–51, 162
Trotskyites, Trotskists, 149, 151, 166
Trubetskoi, E. N., 187
tsar', tsars, tsarina, 5–6, 8–11, 13, 15, 19, 21, 27, 33–5, 39–40, 59, 61, 71, 77, 80, 97, 136–7, 205, 207; see also Belyi tsar', basileus, empress
Tsiolkovskii, K. È., 107
tyranny, 154
  majority tyranny, 96, 157

unassisted human mind [Strauss], 14, 127–8, 182, 210
unchaining of the political, 20, 100, 105, 194, 206
underground, 18–19, 42–4, 49, 51, 96, 107–8, 131, 145, 179, 209
universal homogeneous state [Kojève], 159, 162–3, 177, 179, 206

universalism, universalist, 20, 23, 35, 68, 78–9, 88, 130, 179, 193
Union of Soviet Socialist Republics, USSR, xi, xiii, xiv, 52, 91, 101, 107, 111–13, 115, 117, 119–21, 123–8, 131, 145, 148–9, 151, 154–5, 158, 162, 166–9, 172, 175, 179–80, 185, 188
uprising(s), 11, 13, 16, 19–20, 26, 30, 104
utilitarianism, 29, 32, 67, 73
utopia, utopian, 39, 41, 70, 94, 107, 117, 138–9, 155, 204
utopian socialism see socialism
Uvarov, S. S., 23, 38

Vaizer, T. V., 197
value pluralism, 152–3
Vasilios Blazhennyi, 7, 193
veche, 2–3, 5, 17, 17n, 23, 100, 206
vekha, vekhi, xi, 73, 82, 94–5, 101–2, 106, 124, 174, 183–4
Verbitskaia, A. A., 98
violence, 26, 32–3, 41, 64, 71, 95, 102, 119, 134–5, 186, 194, 198, 202
Viskunov, S., 199
volia, 203
Volokolamskii, I., 6
Voltaire [Arouet], F. M., 13–14
Vorontsova–Dashkova, E. R., 14
Vperëd [Forward], 40, 70
Vygotskii, L. S., 129

Walzer, M., 59, 153, 199
war, 64, 71, 92, 166 see just war
war communism see military communism
we versus them, 142

Weber, M., 85–7, 104, 141
Westernizer, Westernizing *see*
　zapadnichestvo
White Tsar *see Belyi tsar'*
withering away of the state
　[Marxism], 91, 110, 128
Wolff, Chr., 14
women's question [*zhenskii*
　vopros], 98, 114–15
women's rights *see* liberation of
　women
Workers' Opposition, 114
world revolution *see* revolution
World War I, 83, 158
World War II, xi, 2, 111, 117,
　121, 129, 137, 148–9, 152,
　162–3
world-view, *mirovozzrenie*, 32,
　50, 69, 115, 124, 132

xenophobia, 193

zakon, 82, 91n
Zamiatin, E. I., 72, 139, 155, 159,
　162, 207
zapadnichestvo, zapadnik(i), 19,
　22–3, 25, 27–8, 40, 203
Zasulich, V. I., 34, 40–1, 48–9
Zemlia i Volia [Land and
　Freedom], 30, 32–3, 40–1
zemstvo, 2–3, 20, 75, 77–8, 82,
　89, 177, 206
Zetkin, C., 99
zhdanovshchina, 113
Zhenotdel [Women's
　Department], 114
Ziber, N. I., 43, 45
Zinov'ev, A. A., 169, 172, 187,
　199, 200, 208
Žižek, S., 120, 187, 193
zolotaia kletka see Golden Cage
zolotoe desiatiletie see Golden
　Decade